Palgrave Studies in Ancient Economies

This series provides a unique dedicated forum for ancient economic historians to publish studies that make use of current theories, models, concepts, and approaches drawn from the social sciences and the discipline of economics, as well as studies that use an explicitly comparative methodology. Such theoretical and comparative approaches to the ancient economy promotes the incorporation of the ancient world into studies of economic history more broadly, ending the tradition of viewing antiquity as something separate or 'other'.

The series not only focuses on the ancient Mediterranean world, but also includes studies of ancient China, India, and the Americas pre-1500. This encourages scholars working in different regions and cultures to explore connections and comparisons between economic systems and processes, opening up dialogue and encouraging new approaches to ancient economies.

More information about this series at
http://www.palgrave.com/gp/series/15723

Cristina Rosillo-López
Marta García Morcillo
Editors

Managing Information in the Roman Economy

palgrave
macmillan

Editors
Cristina Rosillo-López
Universidad Pablo de Olavide
Sevilla, Spain

Marta García Morcillo
University of Roehampton
London, UK

Palgrave Studies in Ancient Economies
ISBN 978-3-030-54099-9 ISBN 978-3-030-54100-2 (eBook)
https://doi.org/10.1007/978-3-030-54100-2

This Palgrave Macmillan imprint is published by the registered company Springer Nature Switzerland AG.
The registered company address is: Gewerbestrasse 11, 6330 Cham, Switzerland

Contents

Contributors

Jean Andreau École des Hautes Études en Sciences Sociales, Paris, France

Alejandro Díaz Fernández Universidad de Málaga, Málaga, Spain

Miko Flohr Universiteit Leiden, Leiden, The Netherlands

Marta García Morcillo University of Roehampton, London, UK

Claire Holleran University of Exeter, Exeter, UK

Myles Lavan University of St Andrews, St Andrews, UK

François Lerouxel Université Paris-Sorbonne, Paris, France

Dario Nappo Università degli Studi di Napoli Federico II, Naples, Italy

Francisco Pina Polo Universidad de Zaragoza, Zaragoza, Spain

Pablo Revilla Universidad Pablo de Olavide, Sevilla, Spain

Saskia T. Roselaar Independent Scholar, Delft, The Netherlands

Cristina Rosillo-López Universidad Pablo de Olavide, Sevilla, Spain

Nicolas Tran Université de Poitiers, Poitiers, France

Koenraad Verboven Universiteit Gent, Ghent, Belgium

List of Figures

PART I

Information, Economic Theory and the Roman World

CHAPTER 1

Managing Information in the Roman Economy: Introduction

Marta García Morcillo and Cristina Rosillo-López

Knowledge is a form of power that can easily lead to abuse. This idea is deeply discussed in Plato's dialogue *Protagoras* in connection with the eloquence of the sophists. In Socrates' eyes, the sophist, like the food merchant and seller, can deceive his customers when praising his wares (the doctrines).[1] Those trading with food, insists Socrates, tend to ignore whether the product is good for the body, and because they commend all

[1] Pl. *Prt.* 313b-c.

This research and the conference in which the papers were first presented were financed by the project "El sector inmobiliario en el mundo romano: un análisis económico; s. II a.C.-s. II d.C." (HAR2016-76882-P), Ministerio de Ciencia, Innovación y Universidades, Spain.

M. García Morcillo (✉)
University of Roehampton, London, UK
e-mail: Marta.Garcia-Morcillo@roehampton.ac.uk

C. Rosillo-López
Universidad Pablo de Olavide, Sevilla, Spain
e-mail: mcroslop@upo.es

C. Rosillo-López, M. García Morcillo (eds.), *Managing Information in the Roman Economy*, Palgrave Studies in Ancient Economies,
https://doi.org/10.1007/978-3-030-54100-2_1

the products they sell, the purchasers remain uninformed, unless they are trained in the matter. The same lack of discrimination is attributed to the itinerant sellers of doctrines.[2] The dialogue situates the rhetoric of both the sophist and the trader as strategies that are driven by similar principles of economic competition, in which advantage and profit are prioritised over cooperation and honesty. In contrast to practically applied *techné*, this form of unverifiable knowledge can easily generate inequality, as purchasers are prevented from accessing information that could be relevant to their decision-making.[3] In this way, Plato portrays the essential problem of asymmetric information in transactions and market relationships that are not or cannot be submitted—at least in advance—to 'fact-checking' scrutiny or,—to borrow a term from information economics—to signalling messages and mechanisms that allow buyers to test the quality of the items or services offered by the informed party.

The issue of private or hidden knowledge is an economic concept often encapsulated by the idea 'I know something that you don't know'; the opposite would thus be information that is 'publicly observable'. Informational asymmetry is not only a frequent phenomenon in market activities, but is a distinguishing trait of human relationships, and can be identified in numerous parts of our daily life. As Plato shows, the study of this idea—ancient and modern—requires a more complex understanding of the social and cultural structures that influence human behaviour. To what extent should the bearer of relevant information—seller or trader—reveal it to the other party? How can profit coexist alongside good faith and the moral obligation to share knowledge? These generic ethical considerations lead us to the fundamental question of how information is acknowledged and managed by the parties involved in such exchanges. In ancient Rome, philosophical treatises such as Cicero's *On Duties* (*De Officiis*) and Seneca's *On Benefits* (*De Beneficiis*) discussed these issues in relation to economic matters and behaviour, providing answers that matched the social and collective codes and concerns rather than the legal requirements and enforcement norms.

Seneca's *Letters to Lucilius* specifically address the problem of those who transformed the old virtue of wisdom into an obscure and skilful

[2] Pl. *Prt.* 313d.

[3] The problem of rhetoric not associated with virtue as a form of knowledge that generates inequality and power in the dialogue is discussed by Garver (2004).

science to exclusively serve their purposes.[4] One of the consequences of such an instrumentalisation of knowledge is a restricted access to information. In his defence of the transparency of the Stoic doctrines, Seneca resorts to the useful comparison between the philosopher and the seller (as did Plato), and pictures a hypothetical scene in a retail shop: "we have nothing that catches the eye (*ocliferia*), we do not deceive the purchaser; what he will find inside is nothing more than what is exhibited outside (*in fronte suspensa*): we allow the people themselves to select the exemplar from anywhere they wish (*ipsis permittimus unde velint sumere exemplar*)".[5] The marketplace features again as a didactical example of Seneca's battle of discreditation against those who twist or obscure the truth: "when you buy a horse you order to remove its blanket, you pull off the cloths of the slaves for sale (*detrahis vestimenta venalibus*) so that no defects of the body remain out of sight (*ne qua vitia corporis lateant*): how can you evaluate a man that is covered (*hominem involutum aestimas*)?" The philosopher's reasoning specifically refers to the pimping tactics of slave-dealers (*mangones*), and how their use of ornaments raises the suspicion of purchasers, who should thus demand that any clothed parts be removed from the slave's body.[6] These ethical considerations about issues that concern a lack of honesty and transparency, but also about the need to act proactively in the search of truth (and knowledge), are not by chance discussed by Seneca using examples from everyday life in which asymmetric information enables licit profit yet also opens the door to dubious and fraudulent behaviour. These concerns ultimately reflected situations in which all members of society were or had been involved, whether directly or indirectly. Responses by public authorities included specific regulations (such as the edict of the curule aediles), which introduced mechanisms to make the seller liable for any undeclared vice of the merchandise. Other public and private enforcement instruments and forms of information management, such as encoded systems of commercial advertising, contracts, public records of transactions, taxes and market structures, to a certain degree compensated for the essential problems of uncertainty. They also

[4] Sen. *Ep.* 95.13: *'Antiqua' inquit 'sapientia nihil aliud quam facienda ac vitanda praecepit, et tunc longe meliores erant viri: postquam docti prodierunt, boni desunt; simplex enim illa et aperta virtus in obscuram et sollertem scientiam versa est docemurque disputare, non vivere'.*

[5] Sen. *Ep.* 33.3.

[6] Sen. *Ep.* 80.9: *Mangones quidquid est quod displiceat, id aliquo lenocinio abscondunt, itaque ementibus ornamenta ipsa suspecta sunt: sive crus alligatum sive brachium aspiceres, nudari iuberes et ipsum tibi corpus ostendi.*

functioned as a counterbalance to the unequal access to information that generated business opportunities, yet also disadvantaged economic actors, and were essentially a source of transaction costs.

One economic sector that was particularly affected by this disparity in the management of information was the real estate market. A famous anecdote narrated in a letter from Pliny the Younger reveals the story of a large house situated in Roman Athens, which was either put up for sale or let by the owners. However, the advertisement omitted an important defect: the house had been haunted by a ghost that made the place uninhabitable. Regardless of the veracity of the story, Pliny reveals the important detail that the owners hoped someone who was ignorant of the disturbing circumstances would accept the offer. Someone did, in fact: the Stoic philosopher Athenodorus became intrigued by the suspiciously low price of the house and accepted the offer. Led by his curiosity concerning the mystery of the deserted house, he encountered the ghost and helped him to make peace with the spirit that had caused the problem.[7] Aside from the fame of the passage (which is often evoked as the earliest documented ghost story), Pliny reveals a typically speculative performance of sellers in the sector, as well as the function of prices as signals of irregularities or uncommon circumstances. The anecdote also shows, similar to the Senecan examples discussed above (which are also framed by Stoic doctrines), how knowledge of price behaviour within a specific market, as well as a proactive attitude by the uninformed party to test the data provided by the informed one, can to a certain extent compensate for the problem of uncertainty. Athenodorus' awareness of the average prices of houses in Athens during the Augustan age was not an extraordinary circumstance.

The alteration of prices in other sectors also drew the attention of Pliny the Elder. In his attempt to explain the variability of market prices (*pretia rerum*) of certain commodities in Rome and other places almost every year, Pliny provides a valuable reasoning that points to the effects of "shipping costs or the terms on which a particular merchant has bought them, or at some dealer dominating the market may whip up the selling price".[8]

[7] Plin. *Ep.* 7.27: *Deserta inde et damnata solitudine domus totaque illi monstro relicta; proscribebatur tamen, seu quis emere seu quis conducere ignarus tanti mali vellet. Venit Athenas philosophus Athenodorus, legit titulum auditoque pretio, quia suspecta vilitas, percunctatus omnia docetur ac nihilo minus, immo tanto magis conducit.*

[8] Plin. *HN* 33.164: *Pretia rerum, quae usquam posuimus, non ignoramus alia aliis locis esse et omnibus paene mutari annis, prout navigatione constiterint aut ut quisque mercatus sit aut aliquis praevalens manceps annonam flagellet.*

One of these dealers, a certain Demetrius, appears to have provoked a large scandal in the Seplasia, a commercial street in Capua known for its specialised market in expensive aromatic products, and for this reason was prosecuted under Nero. Pliny's proposal to mitigate this problem was to provide a list of prices that were usual in Rome (*poni tamen necessarium fuit quae plerumque errant Romae*) and thus establish a standard value (*ut exprimeretur auctoritas rerum*) that could be used as a reference for all actors involved in the business, including ignorant purchasers. In this regard, Pliny also notes that purchasers who pay exaggerated prices for dye should know that the cost of its production changes according to the season of the shellfish harvest, and its consequently variable supply.[9] Pliny's proposal to fix scales of prices and explain the mechanisms of transaction costs to battle speculation followed the didactic scope of the *Natural History*. In the Preface of the work, Pliny declares that among his aims was to provide judgement to what was new (*novis auctoritatem*), and bring light to what was dark (*obscuris lucem*).[10] The private use of information and restricted knowledge as a source of unjust profit could also impact the labour market. In this regard, Pliny the Elder complains that other kinds of speculators, namely doctors from Egypt who specialised in lepra, used their exclusive knowledge and experience to demand exaggerated wages for their services.[11]

The contributions that make up the present volume aim to deepen our understanding of the ancient Roman Economy by identifying and dissecting the information systems, networks and dynamics that both enabled and conditioned business and financial relationships. The study of knowledge as an economic source, but also as an instrument of power, invites us to evaluate economic activities within a larger collective mental, social and political framework.

The ancient texts seen above illustrate the Romans' awareness of the power of information, as well as the effects of informational differentiation on economic performance and fairness. To what extent did this understanding transcend the ethical level reflected in philosophical writings, and which was also discussed in legislative texts? We will, as far as is possible,

[9] Plin. *HN 9.138*. These cases are analysed by Lao (2011: 44–48), who demonstrates the advisory function of the work against ignorance and speculatory profiteers.

[10] Plin. *HN Praef.* 15.

[11] Plin. *HN* 26.4: *Adveneruntque ex Aegypto genetrice talium vitiorum medici hanc solam operam.*

disclose the complex connections between specialised knowledge, access to and use of information, and its impact on the strategies of economic agents. The volume also discusses the creation of innovative institutions aimed to improve and regulate such performances, yet also keep them under control. Our book builds upon, and is greatly indebted to, the remarkable previous scholarly research on economic theory, specifically on the economics of information, but also on associated theories such as New Institutional Economics (NIE), which have significantly impacted recent studies on the Ancient economy.

In a seminal article published in 1961, George J. Stigler advocated for considering information a key resource to understand the frequent problems attached to economic practices. The dispersion of prices that were often detected within various types of markets, even in the case of products of equal quality, is a phenomenon that Stigler attributed to ignorance and a lack of understanding of certain factors, such as the cost and value of the search, the changing conditions of supply and demand, and the potential effects of advertising. One of the battlegrounds of economic research in the 1960s was the elusiveness of the search for knowledge concerning the quality of goods.[12] Stigler's observation takes us all the way back to Plato's *Protagoras* and to the discussion on the problem of ex-ante unverifiable commodities, a pervasive issue in markets and economic thought, both ancient and modern.

Economic activities and relations necessarily generate situations in which one party is better informed than the other. The job applicant, the seller, the money lender, and the client of an insurance company are all in possession of relevant, exclusive information that is not necessarily shared with or known by their counterparts: the employer, the buyer, the money borrower and the insurance company, respectively. Since the 1970s, research into asymmetric information has occupied a major position in economic theory and challenged traditional assumptions of Neoclassical Economics about the existence of markets shaped by perfect information. Information asymmetry reveals the essential contradictions within theories such as the Walrasian equilibrium, based on the ideal existence of a perfect balance between supply and demand in economic markets. In 2001, the Nobel Prize in Economic Science recognised the substantial and

[12] Stigler (1961: 224) refers to how department stores invest in guaranteeing the quality of their products, and criticises economists who often assume that consumers accept the reputation of a seller on the basis of full knowledge.

innovative research developed by George Akerlof, Michael Spence and Joseph Stiglitz in the field of modern market theory and the impact of economies of information on our understanding of the functioning (and malfunctioning) of market structures, the interactions between actors and agents, and the economic consequences of these phenomena.[13]

The prolific amount of theoretical and empirically based research on the consequences of such asymmetries has led to remarkable outcomes. In Akerlof's famous and fundamental article "The Market for 'Lemons'" (1970), the trade in second-hand cars becomes a case study of private information as a source of adverse selection and its far-reaching effects. The impossibility for a buyer to gain reliable information about the quality of a specific car triggers a lowering of the average prices of all second-hand cars within the market, which ultimately works against anyone willing to sell good quality cars at a fair price, while creating a situation where it is only viable to trade in poor quality cars. Economic institutions that regulate markets and moderate the consequences of asymmetric information are identified by the author as an effective mechanism to palliate this problem.

Another way of mitigating the effects of asymmetric information and adverse selection is signalling, a mechanism that involves setting observable actions and signs that transmit private information to the uninformed party. The labour market is one field in which signalling has become a standard way for employers to compensate for the impossibility of observing the employee's productivity before hiring them.[14] An analysis of private information in the insurance market led Michael Rothchild and Joseph Stiglitz to identify a form of signalling known as screening. One screening method used by insurance companies with no information on customers or their risk situation is to offer various types of contracts and premiums that are subject to certain conditions. This form of self-selection also applies to the labour market, although here it is the employer who specifies the wage and signal—e.g. the level of education—within the contract.[15]

[13] On the contributions of these three key authors, see Löfgren, Persson, Weibull (2002). A general insight into economics of information is provided by Molho (1997).

[14] Spence (1973). In a more recent article, Spence (2002) discusses factors such as the allocation of time as a signal of interest and a screening device, as well as the impact of the internet on the changing information structures, as well as increasing practices such as outsourcing by firms and its effects on transaction costs.

[15] Rothchild and Joseph Stiglitz (1976). See also Wilson (1977) and Wolpin (1977).

While the economics of information is integral to the foundation of Microeconomics, it is only in more recent years that the field has found an echo in historical research. For example, the applicability of Ackerlof's theory, as well as the problem of adverse selection on the Roman slave and livestock market, has been analysed by Bruce W. Frier and Dennis P. Kehoe.[16] The authors show how the Roman legal system established rules that attempted to mitigate the problem of a lack of protection for uninformed purchasers by introducing liability mechanisms affecting the seller. The use of signalling devices was fairly widespread in Roman markets, and recent research in this direction has guided the scope and aim of the present volume. The management of information in the slave and labour markets will be the focus of detailed attention in two contributions of this book.[17]

A relevant aspect discussed throughout this volume is the economic impact of institutional measures such as guarantees, public records and contract clauses, which aimed to compensate and alleviate information asymmetries and reduce transaction costs. Following a NIE perspective, and more specifically, Douglass North's proposed definition of institutions, these can be understood as norms or rules, either formal or informal, that attempt to regulate human relationships.[18] Informal rules, shaped by cultural beliefs and traditions and shared normative frameworks, are regarded as particularly powerful vectors for the consolidation of institutions, but also for institutional change.[19]

NIE approaches have notably influenced the study of the Ancient economy in recent years. North's understanding of institutions and their relation to transaction costs—which refers to any factor or constraint that generates uncertainty and unpredictability in economic trade—plays a central role in NIE. The study of the cost of transactions evolved as an alternative to the postulates of Neoclassical Economics, dominated by the perfectly informed actor known as *homo oeconomicus*. Problems linked to information are indeed a major cause of transaction costs. This aspect, in relation to the question of economic rationalism, has been analysed by Jean Andreau and Jérôme Maucorant.[20] Following the work of economists

[16] Frier and Kehoe (2007).

[17] See in particular the chapters by Lavan and Holleran, and below.

[18] North (1990: 3–4).

[19] North (2005).

[20] Andreau and Maucourant (1999).

such as Oliver E. Wiliamson, Alain Bresson has explored the possibilities of NIE for the study of the Ancient Greek Economy.[21] Transaction costs and institutions that contributed to reducing them and improving the functionality of Roman society and economy, have been scrutinised by Frier and Kehoe in their aforementioned chapter in *The Cambridge Economic History of the Greco-Roman World* (2007). The authors investigate 'the rules of the game'—the institutional environment and norms present in economic organisations and structures that facilitated and regulated commerce in ancient Rome.[22] In his influential *The Roman Market Economy*, Peter Temin applies NIE to discuss the importance of contractual relationships and legal enforcement in the Roman grain market, in which traders had to face the endemic problem of hidden and asymmetric information, and circumvent issues such as adverse selection and moral hazard.[23]

A collective volume edited by Kehoe, David M. Ratzan and Uri Yiftach (2015) has scrutinised the often overlooked contribution of law to the Ancient Economy, and more specifically to an understanding of transaction costs and the institutional efforts to minimise and compensate them. Contracts, firms, agency, coinage and public archives are some of the mechanisms and instruments studied in this fundamental work, which also analyses the concept of knowledge applied to economic performance from the perspective of 'bounded rationality'.[24] The impact of public institutions and the state on the private market in relation to the theory of transaction costs has gained significant ground in recent years. Elio Lo Cascio has drawn attention to the constant preoccupation of Roman authorities about the negative effect of price speculation on the market. Enforcement strategies (the 'rules of the game') were thus put in place to control such practices and guarantee free competition.[25] One of these institutions, the *bibliothêkê enktêseôn*, operated, as François Lerouxel has shown, as a public archive that managed fundamental information for the regulation of the

[21] Bresson (2016 (2007–2008): 15–27; 415–438).

[22] The authors follow North (1991) and Klein (2000) in their examination of the 'rules of the game'.

[23] Temin (2013: 97–113).

[24] Kehoe, Ratzan and Yiftach 2015 (eds.). On the concept of 'bounded rationality', coined by Herbert Simon, see Frier and Kehoe (2007: 121–122).

[25] Lo Cascio (2018).

credit market in Roman Egypt, which contributed to reduce uncertainty, and thus transaction costs.[26]

One of the flaws of NIE, however, is the risk to overestimate the capacity of the state and its structures to enforce contracts and transactions.[27] Taco Terpstra has recently addressed this critical issue, as well as the importance of considering private order mechanisms and their interaction with public institutions as key factors to understand economic performance and the functioning of markets.[28]

Recent research on the role of informal institutions has shown the relevance of social relationships reinforced by shared mental models in the management of information and the minimisation of uncertainty in cross-cultural and long-distance structures of trade.[29] This avenue of research explores the impact of psychology on economic studies, an aspect that has been the focus of major attention in recent studies in the field of behavioural economics, and which investigates factors such as the process of decision-making and the complex ways in which information feeds and contributes to knowledge.[30] Koen Verboven has identified promising lines of research in this direction applied to the Greco-Roman world, as well as in fields such as development economics, as fruitful areas of future study to grow in parallel and complementarily to NIE.[31] From an economic behavioural perspective, it is central to understand how information is received and processed, namely how to recognise the mental mechanisms—including motivation and emotions—that lead to the formation of choices, preferences and decisions.[32] The perspective of performers and

[26] Lerouxel (2015). On the specific case study of real estate and the legal consequences of marriage, see the contribution of the author in this volume, and below.

[27] A nuanced criticism of NIE's model of institutional efficiency is discussed by Verboven (2015).

[28] Terpstra (2019: 13–32).

[29] See in particular, Broekaert (2017: 1–22). On the concept of shared mental models, see Denzau and North (1994).

[30] The way individuals process information is considered by 'prospect theory', a term coined by Kahneman and Tversky in 1979 which encapsulates the idea that real-life decisions very often deviate from expected utility theory.

[31] Verboven (2015). On the further recent applications of NIE, see also Droß-Krüpe, Föllinger and Ruffing (2016).

[32] On the main areas studied by behavioural economics, see Camerer, Loewenstein and Rabin (2004). Cicero's correspondence provides for instance a valuable corpus of materials to explore in detail these mental frameworks in interaction with elite social norms, see García Morcillo (2020).

the influence of the social environment in the handling of information and uncertainty feature strongly in the present book.

The contributions within this volume address the subject of asymmetric information and information management from a variety of complementary perspectives. The book is divided into four parts, each of which reflects distinct approaches, sectors and types of practices in which the economics of information can be tested. These are: (1) Information Management; (2) The Real Estate and Land Property Market; (3) The Labour Market; (4) Trade and Financial Markets.

The first chapter of our book, by the economist Pablo Revilla, provides a survey of key theories regarding information management and markets of incomplete information, which have shaped the field since the second half of the twentieth century, including Friedrich Hayek's "The Use of Knowledge in Society" (1945). Hayek's pioneering work identified market price mechanisms that functioned as a system of information exchange to allow coordinated decision-making within a decentralised system. Revilla goes on to discuss the theory of transaction costs, originally formulated by Ronald H. Coase (1937), as well as the problems and consequences of dysfunctional or incomplete information mechanisms such as moral hazard, leading to economic inefficiency and impacting wealth.

Following Revilla's contribution, the first section provides an in-depth discussion of two case studies of information management. Alejandro Díaz Fernández and Francisco Pina Polo engage with the question of what kind of public and private documents were available in the Roman official archives, particularly the *aerarium populi Romani*. How relevant was access to that information for the development of economic activity? The *aerarium* housed all official documents (*tabulae publicae*) generated by the Roman administration, which included, among others, lists of debtors and creditors of the state, lists of citizens with their tax obligations, and accounts of magistrates abroad. But to what extent was this documentation publicly accessible? Was it available only to magistrates, or to all citizens? Evidence from trials suggests that in theory, private citizens could also gain access. If so, the *aerarium* contributed to reducing the risk of asymmetric information in cases such as concessions to *societates publicanorum*. The consultation of this archived information, which would have included useful financial data such as the outcome of previous allocations, would have allowed these companies to bid more effectively.

The role of knowledge management in the functioning of Roman auctions—public and private—and the impact of asymmetric information on the actors' behaviour is the subject of the second chapter in this section, written by Marta García Morcillo. The auction system was, by its very nature, exposed to uncertainty and manipulation, which resulted in substantial information gaps and inequalities that could affect both sellers and purchasers. The applicability of modern auction theory, game theory and empirical studies are tested by the author in a series of well-documented case studies, which show how the Romans built a reliable information system for this kind of competitive sales, using marketing and enforcement mechanisms, as well as social norms. Ancient authors highlighted the importance of publicity, transparency and control of information as key factors within auctions. The presence of the auctioneer or *praeco*, the requirement of securities and guarantors, the Aedilician regulations, and registers of sales, among others, all ensured this. Yet these efforts faced also complex legal challenges, such as the formation of bidding rings or collusions, and the practice of shill bidding (which involved at least one fake-bidder).

The real estate market and the transfer of land titles are examined in the next section of the book. Saskia T. Roselaar discusses asymmetric information in transactions of land during the Roman Republican period, especially during the second century BC. Arguing for the existence of a free land market, Roselaar demonstrates how transactions in this sector were subjected to problems of unequal information, particularly affecting the relationships between buyers and sellers, and landowners and managers. There were also issues of asymmetric information in cases where land was worked by caretakers for absentee landowners. In the case of the *ager publicus*, a lack of information, and specifically uncertainty regarding its legal status, may all have impacted willingness to invest in state-owned land.

Cristina Rosillo-López studies the real estate market as a sector in which information asymmetries played a fundamental role, as was acknowledged by both Roman jurists and Cicero. The seller generally knows more than the buyer, not only about the item up for sale, but also about the characteristics of the neighbourhood and the prices within the area. In addition, the asymmetry is not equal in all cases, since some sellers and buyers are better informed than others. These disparities in information represent a unique feature of the real estate market compared to other markets, in which the mobility of commodities alters their transaction costs differently. In her contribution, Rosillo-López studies the legal, social and economic measures that attempted to bridge the gap of information asymmetry, both in renting houses or apartments and in letting. Screening and other similar strategies were practiced by buyers and sellers, while Roman law established measures that punished those who did not declare defects in real estate transactions, or who incentivised control over sub-letters.

Roman Egypt provides highly valuable evidence about the effects of state intervention in the property market. François Lerouxel examines two prefectoral edicts from AD 89 and 109 concerning a general register of individuals' property rights, the *bibliothêkê enktêseôn*, which dealt mostly with real estate. One of the main issues within these two edicts was the rights that some wives could have over pieces of real estate owned by their husbands. This public information was, however, not self-evident or automatically transmitted to the widow, which often provoked a problem in the case of a transfer, as the new purchaser may have ignored the widow's rights to the house; a wife might also discover that her husband had sold a house to which she held the rights. These two edicts attempted to tackle this issue in order to prevent long, complex lawsuits and to maintain the social and legal hierarchies by protecting the patrimonial order.

In the third section of the volume, two contributions offer a complementary insight into the labour market. Claire Holleran's chapter looks at factors such as market intermediaries (e.g. contractors), signalling mechanism such as qualifications, apprenticeships, letters of recommendation, and the membership of informal and formal associations as instruments to solve the problem of information asymmetries. Skilled workers, such as doctors and specialised craft workers, relied on signalling devices and the membership of professional associations to display their proficiency. For the employer, these signals also served as a screening model, in which wages were offered according to specific requirements and interpretable signals. Roman law protected buyers against the *imperitia* of poorly skilled workers by liability under contracts of *locatio conductio operis* and the *lex Aquilia*. Enslaved people were hired and borrowed for both skilled and unskilled work, which raised further questions of liability. Holleran clearly points out how these observable signalling devices and strategies to overcome information asymmetries in the labour market were used in both rural and urban areas.

In a similar vein, Lavan deliberates on the sale of slaves and the issues of asymmetric information that this created. Roman law devised strategies to solve the problem of slaves who turned out to have a disease or 'defect' in the buyer's eyes, including a lack of specific behavioural characteristics, such as obedience, diligence and entrepreneurship. Faced with this situation, the buyers paid particular attention to proxies for quality, such as the distinction between new and old slaves. The commodification of human beings and bodies cannot be successful, states Lavan, especially when mental and moral qualities need to be assessed. The antebellum US South provides a useful comparison with the Roman case, since similar questions regarding information asymmetries and slaves were raised and Roman legislators were used as models for norms in the profitable American market for slaves.

The fourth and final section of the book is dedicated to trade relationships, markets and the role of merchants and financial intermediaries in commercial enterprises. Mico Flohr focuses on space as a touchstone of information. How did developing urban networks and landscapes change the way in which economic information circulated? How could people obtain market information if they were strangers in a new place? The uneven distribution of *tabernae* outside Italy, in comparison with *porticus* and *basilicae*, provides a widely divergent picture. In regions like Baetica, Africa Proconsularis and Italy, a dense network of communication facilitated the circulation of information, while in less densely urbanised areas, information asymmetries (e.g. knowledge of products and prices) could be more easily exploited.

The control exercised by associations over economic life through information management is examined by Nicolas Tran in the next chapter. If a so-called de facto monopoly on activities existed, to what extent did it result from an unequal access to information, which depended on membership to a professional association? Roman *collegia* were able to foster and facilitate exchanges of information amongst traders concerning multiple, at times complex, commercial patterns. Yet while associations offered integration to their members, they also organised the exclusion of outsiders. This was especially relevant in the long-distance trade. Tran considers two trading communities attested during the second and early third centuries: the *corpus splendidissimum Cisalpinorum et Transalpinorum*, an association of merchants from both sides of the Alps, and long-distance merchants trading olive oil from the province of *Baetica*.

Long distance trade was an economic sector that demanded a high level of organisation and communication networks across large geographical areas. This is also one of the areas of study of the ancient economy that is most affected by a lack of evidence. Dario Nappo tackles the case study of commerce between the Roman Empire and India, including the issue of information gained through Roman coins found in India. The paper proposes that Roman coins were only exported to India when it was profitable, namely when the ratio between silver and gold in the two regions differed, which allowed merchants who benefited from the arbitrage to make large profits. This sophisticated financial action required great skill to overcome the lack of the necessary information to complete the transaction.

The role of information as a determinant of growth in general, and of the performance of the Roman financial system in particular, is discussed by Koen Verboven in the last chapter of this section. What opportunities and constraints determined the generation, codification, storage and transmission of information in the relationship with economic performance, i.e. the 'Information Governance System' (IGS)? Private order information governance systems included personal networks, communities and *collegia*, as well as practices such as accounting, registration offices and various financial instruments. While the dominant paradigm for long-distance trading organisations remained that of personal trust networks, the public order IGS underlying the credit market allowed these organisations a broader scope in arranging and handling their financial needs. Ethnically based communities and guilds did not control credit provisioning in long-distance trade ventures. Verboven argues that the institutional framework of the Roman empire offered procedures for information governance that supported the development of a market for financial services to long-distance traders, since the efficiency of a credit market depended on access to reliable information. The limitations of close-knit social groups as a credit system stimulated the use of specialised intermediaries (deposit bankers and businessmen who provided financial services) in long-distance trade.

Jean Andreau's concluding remarks reflect on the different ways in which information has been analysed in the present book. Firstly, he looks at specific types of transactions, which bring the protagonists together but also against each other (e.g. seller and buyer, or lender and borrower) and in which information asymmetry is clearly present. Secondly, he discusses from a more general perspective the primary role of information and its diffusion in Roman economic life.

All in all, the papers gathered in *Managing Information in the Roman Economy* offer a multifaceted view of asymmetric opinion, one that spans several centuries and fields of influence. One of the objectives of this volume is to demonstrate the productive and promising application to the Roman world of ideas and theories supplied by the flexible and prolific field of the economics of information, as well as those from other complementary perspectives that have proved highly useful for historical research, such as NIE. Our approach aims to demonstrate that information was not merely a vehicle and a source of profit, but also an instrument that provoked inequality and disadvantage, and which could also destroy the balance of functioning market structures and relationships. The Romans' awareness of this problem boosted the creation of a series of institutions that regulated, restricted and promoted public information and, in the long term, also contributed to the stability and improvement of markets. We are further interested in revealing the key factors that transformed information into knowledge, which involved an interpretative awareness of the use of such information, and the consequences of this process on the creation of institutions and mechanisms that reduced uncertainty and improved economic performance. Still, certain types of information inevitably escaped the control of legal enforcers and regulators. Should we simply consider this issue as an inherent risk and a detrimental factor to economic efficiency? Only through a deeper understanding of social and political structures, of the interactions between public and private actors and institutions, and of the collective and individual rules and mentalities that conditioned economic performance, we can get closer to assessing the complexity of the Roman economy. Ultimately, we hope that this volume will serve as a useful tool for comparative studies of economic history, and for research that explores the possibilities and challenges of modern theories in ancient economies.

Bibliography

Andreau, J., and J. Maucourant. 1999. À propos de la rationalité économique dans l'Antiquité gréco-romaine. Une interprétation des thèses de D. Rathbone (1991). *Topoi. Orient-Occident* 9 (1): 47–102.

Bresson, A. 2016. *The Making of the Ancient Greek Economy. Institutions, Markets and Growth in the City-States* (Published in French in 2007 and 2008). Princeton: Princeton University Press.

Broekaert, W. 2017. Going Mental: Culture, Exchange and Compromise in Rome's Trade with the East. In *Sinews of Empire. Networks in the Roman Near East and Beyond*, ed. H.F. Teigen and E.H. Seland, 1–22. Oxford/Philadelphia: Oxbow Book.

Camerer, C.F., G.F. Loewenstein, and M. Rabin, eds. 2004. *Advances in Behavioral Economics.* Princeton: Princeton University Press.

Coase, R.H. 1937. The Nature of the Firm. *Economica New Series* 4 (16): 386–405.

Denzau, A., and D.C. North. 1994. Shared Mental Models: Ideologies and Institutions. *Kyklos* 47: 3–31.
Droß-Krüpe, K., S. Föllinger, and K. Ruffing, eds. 2016. *Antike Wirtschaft und ihre kulturelle Prägung/The Cultural Shaping of the Ancient Economy.* Wiesbaden: Harrassowitz Verlag.
Frier, B.W., and D.P. Kehoe. 2007. Law and Economic Institutions. In *The Cambridge Economic History of the Greco-Roman World*, ed. W. Scheidel, I. Morris, and R.P. Saller, 113–143. Cambridge: Cambridge University Press.
García Morcillo, M. 2020. Mentality, Motivation and Economic Decision-Making in Ancient Rome: Cicero and Tullia's Shrine. *The Economic History Review* 73 (3): 623–643.
Garver, E. 2004. Can Virtue Be Bought? *Philosophy and Rhetoric* 37 (4): 353–382.
Kahneman, D., and A. Tversky. 1979. Prospect Theory: An Analysis of Decision Under Risk. *Econometrica* 47: 263–290.
Kehoe, D.P., D.M. Ratzan, and U. Yiftach, eds. 2015. *Law and Transaction Costs in the Ancient Economy.* Ann Arbor: University of Michigan Press.
Klein, P.G. 2000. New Institutional Economics. In *Encyclopaedia of Law and Economics*, ed. B. Bouckaert and G. De Geest, vol. 1, 56–489. Cheltenham/Northampton: Edward Elgar.
Lao, E. 2011. Luxury and the Creation of a Good Consumer. In *Pliny the Elder: Themes and Contexts*, ed. R. Gibson and R. Morello, 35–56. Leiden: Brill.
Lerouxel, F. 2015. The βιβλιοθήκη ἐγκτήσεων and transaction costs in the credit market of Roman Egypt (30 b.c.e. to ca. 170 c.e.). In *Law and Transaction Costs in the Ancient Economy*, ed. D.P. Kehoe, D.M. Ratzan, and U. Yiftach, 162–184. Ann Arbor: University of Michigan Press.
Lo Cascio, E. 2018. Market Regulation and Transaction Costs in the Roman Empire. In *Trade, Commerce and the State in The Roman World*, ed. A. Wilson and A. Bowman, 117–132. Oxford: Oxford University Press.
Löfgren, K.-G., T. Persson, and J.W. Weibull. 2002. Markets with Asymmetric Information: The Contributions of George Akerlof, Michael Spence and Joseph Stiglitz. *The Scandinavian Journal of Economics* 104 (2): 195–211.
Molho, I. 1997. *Economics of Information. Lying and Cheating in Markets and Organisations.* Oxford/Malden: Blackwell.
North, D.C. 1990. *Institutions, Institutional Change, and Economic Performance.* Cambridge: Cambridge University Press.
———. 1991. Institutions. *Journal of Economic Perspectives* 5: 97–112.
———. 2005. *Understanding the Process of Economic Change.* Princeton: Princeton University Press.
Rothschild, M., and J. Stiglitz. 1976. Equilibrium in Competitive Insurance Markets: An Essay on the Economics of Imperfect Information. *The Quarterly Journal of Economics* 90: 629–649.

Spence, M. 1973. Job Market Signaling. *The Quarterly Journal of Economics* 87 (3): 355–374.

———. 2002. Signaling in Retrospect and the Informational Structure of Markets. *The American Economic Review* 92 (3): 434–459.

Stigler, G.J. 1961. The Economics of Information. *The Journal of Political Economy* 69 (3): 213–225.

Temin, P. 2013. *The Roman Market Economy*. Princeton: Princeton University Press.

Terpstra, T.T. 2019. *Trade in the Ancient Mediterranean: Private Order and Public Institutions*. Princeton: Princeton University Press.

Verboven, K. 2015. The Knights who Say NIE. Can Neo-Institutional Economics Live up to Its Expectation in Ancient History Research? In *Structure and Performance in the Roman Economy*, ed. P. Erdkamp and K. Verboven, 33–57. Bruxelles: Latomus.

Wilson, Ch. 1977. A Model of Insurance Markets with Incomplete Information. *Journal of Economic Theory* 16: 167–207.

Wolpin, K. 1977. Education and Screening. *American Economic Review* 67: 949–958.

CHAPTER 2

Economics and Information: Asymmetries, Uncertainties and Risks

Pablo Revilla

This chapter attempts to present the main concepts that economists use to explain the role of information in economic environments, and is organised as follows. We first introduce the need for information for economic agents, then present the model of perfect competition. We continue by explaining the difference between perfect and imperfect information, before defining the information problems that arise due to incomplete contracts. We then distinguish between risk, uncertainties and asymmetric information problems, before exposing the main asymmetric information model, before developing the problems derived from asymmetric

I wish gratefully to acknowledge the comments by Marta García Morcillo, Cristina Rosillo-López, Guadalupe Valera, the participants in the workshop "Managing Asymmetric Information in The Roman Economy" and the two anonymous referees. The financial support from grant ECO 2017–86,245-P Plan Nacional de Investigación. Ministerio de Economía y Competitividad is also acknowledged. The remaining errors are my own responsibility.

P. Revilla (✉)
Universidad Pablo de Olavide, Sevilla, Spain

C. Rosillo-López, M. García Morcillo (eds.), *Managing Information in the Roman Economy*, Palgrave Studies in Ancient Economies,
https://doi.org/10.1007/978-3-030-54100-2_2

information, as well as their solutions. We then explain auctions, and the relevance of asymmetric information within this process. Finally, we conclude.

2.1 Introduction

In any economic decision, economic agents (individuals, consumers, workers, companies, governments, etc.) must consider the information available to them. Often, a part of that information corresponds to the personal requirements of the agent, and is thus available without issue. For example, the buyer must consider their tastes and needs before making their purchase, as well as the available budget given their income and wealth. However, they must also consider other relevant information that comes from third parties. This information may be difficult or expensive to obtain, and may even be partially or entirely unknown. The buyer may examine the object to be purchased to assess its quality, but sometimes this requires an expert, and even in these cases there are certain aspects that may remain hidden without further tests. There may also be unknown circumstances, both current or future, that can affect the value of the object (such as undesirable neighbours or facilities surrounding a house), or the conditions that determine the need for that good (a health condition that changes the need for an elevator in an apartment block, for example). In the case of a service, it is difficult to evaluate the quality a priori before hiring it (the skill of a hairdresser, the oratory and dedication of a lawyer, or the pedagogy of a teacher). Moreover, we must rely on their reputation, or the recommendations of former clients. In addition to this, the decision also requires information about alternative possibilities that may exist. The buyer may find a seller with a better or cheaper product, but would then have to devote time and effort to finding them, which may not be worth it. The buyer may be able to satisfy the same need with an alternative product (a good or service) that is equally satisfactory. There may be several ways to make a trip or transport goods, and the buyer may not know of the new options (e.g., Uber and Cabify are now available in many cities as an alternative to a traditional taxi service). We could use similar examples with respect to vendors, workers, companies that hire and sell, investors, and so on. It is thus common for economic agents to have to devote effort, time and even money to obtaining relevant information to make their decisions, without having all the relevant information.

2.2 Perfect Competition Model

Economists work with models to simplify a complex reality and analyse the principal issues of interest. The paradigmatic model is that of the perfectly competitive market. This model is used to describe how a market would function, as a sphere of relationship and exchange suppliers and demanders of a product, as well as the beneficial effects of the market as a system for generating and distributing goods or services that satisfy a human need. In this model, everything is perfect. In addition to perfect information, the assumptions used to describe the basis of the model include: perfect price flexibility; the behaviour of suppliers and price-taking behaviour of consumers and suppliers; profit or personal interest maximisation; and the existence of a homogeneous good (although this is produced by different suppliers and may thus have slight differences that are irrelevant to consumers). This assumption of perfect information also includes several features. First, all market participants have information (immediately and without cost or effort) on all the transactions that take place in the market, as well as their price. Second, everyone has all the necessary (reliable) information concerning the characteristics and quality of the product being exchanged. In other words, it is as if both buyers and sellers were experts in the product, capable of recognising its quality with the naked eye, with no hidden vices or defects, and the evolution of the product (durability, performance, etc.) is also perfectly foreseeable and known. Obviously, real-world examples in which these assumptions can be fulfilled are relatively rare. It is possible to find examples of goods exchanged between experts whose quality is easily identifiable, such as collectors of certain goods (stamps, coins, etc.). We can also find markets in which the information available on all exchanges and their price is accessible in real time, as is the case for financial markets of stocks and other assets, and even for raw materials markets. However, it is difficult to find examples that satisfy all these assumptions at once. If all participants in financial markets naturally and simultaneously knew the characteristics of the traded assets as soon as they changed, it would not be necessary to prohibit insider trading. In the real world, it is far more common to find situations in which the information is not perfect. The causes of this imperfection are many, as we will describe later.

The perfectly competitive market model could therefore be considered unrealistic in terms of how it treats information. Economists use it as a frame of reference, not only because of its simplicity, but also because it describes an ideal market that obtains an optimal allocation in terms of the welfare it provides to participants. In the words of economists it is *efficient,* in the sense that no other system of allocation and distribution of goods or services could improve the welfare of the participants without some of them getting worse. Therefore, by comparing what is envisaged within this model, economists can analyse what would be the potential loss of welfare or efficiency attributable to each different aspect or characteristic of the model's assumptions, such as information problems. Normally, economists identify the welfare generated with the concept of surplus, which can be understood as the difference between the value of the goods for final users and the value of the original resources used to produce those goods. Many other models related to this have been developed, which analyse situations of imperfect information. These would include all situations that, to a greater or lesser degree, do not satisfy the assumptions of perfect information.

2.3 Perfect and Imperfect Information in Models

In order to present what economists can contribute to the concept of imperfect information, it is first necessary to briefly understand the role that perfect information plays in the model of perfect competition. This model, as we mentioned before, predicts that the allocation of goods in a market such as that described in the last section will be efficient. If all the markets within the economy were adjusted to this, model efficiency could be described by achieving three objectives: goods would be allocated to the consumers who value them the most (i.e. those who would need them most if they could afford them); goods would be produced using the least valuable resources, which would be the most abundant or available; and the combination of goods that would be produced would be the best in terms of satisfying the most valued needs using the least valuable resources.

However, there are no agents who decide or plan using these objectives. This model describes a decentralised decision-making system in which each agent (buyers, sellers, consumers, businesses, workers, etc.) decides selfishly. The coordination of these decisions is achieved through the pricing system. As F. Hayek describes: "…the price system as such a mechanism for communicating information if we want to understand its real function".[1] Hayek's contribution was that prices would constitute a

[1] Hayek (1945).

system of messages that allows information to be transmitted so that each agent could make his own decisions in a coordinated way, and that this would be the main function of prices in a market mechanism or economy. High (or rising) prices proposed by buyers would signal a greater desire or need for goods, and given this information the producers of those goods would increase their activity and contract more resources (or resources of greater value) for the production of goods. In turn, the holders of the resources would dedicate them (by selling, leasing or directly employing) to the production of those goods in which they are most valued. Symmetrically, the high (or rising) prices proposed by sellers would report goods shortages and thus the higher value of the resources needed for their production, which is ultimately due to the scarcity or unavailability of those resources. This information would guide the consumers who need or value these goods the least to try to replace them with others of a lower price, which would be more abundant or easier to produce with less valuable resources. In order for this mechanism to function properly, agents must have the correct information on various aspects. First of all, agents must have perfect knowledge of the quality of the goods, in order to be able to express the value they attribute to those goods through prices. Secondly, all prices should be perfectly understood without delay, so that the most profitable options can be chosen (the highest or lowest price according to the buyer or seller) at the time the decision is made. Finally, agents must know all the transactions that take place in the market in order to be able to choose the most profitable buyer or seller. Any absence or limitation to the information available regarding these aspects is considered a situation of imperfect information, and would result in a malfunctioning of the market (with respect to that described in the reference model). Such a malfunctioning would result in a loss of efficiency; this is to say that if the agents ignore the options of transactions or prices, they will probably stop carrying out activities that could be profitable and instead will carry out other, less profitable activities because they ignore the existence of the previous ones. All of this results in a loss of value that could have been generated, that is in satisfying needs using the least valuable resources.

Imperfect information thus generates a loss of efficiency—there is a surplus that is lost, in the sense that it has not been generated when it could have been in the absence of this problem. This loss of surplus justifies the generation of solutions that, although costly, make it possible to solve, entirely or in part, these information problems and recover that lost surplus. Examples of such solutions would be intermediaries, regulations, laws or registries, complex contracts, and so on.

2.4 Information Problems and Incomplete Contracts

For this reason, economists try to distinguish the different information problems and the solutions to each of them. In this sense, it is necessary to differentiate between the problem of incomplete contracts and those of imperfect information. The problem of incomplete contracts can occur even when there are assumptions that create perfect information. Incomplete contracts are cases in which contracts cannot specify all the relevant aspects of the agreement between the parties, for several reasons. One reason would be the high transaction costs of a complete contract (as described by Coase, although Coase did not use such an exact term until years later).[2] The design of a complete contract and the mechanisms necessary to ensure its fulfilment in all cases may involve very high costs relative to the value of the contract itself, and therefore the parties may prefer an incomplete contract. When you buy a book or a newspaper, for example, you don't check if some pages are badly printed, and you also don't bargain about the contract with the seller concerning the consequences if your expectations aren't satisfied.

Another reason would be the existence of relevant information that cannot be verified by third parties, such as courts, thus making it impossible to ensure compliance with the contract in relation to this information (which may nonetheless be known by the parties to the agreement—marriage and divorce agreements may often include examples of this). Other examples would include uncertainty about the future, which may mean that the contract cannot include provisions for all possible events that could affect it, or at least could not be made without cost, or the absence of reliable courts; it may even mean that an incomplete contract is preferable (many people would not want the ticket of a film or play to include spoilers about the outcome—surprises are sometimes welcome). Therefore, although uncertainty or information problems may aggravate the incompleteness of contracts, this is in principle a different concept to problems of imperfect information.

[2] Coase (1937).

2.5 Asymmetries, Uncertainties and Risks

When considering the problem of imperfect information, it is necessary to distinguish three distinct concepts: information asymmetries, uncertainties and risks. Information asymmetries are situations in which one side of the market (usually sellers) has more information than the other side. This imbalance may be due to hidden actions (past or future) regarding the signing of the contract, or hidden information (e.g. concerning the quality or characteristics of the goods). Uncertainties are situations that may lead to different consequences with different probabilities of occurrence. These probabilities may not be well known, or may even be subjective probabilities (each individual may give different probabilities to the same consequence). Unlike uncertainties, risks are situations that can lead to a finite and known number of alternative consequences whose probabilities are well defined and known to everyone (the probabilities of each result when rolling a die, or of winning the lottery, for example). The difference between the uncertainties established here is common when considering decision problems with imperfect information, although not all authors make a clear distinction in this regard, nor do they universally refer to uncertainty as situations in which the probabilities may or may not be well known, or even subjective.

The treatment of decisions in situations of uncertainty or risk has been widely developed in the literature from the work of F. H. Knight.[3] In general, risk treatment considers which is the expected value (among various different alternatives) by means of an arithmetic mean of the value of each possible consequence, weighted by probabilities. An agent whose preferences are risk neutral will always choose the alternative that provides them with the highest expected value. However, it has been proven that there are agents who are risk-averse, and to a certain degree prefer safe or certain alternatives with a value lower than the expected value of alternatives with uncertainty. The degree to which they prefer these safe options can be measured by the difference between the true value and the expected value (some workers prefer a fixed wage job rather than a variable wage, even if the expected value of the variable one would be greater; if these individuals say that they are indifferent between a fixed wage of A and a variable

[3] Knight (1921): "The practical difference between the two categories, risk and uncertainty, is that in the former the distribution of the outcome in a group of instances is known (either through calculation a priori or from statistics of past experience), while in the case of uncertainty this is not true ..."

one of expected value B, then the difference (B-A) is a measure of their risk aversion). There are also other cases where agents prefer risky options, and these are called risk takers or risk lovers. In these cases, the agents prefer a risky option with an expected value lower than the safe value. This would be the case of the person who buys a lottery ticket or participates in a game of chance while knowing that the odds are against him. In economics, it is more common (especially in decisions involving high value) for agents to have risk averse preferences. In these cases, agents can take out insurance or establish contracts in which they pay a price or give up part of the expected value in exchange for reducing the risk. This willingness to reduce risk allows insurance companies or agents with less risk aversion to make a profit by signing contracts. In the case of insurance companies, the benefit is obtained by insuring a large number of agents for whom the chances of the alternatives they wish to avoid are independent of each other. In other words, the insurance company estimates that it will have to compensate some of the individuals, but not all of them at the same time; its risk is thus reduced by adding contracts and the value that it can obtain is similar to the expected value. Its benefit is obtained from the difference between the expected value and the certain value that agents are willing to pay in exchange for obtaining security. However, in the case of contracts between two individuals (e.g., a lessor of a piece of agricultural land and a lessee who will directly exploit the land), it is possible that one of them has a greater aversion to risk than the other (the lessor is averse and the lessee is risk neutral), and it is this fact that allows both to benefit from the contract. The same applies to other cases where the management or exploitation of a resource or business is ceded. In this case, although there is risk, there are no differences between the information available to one participant in the contract or the other, and the probabilities of each possible alternative would even be known by both parties. Interested readers can find a good discussion on this subject and alternative models of risk aversion in a recent paper by T. O'Donoghue and J. Somerville.[4]

In addition to analyses of agents' preferences regarding risk, there is a broad range of literature regarding uncertainty situations. However, in this case the probabilities are not well known, so they may be different for each individual, or even subjective (i.e. influenced by value judgements or

[4] O'Donoghue and Somerville (2018).

opinions concerning the behaviour of third parties or future circumstances). The quantitative treatment in these cases is more complex, and usually requires more advanced probabilistic calculations. Another approach on the part of economists is to consider that in these cases, the preferences of the agents do not depend so much on the calculation of the expected value, but are rather established directly by considering the possible options that include different alternatives (e.g. the decision to participate in a sports bet does not depend on an exact calculation of the expected value with respect to the cost of the bet, but on the intention to participate in the match or to add a material gain to the emotion of the sports result). In these cases, what was previously indicated regarding the possible existence of contracts between individuals is more evident, and may be due not only to the difference in preferences regarding risk, but also to differences in the perception or consideration of probabilities, or even to the desires included in the preferences regarding options in uncertainty. In general, we could affirm that in any human decision the main source of uncertainty is the future. Any human decision involving future events involves deciding under uncertainty. In this sense, all investment decisions include uncertainty and would exceed the scope of the decision with risk. Indeed, Keynes uses the term *animal spirits* in his General Theory of Employment, Interest and Money to refer to the factor that guides the actions of economic agents and, in a certain sense, investment decisions.

2.6 Asymmetric Information

So far, with the exception of subjective probabilities (which are equally unknown to all agents), the aforementioned cases of imperfect information do not consider the substantial differences in information available to one participant or another in contracts or agreements. This would be the realm of asymmetric information, which is compatible with the absence of uncertainty or risk, that is alternative scenarios with different probabilities of occurring. The classic contribution on this is by Akerlof, who presents a market model in which sellers have more information concerning the quality of the goods than buyers, and discusses the consequences that this assumption has on the efficiency of the market (in this case second-hand cars sold between private individuals).[5] It should be recalled that the

[5] Akerlof (1970).

reference framework for this is the model of perfect competition. Buyers will generally value goods differently according to their quality, and the price they are willing to pay will thus depend on the quality they believe the goods have. However, in the situation where buyers cannot distinguish this quality, they must decide what price they are willing to pay, and prudent behaviour advises that they not pay a price equivalent to what they would pay for higher-quality goods.

Therefore, when faced with such asymmetric information, buyers will be willing to pay a lower price. In this context, sellers who own high-quality goods and are aware of this will find that buyers are unwilling to pay a high price, and in many cases sellers will choose not to sell their goods for a lower price and will withdraw them from the market. This initiates a phenomenon called adverse selection, which is characterised by the withdrawal of higher-quality sellers in favour of lower-quality sellers. The withdrawal of these higher-quality sellers should lead consumers to perceive (either by subsequent verification of the quality of the goods purchased or by logical reasoning) that the overall quality of the goods offered has decreased, and therefore the value that can be attributed to them (and consequently the price that they must be willing to pay) should be lower than that considered before the withdrawal of higher-quality goods. This price reduction will lead to the withdrawal of the highest-quality goods remaining on the market and consequently reinforce the adverse selection process. This adverse selection process would, in theory, end when only sellers of goods of the lowest possible quality remain on the market (*lemons*, in the case of used cars). This results in the market being inefficient, because there are transactions of high-quality goods that are not produced and that would have been beneficial to some sellers and buyers. Both parties would thus be interested in solving the problem of asymmetric information generated by this inefficiency.

The problem is that the information revealed by the high-quality seller is not reliable by itself if the other sellers can reproduce the same information (all sellers will claim that their product is of high quality). Therefore, to solve the problem, there must be some signal that sellers of high-quality goods can use to convey the information to buyers; however, this should be a signal that sellers of low-quality goods cannot imitate, or which is so difficult to imitate that it makes it unprofitable for them to do so. This would be the case for product performance guarantees. Ensuring the repair of high-quality goods that are infrequently damaged would be relatively inexpensive, but to do the same with low-quality goods that are very often damaged would be very expensive for sellers. The theoretical explanation for these signals is provided by Spence in a work on signalling in the labour market.[6] He argues that recruiters have a problem because they cannot observe candidates' skills for a job, but that this problem has been solved in part through non-compulsory educational qualifications. Spence believes that these qualifications would be observable signals by employers, which are more costly for workers who have intrinsically fewer skills to perform a job. In this context, non-compulsory education does not increase the ability or capabilities of students, it simply involves an effort to obtain a degree that becomes greater the lower the skills or capabilities of a student are. There would, therefore, be a certain level of education that would discourage low-skilled candidates from obtaining the degree, which would not be the case for higher-skilled candidates because they can obtain the same degree with less effort. In this way, employers can distinguish one type of worker from another and offer higher-paying jobs to those with the required degree (and therefore higher skills), while offering only lower-paying jobs and requirements to workers without the required qualification. Therefore, according to Spence, a signal can solve the problem of asymmetric information as long as it meets three conditions: it is easily observed by buyers; its cost is inversely related to the quality of the goods; and a level of signal is found that discourages lower-quality agents from sending the signal—in spite of the higher price—but does not do so with higher-quality agents. There are then examples of such signals as guarantees, educational levels, deposits or sureties, and so on. However, all these signals imply costs and therefore—even if they solve the problem of inefficiency of the asymmetric information—it is necessary to subtract the costs imposed by this system from the welfare gained. Sometimes the benefits of these signals do not outweigh the costs generated by solving the inefficiency, and thus it is not worthwhile to implement these solutions. In low-value products, the difference in quality may be small and buyers will thus prefer to buy cheap rather than attend to complex signals or contracts, or seek out other products. At other times, these signals can generate or encourage bad behaviour on the part of the buyers themselves. The greater and broader the guarantee or insurance, the less the incentives there are for buyers to take care of their products. This phenomenon, which incentivises bad behaviour on the part of the agents, is called a moral hazard, and we will deal with it later on.

[6] Spence (1973).

Other solutions that have arisen to solve problems of asymmetric information (and which can replace the existence of a signal like that described by Spence) would be a reputation or brand-name. This reputation can involve a cost for the reputed agent (through advertising or dissemination activities, sponsorship, social responsibility, etc.) or no cost (press reports, criticism, social networks, word of mouth, etc.). Normally, these days it implies a certain amount of cost as it requires a combination of these means, and in general to acquire a good reputation (and ensure it is spread around) implies a great deal of time and activity. For this reason, only companies or agents with a prolonged activity reputation can replace other signals. New entrants have to resort to other solutions, such as those described above.

There are also solutions to the problems of asymmetric information from an institutional perspective. These involve the establishment of public or private institutions of a general or mandatory nature, which contribute to reducing the problem of asymmetric information in certain activities. Some examples would be laws or regulations imposing a minimum quality of goods or services, public registries or archives, the establishment of professional standards, compulsory activity licenses supervised by public authorities or professional associations or colleges, and so on. All these mechanisms avoid or reduce the phenomenon of adverse selection by establishing a minimum quality to be met by bidders or by providing a reliable information system that buyers can consult at a relatively low cost. In general, the emergence and durability of these solutions indicates that, whether created by public or private initiatives, the cost of maintaining these institutions (registries, inspection of licences, etc.) is less than the benefits they can generate and is largely due to the efficiency gained by avoiding the problems of adverse selection. However, in the case of public institutions, it is true that in certain cases these institutions may be maintained not so much for their economic value as for their value as instruments of political control.

In the absence of solution mechanisms on the part of sellers or third parties, buyers can try to solve asymmetric information problems by searching for information, although this takes time, resources and effort to conduct a screening process, hire technical advisors or experts, and so on. Evidently, this will only be worthwhile for products with a high value and for which there are no viable alternatives to avoid these asymmetric information problems.

2.7 Reputation, Moral Hazard and the Principal-Agent Model

None of these solutions are without their problems. In general, from the point of view of economists, we consider that these solutions will only be used or maintained over time if their use is rational, that is to say if the benefits of their use outweigh their costs. For example, a new company within a market (i.e. an Asian car brand entering a European market) can initially offer very broad product warranties free of charge and conduct strong advertising campaigns to solve the information problem of being unknown to buyers, while other companies that are already established do not need to do so due to their pre-established reputation. It is likely that over the years, the new company will gain a reputation and then reduce its guarantees and advertising expenditure.

There is a problem that arises with the solution of the signals advocated by Spence in some cases and referred to above: this is the moral hazard. The concept of moral hazard has been elusive for economists, as the controversy between Arrow and Pauly demonstrates.[7] Grubel attempted to precisely define the term, as well as analysing its effects on welfare.[8] A moral hazard can appear in any contract in which one party may behave improperly without the other party being able to control or monitor that behaviour. This would be insurance fraud (ex post) or negligent behaviour (ex ante), as well as lazy or neglected workers, and so on. In all these cases, the improper behaviour of one party has a negative impact on the outcome of the contract for the other party, although sometimes only in terms of probability. For example the user of an electronic device with full warranty and no extra cost for any damage caused may use the device neglectfully, increasing the likelihood that it will accidentally be lost, broken or stolen when compared to the absence of a warranty. As Grubel states, "It is a well-known fact that insured bankrupt retail stores and restaurants tend to go up in flames more often than do financially sound establishments of this type. [...] However, the moral hazard phenomenon, probably most often and quantitatively most significantly, is due to behaviour which only in a very special sense can be considered to be against society's moral norms".[9] Solutions to these problems involve monitoring

[7] Arrow (1963); Pauly (1968).
[8] Grubel (1971).
[9] Grubel (1971: 101).

the other party, imposing behavioural clauses within the contract that can be controlled (hourly controls, inspections, mandatory fire-extinguishing systems, etc.) or alternatively designing a contract that incentivises good behaviour. This proposal to design a contract is one that describes the principal-agent model. In this model, it is assumed that there is a principal whose interest is conditioned by the behaviour of an agent who cannot directly observe it (or would find it very costly to do so). This could be an employer and an employee, a shareholder and the director of a company, and so on. These contracts would have to establish a different system of remuneration (bonuses, commissions, etc.) related to an observable variable (sales, profits, value of shares, etc.), which would likely be related to unobservable behaviour (effort, dedication, care, etc.). In general, the relationship in terms of probability implies that the observable results may be better or worse (even though the agent has behaved correctly), but the probability that the results are good increases with good behaviour. In other words, it is possible to obtain a good sales result whether the employee has made an effort or not, but it would be more likely when he makes an effort. In this case, and since this probabilistic relationship between behaviour and results generates uncertainty that also affects the agent, the retribution should be established in such a manner that the agent has incentives to make an effort, while also taking into account that he may make an effort and the results will still be bad.

The remuneration must thus satisfy two conditions, the first being that the expected *ex ante* value of the remuneration if the staff member makes an effort (a value for the staff member that factors in his assessment of the personal cost of his effort) must be higher than the expected value of the remuneration if he does not make an effort. In addition to this condition on incentives, a participation condition is added, which is usually set out in the following terms. The expected ex ante value of the remuneration if the staff member makes an effort must be higher than the value of the remuneration of an alternative activity (other work with a fixed salary, e.g., or engaging in another activity without uncertainty regarding the result). The combination of these two conditions usually means that the remuneration must include a fixed amount (even if the results are poor) and a bonus (which may be proportional or related to the results) if the results are good. However, there may be occasions when the contract is designed with a remuneration that consists of only a bonus, that is the fixed remuneration is zero and everything is a commission or bonus depending on the results (sales, company profits, etc.). The optimal design of these contracts would imply finding the retributive combination that satisfies these two conditions with the lowest cost for the principal. It should be considered that both the principal and the agent may have different preferences regarding risk, which may influence the optimal remuneration design. It is usually assumed that the agent may be averse to risk while the principal may not, so for the agent it may be very important to have a high fixed amount while the bonus may be lower, but there may be cases in which the agent has different preferences and the optimal contract is structured differently.

2.8 Auctions

We have briefly described the main economic problems generated by imperfect information, as well as some mechanisms created to deal with these problems. There are also other institutions or contracts that, although they are not specific to information problems, become more relevant in these situations. The case of auctions is particularly noteworthy. An auction is a mechanism of competition between buyers, a form of contest that allows the seller to determine who they sell their product to and at what price. In general, it makes it possible to discover who is able or willing to pay a higher price, and to set the price to be paid at the highest valuation of the last bidder to leave the auction. In the case of a single good to be auctioned, it can be said that the auction allocates the good to the potential buyer who values it most, and that the price is equivalent to the value that would be assigned to the second buyer who values it most (the second buyer at that moment), since when the bids reach that value the second buyer will stop participating in the auction. This theoretical result is common to all types of auctions.

The most common type, the English auction (in which the bidders compete to offer higher bids until only one remains unchallenged), ends when the last bid is equal or slightly higher than the maximum value of the good for the second buyer. The second buyer resigns because the price to be paid would be higher than the subjective value, so to buy the good paying this price would mean a loss. The buyer who values the good most wins the auction and obtain the object for this price. Theoretically, if every buyer knows every other buyer—their valuations, and so on—then the optimal strategy for everyone would lead to this result in all kinds of auctions, even the first price auction (in which the buyers bid using closed envelopes and the winner has to pay exactly their own bid). However, in situations of complete information this would not be necessary, because the seller could easily identify the buyers who most valued the goods. If the goods were easily reproducible (manufactured or harvested, etc.), then an auction would be an excessively complex method. The use of auctions makes more sense when it comes to unique objects or those whose value has a large subjective component (works of art), because it can be very difficult to find out which buyer can and is willing to pay more, as well as how much the second buyer would be willing to pay.

However, there is another case in which auctions have a prominent role, one in which the value of the good does not have a subjective component, but is for some reason unknown. Here, the valuation of potential buyers differs because the information they have is different. One example would be the auction of concessions to exploit oil fields, the value of which is unknown (although there are estimates). Another would be the auction of 3G mobile phone licenses in Europe. In these cases, companies or buyers wish to buy goods whose value has no subjective component, but is nonetheless unknown. These are called common value auctions, and involve characteristics that cannot be precisely known, or future circumstances that have no precedent. Different firms may have different studies or measurements that lead them to make different estimates of the target value. In this case, the auction allows the object to be acquired by the company or the buyer with the highest value estimate, although in statistical terms this will not be the most correct estimate, but the one with the greatest upward error. Therefore, the bidder who has overestimated the value of the good will take the good and will have to pay a price equivalent to that of the second most overestimated value. In these cases, this may lead to what is known as the winner's curse, that is the winner in an auction may end up acquiring the good but paying a price higher than the real target value of the good, so that winning the auction and the consequent acquisition is actually a loss. An example of this is the auction of 3G mobile phone licenses, mainly in the European countries, because the revenues for the governments were unexpectedly high. A comparative research across countries has showed only short-term evidence of this phenomenon.[10] The auctions of 4G and 5G licenses have obtained less revenues for the government, i.e. Germany obtained €50 billion with 3G auction in

[10] Cable, Henley and Holland (2002) have analysed the case of the UK, whilst Mackley (2008) has studied the auctions of such licenses in other European countries.

2000, €5.1 billion with 4G in 2015 and €6.5 billion with 5G in 2019, according to DW.[11]

These characteristics are common to all types of auctions—English auctions, Dutch auctions, and auctions sealed at the first or second price—and imply some common biases in the behaviour of the agents. Sellers are interested in having as many potential buyers as possible attending the auction, not only because one can outbid the other, but also because statistically it increases the likelihood that the price will rise. On the other hand, buyers should try to avoid the winner's curse, that is they should bid below their own valuation of the good (or their estimate, in the case of goods with an unknown common value), and if possible bid slightly above the valuation of the next bidder. In the case of English auctions, this process is simpler because it is sufficient to decide a limit value for the bid itself and to increase your bid as little as possible up to that limit value, at which point it is withdrawn from the auction. The limit value would be the valuation of the asset itself, in cases of subjective value. However, in cases of unknown common value it is necessary to discount the probable statistical error—assuming you are the winner of the auction—from the estimated value. In other words, making the greatest statistically possible error will lead to you become the buyer who has most overestimated the real value of the goods. In these cases, sellers are interested in the fact that buyers, in addition to their quantity, can observe the behaviour of others and their real estimates, so that they have more information and can better adjust their own estimate with a lower statistical error of estimation. For this reason, auctions are today often designed in several rounds with limited bids at the end of each round, and all participants are provided with data on the bids placed before they decide whether to withdraw. Interested readers may consult the recent paper by Milgrom about the last developments on auction theory in economics.[12] A more extensive analysis can be found in the book edited by Klemperer and his more recent work with a non-technical introductory curse about auctions.[13]

[11] Retrieved from https://www.dw.com/en/5g-auction-in-germany-raises-65-billion-from-four-telcoms/a-49168657 July 2020

[12] Milgrom (2019).

[13] Klemperer (2000, 2004).

2.9 Conclusion

In conclusion, economists have described and classified the problems generated by imperfect information and have valued the loss of efficiency and well-being that these problems entail. They have also collected the solutions that have spontaneously appeared, and proposed new solutions that evaluate to what extent they would solve the loss of well-being generated by the problems, as well as what the cost of these measures would be. For the most part, these are problems and solutions that arise naturally in economic activities and are not exclusive to the contemporary economy. As can be seen in the following chapters, these problems also arose in antiquity, and many of the solutions mentioned here were then implemented, in one form or another. However, it should be noted that although economists always try to simplify complex economic realities by developing stylised models (and the concepts and categories defined by them respond to this methodology), in real, current or historical cases, complexity nonetheless persists. Very often, we find situations that combine different concepts or information problems, as well as more complex solutions adapted to real cases.

The literature about information problems and about the use of these concepts in economics is huge, technically complex and spreads over many branches. Economists try to design models about how the provision of information can modify the behaviour of agents using game theory.[14] If information is valuable and its absence provokes a loss of welfare, this can generate not only a demand for information, but also a proper market for information.[15] The study of information markets is one of the most dynamic and innovative areas of research in modern economics thinking.

Bibliography

Akerlof, G.A. 1970. The Market for 'Lemons': Quality Uncertainty and the Market Mechanism. *Quarterly Journal of Economics* 84: 488–500.

Arrow, K.J. 1963. Uncertainty and the Welfare Economics of the Medical Care. *American Economic Review* 53: 941–973.

Bergemann, D., and A. Bonatti. 2019. Markets for Information: An Introduction. *Annual Review of Economics* 11: 85–107.

[14] An introduction about this can be found in Bergemann and Morris (2019).

[15] Bergemann and Bonatti (2019).

Bergemann, D., and S. Morris. 2019. Information Design: A Unified Perspective. *Journal of Economic Literature* 57 (1): 44–95.

Cable, J., A. Henley, and K. Holland. 2002. Pot of Gold or Winner's Curse? An Event Study of the Auctions of 3G Mobile Telephone Licences in the UK. *Fiscal Studies* 23 (4): 447–462.

Coase, R.H. 1937. The Nature of the Firm. *Economica New Series* 4 (16): 386–405.

Grubel, H.G. 1971. Risk, Uncertainty and Moral Hazard. *The Journal of Risk and Insurance* 38: 99–106.

Hayek, F.A. 1945. The Use of Knowledge in Society. *American Economic Review* 35: 519–530.

Keynes, J.M. 1936. *The General Theory of Employment, Interest, Money.* London: Macmillan.

Klemperer, P.D., ed. 2000. *The Economic Theory of Auctions.* Cheltenham: Edward Elgar.

Klemperer, P. D. 2004. *Auctions: Theory and Practice (The Toulouse Lectures in Economics).* Princeton: Princeton University Press.

Knight, F.H. 1921. *Risk, and Uncertainty and Profit.* Boston/New York: Houghton Mifflin Co.

Mackley, J.R.K. 2008. European 3G Auctions: Using a Comparative Event Study to Search for a Winner's curse. *Utilities Policy* 16 (4): 275–283.

Milgrom, P. 2019. Auction Market Design: Recent Innovations. *Annual Review of Economics* 11: 383–405.

O'Donoghue, T., and J. Somerville. 2018. Modelling Risk Aversion in Economics. *Journal of Economic Perspectives* 32: 91–114.

Pauly, M. 1968. The Economics of Moral Hazard: Comment. *The American Economic Review* 58: 531–537.

Spence, M. 1973. Job Market Signalling. *Quarterly Journal of Economics* 87: 355–374.

Stigler, G.J. 1961. The Economics of Information. *Journal of Political Economy* 69: 213–225.

PART II

Information Management

CHAPTER 3

Managing Economic Public Information in Rome: The *Aerarium* as Central Archive of the Roman Republic

Alejandro Díaz Fernández and Francisco Pina Polo

In the beginning, Rome was a small town in Latium struggling to survive among others. Rome had a small territory, in which a limited number of citizens lived and worked; its army was also limited, its political system was under construction, and its relationship to other towns and countries was likewise constrained. Under these circumstances, it is reasonable to assume that Rome had not yet reached a high level of bureaucratisation, although a treasury and a modest archive must have already existed. However, the small Latin town became, throughout the Republic, first the ruler of Italy and then of the whole Mediterranean, which led to the creation of a huge empire. Under these new circumstances it also seems reasonable to assume that bureaucracy increased exponentially, giving birth to countless documents and needing hundreds of servants and officers. This is a far cry from

A. Díaz Fernández
Universidad de Málaga, Málaga, Spain

F. Pina Polo (✉)
Universidad de Zaragoza, Zaragoza, Spain
e-mail: franpina@unizar.es

C. Rosillo-López, M. García Morcillo (eds.), *Managing Information in the Roman Economy*, Palgrave Studies in Ancient Economies,
https://doi.org/10.1007/978-3-030-54100-2_3

the false idea of Rome as a great empire virtually without documents—a view that appeared to flourish several decades ago—as scholarship has progressively adopted the perspective that a deep level of bureaucratisation was necessary within a wide and powerful administration, both within Rome and in the provinces.[1]

What kind of public documents can we expect to have been recorded in the Roman official archives, in particular in the *aerarium populi Romani*? To what extent were these documents accessible? How relevant was access to this information for the development of economic activity? For example, what kind of information did a *societas publicanorum* have when they intended to obtain a public contract in a province of the empire, and to what extent was the *aerarium* a source of information on this? This essay aims to reflect on the *aerarium populi Romani* as a possible public source of economic information. In this respect, it is necessary to keep in mind that the evidence available to us is (very) limited and partial. That is why our proposal for reconstruction is, at least in part, hypothetical if not conjectural, although it may open up new perspectives.

According to tradition, the temple of Saturn at the Forum was, from the beginning of the fifth century, the location of the public treasury and archive of Rome, the so-called *aerarium populi Romani*.[2] This seems to mean that the idea of a general archive existed in Rome from the very beginning of the Republic, and from then on its complexity and magnitude increased in line with Roman expansion.[3]

The administration of the *aerarium populi Romani* was the main duty or *provincia* of the *quaestores urbani*.[4] Tacitus will refer later to the general

[1] In this regard, the works and publications of Claude Nicolet (and those inspired by him) have been decisive: Nicolet (1988); Demougin (1994); Moatti (1998, 2011). See now David (2019: 65): "l'élargissement de l'Empire, les nécessités de son administration et la pratique de la codification qui se fit jour donnèrent au document écrit un poids croissant. Il fallait connaître, archiver, classer, retrouver des documents dispersés, hors de portée désormais de la mémoire collective."

[2] Liv. 2.21.2; Plut. *Publ.* 12.3.

[3] This is not the place to develop the discussion on other buildings in which official documents must have been collected and preserved, such as the Tabularium and the Atrium Libertatis. The point is that various different archives existed during the Republic. See Purcell (1993); Tucci (2005); Coarelli (2010).

[4] This is attested by a number of Republican legal documents. See for instance the following paragraph from the *lex Cornelia de XX quaestoribus*: *q(uaestorem) urb(anum), quei aerarium provinciam optinebit, eam mercedem deferto, quaestorque quei aerarium provinciam optinebit, eam pequniam ei scribae scribeisque heredive eius solvito, idque ei sine fraude*

duties of the urban quaestors as *cura tabularum publicarum*;[5] although he is speaking of the Principate, this terminology can also be likely applied to the Republican period. This meant the management and control of the money and the metals reserves, in particular gold, which were deposited in the treasury. It also meant the supervision of all public expenses and incomes in Rome was in the hands of the urban quaestors, always under the command of the Senate,[6] as well as the validation and archiving of all official documents generated by the Roman bureaucracy and administration.[7] The quaestors were of course given support by assistants (*apparitores*), whose numbers increased considerably throughout the Republic as Rome's administration became more and more complex.[8] The *Lex Cornelia de XX quaestoribus*, promulgated by the dictator Sulla in 81, offers some information on how the quaestorian *apparitores* (*scribae*, *viatores* and *praecones*) were nominated.[9] Among them, the *scribae* enjoyed a higher status that corresponded to their greater responsibilities.[10] In fact, the many complex functions of the urban quaestors during their term of

sua facere liceto, quod sine malo pequlatuu fiat, olleisque hominibus eam pequniam capere liceto. (*Lex Cornelia de XX quaestoribus ll.* 1–6. Crawford 1996: 1.294 and 297: "[---] he is to register [with] the urban quaestor, who shall have the treasury as his province, that fee, and the quaestor, who shall have the treasury as his province, is to pay that sum to that scribe, or (those) scribes, or to his heir, and it is to be lawful for him to do so without personal liability, in so far as it be done without wrongful enrichment, and it is to be lawful for those persons to accept that sum"). In general, on the tasks performed by the urban quaestors see Mommsen, Röm.St. II 523–541; Kunkel – Wittmann (1995: 515–523); Lintott (1999: 136–137); Muñiz Coello (2014: 512–520), and now Pina Polo – Díaz Fernández (2019: 79–124). On the *aerarium* in the Imperial period, see Corbier (1974).

[5] Tac. *ann.* 13.28: *dein princeps curam tabularum publicarum a quaestoribus ad praefectos transtulit.* Cf. Ps.-Ascon. *in Verr.* 1.11 p.226 St.: *Quaestores urbani aerarium curabant, eiusque pecunias expensas et acceptas in tabulas publicas referre consueverant.*

[6] See Pol. 6.13.2: οὔτε γὰρ εἰς τὰς κατὰ μέρος χρείας οὐδεμίαν ποιεῖν ἔξοδον οἱ ταμίαι δύνανται χωρὶς τῶν τῆς συγκλήτου δογμάτων πλὴν τὴν εἰς τοὺς ὑπάτους ("the quaestors are not authorised to make any expenditure without a decree of the Senate, except for the service of the consuls"). There is no doubt that Polybius is speaking at this point about the urban quaestors, whereas he refers to the consular quaestors in 6.12.8.

[7] Pina Polo – Díaz Fernández (2019: 84–97).

[8] On the selection, duties and careers of *apparitores*, see Purcell (1983); Muñiz Coello (1982; 1983, esp.119–125).

[9] See Keil (1902); Gabba (1983); Varvaro (1995); Crawford (1996). See especially now David (2019).

[10] Gabba (1983: 489); Purcell (2001). On the importance and excessive influence of the *scribae* working in the *aerarium* see Plut. *Cat.min.* 16.2 (cf. David 2019: 63–65 and 224–225). Nonetheless, the *scribae* were of course subject to controls, and could be brought

office could not have been properly developed without the continuous intervention of the scribes, who very likely served for several years, allowing them to get to know the administration well—at any rate much better than the inexperienced young quaestors who remained in office for just a year.[11]

All official documents (*tabulae publicae*) generated by the Roman republican administration (Senate, magistrates, assemblies, courts, etc.) were recorded and kept in the *aerarium*, and were consequently the direct responsibility of the urban quaestors, the magistrates who ensured their accuracy and preservation.[12] It was the act of depositing a document in the *aerarium* that made it a public document. In this way, the urban quaestors became general public notaries of the Republic. To provide a complete inventory of documents registered in the public treasury is beyond the scope of this article.[13] However, at least some of them will be mentioned in order to better understand the vastness of the documentation and the complexity of the functions for which the urban quaestors—and ultimately their assistants in the *aerarium*—were responsible.

To begin with, senatorial decrees had to be registered in the *aerarium*, including the name of the proposer, the content and the date of issue;[14] in fact, the date of a *senatus consultum* was probably the reference used to archive the decrees in chronological order.[15] In a letter to Atticus, Cicero alludes to the volume (*liber*) containing the senatorial decrees approved during the consulship of Cn. Cornelius and L. Mummius, which suggests

to trial for fraud. Cf. Plut. *Cat.min.* 16.3; Cic. *Mur.* 42: *scriba damnatus, ordo totus alienus.* On scribes brought to trial see Rosillo-López (2010: 127–131).

[11] The continuity in their office can be deduced from Plutarch's narration of how Cato struggled against the corruption of the scribes of the *aerarium* (Plut. *Cat.min.* 16). Cf. Gabba (1983: 489); David (2007: 44); Pina Polo – Díaz Fernández (2019: 84–85).

[12] A survey of the type of documents kept in the *aerarium*, in particular during the Principate, can be found in Millar (1964). See now Pina Polo – Díaz Fernández (2019: 112–115).

[13] See Mommsen, *Röm.St.* II 532–535; Kunkel – Wittmann (1995: 518–521). The scarcity of concrete references to these documents in the ancient sources should be emphasised.

[14] A general reference is found in Liv. 39.4.8: *...senatus consultum factum ad aerarium detulerit.*

[15] The existence of that register is proved by Josephus, who quotes a senatorial decree from 44 copied from the treasury, from the *tabulae publicae* belonging to the urban quaestors of that year, Quintus Rutilius and Gaius Cornelius (Ios. *AJ* 14.219). Cicero, for his part, accuses Antonius of bringing *senatus consulta* that had never existed to the *aerarium*:*...senatus consulta numquam facta ad aerarium deferebantur* (Cic. *Phil.* 5.12). Cf. Cic. *fam.* 12.1.1.

that each year the decrees were compiled and archived in a book.[16] The exact texts of the laws that were passed in the popular assemblies were also registered in the *aerarium*, a procedure that was necessary to ensure the impossibility of a falsification or alteration of their contents.[17] This legal provision was supplemented in 62, when the *lex Iunia Licinia*, sponsored by the consuls D. Iunius Silanus and L. Licinius Murena, was passed. Although its content has been the subject of debate, the law probably set forth that it was mandatory to submit to the *aerarium* a copy of every bill (*rogatio*) when it was made public, before its discussion in *contiones* and the vote in *comitia*.[18] Lists of the allies and friends of the Roman people (*formula sociorum* and *formula amicorum populi Romani*) were also kept in the *aerarium*.[19] The *SC de Asclepiade* makes it clear that this list of friends did exist: "[Uteiq]ue Q. Lutatiu[s M.] Aemilius co(n)s(ules) a(lter) a(mbove), s(ei) e(is) v(ideretur), eos in ameicorum formulam referundos curarent...."[20] Even though direct evidence does not always exist in the ancient sources, the *aerarium* must have contained many other public documents, such as census lists,[21] and perhaps the minutes of magistrates,[22] comitia,[23] and trials or legal processes.

The urban quaestors had a number of assignments that were directly related to the public finances. To begin with, it was through their assistants in the *aerarium* that the magistrates were responsible for the general accounting of the Roman state—its supervision, control and preservation. One of their most important tasks was the supervision of all public income

[16] Cic. *Att.* 13.33: *...reperiet ex eo libro, in quo sunt senatus consulta Cn. Cornelio, L. Mummio coss.*

[17] Cf. Sisenna fr. 117 P.: *idemque perseveraverunt, uti lex perveniret ad quaestorem ac iudices quos vellent instituerent praefestinatim et cupide.*

[18] See Gagliardi (2009), with supplementary bibliography. Cf. Mommsen (1858: 186) (294).

[19] Kunkel – Wittmann (1995: 521).

[20] *S.C. de Asclepiade l.*17 (= *l.* 25 of the Greek text). This list of allies and friends is likewise implied in a text from Livy which refers to 170. An embassy from Lampsacus declared that they had revolted against Perseus as soon as the Roman legions appeared in Macedonia and had given all possible assistance to the Roman commanders. As a reward for their behaviour, they requested the Senate to be included amongst the friends of Rome, and the Senate instructed the praetor Q. Maenius to enrol the Lampsacans among the states allied to Rome: *Lampsacenos in sociorum formulam referre Q. Maenius praetor iussus* (Liv. 43.6.10).

[21] Kunkel – Wittmann (1995: 518).

[22] Mommsen, *Röm.St.* II 533.

[23] Cic. *Pis.* 15.

and expenses—thus assuming the role of comptrollers of the Republic—and each operation had to leave a documented trail.[24] The money for every payment the state made came from the treasury, and as a result it was expected that all expenses were to be controlled by the urban quaestors. They did not take the initiative to pay a public expense, as they simply followed orders given by the Senate, or directly by a higher magistrate in the name of the Senate. Nevertheless, all public expenses required authorisation for payment by the urban quaestors, who had the ultimate accounting responsibility.[25] They also supervised all the public income that ended up in the *aerarium*. First, the extraordinary types of income, including: war reparations that defeated peoples or cities were obliged to pay to Rome, as well as those derived from auctions in which different items were sold; part of the spoils, such as prisoners of war; the property of individuals who declared themselves insolvent, or became outlaws by proscriptions; and public land.[26] The urban quaestors also supervised the regular forms of income, such as the *tributum* paid by every Roman citizen, and consequently the amount paid by every citizen had to be registered in the *tabulae publicae*.[27]

The urban quaestors also had to supervise the accounts of all magistrates after they completed their offices, both in Rome and in the provinces of the empire.[28] Every magistrate who handled public money during his term in office was obliged to put in writing and bring to the *aerarium* detailed accounts after returning from his province.[29] The *scribae* working

[24] Pina Polo – Díaz Fernández (2019: 95–97).

[25] Trisciuoglio (1998: 102). Cf. Mommsen, *Röm.St.* II 541.

[26] Pina Polo – Díaz Fernández (2019: 91–94).

[27] Tributes brought by an embassy to Rome were also given to the urban quaestors for the *aerarium*, for example the *stipendium* of Antiochus brought by the leader of the envoys of the king, Apollonius: *quaestores urbani stipendium, vasa aurea censores acceperunt*... (Liv. 42.6.11).

[28] Let us take as an example Verres' accountability after his quaestorship. Verres was quaestor in 84 and proquaestor probably in 83–82. After his return to Rome, he was obliged to present his accounts (*rationes*) in detail to the urban quaestors. Cicero reproduces the heading of Verres' report: "Accounts related to the urban quaestors P. Lentulus and L. Triarius." (Cic. *Verr.* 2.1.37: *P. Lentulo L. Triario quaestoribus urbanis res rationum relatarum*). Lentulus Sura and Triarius were the urban quaestors in 81.

[29] In general, on the rules about bookkeeping in the late Roman Republic, see Fallu (1979) and now Pina Polo – Díaz Fernández (2019: 86–90). Cf. Rosillo-López (2010: 110–111); Cuomo (2011: 198).

in the treasury had to check these,[30] and the urban quaestors had to give their approval to say that the accounts were appropriate.[31] The presumed inaccuracy of the *rationes* submitted by a magistrate could obviously be used as a weapon for a political attack or even for a judicial process, as was habitual in the last two Republican centuries. Some testimonies show that these *rationes* could indeed be decisive proof in a trial.[32] For example, Ti. Sempronius Gracchus was concerned by having lost his tablets of accounts (πινακίδες) after the Numantines surrounded the army of his consul, C. Hostilius Mancinus, in 137, as he knew he risked being attacked by his political enemies in Rome for not being able to give an account of his quaestorship in Hispania.[33] When referring to the supposedly imprecise accounts presented by Verres after his quaestorship, Cicero hints at how these *rationes* had to be structured. There were three major sections: the income that the magistrate had at the beginning of his office; the expenses throughout his mandate; and the final balance.[34] Within these sections, every element had to be described item by item, something that undoubtedly implied a considerably complex process.[35]

The *lex Iulia de repetundis*, which was passed in 59, signified a concerted effort to avoid the manipulation of public accounts. Cicero alludes to this law in his correspondence, both during his stay as governor in Cilicia and after his return to Rome, which allows us to see broadly how

[30] Cf. Cic. *Pis.* 25: *Ita enim sunt perscriptae scite et litterate ut scriba ad aerarium qui eas rettulit perscriptis rationibus secum ipse caput sinistra manu perfricans commurmuratus sit...*

[31] According to Callistratus, a Roman jurist of second-third century AD, the accountability followed several stages: a review of the documentation (*legendas rationes*); a supervision of the calculations (*computandas rationes*) as well as a delivery of the remains (*reliqua solvere*); and finally an approval and closure of the accounts (*subscribere rationes*) (*Dig.* 35.1.82). These stages may also have existed during the Republic. See Rosillo-López (2010: 112 n.176).

[32] The quaestor P. Albius had to present his accounts in the trial against his superior, Q. Mucius Scaevola Augur, for the maladministration of the latter in the province of Asia, ca. 120–119 (Cic. *de orat.* 2.281); see Alexander (1990), no. 32. On the importance of these *tabulae* in trials, cf. also Cic. *Scaur.* 18; *Att.* 1.16.4; Val. Max. 2.10.1.

[33] Plut. *Ti. Gr.* 6.1–3.

[34] Cic. *Verr.* 2.1.36: *Accepi...viciens ducenta triginta quinque milia quadringentos decem et septem nummos. Dedi stipendio, frumento, legatis, pro quaestore, cohorti praetoriae hs mille sescenta triginta quinque milia quadringentos decem et septem nummos. Reliqui Arimini hs sescenta milia.* Cf. Fallu (1979: 102).

[35] Cicero reproaches Verres for the excessive conciseness of his accounts, an unmistakable proof of his culpability according to him, and wonders: "Is this the way of presenting accounts?" (Cic. *Verr.* 2.1.36: *Hoc est rationes referre?*).

the procedure worked.[36] In agreement with the *lex Iulia*, it was compulsory to deposit two copies of the accounts in two cities within the province.[37] This meant that accounts had to be in their final form before the governor left his province and returned to Rome. An exact duplicate had to be brought as a third copy to the *aerarium* in Rome, for supervision by the urban quaestors through their scribes.[38] The purpose of this measure was to make it possible to compare the different copies, if necessary. The accounts could not be amended once deposited in the provincial cities.[39] Cicero claims the accuracy and integrity of his accounts, but in any case he places the greater responsibility on his *scriba*, M. Tullius. This was obviously a way for Cicero to distance himself from any potential irregularities, but it also shows that in practice the *scribae* were in charge of all the bureaucratic issues.[40]

The final task performed by any Roman commander after his return to the *Urbs* ought to be a presentation to the urban quaestors of a thorough catalogue of spoils taken from the enemy: money, gold, silver and every kind of asset.[41] This documentation, kept in the *aerarium*, should be implicitly considered as a statement of public ownership. As in other cases, the duty of the urban quaestors was consequently to act as public notaries

[36] See Cic. *fam.* 5.20.1, where Cicero contrasts the *ius vetus et mos antiquus* with the new regulations introduced by the Iulian law. Cicero sent this letter to L. Mescinius Rufus, his quaestor in Cilicia. Cf. Venturini (1979: 471–477); Coudry (2009: 58–59); Rosillo-López (2010: 112); Pina Polo – Díaz Fernández (2019, 87–88).

[37] Cic. *Att.* 6.7.2: *ego Laodiceae quaestorem Mescinium exspectare iussi, ut confectas rationes lege Iulia apud duas civitates possem relinquere*; *fam.* 2.17.4: *Rationes mei quaestoris nec verum fuit me tibi mittere nec tamen erant confectae. Eas nos Apameae deponere cogitabamus.*

[38] Cic. *fam.* 5.20.2. It seems that the *scribae* of the *aerarium* made themselves one further copy of the accounts, which suggests that the magistrate kept the original in his personal archives. Cf. Rosillo-López (2010: 112).

[39] Cic. *fam.* 5.20.8.

[40] Fallu (1979: 110); Cuomo (2011: 190).

[41] In a letter written to Caninius Sallustius, Cicero declares categorically that the booty he had been able to acquire during his expedition in Cilicia was to be sent to the urban quaestors, that is, to the Roman people, without anyone else touching it, he says. Cicero adds that in Laodicea he would take all necessary measures to ensure that the public money would reach Rome without problems in its transportation (Cic. *fam.* 2.17.4: *De praeda mea praeter quaestores urbanos, id est populum Romanum, terruncium nec attigit nec tacturus est quisquam. Laodiceae me praedes accepturum arbitror omnis pecuniae publicae, ut et mihi et populo cautum sit sine vecturae periculo*).

on behalf of the *civitas*,[42] and failure to do so could result in prosecution.[43] Cicero forcefully contrasts the behaviour of Verres in Sicily with that of P. Servilius Vatia Isauricus—not only had Verres illegitimately plundered Sicily, he also kept the spoils for himself and his friends instead of giving them to the public treasury. On the contrary, Servilius had obtained his booty in accordance with the law of war ("imperatorio iure"), brought it to Rome, exhibited it in his ceremony of triumph, and eventually "took care of registering all in public documents in the treasury."[44] These documents, under the heading "Rationes relatae P. Servili" ("The accounts delivered by Publius Servilius"), were available, since Cicero specifically mentions their contents: "You see not only the number of the statues, but the size, the form, and the state of each one accurately characterised in writing."[45]

The *aerarium populi Romani* thus collected and preserved an impressive compilation of official political, administrative and civil documents (lists of citizens, senatorial decrees, texts of laws, lists of allies and friends of Rome, etc.), as well as financial and fiscal documents (accounts of magistrates within Rome and abroad, public income and expenses, taxes, etc.). It should be added that among these financial documents were the lists of debtors and creditors of the state (as the activity of Cato during his

[42] See Churchill (1999: 103): "This document would serve as a concrete record of what the public had already seen (*during the triumph), and would make it possible for those with access to the *aerarium* to confirm their recollections." On the accounts of booty, see Coudry (2009: 52–60); Pina Polo – Díaz Fernández (2019, 88–91).

[43] For example, Manius Acilius Glabrio was prosecuted because a part of the booty that had apparently been taken from Antiochus' camp was not exhibited in the procession of triumph and was not brought to the *aerarium*. See Liv. 37.57.12: *...quod pecuniae regiae praedaeque aliquantum captae in Antiochi castris neque in triumpho tulisset, neque in aerarium rettulisset.*

[44] Cic. *Verr.* 2.1.57: *P. Servilius quae signa atque ornamenta ex urbe hostium vi et virtute capta belli lege atque imperatorio iure sustulit, ea populo Romano adportavit, per triumphum vexit, in tabula publica ad aerarium perscribenda curavit.* Cf. Coudry (2009: 53).

[45] Cic. *Verr.* 2.1.57: *Non solum numerum signorum, sed etiam unius cuiusque magnitudinem, figuram, statum litteris definiri vides.* Cf. Liv. 39.7.1, where a detailed list of what Cn. Manlius Vulso contributed to the treasury on the occasion of his triumph is given: 200 golden crowns, 220.000 pounds of silver, 2103 pounds of gold, and so on. It is obvious that this information comes from the official report delivered by Manlius Vulso.

quaestorship shows),[46] as well as certificates of property,[47] and no doubt public contracts.[48] This all set up an extraordinary and essential source of information for the Roman administration.

Was this documentation accessible? Was it available only to magistrates and senators, or open to all citizens? Due to the lack of evidence, these questions are difficult to answer conclusively. In his biography of Cato Uticensis, Plutarch offers the first possible answer. He states that once Cato laid down his quaestorship in 64, he made some of his slaves go to the archive every day and copy the new transactions. Additionally, Cato himself paid five talents for a copy of the books containing accounts of the public business from the times of Sulla to his own quaestorship.[49] Five talents is a considerable amount of money for a copy, which must have been made by *librarii* in the service of Cato.[50] Were these *librarii* professional copyists belonging to the staff of the *aerarium* and working according to the demands of customers who requested copies of documents? Were they slaves or freedmen of Cato, and five talents was the price paid to the *aerarium*? Was there a market for financial information services? In any case, this passage from Plutarch implies that public documents in the *aerarium* were available for private use, and were accessible to citizens who did not hold office, since Cato was certainly a senator after his quaestorship, but he was not a magistrate at the moment.

In the trials that took place in the *quaestiones perpetuae* during the second and first centuries, defendants were accused of misconduct as governors of a province, corruption, illegal access to Roman citizenship, and

[46] According to Plutarch's account, when Cato found in the archive that many persons owed debts of long standing to the public treasury and the treasury to many persons, he immediately demanded payment from debtors and made payment to creditors (Plut. *Cat. min.* 17). Cf. Millar (1964: 35–36).

[47] Cic. *Flacc.* 80: *illud quaero sintne ista praedia censui censendo, habeant ius civile, sint necne sint mancipi, subsignari apud aerarium aut apud censorem possint.*

[48] Plut. *Quaest.Rom.* 42. Cf. Millar (1964: 35).

[49] Plut. *Cat.min.* 18.5: οὐ μὴν οὐδὲ ἀπαλλαγεὶς τῆς ταμιείας ἀφῆκε τῆς φρουρᾶς ἔρημον τὸ ταμιεῖον, ἀλλ᾽ οἰκέται μὲν αὐτοῦ καθ᾽ ἡμέραν ἀπογραφόμενοι τὰς διοικήσεις παρῆσαν, αὐτὸς δὲ βιβλία λόγους περιέχοντα δημοσίων οἰκονομιῶν ἀπὸ τῶν Σύλλα χρόνων εἰς τὴν ἑαυτοῦ ταμιείαν ὠνησάμενος πέντε ταλάντων ἀεὶ διὰ χειρὸς εἶχεν.

[50] The use of copyists was common. For instance, once the tribune of the plebs Rullus presented his agrarian *rogatio* in December 64, Cicero, who was still a *consul designatus*, immediately ordered several *librarii* to transcribe the text of the bill and had it sent to him (Cic. *leg.agr.* 2.13). On the use of *librarii* to obtain copies of public documents, see Cic. *leg.* 3.46, where Cicero shows distrust towards *apparitores* and *librarii*.

more, and it was thus essential that prosecutors and advocates were as prepared as possible for their intervention before the court. This implied a careful knowledge of economic, technical and juridical information, which could in part be obtained from oral evidence given by witnesses, but a large part of which had to be extracted from documents. When Cicero explains in *De oratore* that in the first phase of the work carried out by an advocate it is necessary to collect proofs and establish facts, he mentions as sources "documents (*tabulae*), testimonies, agreements, examinations, laws, senatorial decrees, court decisions, magisterial decrees, reports, and whatever else is not produced by the orator but it is supplied to the orator by the case itself or by the parties."[51] Cicero first mentions *tabulae*, a presumably general reference to official documents recorded in the *aerarium*, but later refers to other kinds of information that, as we have seen, could also be found in the general archive of Rome.[52]

The correct preparation of a trial thus involved a previous investigation by the orators who were going to intervene in it, which presumably in most cases meant carrying out, at least partially, an inquiry in the *aerarium*, which was very likely accomplished by slaves or freedmen at the service of prosecutors and advocates, just as Cato used his slaves to be updated. Many of the discourses delivered by Cicero at the court—and also in the Senate or before the people—such as the *Verrinae*, *De lege agraria* and others, are a good example of how thorough research work should be done beforehand. In order to prepare his *Verrinae*, as an advocate Cicero would have utilised a great number of fiscal and financial documents generated by the administration in Sicily, which means that local and provincial archives were also open to obtain information. In fact, Cicero alludes to an article of the *lex Cornelia repetundarum* according to which he, as prosecutor, was allowed to consult all documents and records (*tabulae et litterae*).[53] Something similar can be said about the agrarian *rogatio Servilia*, which must have implied previously meticulous work on the part of the tribune Servilius Rullus, as it was an agrarian law that was

[51] Cic. *de orat.* 2.116: *...ut tabulae, testimonia, pacta conventa, quaestiones, leges, senatus consulta, res iudicatae, decreta, responsa, reliqua, si quae sunt, quae non reperiuntur ab oratore, sed ad oratorem a causa [atque a re] deferuntur.* Cf. Pugliese (1964: 308–310).

[52] This could perhaps explain the arson of certain archives with the purpose of destroying evidence, something that would indirectly support open access to archives to obtain copies of documents. Cf. Moreau (1994: 141–143).

[53] Cic. *Verr.* 4.149: *Ego legem recitare, omnium mihi tabularum et litterarum fieri potestatem.*

required to precisely designate the public lands to be distributed, and Cicero answered in his speeches against the bill with the same degree of precision, using information that was obviously taken from official documents.[54] As Nicolet presumed, this may signify that the *aerarium* contained detailed information about the territories under Roman control, including cadastral-type figurative documents.[55]

Once again, the important point is that the information brought together within the *aerarium* had to be available to *privati*, presumably including men who had not held yet a magistracy—and were thus not senators—and used trials as a springboard for their political careers. This does not necessarily mean, however, that the Roman general archive was open to queries from any citizen. In the case of trials, it seems likely that an authorisation from the praetor presiding over the *quaestio* was needed to gain access to official documents. In any case, it is probably realistic to assume that only educated well-off people of prominent social (and political) standing were regular customers of the *aerarium*.[56]

Having established the at least partial availability of the information contained in the archive, the next and final question is to explore how this affected economic and financial transactions, and once again the problem is the paucity of evidence. Asymmetric information can lead to market failure and inefficient economic results. These asymmetries of information are at times difficult to avoid in certain markets, for example the real estate market, in which it is very common that one party involved in the transaction, usually the seller, has more complete information than the other.[57] Asymmetric information in this field can stimulate deception on the part of the seller and annoyance on the side of the buyer, whose outlay may result in disaster.

If this principle is applied to the investments implemented by a large company, then the risk of failure and negative economic implications is multiplied, as companies—whether large or small—cannot afford to lack

[54] See Roselaar's article in this volume.

[55] Nicolet (1994: 153–155). Nicolet even asserted that "les archives romaines étaient donc exactes."

[56] In a passage from *De legibus* (*leg.* 3.46), Cicero refers to copyists who made copies of the texts of laws on request (*a librariis petimus*). The text once again shows the practice of copying official documents contained in the *aerarium* for private individuals, although it does not seem realistic to read *petimus* as an allusion to all Roman citizens; rather, Cicero is thinking exclusively of people like himself, that is of his social class.

[57] See Rosillo-López in this volume.

up-to-date information if they wish to succeed as a business. Let us take the *societates publicanorum* as an example. There were obviously companies of very different size and prominence in Rome, but they all had the goal of gaining a concession in a province, for example to exploit a mining district or salt mines, to collect taxes, and so on. The *locatio* to exploit these business opportunities was obtained or renewed through public auction, usually every five years. A company had to make an economic proposal to win the auction against other companies and obtain the benefits for the following period, which was not possible without a market study, or without having all the information.[58] It is reasonable to assume that the *societates publicanorum* had their own *scribae*, who were permitted—and perhaps even had privileged contacts—within the archives. Nicolet has argued that documents in the *aerarium* were classified by chronologically and by category—which would certainly have been the case for *senatus consulta* and laws—but not geographically, a fact that would have made researching a particular territory problematic.[59]

However, before a company assumed any financial risk, it would need to have as accurate an idea as possible of the potential market it aspired to exploit; without this, its financial proposal would have been made blind, and the *societas* would have run a serious risk of failing. First, the company needed to know the situation in the territory where the *locatio* would be auctioned: was the situation stable? Was there any risk of military conflict or destabilisation? What was the relationship between the *publicani* and the local people? How was the economic situation? What was the financial situation of the cities that had to pay taxes to the company?

In this respect, the company could gather information from their business networks and could talk to recent governors and *publicani* who had been involved in the province to know their opinions first-hand, but they could also consult the reports from these governors and their financial accounts kept in the *aerarium*, in which it was possible to find objective economic and financial information.[60] If the auction dealt with the renova-

[58] Of course the calculations could be wrong, as seems to have occurred in 61 with the publicans of Asia, who claimed from the Senate a relaxation of the conditions of the *locatio* (*remissio mercedum*), adducing that they had paid too high a price. See Cic. *Att.* 1.17.9; Suet. *Caes.* 20.

[59] Nicolet (1988: 137; 1994: 151).

[60] Nicolet (1994: 163), considered that before the *lex Iulia* of 59 the *rationes* of a governor had to be sent or brought to Rome, and served as a source of information about the economy of a province.

tion of a *locatio* that was already underway, it was even more important to know as accurately as possible how the concession had functioned in the last few years, as well as how much rent the *societas* in charge of it had obtained. Otherwise, there would be asymmetric information between the *societas* in charge of the *locatio* and its potential rivals. However, it is almost certain that the *societates publicanorum* were controlled by the Roman administration. They had to declare their earnings to the state, either through annual accounting balances (*rationes*) or at the very least every five years when the *locatio* was renewed.[61] It seems probable that such official reports would have had to be delivered to the *aerarium populi Romani*.[62] Were these accessible to other *societates*? In this respect, one can only conjecture, but it appears reasonable that legal agents of *societates* who were interested in competing for a public contract would be authorised to obtain copies of those reports, and in general to get as much information as possible. This official information, if it was accessible to all competitors, was certainly not the only source the *publicani* had to base their bidding strategy on, but it would have helped to reduce the uncertainties and make the competition fairer. Ultimately, this benefitted the state: the greater the competition, the greater the profits could be.

Every state needs a central archive to record and preserve its bureaucratic production. In Rome, the *aerarium populi Romani* was the depository for official documents throughout the Republican period. Among these documents, we can reasonably conclude that there were global accounts, both at a provincial and Roman level, which were accessible under certain circumstances and for certain individuals. As Nicolet has correctly asserted: "les chiffres n'étaient apparemment pas des secrets d'État."[63] The *aerarium* has been overlooked as a location where magistrates and senators—but also at least some influential private citizens—could go to look for economic and financial information, for example to be used in a trial or to make an investment. If this partially hypothetical

[61] Cf. Cic. *Att.* 4.11.1: *dixit mihi Pompeius Crassum a se in Albano exspectari ante diem IIII Kal.; is* cum *venisset, Romam (eum) et se statim venturos ut rationes* cum *publicanis putarent.*

[62] Nicolet (1994: 164–168). The accounts of the *societates publicanorum* certainly existed and were deposited where they were acting, as Cicero, who speaks of *tabulae publicanorum*, shows (Cic. *Verr.* 2.187). Cicero adds in this context that it was forbidden to bring the accounts to Rome, as they were essential for the Sicilian administration (Moreau 1994: 133), but these accounts do not necessarily coincide with the annual balances.

[63] Nicolet (1994: 171).

but in any case worth exploring interpretation is correct, the access to the data contained in the general archive of the Roman Republic would have likely reduced the risk of asymmetric access to information and its potential economic effects.

Bibliography

Alexander, M.C. 1990. *Trials in the Late Roman Republic, 149 BC to 50 BC.* Toronto: University of Toronto Press.

Churchill, J.B. 1999. *Ex qua quod vellent facerent*: Roman Magistrates' Authority over *Praeda* and *Manubiae*. Transactions and Proceedings of the American Philological Association, 129, 85-116.

Coarelli, F. 2010. Substructio et Tabularium. *Papers of the British School at Rome* 78: 107–132.

Corbier, M. 1974. *L'Aerarium Saturni et l'Aerarium Militare. Administration et prosopographie sénatoriale*, Rome: École Française de Rome.

Coudry, M. 2009. Partage et gestion du butin dans la Rome républicaine: procédures et enjeux. In *Praeda. Butin de guerre et société dans la Rome républicaine*, ed. M. Coudry and M. Humm, 21–79. Stuttgart: Franz Steiner Verlag.

Crawford, M.H. (ed.). 1996. *Roman Statutes*, 2 vols. London: Institute of Classical Studies.

Cuomo, S. 2011. All the Proconsul's Men: Cicero, Verres and Account-Keeping. In *L'insegnamento delle technai nelle culture antiche: atti del convegno, Ercolano, 23–24 marzo 2009 AION, Quaderni 15*, ed. A. Roselli and R. Velardi, 165–185.

David, J.-M. 2007. Ce que les *Verrines* nous apprennent sur les scribes de magistrats à la fin de la République. In *La Sicile de Cicéron: lecture des Verrines. Actes du colloque de Paris (19–20 mai 2006)*, 35–56. Besançon.

———. 2019. *Au service de l'honneur. Les appariteurs de magistrats romains*, Paris: Les Belles Lettres.

Demougin, S. (ed.). 1994. *La mémoire perdue. À la recherche des archives oubliées, publiques et privées, de la Rome antique*, Paris: Publications de la Sorbonne.

Fallu, E. 1979. Les règles de la comptabilité publique à Rome à la fin de la République. In *Points de vue sur la fiscalité antique,* ed.H. van Effenterre. Paris.

Gabba, E. 1983. Lineamenti di un commento alla *Lex Cornelia de XX quaestoribus. Athenaeum* 61: 487–493.

Gagliardi, L. 2009. La *lex Iunia Licinia* e le procedure di pubblicazione e di conservazione delle leges nella Roma tardo-repubblicana. *Diritto@Storia* 8. www.dirittoestoria.it/8/Tradizione-Romana/Gagliardi-Lex-Iunia-Licinia.htm

Keil, J. 1902. Zur *lex Cornelia de viginti quaestoribus. Wiener Sudien* 24: 548–551.

Kunkel, W., and R. Wittmann. 1995. *Staatsordnung und Staatspraxis der römischen Republik. 2. Die Magistratur.* Munich: C.H. Beck.

Lintott, A. 1999. *The Constitution of the Roman Republic*. Oxford: Clarendon.
Millar, F. 1964. The Aerarium and Its Officials Under the Empire. *Journal of Roman Studies* 54: 33–40.
Moatti, C., ed. 1998. *La mémoire perdue. Recherches sur l'administration romaine*, Rome: École Française de Rome.
———. 2011. La mémoire perdue. À la recherche des archives oubliées de l'administration romaine. *Cahiers du Centre Gustave Glotz* 22: 123–130.
Mommsen, Th. 1858. Sui modi usati da' Romani nel conservare e pubblicare le leggi ed i senatusconsulti. In *Annali dell'Istituto di corrispondenza archeologica* 39, 181–212 = *Gesammelte Schriften*, Berlin/Dublin/Zurich (1965) (first edition 1907) III, 290–313.
———. 1876–1888. *Römisches Staatsrecht*, 3 vols. in 5, Leipzig: Hirse.
Moreau, Ph. 1994. La mémoire fragile: falsification et destruction des documents publics au Ier s. av. J.-C. In *La mémoire perdue. À la recherche des archives oubliées, publiques et privées, de la Rome antique*, ed. C. Nicolet, 121–147. Paris: La Sorbonne.
Muñiz Coello, J. 1982. *Empleados y subalternos de la administración romana. I. Los* scribae. Huelva: Colegio universitario de la Rabida.
———. 1983. Empleados y subalternos de la administración romana. II. Los *praecones. Habis* 14: 117–146.
———. 2014. Los cuestores republicanos. Origen, funciones y analogías. *Klio* 96: 500–536.
Nicolet, C. 1988. *L'inventaire du monde. Géographie et politique aux origines de l'Empire romain*. Paris: Hachette.
———. 1994. Documents fiscaux et géographie dans la Rome ancienne. In *La mémoire perdue. À la recherche des archives oubliées, publiques et privées, de la Rome Antique*, ed. C. Nicolet, 149–172. Paris = 2000. *Censeurs et publicains. Économie et fiscalité dans la Rome antique*, 247–264. Paris: Arthème Fayard.
Pina Polo, F., and A. Díaz Fernández. 2019. *The Quaestorship in the Roman Republic*. Berlin: Boston De Gruyter.
Pugliese, G. 1964. La preuve dans le procès romain de l'époque classique. In *La preuve. 1. L'Antiquité. Recueils de la Société Jean Bodin* 16, 277–348. Brussels: Éd. de la Librairie encyclopédique.
Purcell, N. 1983. The *apparitores*: A Study in Social Mobility. *Papers of the British School at Rome* 51: 125–173.
———. 1993. Atrium Libertatis. *Papers of the British School at Rome* 61: 125–155.
———. 2001. The *ordo scribarum*: a study in the loss of memory. *Mélanges de l'École française de Rome. Antiquité* 113 (2): 633–674.
Rosillo-López, C. 2010. *La corruption à la fin de la république romaine (IIe-Ier s. av. J.-C.): aspects politiques et financiers*. Stuttgart: Steiner.
Trisciuoglio, A. 1998. *Sarta tecta, ultrotributa, opus publicum faciendum locare. Sugli appalti relative alle opere pubbliche nell'età repubblicana e augustea*. Napoli.

Tucci, P.L. 2005. Where High Moneta Leads Her Steps Sublime. The 'Tabularium' and the Temple of Juno Moneta. *Journal of Roman Archaeology* 18: 6–33.

Varvaro, M. 1995. Per una interpretazione della *Lex de XX quaestoribus*. *A.S.G.P.* 43: 577–588.

Venturini, C. 1979. *Studi sul 'crimen repetundarum' nell'età repubblicana*. Milano: Giuffrè.

CHAPTER 4

Managing Uncertainty and Asymmetric Information in Roman Auctions

Marta García Morcillo

4.1 Introduction

An auction can be defined as a market structure that allocates rights through a process of price competition, in which bidders make offers. A distinguishing trait of this procedure is the uncertainty over the final price, which determines the strategy of the actors and their management of both public and exclusive information, before and during the bidding. The winning offer depends on rules established in advance, so auctions are typically either price ascending or descending.[1] There is a widely accepted view that the bidding competition represents a fair and reliable system for valuing a good or service and for fixing its price at a given moment and

[1] Descending price auctions are conducted in the allocation of certain types of public contracts, such as procurement auctions, or in the sale of perishable products, such as fresh fish, fruits and vegetables, and flowers. Alternatives to these systems are the second-bid and the sealed auctions; see Milgrom (1989); Kemperer (2004: 14–15).

M. García Morcillo (✉)
University of Roehampton, London, UK
e-mail: Marta.Garcia-Morcillo@roehampton.ac.uk

C. Rosillo-López, M. García Morcillo (eds.), *Managing Information in the Roman Economy*, Palgrave Studies in Ancient Economies,
https://doi.org/10.1007/978-3-030-54100-2_4

place.[2] Auctions have a reputation for effectiveness and flexibility, and have become the most common systems of price setting for multilateral trading today. The volume of trade and monetary transactions that they generate in modern economies is unparalleled in world history. Due to their allocative efficiency, auctions have also become increasingly important in game and economic theory.[3] From this standpoint, they are regarded as non-cooperational games of incomplete information.[4] Certain theoretical approaches to auctions specifically aim to improve our capacity to predict choices, reduce uncertainty, and ultimately calculate winning strategies for bidders and sellers.[5] Despite the unquestionable impact of these studies on our knowledge of the decision-making process, there is no exact science behind this practice. Incomplete knowledge remains, after all, a distinctive trait of auctions. From the perspective of New Institutional Economics (NIE), auctions can also be considered as institutions that combat uncertainty with encoded information that aims to boost price competition, which also regulates and enforces the actors' performance.

Empirical and theoretical studies of modern auctions have provided valuable tools for comparative analysis in historical research. The great variety of ancient evidence available, despite unavoidable gaps, permits us to draw a chromatic picture of Roman auctions, and to attest their popularity as a system of price allocation, both in the public and the private sphere.[6] In the first part of this study, using a concept coined by Douglass North, I will look at the 'rules of the game': the enforcement and marketing mechanisms, as well as the social norms that shaped the information systems of Roman auctions. In the second part, I will attempt to reveal the shadows of this information system, and how they triggered morally ambiguous performances by actors. Two specific dysfunctional conspiracies will be analysed (which are also typical of modern auctions): the

[2] However, the auction's value does not necessarily represent the market value of an item, the dynamics of supply and demand, or the valuation estimated by the actors.

[3] See on this point also Revilla's chapter in this volume.

[4] See Hubbard and Paarsch (2015: 34–42). The Nash equilibrium and the prisoner's dilemma are two well-known theorems developed by game theory that have also been applied to the analysis of auctions.

[5] Risk aversion and anchoring are two phenomena studied by behavioural economics that seek to understand the bidder's mental framework in the process of valuation and decision making.

[6] In general, on Roman auctions, see Talamanca (1954); Thielmann (1961); Ankum (1972); Andreau (1974, 1987, 1999a, 2018); García Morcillo (2005).

formation of bidding rings or collusions, and the practice of shill bidding, which involves the seller and at least one fake-bidder. The aim of the chapter is to demonstrate that ancient Romans had a profound understanding of the complexities and risks of this versatile market structure, of the issues and opportunities generated by its transparency, its opacity and, ultimately, by games of information that did not always match the restrictions imposed by law and morality.

4.2 Information Against Uncertainty: Setting the Rules of the Game

From a NIE perspective, auctions are institutions that not only constrain the actors' performance, but also supply encoded information aimed at constructing an attractive market environment to encourage fair price competition and secure the payment and transfer of rights to the holder of the best bid. In this sense, institutions have both a restrictive and a cognitive-informational function. This means that they constrain the actor's behaviour, but also facilitate the access to relevant information that influences strategies, decisions and performance; both functions help reduce uncertainty and ambiguity.[7] Some scholars differentiate between types of uncertainty: substantive uncertainty, for instance, refers to the lack of available information that affects the decision-making process, while procedural uncertainty concerns the cognitive limitations and the lack of ability of actors to process and make the best use of the information available.[8] From the perspective of the purchaser, the regulated publicity of auctions supplies information that is essential—even if not necessarily sufficient—to plan and organise the bidders' strategies. Still, the very nature of the price competition is a factor that challenges the capacity of bidders to interpret and complete the information needed to evaluate the most successful action point. Auctions' performers are thus affected both by substantive and by procedural uncertainty. Beyond the mechanisms of enforcement and the capacity of performers to deal with different types of uncertainty, the effective functioning of this market environment depends in the end on its capacity to generate confidence in both sellers and

[7] On the informative function of institutions see North (1990: 3, 25); Knight (1997) and Dequech (2004).

[8] On the differentiation between both types of uncertainty, see Dosi and Egidi (1991); and Dequech (2006).

potential purchasers and, more generally, to project an image of credibility on this particular framework of exchange.

How did the Romans build a reliable information system for auction sales? As we will see next, publicity, transparency and control of information are the key factors that ancient authors associated with the efficiency of this institution.[9]

Cicero's speeches in the *De lege agraria* (63 BC) discuss the bill proposed by the tribune of the plebs P. Servilius Rullus to allow a commission of *decemviri* to sell public land and *vectigalia* in Italy and the provinces. Part of the orator's rhetoric argument revolves around the lack of transparency and irregularities of these sales.[10] In his speech to the Senate, Cicero compares the opacity of these sales with the regulated apparatus of publicity attached to state auctions: "The censors may not let the farming of the revenues except in the sight of the Roman people; shall these men be allowed to sell them even at the ends of the earth?"[11] The comparison continues by recalling the miserable men who, after wasting their patrimonies, sold their property at the auction hall (*atria auctionaria*), rather than at crossroads and bifurcations, while the *decemviri* were ready to sell property of the Roman people in whatever dark or isolated place they chose.[12] The second speech, addressed to the people from the Rostra, deepens the argument concerning the lack of visibility, and thus the trustworthiness of the proposed decemviral sales, which—contrary to the norm—were not planned to take place in Rome, or from the Rostra, or in front of the people, or through a public auctioneer or *praeco*.[13] Cicero's powerful rhetoric imagery associates a centralised and freely accessible topography of

[9] In his chapter about Roman finances in the present volume, Koen Verboven uses and discusses the term 'information governance system' to refer to the set of restrictions and opportunities that determine the perception and use of information and that contribute to reduce transaction costs.

[10] Cicero complained, for instance, that territories in Paphlagonia, Pontus and Cappadocia had already seen the *hasta praeconis*, and thus been apportioned to purchasers, even if Pompey's army was still active in the region, *Leg. Agr.* 1.6; 2.53–54.

[11] Cic. *Leg. agr.* 1.7: *Censoribus vectigalia locare nisi in conspectus populi Romani non licet; his vendere vel in ultimis terris licebit?* (transl. J. H. Freese).

[12] Cic. *Leg. agr.* 1.7: *At hoc etiam nequissimi homines cinsumptis patrimoniis faciunt, ut in atriis auctionariis potius quam in triviis aut in compitis auctionentur; hic permittit sua lege decemviris, ut, in quibus commodum sit tenebris, ut, in qua velim solitudine, bona populi Romani possint divendere.*

[13] Cic. *Leg. agr.* 2.55–56. The argument is strengthened by evoking the feared Sullan proscriptions and the subsequent sale of confiscated properties. Despite the opposition they

auctions with recognised norms of publicity as the pillars of the legitimacy for this type of sale. The message is clear: no licit auction should take place in darkness because this opacity would hinder the right of bidders to access equal information and the presence of witnesses to validate the price competition. Cicero defends the importance of the mechanisms of publicity of auctions—even for sales that had a negative impact on the reputation of citizens, such as those provoked by the insolvency of debtors. The regulated process of the *venditio bonorum*, which was initiated by a creditor and authorised by a magistrate, is described in detail in Cicero's earlier speech *Pro Quinctio* (81 BC).[14] From this case, we learn that the authorisation to seize goods (*missio in bona*) by the praetor implied an official valuation of the property, which was the basis for the information of the *proscriptio*, the pre-announcement of the sale that lasted thirty days. This procedure appears to have been modelled on the Athenian praxis,[15] and consisted of a transitional phase led by an administrator (the *magister bonorum*) that fulfilled two purposes. First, the debtor could, during this period, still pay off his debts and recover his properties. Second, the *missio in bona* was an effective marketing mechanism that allowed potential bidders to check the items listed in the register, gather further information, test potential competitors, study the market for similar items, and last but not least, establish an adequate strategy for the auction. Once the deadline was passed and the debt remained open, the proper sale was advertised.[16] The importance of this marketing strategy is highlighted by the fact that, according to Cicero, numerous written announcements (*libelli*) reproducing the *proscriptio* were posted throughout the city, *in celeberrimis locis*, thus generating a form of negative publicity for the debtor, equivalent in

generated, these sales were announced and conducted from the Rostra, and were thus in the public eye; see further García Morcillo 2016: 121–125.

[14] An in-depth analysis of this episode and its legal complications is provided by Hinard (1975); Platschek 2002 and Lintott (2008: 43–59). On the *venditio bonorum* see Giuffrè (1993: 317–364).

[15] In the sale of public land in fourth-century Athens, the *prokyrexis* or written announcement commenced a period of sixty days, during which inspections and claims could be made. The oral announcement of the *keryx*, five days before the actual auction, opened the acceptance of bids, which were introduced in written form on the agora, Thphr. *Frg.* 97 (*Stobae. Serm.* 42), 1–3. Similar regulations are attested throughout the Greek world, and particularly in Ptolemaic and Roman Egypt, see Talamanca (1954); Alessandrì (2005, 2012, 2017); Monson (2012).

[16] The jurist Gaius confirms the testimony of Cicero and attests the prevalence of this practice during the Principate, see Gai. 3.79.

his view to that of the condemned citizens, victims of confiscations and the *sectio bonorum*.[17] The very common expression *celeberrimus locus* synthesises a key principle of advertising that was deeply embedded in the everyday Roman praxis.[18]

The financial archive of the Sulpicii from Puteoli, dated to mid-first century AD, provides an extremely valuable, complementary testimony to Cicero's description of the procedure preceding the *venditio bonorum*. The Sulpician documents concern information for future announcements of auctions of pledged goods (*fiducia* or *pignus*).[19] Several *tabulae* detail that *libelli* reproducing the *proscriptio* of the sale should be posted thirty days before the auction in a specific area of the Forum of Puteoli, a wall or *parastatica* located within the *porticus Augusti Sextiana*.[20] The sales took place *ante chalcidicum Caesonianum*, a specific building that was also on the Forum of the city.[21] The prospects of profit for the sellers increased when the sale took place during the weekly markets or *nundinae*.[22] This connection enabled ties with other market environments, thus generating multilateral networks of information. The market day was also, not by chance, the day on which contracts were often concluded. The management of time (and times) and a clear communication policy were also essential for the consolidation of these practices as reliable and respected market structures. Rules were obviously different in auctions in which price estimations depended on daily, unpredictable circumstances and quick-check evaluations, such as the markets for perishable goods, and for those depending on particular transport dynamics, such as temporary markets of livestock and slaves. The Aedilician regulations recorded in the legal sources detail the procedures to be followed by sellers of slaves, as well as the immediate publicity that characterised these markets. These

[17] Cic. *Quinct.* 27; 73.

[18] The expression is well attested in public announcements preserved in epigraphic documents—see for instance the *Senatus Consultum de Cn. Pisone Patre* (*AE* 2008, 651); the *Lex Irnitana*, (*AE* 2008, 63). Further examples: *AE* 1984, 250; 2003, 359; 2008, 417; *CIL* X, 4643; *CIL* XII, 4393. See Corbier (2013), 25; Rosillo-López (2003), 63–65. Specific recommendations to increase the visibility and clarity of the announcements posted are mentioned by Ulpian, *Dig.* 14.3.11.3 (Ulp. 28 *ad. ed.*).

[19] *TPSulp.* 83–93, cf. Camodeca (1999: 185–204).

[20] *TPSulp.* 83–86; 88; 90–92, cf. Camodeca (1999: 189).

[21] *TPSulp.* 85; 87; 90–92, cf. Camodeca (1999: 185–204). The *chalcidicum* was a columned *porticus*.

[22] Two tablets indicate that the auction would have taken place on the town's market day (*in nundinas proximas*), *TPSulp.* 87 and 89.

entailed the precise written information to be included in the *titulus* and the announcement of the *praeco*. Any omission or manipulation of the relevant information could bring about the *actio redhibitoria*, or cancelation of the transaction.[23] In contrast to these short-term mechanisms of advertising, other types of auctions permitted potential bidders to plan their strategy ahead of time by carefully inspecting properties and movable goods some time before the sale. In the famous auction of Pompey's goods, the morally objectionable display of his personal objects was not only a highly ideological act aimed at humiliating a defeated political leader and faction, but also offered first-hand information on the state of the items to complement the official sale-register (*tabula*); this permitted buyers to more closely estimate the potential prices.[24] In a similar way, Cassius Dio reports that after the death of Commodus, Pertinax ordered the objects and slaves linked to gladiatorial games that had belonged to the Emperor to be displayed in the sale-room (*pôlêtêrion*). The author adds that the exhibition intended to expose Commodus' luxurious lifestyle, but also to identify those who might have been interested in purchasing the devalued items.[25]

The *praeco*, acting as an *apparitor* for the magistrates (or simply as an agent of the seller), was a key figure in the publicity process. Besides an oral reproduction of the written announcement, his active role as moderator and animator of bids in the price competition established him as a manager of selected information, who could influence the response of the bidders and their own valuation. The *praeco* was in control of the rhythm of the sale, and could thus accelerate bids and encourage competition, but also generate suspicion and caution. The *praeco*'s mission was to promote the sale, create anticipation and assign the goods to the best bidder. His priority was ultimately to get the best possible deal for the seller, the *dominus auctionis*, who was not necessarily the item's owner (*dominus rei*)—the seller might also be an agent, whose reward would be a percentage of the price obtained in the sale.[26] This explains why we find frequent literary allusions to the *praecones* as masters of ceremonies, but also as morally dubious characters, able to exaggerate and lie about the quality of goods.[27]

[23] *Dig.* 21.1.31–32 (Ulp. *1 ed. aed. Cur.*) See Jakab (1997: 45–49); Lavan in this volume.

[24] Cic. *Phil.* 2.73.

[25] D.C. 75.54–55.

[26] See the *Lex metalli Vipascensis*, lin 10–11, and García Morcillo (2005: 145–147).

[27] See for instance Mart. 6.66; Apul. *Met.* 23–25, Cic. *Off.* 3.55–56 (on this particular case, see Rosillo-López, in this volume), further Hinard, F. (1976); Rauh (1989b); García Morcillo (2005: 137–156); Bond (2016: 21–58).

Aside from the mechanisms of publicity, for the auction to appear effective it also relied on the generally applied requirements of security and guarantees (*fideiussores* or *cognitores*) to bidders and purchasers. This obligation was clearly mentioned in the regulations for the allocation of public contracts,[28] and resulted from the nature of the payment agreements, which were often delayed or promised in instalments, and sometimes linked to loans provided to purchasers by bankers and financial intermediaries.[29] The registers of the sales were also recorded in *tabulae* that could be publicly consulted; these could also have a probatory value in case of legal conflicts.[30] Registers exclusively linked to auctions are attested in several sources.[31] In the private sphere, bankers kept a record of the sales and payments of purchasers. The *tabulae argentariorum* or *argentariae* included the name of the successful bidder, the object sold and the price reached at the auction.[32] The documents of private bankers were also used by the state to collect the percentage tax rate imposed on any private auction from the age of Augustus onwards.[33]

All in all, Roman auctions put in place effective and recognisable mechanisms of information, as well as enforcement strategies that, based on the experience of long-established practice, contributed to substantially reducing the uncertainty and promoting secure and transparent spaces of economic exchange.

[28] On the handling of security by public contractors, see the *Lex pareti faciundo* (1.5; 3.54); *Lex portorium Asiae* (e.g. 43.101–103) and the *Lex Flavia Municipalis*. See also *Dig*. 39.4.9 pr.1 (Paul. 5 *sent.*).

[29] On the use of promises of payment or stipulations and the participation of bankers and financial intermediaries in private auctions, see Andreau (1974: 88–103; 1987: 174–176; 658); García Morcillo (2005: 120–128); Petrucci (2016).

[30] See Cic. *Ver.* 3.77; and the *Lex Flavia Municipalis*.

[31] *Dig.* 27.3.1.3 (Ulp. 36 *ad ed.*): cum *neque inventaria neque auctionalia proferentur*; Ambr. *Epist.* 37.13: *tabulae auctionales*.

[32] See for instance Cic. *Cluent.* 64.80; *Caec.* 6.17; Quint. *inst.* 11.2.24; Sen. *contr.* 1 pr. 19. The tablets containing the payment receipts from auctions in the archive of the Pompeian banker Iucundus were confirmed by a number of witnesses, Andreau (1974: 86–87).

[33] The *centesima rerum venalium* or *centesima auctionis*. The deduction of this tax from the tablets of Iucundus is convincingly argued by Andreau (1974: 81–86). The tax is explicitly mentioned in the *Lex metalli Vipascensis* as *centesima argentariae stipulationis*, lin. 6–8; Talamanca (1954: 147); Thielmann (1961: 68–69); Andreau (1987: 134–136). Traces of the collection of this tax by private bankers in Roman Egypt are discussed by García Morcillo (2008: 271–274).

4.3 Challenging the Rules of the Game

In stark contrast to the auctions' transparency were episodes in which abuse of power and corruption transformed these processes into illegal forms of profit. In the case of the auction of public contracts, system failures and dysfunctions revealed the manipulation by those who enforced the rules. Verres' abuses in the auctions for leasing out of the *decuma* in Sicily, along with the prior episode of the *locatio* of the contract for the reparation works of the temple of Castor and Pollux in Rome (70 BC), reveal a varied catalogue of such fraudulent practices. In the case of the temple, Cicero denounced a secret agreement between the urban praetor and adjudicator, Verres, and an allied bidder (Habonius), to artificially increase the price of a descending auction, in order to prevent the other bidders from succeeding.[34] Habonius, who was one of the tutors of the heir of the former contractor, P. Junius, agreed to participate in a conspiracy against the interests of the heir and the other tutors. In order to achieve his objective, Verres disregarded the rules on publicity, as neither the day nor the place of the sale were announced in advance.[35] Despite this irregularity, the other tutors managed to attend the auction, placed a bid substantially lower than that offered by Habonius and won the competition; their properties were accepted as security for their payment.[36] However, public records (along with Verres' accounts) revealed that he had manipulated the registers of the *locatio*, added Habonius as the contractor, and retained the pledge handed in by the bidders—the real bounty for both conspirators.[37] This was possible because the reparation works were never accomplished. When the falsification of the registers was discovered, Verres was forced to return 110,000 sesterces to one of the tutors, D. Brutus.[38]

The same pattern was replicated by Verres in the adjudications of the *decuma*, the tithe paid by the Sicilian farmers. After abolishing the old *Lex Hieronica*, which regulated the leasing of the *vectigalia* on the island,

[34] Cic. *Ver.* 1.130–132.

[35] Cic. *Ver.* 1.140–145.

[36] Cic. *Ver.* 141.

[37] Cic. *Ver.* 1.144–5.

[38] Cic. *Ver.* 1.149–150. The security had not been returned because Verres' departure avoided the *probatio* of the accomplishment of the works, see Rosillo-López (2003: 61). *Ver.* 1.149–150.

Verres manipulated the new auctions to benefit his own candidates.[39] In Leontium, Verres sold the *decuma* to his accomplice Apronius for a price that, according to Cicero, would have been much higher if a real competition with other bidders had taken place.[40] The suspicious prices registered by Verres in the public *tabulae,* along with his own records, once again demonstrated the efficient probatory utility of these registers to discover fraud and protect the system.[41]

Verres' abuses also reveal the problem of shill bidding, a practice defined as the intrusion into an auction of a fake bidder who—generally in partnership with the seller—works to artificially raise or lower the price at an auction. These cases show how the rules of the game were broken by the same authorities and magistrates who were supposed to regulate the system. Something similar is recorded in the auctions of confiscated properties held during the Second Triumvirate, which intentionally made it difficult for external bidders—including the relatives of proscribed citizens—to participate in them, with the objective of benefiting and encouraging soldiers to buy the properties at low prices.[42] These manipulations destroyed the reputation of auctions as trustworthy, freely competitive markets.

So, what happened when actors took advantage of information asymmetries and legal loopholes within the system at the expense of other parties? The ancient sources reveal traces of secret agreements, conspiracies and the selective management of information to manipulate the bidding process. These strategies often operated on the margins of legality and could ultimately generate moral concerns, even if they appear to have been relatively common. I will now examine several situations in which bidders colluded to control or destroy price competition, as well as cases of shill bidding in which a secret agreement between a seller and a bidder conspired to alter the price at the expense of other bidders.

[39] *Ver.* 3.13–14; 18–27; 36; 42; 51; 150. On the leasing out of the contract of the *decuma*, see Nicolet (2000: 277–293). Former contractors tried to organise themselves to offer higher bids than Verres' candidates, *Ver.* 3.99.

[40] Cic. *Ver.* 3.110; 148.

[41] Cic. *Ver.* 3. 111–113. See also 3.48–49; 70–76; 90–91. On the importance of these documents, see Butler (2002: 35–60); Andreau (2007: 81–92). The suspiciously cheap prices written down in Verres' private records for three famous artworks supposedly bought at an auction were used by Cicero as evidence of fraud, a *simulatio emptionis*, *Ver.* 4.12.

[42] App. *BC.* 4.29; D.C. 47.17. Exceptions were made for those who would buy at high prices and not just speculate on the price, D.C. 47.14.

4.3.1 Malus Emptor Alienus*: Bidders' Collusion and Rings*

In auctions, bidders generally do not have a dominant strategy. Their access to information is limited, as they need to overcome the problems of not only ignoring the valuation of the goods and their competitors' strategies, but also of possible intentional omissions by the seller. Exceptions to these situations are cases in which the lack of bidders, time pressures and other circumstances inhibit price competition, situating bidders in an advantageous position.[43] Sellers are naturally interested in maximising the publicity of auctions to attract a large number of bidders, yet they also fear that bidders will share information with each other, which can lead to cooperation, collusion and rings. Collusion is a particularly dysfunctional—and typical—phenomenon within auctions. Bidding rings can also lead to the formation of more or less formalised cartels. Collusion is thus a price-fixing conspiracy. The more impenetrable a ring is, the more successful it will be in achieving its goals. Generally, the suppression of competition decreases the possibility of high profits for sellers, but also for potential purchasers, who will now have to share any gains.[44] The risk of collusion is higher in the case of public contracts, but also within sectors in which potential bidders share fluid, secure spaces of communication, which can strengthen trust among them. When secret, negative forces against profitability threaten the cartel from inside, its ring-structure collapses. External bidders and enforcement institutions can also fracture cooperative conspiracies.[45] The creation of industrial cartels is an extremely widespread practice within the vast business of major procurement contracts today.[46] Even if collusion can be effective in the short-term, in the long run cartels will encounter increasing difficulty to keep the conspiracy secret without the knowledge of the seller or external bidders. Only by creating a powerful apparatus of information control and attractive incentives for bidders participating in the ring can the cartel guarantee its continuity. Nonetheless, collusion was (and still remains) a difficult practice to detect, which opens the door to strategies that explore the grey zones of legality.

[43] On the devaluation of prices and the unfavourable market for sellers of spoils in certain military campaigns, see Plut. *Luc.* 14.1.

[44] On ring bidding, see McAffee and McMillan (1992).

[45] On the success of cartels, see Levenstein and Suslow (2006).

[46] Several strategies to detect collusion are discussed by Porter and Zona (1993).

In Classical Athens, tax-farmers used to collude to keep prices low and share the benefits, but at times the involvement of external bidders broke these conspiracies, demonstrating a failure to strictly control information.[47] The Milon archive (225–222 BC), an early document that attests the assignation of land in Ptolemaic Egypt, supplies valuable information about a bidders' collusion, as well as hints of the possible involvement in such a conspiracy of the public commissioner (*praktor*), in charge of the sales of the sale.[48] Bidding rings were also recorded in tax-farming contracts auctioned off by the Ptolemaic administration. A well-known instance is recorded in a papyrus from the royal bank of Thebes (131 BC), related to the price of a contract for the farming out of a harbour custom tax. After a failed auction with no bidders, two candidates, who had already farmed out the tax in the past, obtained the contract in a subsequent auction after bidding for a lower price.[49] The lack of competition in the first auction suggests an intentional manoeuvre agreed by the bidders to decrease the adjudication price at the second opportunity. In ancient Rome, tax-farming companies, the *societates publicanorum*, were essentially the end-result and crystallisation of the institutionalisation of this sort of collaborative agreements between public contractors. Their corporative unity could influence the auction price of the contracts, as we saw with the conflict generated by the farming out of the *vectigalia* in Asia in 61 BC. The tax farmers actively campaigned for the cancelation of the contracts of the *locationes*, which from their perspective had been excessively reduced in price by the censors.[50] Their claim was only accepted in 59 BC, when they were also compensated with a *remissio mercedis*, a reduction of their yearly contribution.

The power and excesses associated with the tax farmers within the province of Asia during this period did not wipe out competitive bidding,

[47] Symptomatic cases are detailed in Andocides' *On the Mysteries* 133–134. On the tax-farming process in Athens, see Pritchard (2015). Another famous case of a bidding cartel is discussed in Lysias' speech 22 (*Against the corn dealers*).

[48] *P. Eleph.* 20; *P. Eleph.Gr.* 18–21, see Clarysse (2003). The documents attest that the *praktor* Milon was in charge of the sale, due to financial problems, of the priestly property in the *nome* of Edfu. As Manning (2003: 83–85; 2010: 118–120) plausibly discusses, the family tried to recover the items through a fake purchaser and the probable bribery or mismanagement of Milon, who soon after the scandal ran away to avoid facing responsibilities.

[49] *UPZ* II 224, Talamanca (1960); Bogaert (1998–9: 53–54).

[50] Cic. *Att.* 1.17.9. On this episode, see Nicolet (2000: 310–12). Further, Cic. *Q. fr.* 1.1.33; *Mur.* 62.

however, as it remained an advantageous system for the state.[51] The unpredictability attached to the collection of direct taxes and the constant shadow of collusion that hung over the cooperative behaviour of the *publicani* were compensated by an obligation to provide large security deposits (*praedia*, *cautio*) and guarantees (*praedes*).[52] This obligation also remained crucial during the Principate, and served to counteract the substantive and procedural uncertainties of the bidding process. A passage by the jurist Paulus in the *Digest* specifically states that when, in the heat of the competition (*calor licitantis*), bids go far beyond the usual prices in the *locatio* of the contracts of the *vectigal*, these offers should be still considered, provided the bidder can supply reliable *fideiussores* and a deposit.[53] The use of the verb *inflo* by Paulus suggests that such auctions may have been exposed to manipulation and secret agreements, such as the frauds denounced in the process against Verres.

The capacity of the *publicani* to act as collaborative rings, as well as the risk of unauthorised collusion with the purpose of keeping prices down, are both outlined in a passage from Suetonius' *Life of Augustus*. Following a serious outrage committed by a Roman knight, the Emperor ordered that he and his possessions be put up for sale. In order to help him, his fellow *publicani* colluded to make a single bid at the auction, buy the knight at a low price and liberate him. The ring's control of information was not successful, however. Augustus discovered the manoeuvre, aborted the sale and directly assigned the man to one of his freedmen.[54] The context of this anecdote recalls the patrimonial auctions of insolvent debtors and those of goods confiscated to condemned citizens, both of which were increasingly attested towards the end of the Republic. The latter in particular became, despite their unpopularity, an attractive market for buyers seeking out devalued bargains.[55]

[51] On the continuity of competitive *licitationes* for public contracts, see Nicolet (2000: 311–312).

[52] Tan (2017: 42–50), following Butcher (1993), convincingly states that Roman tax farmers did have a weak position relative to the state, as they were subjected to restrictive regulations but still had to compete for contracts.

[53] *Dig.* 39. 4.9pr. (Paul. 5 *sent.*).

[54] Suet. *Aug.* 24: *Equitem Romanum, quod duobus filiis adulescentibus causa detrectandi sacramenti pollices amputasset, ipsum bonaque subiecit hastae; quem tamen, quod inminere emptioni publicanos videbat, liberto suo addixit, ut relegatum in agros pro libero esse sineret.*

[55] This is the case, for instance, with the auctions held by the triumvirs, App. *BC.* 4.31.

Occasionally, friends and relatives of the former owners would try to reacquire the goods for their benefit.[56] Such efforts, when organised collectively, could lead to collusion. Cicero's correspondence provides us with a first-hand testimony of an insider within a ring-bidding auction. T. Annius Milo's condemnation to exile in 52 BC was followed by the confiscation and announcement of the sale of his possessions. In order to avoid the fatal scattering of Milos' patrimony in the hands of a reseller (*sector bonorum*), Cicero, in accordance with Milo's friend, C. Duronius, decided to acquire the properties for a low price with the intent of helping him keep his slaves and to save a property for Fausta, Milo's wife. The agreement tried to avoid and discourage the potential intervention of an external purchaser (*malus emptor alienus*), which would raise prices within the auction.[57] However, the entire operation came to be threatened by an internal affair: the intervention of Philotimus, the freedman of Cicero's wife Terentia, who was supposedly acting as the orator's agent in the bidding, but who Milo suspected of pursuing his own interests at the auction.[58] Accordingly, Cicero asked Atticus to help him with this delicate issue, not only because it could damage the deal, but because, if it came to be known, would have automatically affected Cicero's own reputation as a trustworthy social and economic actor. Asconius' commentary to Cicero's *Pro Milone* mentions that Milo's properties were auctioned off for a fraction of their true value (*semuncia*),[59] which explains why this affair was also a tempting business opportunity. From the perspective of

[56] Famously, Sextus Pompeius purchased some of the properties that had belonged to his father and then been resold by Antony in this way, Cic. *Phil.* 13.5.10–12. Similarly, Cassius Dio (47.17) reports that during the Second Triumvirate, victims of proscriptions were permitted to reacquire one-third of their own patrimonies, yet encountered difficulties doing so due to the highly devaluated prices at auctions, which attracted external bidders, and the fact that entire lots were sold at a single auction.

[57] Cic. *Att.* 5.8.2: *id ego ita fieri volui de C. Duroni sententia quem et amicissimum Miloni perspexeram et talem virum qualem tu iudicas cognoram. Eius autem consilium meumque hoc fuerat, primum ut in potestate nostra esset res, ne illum malus emptor alienus mancipiis quae permulta secum habet spoliaret, deinde ut Faustae. quoi cautum ille esse voluisset ratum* esset. *Erat etiam illud ut ipsi nos si quid servari posset quam facillime servaremus.*

[58] Cic. *Att.* 5.8.2: *tu si modo es Romae (vix enim puto), sin es, hoc vehementer animadvertas velim. Roma acceperam litteras Milonem meum queri per litteras iniuriam meam quod Philotimus socius esset in bonis suis.*

[59] Ascon. *tog. Cand. in Mil.* 54, 20–21: *Milo in exilium Massiliam intra paucissimos dies profectus est. Bona eius propter aeris alieni magnitudinem semuncia venierunt.* As has been noted by Shackleton Bailey, *Atticus III* (1966: 202).

collusion theory, but also of behavioural economics, this case shows the problem of distrust within weak auction rings. The presence of the suspicious Philotimus as Cicero's agent was viewed by Milo as a destabilising element, and ultimately also threatened to cast a bad light on Cicero's behaviour. The entire letter is permeated by Cicero's suspicion and fear, but also by the absolute confidentiality of the information he shared with Atticus.

Bidder's collusions, such as that attempted in Milo's case, primarily affected the seller, in this case the state. Legal responses to this and other issues linked to bidding conflicts show an understanding of the complex, often opaque and frequently quite sophisticated strategies and manoeuvres of colluders. In seeking to characterise the forms of profit irregularly generated from auctions, Roman jurisconsults faced the difficulty of controlling a process that was shaped by numerous uncertainties and information asymmetries, all of which conditioned the price-competition. The term *collusio* as a conspiracy to keep prices low is explicitly mentioned by Ulpian in a passage of the Digest concerning a hypothetical disadvantaged sale of the property of a *pupillus* or ward.[60] The third century AD jurist Callistratus lists among potentially reportable irregularities the performance of those who bought from the *fiscus* something of great price for a lesser one.[61] In a similar vein, a rescript of the Emperor Gordian III (AD 239) refers to the possible fraud signalised by the suspect low price paid for a pledged property linked to a small debt. The expression *gratiosa emptio* denounces here a sale unfairly advantageous to the purchaser at the expense of the debtor.[62] More specifically, an imperial decree of the emperors Valentinian, Theodosius and Arcadius that was sent to the *vicarius Africae*, Magnillus, in AD 392 urged him to undertake a complete appraisal or valuation (*aestimatio*) of the properties and revenues of debtors whose goods were about to be auctioned off by the state (*subhastatio publica*) in order to prevent fraud.[63] The text observes that such irregularities were particularly suspected when prices were low and the property had been sold *sub gratiosa auctione*, namely when little benefit remained for the state (since the debtor had lost everything). Similarly than in Gordian's rescript, the term *gratiosa auctio* seemed thus to describe a non-competitive

[60] *Dig.* 4.4.49 (Ulp. 35 *edict.*).

[61] *Dig.* 49.14.1 pr. (Callist. 1 *De iure fisci*): *vel magni pretii rem minoris ex fisco comparasse.*

[62] *Cod. Iust.* 10.3.2. Similarly, *Cod. Iust.* 10.1.3.

[63] *Cod. Theod.* 10.17.3 (AD 392) = *Cod. Iust.* 44.16.

auction in which the bidders had colluded.[64] This practice is labelled by the Augusti as unfair (*periniquum*), yet the text offers no clear solution of how to avoid its damaging outcomes for the state's interests as creditor and seller. An accurate appraisal of the debtors' properties may have helped to ascertain whether the debtor had been the ultimate beneficiary of a conspiracy that aimed to repurchase his former properties for a devalued price. The *aestimatio* was also useful to identify whether properties were being sold below their real value, and to take measures against these practices. The imperial requirements to increase control over private patrimonies appear to have been the only efficient enforcement strategies against secret conspiracies, which would otherwise have been very difficult to prosecute from a legal perspective. The use of the term *gratiosa auctio* or *emptio* denotes thus the legislators' recognition of an ambiguous, albeit not necessarily fraudulent, behaviour. An imperial rescript of AD 294 confirms that a debtor affected by the low price at which his properties were sold could present allegations of *collusio* or *fraus* (fraud) against the procurator of the imperial fiscus.[65] This shows that when the collusion came to the light and could be proved, this action was explicitly named and typified.

Overall, these instances show to what extent price competition and uncertainty challenged public and legal enforcers. A profound knowledge of the mechanisms and behaviour patterns of sellers and bidders in specific types of auctions was an extremely valuable information for Roman legislators to consider when they were confronted with these practices.

4.3.2 **Falsus emptor et illicitator:** ***Lying by Omission and Shill Bidding***

Despite the strong apparatus of publicity of Roman auctions, unequal access to relevant information was a constant issue, which opened the gateway for situations whereby the principle of the open price-competition could be manipulated at the expense of one or more bidders. The intrusion of fake bidders to artificially alter the competition of an auction in favour of the seller is popularly known as shill bidding. The employment

[64] *Etenim periniquum est, ut, alienis bonis sub gratiosa auctione distractis, parum accedat publico nomini, quum totum pereat debitori.* The expression is translated as a 'rigged auction' in the edition of the *Codex Iustinianus* by Frier et al. (2016). A passage of Ulpian in the Digest (26.7.7.2 (*Ulp. Ed.* 35)) refers to the purchase of *praedia* by a tutor *per sordes aut gratiam*, to describe irregular favours that benefited the *emptor*.

[65] *Cod. Iust.* 2.37.3 (AD 294).

of a 'puffer' to artificially boost price competition on behalf of the seller is an established practice in modern auctions. Even prestigious auction houses occasionally resort to what is known as 'taking bids from off the wall' in order to boost price competition and prevent goods from being sold below their reserve price. The capacity of the auctioneer to manipulate the audience and create the illusion of real competition is essential to the success of this strategy.[66] This practice is not necessarily illegal, provided the genuine bidders are notified about such arrangements in advance.[67] In recent years, the global popularity of online selling intermediaries like eBay has accelerated interest in this phenomenon, not least because the anonymity and opaqueness of such platforms multiplies the risk of fraud.[68] When it remains secret, shill bidding is not considered to be an act of good faith, and in the long run this inexorably affects the reputation of sellers and intermediaries, who base their business on the users' trust in a system that is expected, despite its very selective use of information, to offer a reliable and fair market environment.[69]

Just as is the case today, shill bidding was an evasive and pervasive phenomenon in ancient Rome. Its problematic detection challenged the legislators, who found it difficult to separate what were legal and illegal practices. Beyond the fragrant irregularities and manipulations of public auctions seen above, such conflictive situations also often arose in private sales linked to the extended practice of shared inheritances. Cicero's correspondence is, again, a unique and highly eloquent source to observe the orator as protagonist in auctions that were the result of agreements between coheirs.[70] His 'insider' testimony offers further clues on how shill bidding could operate on the margins of legality.

In a letter dated to 51 BC in response to Cicero's friend M. Marius, we learn of the former's interest in purchasing a property. Marius had asked him to bid on his behalf in the auction, even though Cicero was one of the coheirs of the estate. Despite the evident conflict of interest—as a seller who expected to obtain the highest possible benefit from the sale—Cicero

[66] Among others, large auction houses such as Sotheby's and Christie's frequently resort to these strategies.

[67] Attempts to regulate such ambiguous practices in modern auctions are attested from at least since the eighteenth century, see Meisel (1996: 400–403).

[68] See Steiglitz (2007).

[69] Marshall and Marx (2014: 202–203).

[70] For example Cic. *Att.* 1.14.7; 7.1.9; *Fam.* 14.5.2–3; *Att.* 11.15.3–4; 13.12.4; 13.13–14.4; 13.37.a; 13.45.3; 13.46; 14.9.1; 14.10.3; 14.11.2.

finally accepted the commission (*mandatum*). Marius even gave him a figure that would be his highest bid, which put Cicero in a difficult position. As a potential solution, he agreed to negotiate a fixed price with the other coheirs. Being aware of the contradiction and the irregular situation, Cicero finished the letter with a joke: "since I know now the price you have fixed, I will arrange a sham bidder (*illicitator*) that makes the price lower".[71] The sentence ironically speculates on the possibility that Cicero and Marius would secretly arrange the intervention of a fake bidder without sharing this information with the other coheirs.

The term *illicitator*, derived from *licitatio* (auction/bidding), reappears symptomatically in a passage from book III of the *De Officiis*, in which Cicero censures the speculative *simulationes* between business parties and urges the complete removal of falsehood (*mendacium*) from transactions.[72] The intriguing sentence confronts the reader with two typical sides of auctions and the role of sellers and purchasers in the price competition: "the seller should not engage a sham bidder, nor should the purchaser engage anyone who bids against him" (*non illicitatorem venditor, non qui contra se liceatur emptor apponet*). While the first case defines a form of shill bidding like that described in the Marius affair, the second seems to refer to a collusion conspiracy between bidders. The next sentence suggests a solution to this problem: "If both come to talk, they should do it no more than once" (*Uterque si ad eloquendum venerit, non plus quam semel eloquetur*).[73] Cicero thus proposes an intentional restriction on the communication and exchange of information between sellers and purchasers in order to preserve the fairness of the price competition. Aside from Cicero, the term *illicitator* is mentioned elsewhere only by the second century AD lexicographer Festus, who simply defines it as an

[71] Cic. *Fam.* 7.2.1: *Mandatum tuum curabo diligenter. Sed homo acutus ei mandasti potissimum cui expediret illud venire quam plurimo. Sed eo vidisti multum quod praefinisti quo ne pluris emerem. Quod si mihi permisisses, qui meus amor in te est, confecissem* cum *coheredibus. Nunc, quoniam tuum pretium novi, illicitatorem potius ponam quam illud minoris veneat. Sed de ioco satis est. Tuum negotium agam, sicuti debeo, diligenter.*

[72] Cic. *Off.* 3.61. Festus links *licitatio* with those who compete in the market of fighting: *licitati in mercando sive pugnando contendentes*, Fest p. 83. On *licitatio* as auction as well as bidding, see Andreau (1999b: 179–180).

[73] W. Miller (LCL 1913) translates both sentences less literally: "the seller will not engage a bogus bidder to run prices up nor the buyer one to bid low against himself to keep them down; and each, if they come to naming a price, will state once for all what he will give or take." In my view, Cicero's text does not refer to a discussion on the price between the parties, but rather to negotiations that denaturalise, and thus potentially manipulate the auction.

emptor.[74] The word may have been rarely used in this time, or may have simply been a product of Cicero's own invectiveness to designate a practice not clearly defined by law, yet detectable in the praxis. The fact that Festus seemed to ignore the specific meaning of the word points in this direction.

As we will see below, Roman legislators did use other expressions to identify such sham bidders, or simply resorted to describing the action. Again, this lack of definition points to the elusiveness of a practice that was masked by the asymmetries of information that shaped the bidding process. The suspicion that sham bidders could interfere with and manipulate auctions was always a possibility when bidders did not know each other, or when the intentions of sellers were not clear. The business opportunities generated by inheritances often cast such shadows. For this reason, it was important for bidders to build their strategy with enough information about their competitors, their identity and their financial credibility.

Cicero's correspondence provides, once again, a rather accurate case study on the construction of the bidder's information strategies and the efforts made to compensate the substantive and procedural uncertainty before the auction. By May 45 BC, the strenuous search for a suitable property to build a temple in memory of his daughter led Cicero to negotiate with the heirs on his participation in the auction of the *Horti Scapulani*, an attractive estate located in an exclusive area of the Campus Vaticanus.[75] The long and complex affair of Tullia's fane is an invaluable case study for the impact of social and psychological factors on the process of economic decision-making.[76] The story also reveals the interaction between the formal and informal channels of information that conditioned Cicero's participation in the sale as an external bidder.[77] The auction of the *Horti Scapulani* was surrounded by uncertainties, which caused suspicion over the true intentions of the coheirs of the property, who had originally planned to auction the estate among themselves.[78] Cicero shared his con-

[74] Fest. p. 80.25: *Inlicitator*: *emptor*. On *il-/inlicitator* as mock- or sham-bidders, see also *The Oxford Latin Dictionary* (ed. P.G. Glare 1973), IV, 828; and further editions of the *De Officiis*: M. Testard (CUF) (1970, 101–2): 'enchérisseur'; M.T. Griffin and E.M. Atkins (CUP) (1991, 123): 'artificial bidder'; R. Nickel (Tusculum) (2008, 255): 'Scheinkäufer'.

[75] Cic. *Att.* 12.37.2. For the whole episode, see Shackleton Bailey (1966: 404–413).

[76] An in-depth analysis is provided by García Morcillo (2020).

[77] Rosillo-López discusses in this volume how a crucial confidential information finally ended Cicero's participation in the auction.

[78] Cic. *Att.* 12.38a.2.

cerns with his friend and adviser Atticus, and complained about the insufficient information on the property provided by the coheirs upon his request, which was a relevant factor to making his own economic valuation.[79] The operation required phenomenal financial resources, and Cicero accepted the challenge.[80] One of Cicero's strategies to prepare the auction was to carefully investigate the profile, means and intentions of all four coheirs. This information reinforced his capacity to negotiate a favourable agreement with them concerning a maximum price at the auction, which would have allowed him to secure the acquisition.[81] This information was also key to dissipating certain shadows of suspicion loomed over one of the coheirs—the ambitious and wealthy Roscius Otho—who also intended to bid for the property. In a letter dated May 27, Cicero shared his thoughts on his rival, who he believed he knew well, and suggested that the coheir's finances were not so flamboyant as he pretended. Contrary to the official picture, Cicero doubted that Otho was really so enthusiastic about the purchase (*nec tamen insaniturum*), and that he could hardly be considered a serious competitor. "Why then bother? Why all these interpretations?" (*Att.* 13.29.1). Cicero's doubts over Otho's means and intentions suggests that he suspected a possible conspiracy between the coheirs to artificially increase the price of the auction through Otho, who would have acted as a sham bidder to the detriment of Cicero's interests as a purchaser. It is plausible to believe that Cicero's response to the *illicitatores* in the *De Officiis* was based on first-hand experiences like this one. His formula for avoiding such secret agreements between sellers and purchasers combined the assumption of honesty and the acceptance of specific rules (formal or informal) that would drastically restrict communication between the actors prior to the bidding. These moral guidelines appear unrealistic and contradictory in view of his own performance, however, and according to what seemed to be the customary behaviour of interested parties in these markets.

Secret agreements that altered the natural course of auctions and affected the interests of other parties could also be made public before the *licitatio*. One such case is narrated by Pliny the Younger, in a letter to

[79] This was partially solved by an inspection of the property by his agents, Cic. *Att.* 13.1.3; 13.29.1–2; 13.33.2.

[80] On the financial strategies of this affair, see especially Benöhr (1986); Rauh (1989a: 60–69); Rollinger (2009: 154–60).

[81] Cic. *Att.* 12.5a; 13.31; 13.5.1; 13.7.1.

Calpurnius Fabatus. In the epistle, Pliny tried to morally justify why he opted, by means of his freedman Hermes, to sell his part of an inherited property in Comum to his friend Corellia. This broke a previous agreement with the other coheirs—Fabatus among them—to auction the property off in its entirety, rather than as divided plots.[82] This decision, apparently not motivated by economic reasons, prevented Pliny (as well as the other heirs) from obtaining a higher proportional price at the auction.[83] Pliny insists at the end of the letter that he had the freedom to make the decision, even if the coheirs may not have approved it. While he acted according to friendship (*amicitia*), they were free to pursue profit (*utilitas*). The emphasis on the moral legitimacy of the action and the freedom of choice that the coheirs still had, was an attempt to shift attention from the core of the conflict: the fact that the coheirs had not been informed in advance of Pliny's intentions to sell his portion of the estate. Although this decision was legal, it was clearly disloyal and dishonest and put the coheirs in an economically disadvantageous position.[84]

The first-hand evidence of conspiracies provided by Cicero and Pliny reflect some of the frequent situations that fell outside the boundaries of the specific measures and regulations against substantive uncertainty. This does not mean, however, that the law was blind towards such strategies. The *arbitrium* of the magistrate concerning the partition of a property with several heirs was a typical enforcement mechanism, one that was aimed precisely at preventing any heir from taking decisions that would damage the interest of the others. The chapter entitled *Action for dividing an inheritance* (*iudicium familiae erciscundae*) in the *Digest* (10.2) discusses several cases of irregularities, conflicts and arbitrary decisions that were typically linked with these situations. One of the issues that frequently

[82] Plin. *Ep.* 7.11. The text specifies that Hermes removed his five-twelfth of the property after announcing at the auction: *Miraris, quod Hermes libertus meus, hereditarios agros, quos ego iusseram proscribe, non expectata auctione pro meo quincunce ex septingentis milibus Corelliae addixerit.* On this episode, see Sherwin-White (1966: 415–418); García Morcillo (2005: 245–246).

[83] Plin. *Ep.* 7.11. Pliny admitted that he may have obtained nine hundred thousand sesterces instead of the seven hundred Corellia paid for it. Pliny apologised to Fabatus and the coheirs for having decided to help his friend as a moral obligation.

[84] In a later letter, *Ep.* 7.14, we learn that Corellia insisted to pay nine and not seven hundred thousand sesterces for the purchase of the property. Sherwin-White (1966: 417–418), has noticed that the difference between both is 5%, which coincides with the rate of the inheritance tax, the *vicesima hereditatium*, which Pliny had to pay for the acceptance of his inheritance.

affected this kind of sale was the omission of information by one of the heirs bidding at the auction.[85] One solution to this problem, suggested by Gaius, was easy: to make copies of the will and share them with all the coheirs.[86] The chapter also discusses more complex and ambiguous situations. The jurist Paul reports on a creditor who shared an inherited pledge and decided to buy his coheir's portion at auction. The jurist affirms that if a buyer bids too eagerly (*quod animose licitus sit*), a hearing to return the pledge to the debtor should be considered. The creditor's dishonest profit is merely deduced here from his suspicious attitude as a bidder, rather than any other objective consideration.[87] Auctions generated by the division of properties were a potential realm of fraud. A passage by Marcianus describes the case of someone who, in order to avoid the auction for dividing a common property in accordance with the old *Lex Licinnia*, decided to sell the property. Behind this manoeuvre, the jurist contemplates that "his intention might, for example, be that a buyer with greater resources should bid for it and acquire it cheaply so that he might get it back again".[88] Implicit in the text is that the action of division would have been detrimental to the seller, possibly due to open debts and pledges. This conspiracy reveals another variation of shill bidding.

Suspicious, self-interested behaviour was something carefully observed in property transfers led by tutors. Paul envisages the circumstance in which a tutor became the purchaser of a *pupillus*' property at an auction. Would this action be legal? The response of the jurist is affirmative, yet he also notes an exception established under Trajan: "if the tutor should buy cheaply, he would be liable in the action on tutelage, just as he would if he had knocked the thing down to someone else as a low price".[89] It is remarkable that the only truly detectable sign of shill bidding by tutors appears to have been suspicious prices that did not match the market estimates of similar or equivalent properties.

[85] See *Dig.* 10.2.6 (Ulp. 19 Edict.): *Nam ad licitationem rem deducere, ut qui licitatione vicit hic habeat instrumenta hereditaria, non placet neque mihi neque Pomponio.*

[86] *Dig.* 10.2.5 (Gai. 7 *Prov. ed.*).

[87] *Dig.* 10.2.29 (Paul. 23 *ed.*).

[88] *Dig.* 4.7.12 (Marc. 14 *inst.*): *verbi gratia ut potentior emptor per licitationem vilius eam accipiat et per hoc iterum ipse recipiat* (transl. by A. Watson).

[89] *Dig.* 41.4.2.8 (Paul. 54 *ad. ed.*): *si propius habeat emptorem, et, si minoris emerit, tutelae iudicio tenebitur ac si alii minoris addixisset.* The *iudicium tutelae* meant that the tutor could be condemned in the case of irresponsible management that would cause damage or provoke loss of the pupil's property.

Finally, I would like to discuss a hybrid institution that contained elements of both auctions and consensual sales. The *in diem addictio* was a type of sale in which the contract between the purchaser and seller was conditioned on the submission of a better bid within a limited time-period.[90] This better bid did not necessarily implied a higher offer, but merely present better conditions for the seller (*melior condicio*).[91] Ulpian explains that this new offer could consist of a more suitable form of payment, a payment by a more reliable person, or simply be accompanied by a more attractive guarantee.[92]

These types of private contracts showed some common elements of the fiscal 'open auctions' affecting debtors of the state, as well as of typical forms of allocation of land in Ptolemaic Egypt.[93] The *in diem addictio* is discussed in depth in chapter 18.2 of the *Digest*, and, judging from the caseload, it appears to have been a contractual relationship typically arranged between landlords and farmers. This conditional factor clearly weakened the position of the purchaser during the transitional period between the first purchase and the definitive adjudication. If someone gave a better offer, however, the vendor was obliged to update the first purchaser and give him the opportunity to outbid the new offer.[94] The temporary and conditional nature of these contracts suggest that they were specifically designed to protect the sellers from the potential economic impacts of the changing nature—and consequently also value—of goods, or rather of their market revaluation. This was typically the case with productive land before and after the harvest. However, what happened when a bid that was higher than that of the first purchaser was made after the economic value of the land had increased following a successful harvest? Roman jurists were not unanimous on who should benefit from these fruits.[95] Ulpian, evoking the opinion of Julian, states that "when it is

[90] A definition of the *in diem addictio* is provided by Paul, *Dig.* 18.2.1 (Paul. 5 *ad Sab.*).

[91] *Dig.* 18.2.5 (Pomp. 9 *ad Sab.*): *Quidquid enim ad utilitatem venditoris pertinet, pro meliore condicione haberi debet.*

[92] *Dig.* 18.2.4.6 (Ulp. 28 *ad Sab.*).

[93] See Talamanca (1954: 106–107). The author suggests that sellers may have opted for these alternatives to traditional *auctiones* to avoid the expenses associated with these processes. In sales of unoccupied or abandoned land in Ptolemaic Egypt, the possibility to outbid the highest price after the adjudication (*kuroris*) was generally open until the payment of the final sum and the transfer of the goods (*paradeixis*).

[94] *Dig.* 18.2.7 (Paul. 5 *ad Sab.*); 18.2.8 (*Paul. 33 ad ed.*).

[95] *Dig.* 18.2.6.1 (Ulp. 28 *ad Sab.*). Paul compares the *in diem addictio* with the situation of tenants and landowners, and defends the idea that whoever cultivates the land should benefit from its fruits, *Dig.* 49.14.50 (Paul. 3 *decr.*).

said that interim fruits go to the first purchaser, that holds, whenever there appears no purchaser who makes a better offer (*quotiens nullus emptor existit, qui meliorem condicionem adferat*) or a false purchaser (*vel falsus existit*); but if there be a genuine second purchaser (*sin vero exstitit emptor)*, it is settled that the first purchaser must restore the fruits, but not the vendor".[96] The passage implicitly describes the possibility of shill bidding arranged by the vendor with the purpose of: (a) forcing the bidder to outbid the 'phantom bidder' and thus increase the price of the first offer before the pre-established deadline; or (b) reacquiring the now reappraised land (including its fruits) with the help of a 'straw man'. In both cases, the vendor would benefit from a fraudulent manoeuvre that was difficult to detect. As discussed above in the case of 'off the wall' bids, the *in diem addictio* was a mechanism exposed to potential abuse by sellers who were unhappy with the price competition. As is typically the case in eBay auctions, the time limited nature of these agreements added an element of pressure towards the first purchaser, as the offer of an unknown bidder could be presented at any time, limiting the options of the former to gather information and plan a strategy. How to identify a *malus* or *falsus emptor*? A strict control over the mechanism of guarantees or security required from the bidders was an effective—although not infallible—means of proving the reliability of bidders. Another, no less important means was to test beyond a doubt the *bona fides* of the seller. Certainly, the didactic instances recorded in the legal sources, which reveal a repeated modus operandi leading to suspicious benefit, were precious sources of information that contributed to recognising the signals of such a conspiracy and to building a legal case against it in the long term.[97]

4.4 Conclusions

All in all, the heterogenous evidence analysed above shows the vigour of Roman auctions as effective and attractive market structures and institutions with a solid apparatus of information. The state provided and supervised to a certain degree the structures and enforcement mechanisms that

[96] *Dig.* 18.2.6 pr. (Ulp. 28 *ad Sab.*) (transl. by A. Watson).

[97] Ulpian proposes to investigate the intentions of the vendor to state if he is acting in good faith, *Dig.* 18.26pr. (Ulp. 28 *ad Sab.*). Along with stricter legislation, intensified self-regulation and professional codes or practices are today still suggested as the most effective mechanisms to attenuate this problem, Meisel (1996: 413).

secured an encoded, regulated and time limited publicity, stimulated expectation and interest, assured and facilitated payment, and ultimately contributed to reducing uncertainty. The experience of the actors within this system allows us to explore the dysfunctional elements of auctions, as well as the opportunities—licit and illicit, moral and immoral—generated by asymmetric information and the system's exposure to manipulation. These also reveal the Romans' understanding of the complexities of this practice, of its numerous risks and moral dilemmas, and its social and economic impact. The strengths of Roman auctions as economic but also social institutions lay above all in their flexibility, resilience and capacity to adapt to different environments. As I hope to have demonstrated in this chapter, auction theory and empirical studies can contribute to disclosing the interplay between the institutional framework and control of information, on the one hand, and the opaqueness and ambiguities that shaped the performance and strategies of actors, on the other. Despite their many twilight zones, these market structures remained reliable systems of price competition.

Bibliography

Alessandrì, S. 2005. *Le vendite fiscali nell'Egitto romano.* I. Da Augusto a Domiziano. Bari: Edipuglia.

———. 2012. *Le vendite fiscali nell'Egitto romano. II. Da Nerva a Commodo.* Bari: Edipuglia.

———. 2017. *Le vendite fiscali nell'Egitto romano. III. Da Settimio Severo a Diocleziano.* Bari: Edipuglia.

Andreau, J. 1974. *Les affaires de Monsieur Jucundus.* Rome: École Française de Rome.

———. 1987. *La Vie financière dans le monde romain: les métiers de manieurs d'argent (IVe siècle av. J.-C.-IIIe siècle ap. J.-C.)*. Rome: École Française de Rome.

———. 1999a. *Banking and Business in the Roman World.* Cambridge: Cambridge University Press.

———. 1999b. Licitatio. *Der Neue Pauly* 7: 179–180.

———. 2007. Registers, account-books, and written documents in the *De frumento, In Sicilia Nutrix Plebis Romanae: Rhetoric, Law and Taxation in Cicero's Verrines* (Bulletin of the Institute of Classical Studies, Supplement 97), London: Institute of Classical Studies, 81–92.

———. 2018. Auctions. *Oxford Classical Dictionary.* https://oxfordre.com/classics/view/10.1093/acrefore/9780199381135.001.0001/acrefore-9780199381135-e-8237

Ankum, H. 1972. Quelques problèmes concernant les ventes aux enchères en droit romain classique. In *Studi in onore di Gaetano Scherillo* I, 377–393. Milano: Istituto Editoriale Cisalpino-La Goliardica.

Benöhr, H.-P. 1986. Das Faberianum negotium – Schuldenbereinigung zur Zeit Ciceros. *Zeitschrift der Savigny-Stiftung für Rechtsgeschichte, RA* 103: 275–320.

Bogaert, R. 1998–9. Les opérations des banques de l'Égypte ptolémaique. *Ancient Society* 29: 49–145.

Bond, S. 2016. *Trade and Taboo. Disreputable Professions in the Roman Mediterranean*. Ann Arbor: University of Michigan Press.

Butcher, J.G.D. 1993. Revenue Farming and the Changing State in Southeast Asia. In *The Rise and Fall of Revenue Farming: Business Elites and the Emergence of the State in Southeast Asia*, ed. J.G.D. Butcher and H.W. Dick, 19–44. London: Macmillan Press.

Butler, S. 2002. *The Hand of Cicero*. London: Routledge.

Camodeca, G. 1999. *Tabulae Pompeianae Sulpiciorum (TPSulp.): Edizione critica del archivio puteolano dei Sulpicii* , Vol. I, Roma: Quasar.

Clarysse, W. 2003. The Archive of the Praktor Milon. In *Edfu, an Egyptian provincial capital in the Ptolemaic Period* , ed. K. Vandorpe and W. Clarysse, 17–27. Brussels: Koninklijke Vlaamse Academie van België voor Wetenschappen en Kunsten.

Corbier, M. 2013. "Writing in Roman Public Space", in G. Sears-P. Keegan-R. Laurence (eds.), *Written Space in the Latin West, 200 BC to AD 300*, London/New Delhi/New York/Sydney: Bloomsbury Academic, 13–47.

Dequech, D. 2004. Uncertainty: Individuals, Institutions and Technology. *Cambridge Journal of Economics* 28: 365–378.

———. 2006. New Institutional Economics and the Theory of Behaviour under Uncertainty. *Journal of Economic Behavior & Organization* 59: 109–131.

Dosi, G., and M. Egidi. 1991. Substantive and Procedural Uncertainty – An exploration of Economic Behaviour in Changing Environments. *Journal of Evolutionary Economics* 1: 145–168.

García Morcillo, M. 2005. *Las ventas por subasta en el mundo romano: la esfera privada*. Barcelona: Universidad de Barcelona.

———. 2008. Auctions, Bankers and Public Finances in the Roman World. In *Pistoi dia tèn technèn. Bankers, Loans and Archives in the Ancient World. Studies in Honour of Raymond Bogaert (Studia Hellenistica 44)*, ed. K. Verboven, K. Vandorpe, and V. Chankowski, 257–275. Leuven: Peeters.

———. 2016. Placing the hasta in the Forum: Cicero and the Topographic Symbolism of Patrimonial Sales. In *Ruin or renewal? Places and the Transformation of Memory in the City of Rome*, ed. M. García Morcillo, J.H. Richardson, and F. Santangelo, 113–133. Roma: Quasar.

———. 2020. Mentality, Motivation and Economic Decision-Making in Ancient Rome: Cicero and Tullia's Shrine. *The Economic History Review* 73 (3): 623–643.

Giuffrè, V. 1993. Sull'origine della "bonorum venditio" como esecuzione patrimoniale. *Labeo* 39: 317–364.

Hinard, F. 1975. Le "Pro Quinctio", un discours politique? *Revue des Études Anciennes* 77: 88–107.

———. 1976. Remarques sur les 'praecones' et le 'praeconium' dans la Rome de la fin de la République. *Latomus* 35: 730–746.

Hubbard, T., and J. Paarsch. 2015. *Auctions*. Cambridge, MA/London: MIT Press.

Jakab, É. 1997. Praedicere *und* cavere *beim Marktkauf. Sachmängel im griechischen und römischen Recht*. München: Beck.

Kemperer, P. 2004. *Auctions. Theory and Practice*. Princeton/Oxford: Princeton University Press.

Knight, J. 1997. Social Institutions and Human Cognition. *Journal of Institutional and Theoretical Economics* 153: 693–699.

Levenstein, M.C., and V.Y. Suslow. 2006. What Determines Cartel Success? *Journal of Economic Literature* 44: 43–95.

Lintott, A. 2008. *Cicero as Evidence. A Historian's Companion*. Oxford: Oxford University Press.

Manning, J.G. 2003. *Land and Power in Ptolemaic Egypt. The Structure of Land Tenure 332–30 BCE*. Cambridge: Cambridge University Press.

———. 2010. *The Last Pharaohs. Egypt under the Ptolemies, 305–30 BC*. Princeton: Princeton University Press.

Marshall, R.C., and L.M. Marx. 2014. *The Economics of Collusion. Cartels and Bidding Rings* (1st ed. 2012), Cambridge, MA: MIT Press.

McAfee, R.P., and J. McMillan. 1992. Bidding Rings. *The American Economic Review* 82: 579–599.

Meisel, F. 1996. 'Upping the Ante': Market Distortion in Auction Sales. *The Modern Law Review* 59 (3): 398–413.

Milgrom, P. 1989. Auctions and Bidding: A Primer. *Journal of Economic Perspectives* 3 (3): 3–22.

Monson, A. 2012. *From the Ptolemies to the Romans. Political and Economic Change in Egypt*. Cambridge: Cambridge University Press.

Nicolet, C. 2000. *Censeurs et publicains: Économie et fiscalité dans la Rome antique*. Paris: Arthème Fayard.

North, D. 1990. *Institutions, Institutional Change, and Economic Performance*. Cambridge: Cambridge University Press.

Petrucci, A. 2016. Banquieri e vendite all'asta private tra tarda Repubblica e Principato. *Cultura giuridica e diritto vivente, Special issue*. http://ojs.uniurb.it/index.php/cgdv/issue/view/106

Platschek, J. 2002. Die 'tabula tamquam plaga' in 3.17.68. *Index* 30: 205–214.

Porter, R.H., and J.D. Zona. 1993. Detection of Bid Rigging in Procurement Auctions. *Journal of Political Economy* 101: 518–538.

Pritchard, D.M. 2015. *Public Spending and Democracy in Classical Athens*. Austin: University of Texas Press.

Rauh, N. 1989a. Finance and Estate Sales in Republican Rome. *Aevum* 63: 45–76.

———. 1989b. Auctioneers and the Roman Economy. *Historia* 38: 451–471.

Rollinger, C. 2009. *Solvendi sunt nummi. Die Schuldenkultur der späten römischen Republik im Spiegel der Schriften Ciceros*. Berlin: Verlag Antike.

Rosillo-López, C. 2003. Fraude et contrôle des contrats publics à Rome. In *Tâches publiques et entreprise privée dans le monde romain*, ed. J.-J. Aubert, 57–94. Neuchâtel: Université de Neuchâtel.

Shackleton Bailey, D.R. 1966. Tullia's Fane (Appendix 3). In *Cicero's Letters to Atticus, vol. V, (Books XI–XIII)*, ed. D.R. Shackleton Bailey. Cambridge: Cambridge University Press.

Sherwin-White, A. N. 1966. *The Letters of Pliny. A Historical and Social Commentary*. Oxford: Clarendon Press.

Steiglitz, K. 2007. *Snipers, Shills, and Sharks: eBay and Human behaviour*. Princeton: Princeton University Press.

Talamanca, M. 1954. *Contributi allo studio delle vendite all'asta nel mondo classico* . Roma: Academia Nazionale dei Lincei.

———. 1960. Osservazioni su UPZ 218–226. *Bulletino dell'instituto di Diritto Romano* 63: 250–261.

Tan, J. 2017. *Power and Public Finance at Rome, 264–49 BCE*. Oxford: Oxford University Press.

Thielmann, G. 1961. *Die römische Privatauktion. Zugleich ein Beitrag zum römischen Bankierrecht*. Berlin: Duncker & Humblot.

PART III

The Real Estate and Land Property Market

CHAPTER 5

Asymmetric Information, *Ager Publicus* and the Roman Land Market in the Second Century BC

Saskia T. Roselaar

5.1 Introduction

This chapter will discuss asymmetric information in the land market of the Roman Republican period, especially the second century BC. Assuming that a free land market existed in this period, the paper will discuss whether this market was subject to problems of asymmetric information, and if so, to what extent. Problems may have occurred especially with regard to the sale of land, since it was difficult for potential buyers to accurately estimate the value of a plot. They therefore always had to be on their guard against being cheated. There were also problems of asymmetric information in cases where land was worked by caretakers for absentee landowners. In this case, the principal-agent problem raised its head, since the landowner could never be sure that the agent took the best interests of the owner to heart.

S. T. Roselaar (✉)
Independent Scholar, Delft, The Netherlands

C. Rosillo-López, M. García Morcillo (eds.), *Managing Information in the Roman Economy*, Palgrave Studies in Ancient Economies,
https://doi.org/10.1007/978-3-030-54100-2_5

Finally, the paper will compare the free market for land in general with the market for a specific type of land, namely *ager publicus*, that is land owned by the Roman state. Lack of information, and specifically uncertainty regarding its legal status, may have impacted willingness to investment in buying or renting state-owned land. Therefore, not all land may have been available on the free market, despite the growing demand for land in Italy in the Republican period.

5.2 The Roman Land Market in the Second Century BC

The first part of this paper will focus on the question whether a free land market existed in the second century BC and to what degree it was subject to problems of asymmetric information. With regard to the first issue, almost all scholars agree that there was indeed a free market for land in this period. Important work on the Roman land market has been done by Peter Temin. He suggests that three attributes of land ownership can indicate a functioning market for land. First, there is a price for land that can change freely when conditions in supply and demand change. Second, people can buy and sell land at this price without reference to outside authorities, that is they can make their own decisions rather than reflecting the decisions of people not directly involved in the land sale. Third, there are few restrictions on or obligations for most landholdings and land transfers, other than the payment of taxes. Temin argues that these three conditions indeed applied, and I agree with him that there was indeed a free market for land during most of the Republican period, especially the third and second centuries. The land market experienced little government control, such as debt moratoria, rent control and tenant protectionism. There was much variation in prices and transaction methods were sophisticated, including mortgages arranged by financial specialists.[1]

The fact that land was freely available was welcome in the middle to late Republic, as this period saw great increase in commercial agriculture. I cannot fully describe all economic developments in this period here, but I

[1] Temin (2006: 134–7); Arruñada (2020). Prices, for land especially, could fluctuate wildly. Examples mostly date from the civil wars of the first century, when the ownership of land as a secure possession was coveted more than ever before. See for example Suet. *Aug.* 41.1–2; Plut. *Crass.* 2.3–5; Cic. *Rosc. Am.* passim. See Andreau (1999: 12–16, 108–111); Hollander (2012: 148).

will briefly summarize these,[2] in order to show that demand for land was fairly large in this period. In the second century, commercial agricultural production increased significantly in scale, with both the number of commercial farms and their individual size becoming larger. Although commercial farms were still fairly modest in scale at this time, many show evidence for the commercial production of wine and olives, as is attested by the presence of amphorae, dolia, and wine and olive presses. A famous example is the farm at Moltone di Tolve in Lucania, first built in the third century BC.[3] As shown by the latest research, the performance of the Italian economy and the living standards of people in the Republican period were very impressive. For example in the second century BC Pompeii was a prosperous town, with continuous investments in production and manufacture aimed at maximizing profits. Its prosperity was due mainly to the interconnectedness of its economy, with Vesuvian wine exported through the main harbour at Puteoli. This meant that a large part of the population enjoyed a varied diet and luxury consumer goods, as well as lived in rather large houses.

The fact that agriculture was flourishing and living standards were high raises the question whether Romans in the second century BC consciously aimed to make a profit. In contrast to older literature, which suggested that Romans were not primarily interested in profit,[4] it is now increasingly recognized that profit maximalization was very much an aim for the Roman elite in the Republican period.[5] In general, we can discern a growing rationalism in the second century BC with regard to profit maximalization and the choices that wealthy Romans made in order to make a profit. In land ownership, this is reflected in changes in the organization of farms, with the appearance of growing numbers of larger farms, and changes in the ratio between free and slave workers.[6] Cato the Elder's mindset clearly reflects this. As Plutarch describes: "as he applied himself more strenuously to money-getting, he came to regard agriculture as more entertaining than profitable, and invested his capital in business that was safe and sure. He bought ponds, hot springs, districts given over to

[2] See recent works on the Roman economy in the second century BC: Kay (2014); Flohr (2017); Jongman (2017); Tol and De Haas (2017); Roselaar (2019).

[3] See Isayev (2007: 73–76); Marzano and Métraux (2018); Roselaar (2019: 85–115).

[4] For example Finley (1999); see discussion in Tol and De Haas (2017: 3).

[5] Flohr (2017: 80–81).

[6] Capogrossi (2010: 536). In general, profits from agriculture seem to have been much larger in the second century than in the fourth and third; see the works cited in note 2.

fullers, all of which brought him in large profits."[7] Clearly, making a profit was a foremost consideration in Cato's mind; he did not hesitate to spread out into other branches of real estate, when agricultural land turned out to be not the most profitable enterprise.[8] Varro, writing a century after Cato, similarly stated that: "The Italian seems to have had two things particularly in view in his farming: whether the land would yield a fair return for the investment in money and labour, and whether the situation was healthful … For no sane man should be willing to undergo the expense and outlay of cultivation if he sees that it cannot be recouped."[9]

In the late Republic, the desire for profit can be discerned the most clearly in the investment choices by wealthy Romans in urban property, about which we are fairly well informed by Cicero's works. For example, *insulae* in Rome yielded a high income from rents and were therefore worthwhile objects for investment.[10] The same mentality may have applied to rural properties as well; Cicero's property at Puteoli, for example, was not just a residence, but also included shops, and yielded a profit of 80,000 sesterces in one year.[11] The sheer number of properties owned by Cicero may suggest that he bought them with the intent of making a profit,[12] although he also states: "in making a purchase a man may properly use his friends' means to get what suits his position (*dignitas*)."[13] Thus, the reasons for buying any property were complex: a desire for profit either through speculation, collection of rents (for both urban and rural properties)[14] or long-term improvement that increased the yield of the land (for agricultural properties), a secure investment since wealth was easier to store in land than in valuables, and *dignitas*—a difficult term, incorporating both 'honour', 'reputation' and 'prestige'—that one accrued from owning a large number of well-tended properties.

[7] Plut. *Cat. Mai.* 21.5.

[8] See Rosenstein (2008), who argues that investment in urban property and other commercial enterprises made up a much larger part of elite incomes than land ownership.

[9] Var. *R.* 1.2.8. Cic. *Att.* 9.9.4 similarly describes how Atticus "usually wanted to know how many years' purchase it was worth, and what was the value of the fixtures" before buying any land. See Hollander (2012: 75–76).

[10] For example Cic. *Att.* 1.14.7, 7.3.6–9, 12.32.2, 14.3, 15.17.1, 15.20.4, 16.1.5; *Cael.* 17–18; *Off.* 3.66. See Frier (1978) for urban property management.

[11] Cic. *Att.* 13.46. 3, 14.9.1, 14.10.3. See Frier (1978: 2).

[12] Cic. *Q.Fr.* 3.1 list a number of properties which Cicero owns or is considering buying. See Walcot (1975: 127–8).

[13] Cic. *Att.* 1.13.6.

[14] For the renting of agricultural property, see Kehoe (1997); Roselaar (forthcoming).

This brings us to an important issue related to the subject of asymmetry of information: the decision-making process that a potential buyer of agricultural land faced, and the degree to which this was hampered by an asymmetry of information. In what follows, I will take a closer look at this process in order to determine which considerations played a role in any decision to buy land. Since, as mentioned above, there were various reasons to buy land, it is clear that the decision made by someone looking for land was not easy; his reasoning could vary, depending on his reason to buy. The main issue that all potential buyers of land faced was deciding which land to buy with the budget available. As information theory states, perfect information results in the perfect distribution of goods, as necessitated by the supply and demand of such goods. In the Roman land market, an imbalance of information between buyers and sellers may have led to inefficient outcomes in the market. When information is asymmetric, prices are distorted and optimality in the allocation of resources is not achieved. Problems of information were exacerbated in the Roman era by the problems of long-distance communication, which made it particularly difficult to acquire adequate information.[15] This was a problem both when buying land, as well as selling it.

A Roman looking to buy a farm would ideally have in mind exactly what type of land he wanted to buy, with regard to the soil, elevation, rainfall, distance from the market and from his own home, location in economic networks et cetera. He would also have in mind a maximum price he was willing to pay. Unfortunately, it was impossible to know all plots for sale that fit his requirements, and to establish which one was the closest match, as also discussed by Rosillo-López in this volume for other real estate, such as houses. In any case, a potential buyer would not have unlimited time to spend on researching all options. Furthermore, all plots of land had their own specific qualities, so that it was very difficult to compare them and determine what would be a realistic price. This meant that the buyer would either have to trust the research of an agent, for example a slave or freedman, or that he would have to settle for a plot of land that seemed to fit (most of) his requirements, without having studied all the possible options.

[15] On the speed and costs of travel and communication, see both positive and negative examples in Cato *Agr.* 22. 3; Plin. *HN.* 19. 3–4; see Nicholson (1994); Adams (n.d.), with further references.

The ancient agronomists give some advice about the best land to buy. Cato is our most important source for agriculture in the second century, despite the debate about the aim of his work.[16] He explains in some detail how a buyer should go about selecting a farm: "When you are thinking of acquiring a farm, keep in mind these points: that you be not over-eager in buying nor spare your pains in examining, and that you consider it not sufficient to go over it once. However often you go, a good piece of land will please you more at each visit. Notice how the neighbours keep up their places; if the district is good, they should be well kept." He then goes on to name some of the criteria for good land that a potential buyer should pay attention to: "It should have a good climate, not subject to storms; the soil should be good, and naturally strong. If possible, it should lie at the foot of a mountain and face south; the situation should be healthful, there should be a good supply of labourers, it should be well watered, and near it there should be a flourishing town, or the sea, or a navigable stream, or a good and much travelled road. It should lie among those farms which do not often change owners; where those who have sold farms are sorry to have done so."[17]

Cato in this passage cites a great number of issues that are important in the choice of a farm. Not only the farm itself had to be studied carefully, but especially the area in which it was located. Cato pays attention not only to geographical aspects, such as the climate, soil and exact location, but also to the social aspects of the community, especially whether there are sufficient neighbours who could be hired as wage labourers during the harvest. Furthermore, the community should have some stability, in that the farms remain in the same hands for a significant period of time. Commercially rational aspects also receive attention: the farm should be located in such a location that the harvest can easily be transported to the market.

[16] For which see White (1973: 456–457); Terrenato (2012).

[17] Cato *Agr.* 1.1–5: *1 Praedium quom parare cogitabis,* sic *in animo habeto, uti ne cupide emas neve opera tua parcas visere et ne satis habeas semel circumire. Quotiens ibis, totiens magis placebit quod bonum erit. 2 Vicini quo pacto niteant, id animum advertito: in bona regione bene nitere oportebit. … Uti bonum caelum habeat, ne calamitosum siet, solo bono, sua virtute valeat. 3 Si poteris, sub radice montis siet, in meridiem spectet, loco salubri, operariorum copia siet, bonumque aquarium, oppidum validum prope siet aut mare aut amnis, qua naves ambulant, aut* via *bona celebrisque. 4 Siet in his agris, qui non saepe dominos mutant: qui in his agris praedia vendiderint, eos pigeat vendidisse.*

Varro similarly emphasizes the importance of knowledge about the farm: in fact, he considers "knowledge of the farm, comprising the nature of the soil and its constituents" as the first among the four aspects of agriculture.[18] This "nature of the soil" is further defined as "the conformation of the land, the quality of the soil, its extent, and in what way it is naturally protected."[19] He then subdivides these points into further detailed aspects which should be considered when buying a farm. With regard to conditions outside the farm, Varro advises to investigate "whether the neighbourhood is unsafe; whether it is such that it is not profitable to transport our products to it, or to bring back from it what we need; third, whether roads or streams for transportation are either wanting or inadequate; and fourth, whether conditions on the neighbouring farms are such as to benefit or injure our land."[20]

Most of this advice is fairly general; Cato gives some general rules of thumb about buying land, such as "it should have a good climate" and "it should lie at the foot of a mountain and face south." Another example is the dictum that "a lowland farm that everywhere slopes regularly in one direction is better than one that is perfectly level, because the latter, having no outlet for the water, tends to become marshy."[21] Obviously, in a general handbook it is difficult to be very specific, although these works sometimes offers more detailed advice. Cato advises for example to create a tree plantation on suburban farms, so that the wood may be sold in town.[22] Given the costs of transporting wood over long distances, it would not be profitable to produce firewood (or other types of wood used in towns, e.g. for building) at long distances from the market. Clearly, Cato had a good idea of what made a farm profitable, and aimed for long-term profit maximalization from his agricultural exploits, as is clear from his handbook.[23]

[18] Var. *R.* 1.5.3: *Agri culturae, inquit, quattuor sunt partes summae: e quis prima cognitio fundi, solum partesque eius quales sint.*

[19] Var. *R.* 1.6.1: *Igitur primum de solo fundi videndum haec quattuor, quae sit forma, quo in genere terrae, quantus, quam* per se *tutus.*

[20] Var. *R.* 1.16.1: *Si vicina regio est infesta; si quo neque fructus nostros exportare expediat neque inde quae opus sunt adportare; tertium, si viae aut fluvii, qua portetur, aut non sunt aut idonei non sunt; quartum, siquid ita est in confinibus fundis, ut nostris agris prosit aut noceat.*

[21] Varro *R.* 1.6.6: *Campester locus is melior, qui totus aequabiliter in unam partem verget, quam is qui est ad libellam aequos, quod is,* cum *aquae non habet delapsum, fieri solet uliginosus.*

[22] Cato *Agr.* 7.1.

[23] Martin (1971: 85–7, 92); Dalby (1998: 24).

However, the general knowledge about farming as presented in these handbooks would not be sufficient to judge the quality of a specific plot of land. This would require the buyer to actually come and look at the plot. Cato indeed advises to visit the plot, and not just once, but several times, as in the passage cited above: "[do not] consider it sufficient to go over it once." He apparently assumes that the buyer will visit the farm himself, rather than leaving this task to an agent. This would require a serious investment of time for the future buyer, especially if he was considering several properties. Given the slow pace of travel in ancient Italy, visiting prospective farms several times was no easy task.

The best source of information were landowners who already worked in the area, who could be asked about the circumstances on the ground. For example, local farmers knew best which lands in their village were the best, how much they yielded, how they should be worked et cetera. This indicates the importance of oral dissemination of knowledge, as this kind of information was not written down anywhere in Republican Italy. People who were literate had some advantage in the information market, since they could, for example send out letters in order to collect information, rather than visit their business partners in person. They could also create their own personal archive in which they could store and retrieve information received in the past, and exchange this information with trusted third parties.[24] However, information regarding the quality of land, or about past transactions, was not stored in writing in any kind of central archive, and therefore could not be consulted by all those interested in buying land. Cato, in any case, never refers to any written information to consult, but only to what he could see on the ground, such as the number of oil presses and *dolia*.[25] This allowed him to make a calculation in his head about the possible profitability of the farm, but this could not be checked against actual accounts regarding the yields of the farm in recent years. In many cases, buyers would have bought an estate close to one they already owned, since they knew the local circumstances and it was easier to manage estates that were close together. This was the case for example of M. Fulcinius, who bought an estate in Tarquinii next to his wife's.[26]

This advantage is also present in Pliny the Younger's letter regarding a purchase he was considering. Although his letter is outside the scope of

[24] See Culham (1989) on private and public archives.

[25] Cato *Agr.* 1.4.

[26] Cic. *Caec.* 11.

the period covered in this paper, it is worth citing in some length. Most of Pliny's arguments applied in the second century BC, as well as a few centuries later: "Some land adjoining my own, and even running into mine, is for sale, and while there are many considerations tempting me to buy it, there are equally weighty reasons to dissuade me. I feel tempted to purchase, first, because the estate will look well if rounded off, and, secondly, because the conveniences resulting therefrom would be as great as the pleasures it would give me. The same work could be carried on at both places, they could be visited at the same cost of travelling, they could be put under one steward and practically one set of managers, and, while one villa was kept up in style, the other house might be just kept in repair. Moreover, one must take into account the cost of furniture and head-servants, besides gardeners, smiths, and even the gamekeepers, and it makes a great difference whether you have all these in one place or have them distributed in several. Yet, on the other hand, I am afraid it may be rash to risk so much of one's property to the same storms and the same accidents, and it seems safer to meet the caprices of Fortune by not putting all one's eggs into the same basket. Again, there is something exceedingly pleasant in changing one's air and place, and in the travelling from one estate to another... The land in question is fertile, rich and well-watered; it consists of meadows, vineyards and woods, which are productive and guarantee an income, not large, it is true, but yet sure."[27]

Thus, Pliny cites mainly economical and practical reasons for buying this plot of land: the land will give him a steady income; by buying an estate next to own, he will save on travel time. Moreover, it will be cheaper to maintain just one villa, as well as hire experts for specialised jobs, or buy specialized slaves. At the same time, he was aware of the risks of owning too much land in one place, as a failed harvest or other disaster would

[27] Plin. *Ep.* 3.19.1–5: *[1] Praedia agris meis vicina atque etiam inserta venalia sunt. In his me multa sollicitant, aliqua nec minora deterrent. [2] Sollicitat primum ipsa pulchritudo iungendi; deinde, quod non minus utile quam voluptuosum, posse utraque eadem opera eodem viatico invisere, sub eodem procuratore ac paene isdem actoribus habere, unam villam colere et ornare, alteram tantum tueri. [3] Inest huic computationi sumptus supellectilis, sumptus atriensium topiariorum fabrorum atque etiam venatorii instrumenti; quae plurimum refert unum in locum conferas an in diversa dispergas. [4] Contra vereor ne sit incautum, rem tam magnam isdem tempestatibus isdem casibus subdere; tutius videtur incerta fortunae possessionum varietatibus experiri. Habet etiam multum iucunditatis soli caelique mutatio, ipsaque illa peregrinatio inter sua. [5] Iam, quod deliberationis nostrae caput est, agri sunt fertiles pingues aquosi; constant campis vineis silvis, quae materiam et ex ea reditum sicut modicum ita statum praestant.*

affect both estates. It is clear from his letter that Pliny knew the area well, so that he could judge the economic potential and could weigh the pros and cons of buying the land. He would not have had access to this information if he had not already owned land here.

Still, it is likely that wealthy landowners did not always travel to the area where they wanted to buy land. We know of various people owning land in various parts of Italy, for example Pompey, who owned land in Picenum, Formiae, Alba, Tusculum, Falerna, Lucania, and elsewhere.[28] It is likely that such people were usually reliant on agents. This points to the essential nature of trust in ancient society. For the ancient world, informal social networks played an important role as third parties, as they could supply information about the trustworthiness of business partners, as well as the quality of the goods being traded.[29] As Verboven indicates in this volume, Republican Italy was not a unified entity, so there were many independent communities and thus many different information structures. Of course, even in a unified state, not all information is available to everyone. This means that rationality in economic decisions was always bounded by the limits of the information available at any particular moment. Thus, Roman businessmen relied mostly on private order information governance systems, rather than public, as the state's bureaucracy was limited. Gradually throughout the Republic, Roman law became more important within Italy, as discussed below, leading to a greater importance of the public order information governance system. Still, its power was always supplied by various informal, private networks that disseminated information.[30]

Thus, someone looking to buy land could either approach his network of acquaintances in order to find out more about the quality of the land and the trustworthiness of the seller, and/or he could send a trusted agent to negotiate on his behalf. Much research has been done on the networks of trust that could be utilized in order to gain information about potential business partners.[31] In many cases, the mechanisms were fairly rudimentary: notices about debtors were posted at the *columna Maenia* in Rome;[32]

[28] Cic. *Phil.* 13.6.11; Plut. *Pomp.* 6.1; Vell. 2.29.1. See below for Cicero's multiple business properties.

[29] See Nappo in this volume. Most of the available evidence comes from the early Imperial period, especially the archives of the Sulpicii and of Caecilius Iucundus. For these, see Verboven (2008); Broekaert (2017).

[30] See Verboven in this volume.

[31] Broekaert (2017: 388–399, 406–409).

[32] Cic. *Sest.* 18.

otherwise, personal networks were the most important source of information about potential business partners. Oaths were frequently used in order to bind oneself to an agreement, but apart from the judgment of the gods, mortal means of enforcement were limited. Public shaming of defaulting debtors was also a method frequently used by desperate lenders, as Plautus describes for the second century BC, as well as the organization of businessmen into private, voluntary groups such as *collegia*.[33]

The use of agents in business seems to have become more common in the second century, since in this period the *actiones adiecticiae qualitatis* were introduced into Roman law. The *actio exercitoria* made a father or master responsible for the actions of his son or slave who engaged independently in business matters. The *actio institoria* made fathers and masters responsible for sons or slaves appointed as managers of estates or shops.[34] The fact that an action was necessary in order to appoint responsibility in case of trouble also shows that trust only went so far in facilitating business. This creation of a legal *actio* shows that the Roman state was aware of the principal-agent problem: principals would have trouble selecting reliable agents, and the agents they chose might abuse their powers by acting in their own interest rather than that of their masters or their business partners.[35] This problem could partially be mitigated by choosing trusted family members, friends, slaves or freedmen as agents, but this was not always successful. Other legal innovations occurred at the same time, with the aim of simplifying business transactions that were already taking place in the market, such as the *bonae fidei iudicia*[36] and the possessory interdicts.[37] Thus, the law followed the market in creating new legal instruments for trade.[38] This matches the importance which scholars have placed on the importance of a functioning legal system. The relations between merchants and agents are simplified greatly if they have contractual relations that are enforceable in a court of law,[39] as the Roman state increasingly recognized in the second century BC.

[33] Plaut. *Pseud.* 1145; see *Pseud.* 556, *Curc.* 683, *Epid.* 118, *Men.* pr.48, *Truc.* 759. On *collegia* see Verboven (2007).

[34] Watson (1961: 5–6); Aubert (1994: 46–64); Broekaert (2017: 390–391).

[35] Eisenhardt (1989).

[36] Watson (1961: 12–13).

[37] Kaser (1996: 408–421).

[38] Frier and Kehoe (2007); Roselaar (2019: 125).

[39] North (1990).

Once a sale was concluded, the buyer could only hope that his judgment had been correct and the land was indeed to his expectations. The law stated that defects to real estate should be declared before the sale; if this did not happen, the vendor must pay damages to the buyer. Cicero explains: "In the laws pertaining to the sale of real property it is stipulated in our civil code that when a transfer of any real estate is made, all its defects shall be declared as far as they are known to the vendor. According to the laws of the Twelve Tables it used to be sufficient that such faults as had been expressly declared should be made good and that for any flaws which the vendor expressly denied, when questioned, he should be assessed double damages. A like penalty for failure to make such declaration also has now been secured by our jurisconsults: they have decided that any defect in a piece of real estate, if known to the vendor but not expressly stated, must be made good by him."[40] It is likely that this law also applied to land, so that any defects on land—for example problems with the soil, problems with the local water supply, or the situation of the tenants[41]—should be declared to a potential buyer, although this is not specified. However, in the case of land a defect would be very difficult to prove. A disappointing harvest could be due to many factors, such as the weather or mistakes by the farmer, and it would therefore be impossible to sue the seller for a defect. This made it vital to verify the quality of the land and the farm buildings before the sale.

From this overview we may conclude that asymmetry of information indeed played a role in the free land market in the Roman Republic. When buying land, it was necessary for the buyer to inform himself as much as possible about the qualities of the various plots of land available. The best possible means to do so was autopsy, as there were no archives regarding past sales and prices. This meant that the buyer either had to visit the plot

[40] Cic. *Off.* 3.65: *Ac de iure quidem praediorum sanctum apud nos est iure civili, ut in iis vendendis vitia dicerentur, quae nota essent venditori. Nam,* cum *ex duodecim tabulis satis esset ea praestari, quae essent lingua nuncupata, quae qui infitiatus esset, dupli poenam subiret, a iuris consultis etiam reticentiae poena est constituta; quicquid enim esset in praedio vitii, id statuerunt, si venditor sciret, nisi nominatim dictum esset, praestari oportere.* See also *Dig.* 19.1.38.2 (Proculus), *Dig.* 21.1.19pr (Ulpian. 1 *ad Ed. Cur. Aed.*), *Dig.* 18.1.43pr (Florian. 8 *Inst.*). See Orth (2003); Rosillo-López in this volume. For defects relating to slaves, see Lavan in this volume.

[41] As Pliny the Younger describes (*Ep.* 3.19.6–7), the tenants on the estate he was considering buying had been impoverished by the bad management of the previous owner, so that Pliny would have to invest in slaves to work for them, if he were to buy the estate.

himself, or send an agent to take care of the purchase. Given that the Roman state in the second century introduced various legal innovations increasing the possibilities for agents to do business, it seems likely that the increase in commercial agriculture meant that businessmen delegated more of their tasks to agents.

5.3 The Management of Farms

Once a farm was bought, if the owner could not work it himself, he could appoint an agent to do so. In many cases, this was a slave called the *vilicus*.[42] In this case, the owner was at a disadvantage with regard to information: the *vilicus* was responsible for the daily management of the farm, while the owner, who often lived at considerable distance, could only give general guidance as to how the land should be worked. In case of problems, the *vilicus* was on his own, as he could not easily consult with the owner. The *vilicus* could also cheat the owner, if he so desired, since the owner would not be able to keep a close eye on his agent, illustrating the principal-agent problem in such cases. It was therefore important to pick a reliable *vilicus* and to build up a relationship of trust with him. Varro gives detailed advice about the characteristics of the ideal *vilicus*: "The slaves ought to have men over them who know how to read and write and have some education, who are dependable and older than the hands whom I have mentioned; for they will be more respectful to these than to men who are younger. Furthermore, it is especially important that the foremen be men who are experienced in farm operations; for the foreman must not only give orders but also take part in the work, so that his subordinates may follow his example, and also understand that there is good reason for his being over them—the fact that he is superior to them in knowledge. ... The foremen are to be made more zealous by rewards, and care must be taken that they have a bit of property of their own, and mates from among their fellow-slaves to bear them children; for by this means they are made steadier and more attached to the place. ... They are made to take more interest in their work by being treated more liberally in respect either of food, or of more clothing, or of exemption from work, or of permission to graze some cattle of their own on the farm, or other things of this kind."[43]

[42] For the management of farms, see Maróti (1976); Teitler (1993); Carlsen (1995).

[43] Varro *R.* 1.17.4–7: *Qui praesint esse oportere, qui litteris atque aliqua sint humanitate imbuti, frugi, aetate maiore quam operarios, quos dixi. Facilius enim iis quam qui minore natu*

Thus, it is clear that a relationship of trust should be cultivated between the owner of the farm and his *vilicus*. This required some cost and effort from the owner, for example allowing the *vilicus* better food and giving him time off to work for himself. In the long run this would build up the trust between the two, which would lead to higher productivity, and could prevent the owner from being made responsible for bad management by his *vilicus* under the *actio institoria*. Trust was therefore essential in reaching optimal economic outcomes for both parties.

Although the daily running of the farm was certainly left to a *vilicus*, Cato advises to watch over him closely: "When the master arrives at the farmstead, after paying his respects to the god of the household, let him go over the whole farm, if possible, on the same day; if not, at least on the next. When he has learned the condition of the farm, what work has been accomplished and what remains to be done, let him call in his overseer the next day and inquire of him what part of the work has been completed, what has been left undone; whether what has been finished was done betimes, and whether it is possible to complete the rest; and what was the yield of wine, grain, and all other products."[44] The owner was supposed to visit regularly, and keep a close eye on what happened at the farm, as Cato discusses. Among other things, the owner should set out work schedules, order supplies, sell redundant items, et cetera. While these tasks could conceivably have been carried out by the *vilicus*, Cato assigns them to the master himself.[45] In fact, the *vilicus* "must not plan any sale unknown to

sunt dicto audientes. Praeterea potissimum eos praeesse oportere, qui periti sint rerum rusticarum. Non solum enim debere imperare, sed etiam facere, ut facientem imitetur et ut animadvertat eum cum *causa sibi praeesse, quod scientia praestet .... Praefectos alacriores faciendum praemiis dandaque opera ut habeant peculium et coniunctas conservas, e quibus habeant filios. Eo enim fiunt firmiores ac coniunctiores fundo.... Studiosiores ad opus fieri liberalius tractando aut cibariis aut vestitu largiore aut remissione operis concessioneve, ut peculiare aliquid in fundo pascere liceat, huiusce modi rerum aliis, ut quibus quid gravius sit imperatum aut animadversum qui, consolando eorum restituat voluntatem ac benevolentiam in dominum.* Similar comments are made by Cato *Agr.* 5.1–5, but with less explicit care for the *vilicus*' wellbeing.

[44] Cato *Agr.* 2.1: *Pater familias ubi ad villam venit, ubi larem familiarem salutavit, fundum eodem die, si potest, circumeat; si non eodem die, at postridie. Ubi cognovit, quo modo fundus cultus siet operaque quae facta infectaque sient, postridie eius diei vilicum vocet, roget, quid operis siet factum, quid restet, satisne temperi opera sient confecta, possitne quae reliqua sient conficere, et quid factum vini, frumenti aliarumque rerum omnium.* See Marzano and Métraux (2018: 27) for the variety of issues that the owner had to deal with when arriving at his estate.

[45] Cato *Agr.* 2.

the owner, or any business concealed from the owner."[46] Clearly, Cato is of the opinion that personal supervision—that is the personal collection of information by the owner—is the most reliable source of information. Cato also advises to build a well-planned house, so that the owner can live there comfortably and will be more willing to visit often. Better supervision will in the end lead to a higher profit.[47] In the second century BC, most large landowners owned several farms in various locations, rather than one contiguous very large establishment. This made it impossible for the owner to live at each farm at all times.[48] Still, personal supervision and detailed instructions to the *vilicus* were necessary in order to maximize profits.

Interestingly, urban property was managed in the same way by middlemen, who paid the rent as a lump sum to the owner and then recouped it from the individual tenants. This is clear from Cicero's descriptions regarding the *insulae* he let out in Rome, where he always gives one large sum for the rental income for each property, paid on a particular date.[49]

From this short overview of the management of farms, we may conclude that a principal-agent problem may have arisen. Despite the close supervision which Cato recommends and the importance of trust between owner and manager, discussed by Varro, the *vilicus* would have ample opportunity to act on his own initiative. There was no way to guarantee that he would act in the owner's interests, and so the owner suffered from asymmetry of information: he could not be aware of everything that happened at his farm, in contrast to his *vilicus*, and was therefore at a disadvantage.

5.4 *Ager publicus* and the Land Market

So far, we have seen that the economy in the second century was growing at a fast pace, and that there were many people willing to buy land in Italy. However, there was one complicating factor: the existence of *ager publicus*. This was land owned by the state, which it had confiscated during the conquest of Italy in the fifth to third centuries. Some land had been used

[46] Cato *Agr.* 5.4: *Nequid emisse velit insciente domino, neu quid dominum celavisse velit.*

[47] Cato *Agr.* 4.

[48] Martin (1971, 90–1); Marzano and Métraux (2018: 18).

[49] Cic. *Att.* 12.32.2, 14.10.3, 15.17.1, 16.1.5; *Dig.* 19.2.30 pr. (Alf. 3 *Dig. a Paulo Epit.*); *Dig.* 19.2.60.pr (Labeo). See Frier (1978: 3–4).

to establish colonies, while other land had remained in the hands of the state. There were in fact several types of *ager publicus*. The two largest categories were public pasture lands, which were leased out against the payment of a rent, and arable land. This latter category was the most important for those wishing to invest in commercial agriculture. However, one major problem was that the land owned by the state was not carefully measured and documented. Appian, in his famous description of the *ager publicus*, states: "As they subdued successive parts of Italy by war, the Romans confiscated a portion of the land and founded towns. ... In the case of captured land which became theirs on each occasion, they distributed the cultivated area at once to settlers, or sold or leased it; but since they did not have time to allocate the very large quantity that was then lying uncultivated as a result of hostilities, they announced that this could for the moment be worked by anyone who wished at a rent of one tenth of the produce for arable land and one fifth for orchards. Rents were also set for those who pastured larger and smaller animals."[50] It seems that some land was leased out against a rent, although I believe that this rent was not often collected. In many cases, the land may have remained with the original Italian owners, from whom it had been taken in theory, but not in practice.[51]

Nevertheless, some land was rented out by the state. *Ager publicus* was owned by the state, which meant that it could at any time be reclaimed by the state from its users. In a few cases, the state actually went as far as to reclaim land. For example in 173 "the Senate resolved that, before the magistrates went abroad, Lucius Postumius should go into Campania, to fix the bounds between the lands which were private property and those which belonged to the public; for it was understood that individuals, by gradually extending their bounds, had taken possession of a very considerable share of the common lands."[52] It was proposed that the land would be rented out by the censors, creating a specific type of *ager publicus*,

[50] App. *BC.* 1.7: Ῥωμαῖοι τὴν Ἰταλίαν πολέμῳ κατὰ μέρη χειρούμενοι γῆς μέρος ἐλάμβανον καὶ πόλεις ἐνῴκιζον ... καὶ τάδε μὲν ἀντὶ φρουρίων ἐπενόουν, τῆς δὲ γῆς τῆς δορικτήτου σφίσιν ἑκάστοτε γιγνομένης τὴν μὲν ἐξειγρασμένην αὐτίκα τοῖς οἰκιζομένοις ἐπιδιῄρουν ἢ ἐπίπρασκον ἢ ἐξεμίσθουν, τὴν δ᾽ ἀργὸν ἐκ τοῦ πολέμου τότε οὖσαν, ἢ δὴ καὶ μάλιστα ἐπλήθυεν, οὐκ ἄγοντές πω σχολὴν διαλαχεῖν ἐπεκήρυττον ἐν τοσῷδε τοῖς ἐθέλουσιν ἐκπονεῖν ἐπὶ τέλει τῶν ἐτησίων καρπῶν, δεκάτῃ μὲν τῶν σπειρομένων, πέμπτῃ δὲ τῶν φυτευομένων. ὥριστο δὲ καὶ τοῖς προβατεύουσι τέλη μειζόνων τε καὶ ἐλαττόνων ζῴων.

[51] Roselaar (2010: 83–84, 113–118).

[52] Liv. 42.1.6.

called *ager censorius*.[53] This probably entailed renting out the land for a specific length of time, against the payment of a set amount.

Despite Postumius' efforts, in 165 it was again necessary to reclaim *ager publicus*: "P. Lentulus, ... when he was *praetor urbanus*, the Senate authorized him to buy up the Campanian territory, which had been completely occupied by private individuals, in order that it should become public land. The owners of the land agreed to let Lentulus set the price, and being a just man, he did not deceive them. Such was his moderation that he both served the interests of the Republic and restricted private ownership, and he used public money to buy 50,000 *iugera* of land. He brought the Campanian territory, which had been divided amongst private individuals, into public ownership, and let it out at a fair price. Put in charge of an investigation, he recovered much other land, and left a plan of the territory on a bronze tablet in the temple of Liberty."[54]

Other cases of the sale or lease of *ager publicus* existed, for example the creation of the *ager in trientabulis* in 200. In 210, many citizens had given loans to the state to finance the Second Punic War. It was decided that this money would be paid back in three instalments, but in 200, when the time came for repayment of the second, it transpired that there was no money available. Therefore "since many of these citizens observed that there was, in many areas, land for sale which they needed to buy, the Senate decided that they should be granted the opportunity of using public lands within a fifty-mile radius of Rome. The consuls were to evaluate this land and impose a tax of an *as* per *iugerum* to show that it was public land that was involved. The rationale behind this was that, when the public purse was again solvent, anyone preferring cash to land could restore the land to the people."[55] However, the state was unable to retain control of the *ager in trientabulis*, even though it was expressly stated to have remained *ager publicus*. The land could only be taken away by the state on the initiative of the buyer, and therefore its occupiers acquired virtually complete security of tenure on this land. There is no indication that anyone ever exchanged his land for money, and the *trientabula* are mentioned as an

[53] Liv. 42.19.1–2.

[54] Gran. Lic. 9–10. See Cic. *Leg. Ag.* 2.82. On this episode, see Pina Polo (2011: 170), who states that Cicero specifies that the land was private. However, Cicero says *privatos agros qui in publicum Campanum incurrebant*, which suggests that private individuals encroached on public land, like Granius does.

[55] Liv. 31.13.6–9.

existing category of land in the *Lex agraria* of 111.[56] The creation of this land had been another way for the rich to gain control of *ager publicus* and acquire on it a title which secured their possession.[57]

In these cases, *ager publicus*—at least the land which was known to be *ager publicus*—was not sold and bought on the free market, but by the state. This made sense, as the state was legally the only owner of state-owned land, and therefore every sale would have to be arranged by the state. The existence of *ager publicus* caused problems with regard to information asymmetry. In the case of *ager publicus*, potential users of this land suffered from information asymmetry, as the Roman state may have known the land was to be retaken in the near future, while the users did not know this. As mentioned above, in situations of information asymmetry, and important role is played by information agents, who know more than others. Any information about a change in the status of this land from public to private was relevant for those looking for land to buy. An example could be senators who knew about upcoming decrees of the Senate regarding the sale or distribution of state-owned land, and could either buy this for themselves or tell their business associates about this important opportunity. Cicero relates how he was stopped from acquiring a piece of land, because he gained inside information that Caesar planned a new layout of the area in which it was located: "Capito started talking about the enlargement of the city: the Tiber is to be diverted, starting from the Milvian bridge along the Vatican Hills: the Campus Martius is to be covered with buildings; while the Vatican plain is to become a kind of new Campus Martius. 'What do you say?' said I, 'why, I was going to the auction, to secure Scapula's pleasure-grounds if I could safely do so.' 'Don't do anything of the sort,' said he, 'for the law will be carried. Caesar wishes it.' I didn't betray any annoyance at the information, but I am annoyed at the scheme."[58] The land in this case was not *ager publicus* yet, but was in danger of becoming so, if it were to be confiscated by the state. In this case, a clear information asymmetry existed between those who knew about Caesar's plan and those who did not.

We may conclude that if land was clearly demarcated as *ager publicus*, it would be unattractive to invest in it, as the land could be taken away at any time. From the description that Cato the Elder gives of his ideal farm in

[56] *Lex agraria* ll. 31–2.
[57] Roselaar (2010: 127–128).
[58] Cic. *Att.* 13.33a.

De agri cultura,[59] as well as the archaeological record,[60] it is clear that commercial agriculture demanded a relatively large investment. The owner needed to pay for slaves, equipment, livestock, seeds or plants, building material, transport, wages for free labourers, and any other expenses which one incurred in running a farm. This of course involved a considerable risk: if the harvest failed or the produce could not be sold at a profit, the owner would lose much of the invested capital. The same would happen if the owner held *ager publicus* which was suddenly taken away by the state. It is therefore a reasonable assumption that insecurity of possession would have inhibited a holder from making large investments in the development of the land: one would think twice before setting up an estate if the basic necessity, land, was not securely held. That this was not a completely theoretical possibility is shown by the fact that Cato himself as censor ordered that "structures owned by private individuals that had been built or erected on public land [should be] demolished within thirty days."[61] In this case the builders may not have realised that the land was state-owned, and assumed it was their own. Alternatively, they might have known it was *ager publicus*, but assumed the state would not use it, and simply invested anyway.

Cicero highlights the connection between insecurity of tenure and unwillingness to invest for a later period. He explains that land distributions made by Lucius Antonius could easily be annulled, because "the occupiers will depart with equanimity; they have gone to no expense; have not yet stocked the land, some because they had no confidence, some because they had no money."[62] Apparently the insecurity of their tenure had made the recipients hesitant to invest in the land; of course, this was especially the case in the civil wars of the first century, when no one could be sure that he would keep hold of his land. Nevertheless, this shows that it was undesirable to invest in land of which one did not have a secure title.

[59] Cato *Agr.* 10–13.

[60] Marzano and Métraux (2018).

[61] Liv. 39.44.4. The Latin in fact says *loca publica*, which is not the same as *ager publicus*, but could refer to public places such as roads or fora.

[62] Cic. *Phil.* 6.5.14; apparently, they lacked confidence in the security of their holdings. See App. *BC.* 4.31. Uncertainty about property would cause problems when trying to sell land. For example in 45 Caesar tried to have sales made in Sulla's time ratified, so that he would have more authority over those lands that he had bought himself and was now selling. If his title as owner would remain uncertain, then "what possible right of property can his sales carry?" As long as Caesar's title to the land remained uncertain, he could not transfer its ownership by sale, Cic. *Fam.* 13.8.2.

This means that the use of *ager publicus* for market-oriented production was problematic. Insecurity of tenure would make people reluctant to invest in land, since they could not be sure that their holdings would not be taken away from them. The ancient sources, for example Pliny the Younger's letters, suggest that Roman landowners in the long term preferred a secure income over a high income, so that security of tenure on land must have been essential.[63] Insecurity of possession would limit the desire to investment, and thereby the potential profit to be made from the land. This obviously reduced the market value of the land, to such a degree that we must assume that a free market for *ager publicus*—at least *ager publicus* of which the public status was clear—was virtually absent.

In the cases cited above, the state had been able to demarcate the *ager publicus*, suggesting that there was sufficient information available on which the state could base the demarcation of the land. However, this was not always the case. In 210, for example, the state had declared the land belonging to Capua *ager publicus*, as punishment for Capua's defection to Hannibal. Livy states that in 205 "people were allowed to lay information about lands that had belonged to any Campanian citizen, so that it could become the property of the Roman people."[64] This means that the state had lost track of its *ager publicus* within five years of its appropriation.

From the examples cited above it is clear that private individuals often encroached on the public land and exploited it in much the same way as they would do with their privately owned land. In the cases cited above, the state, after considerable effort, managed to re-establish control over the land it owned. However, there were many other tracts of *ager publicus* which had not been demarcated at all. This land was *ager publicus* in theory, but in practice was used by whoever occupied it. Many users of such land treated it as their private land, and in fact no one may have been aware of its status: neither the state, nor the users nor potential buyers. When the Gracchan land commission started its distribution work in 133 BC, the problems of inadequate administration became very clear. During the second century most holders of *ager publicus* had assumed that their land would not be taken away, and had invested considerable sums of money in it. Appian describes the consternation caused by Tiberius Gracchus' law: "[The users of land] gathered in groups, deploring their

[63] Plin. *Ep*. 3.19, 9.37. See Kehoe (1997: 15).

[64] Liv. 28.46.5. The state often depended on private informers for gathering intelligence on *ager publicus*: App. *BC*. 1.18; *Lex agraria* ll. 90–1.

situation and supporting their case against the poor by pointing to the work they had put in over many years, their planting, their building. Some had bought land from their neighbours; were they to lose the money as well as the land? Some had family tombs on the land or said that holdings had been treated as fully owned and divided up on inheritance. Others claimed that their wives' dowries had been invested in such lands, or that it had been given to their daughters as dowry, and moneylenders could show loans made on this security. In short, there was a babel of protest and lamentation."[65] Clearly, people had been treating the land as privately owned and had bought and sold it as such, or given such land as security for loans.

We noted that land which was known to be *ager publicus* was unattractive for investment, as it could be taken away at any time. However, the fact that land existed of which the status was not known at all was a more serious problem. As is clear from Appian's passage, people had invested in such land and now stood to lose their investments, without adequate compensation by the state. In this case, there was no information asymmetry, but rather a complete lack of information, since no one party knew more than the other. The balance of power swung towards the state, however, as it held the authority and means to retake control over the land. The effect of uncertainty of legal status on the economic value of the land may have been similar to the effect of public status: a lack of reliable information would have led to a lack of investments and a decrease in the value of the land.

The Roman state in fact recognized that the insecurity of titles on land was a problem. It was also aware of the general desire to find land for commercial investments, especially in central Italy. In the late third and second centuries the state attempted to create more possibilities for secure tenure on *ager publicus*, perhaps in response to the demand of commercial producers to buy land. A first step in this process took place in the Second Punic War, when the Roman state turned out to own several tracts of *ager publicus* in central Italy. It now disposed of these in order to raise money for the war through the sale of land by the quaestors as *ager quaestorius*, the lease of land as *ager censorius* and the creation of the *ager in trientabulis*. The latter was located within 50 miles from Rome, and the known tracts of *ager quaestorius and ager censorius* were likewise located near Rome. These three methods of alienation thus created security of tenure

[65] App. *BC.* 1.10.

on highly desirable tracts of land in central Italy. The Gracchan land reform also led to the privatization of a great amount of *ager publicus*, although some land still remained in the hands of the state.[66] Eventually, the unsatisfactory nature of its legal status led to the disappearance of almost all *ager publicus* in Italy by the mid-first century BC, although we cannot follow this development here in detail.[67]

This section has shown that *ager publicus* had a fundamentally inefficient legal status with regards to the economic value of this land in the Roman Republic. Due to the insecurity of the status of this land, it was less suitable for investment, which went against economic developments in the second century BC. In cases where the status of land as *ager publicus* was clear, an information asymmetry existed between the legal owner, that is the state, and potential buyers. In cases where it was not clear that land was *ager publicus*, there was no reliable information available to any party involved. A parallel may be visible in the erroneous marriages between citizens and non-citizens in Egypt, discussed by Lerouxel in this volume: sometimes, no one knew the civic status of a person, including themselves. Therefore, this was not a problem of information asymmetry between two parties, but rather a lack of information due to inadequate record keeping. The clear limits of Roman record-keeping show that asymmetry of information was only one issue that could limit optimal outcomes in the Roman economy.

5.5 Conclusion

The first section of this paper has shown that a free market for land existed in the middle to late Republic, and that this market was not free from problems relating to asymmetry of information. Most important was the asymmetry between buyers and sellers of land, and the asymmetry between landowners and the managers they appointed to work the land. In both cases the party with less information was in danger of being cheated through the problems connected with the principal-agent problem. Legal institutions formed a remedy to some extent, but in the case of land sales it was very hard to prove malice. Therefore, the dangers of an asymmetry of information could not be fully mitigated.

[66] Roselaar (2010: 230–279).

[67] See Roselaar (2010: 278–287).

From the fourth section we may conclude that *ager publicus* was an unsatisfactory legal category of land, given the rising economic value of land in the second century BC. When the status of the land as *ager publicus* was clear, an information asymmetry existed between the state and potential buyers. In other cases it was not clear that land was *ager publicus*, which meant all parties suffered from a lack of information available. This unsatisfactory legal and economic situation in the end led to the privatization of *ager publicus*, first by the creation of new types of state-owned land, which were held with secure titles by individuals, and in the Gracchan period to the distribution of land as private property. Thus, the privatization of public land was not simply the result of the 'greed of the rich', who were trying to monopolize all the land for their selfish gains, as is often argued by the ancient sources, as well as many modern interpretations.[68] Instead, it was a logical conclusion of increased demands placed on scarce resources. The wish of commercial producers to acquire more land undoubtedly played a role, but this was a logical consequence of the wish to buy land on which to produce crops for the growing market in the second century BC.

Bibliography

Adams, C. (n.d.). *Transport in the Roman Empire*. Available at: https://www.academia.edu/10259552/Transport_in_the_Roman_Empire

Andreau, J. 1999. *Banking and Business in the Roman World*. Cambridge: Cambridge University Press.

Arruñada, B. 2020. The Institutions of Roman Markets. In *Roman Law and Economics*, ed. G. Dari-Mattiacci and D. Kehoe, vol. II, 247–299. Oxford: Oxford University Press.

Aubert, J.-J. 1994. *Business managers in Ancient Rome: a social and economic study of institores, 200 B.C.–A.D. 250*. Leiden: E.J. Brill.

Broekaert, W. 2017. Conflicts, Contract Enforcement, and Business Communities in the Archive of the Sulpicii. In *The Economy of Pompeii*, ed. M. Flohr and A. Wilson, 387–414. Oxford: Oxford University Press.

Caprogrossi Colognesi, L. 2010. Appunti per una storia dell'economia agraria romana. *Studia et documenta historiae et iuris* 76: 523–542.

Carlsen, J. 1995. *Vilici and Roman Estate Managers*. Rome: L'Erma di Bretschneider.

[68] For example the passage of Appian cited above; for modern interpretations, see Toynbee (1965: 1); Hopkins (1978).

Culham, P. 1989. Archives and Alternatives in Republican Rome. *Classical Philology* 84: 100–115.

Dalby, A. 1998. *Cato: On Farming.* Totnes: Prospect Books.

Eisenhardt, K.M. 1989. Agency Theory: An Assessment and Review. *The Academy of Management Review* 14 (1): 57–74.

Finley, M.I. 1999. *The Ancient Economy*, Cambridge 1st ed. 1973. University of California Press.

Flohr, M. 2017. Quantifying Pompeii: Population, Inequality, and the Urban Economy. In *The Economy of Pompeii*, ed. M. Flohr and A. Wilson, 53–84. Oxford: Oxford University Press.

Frier, B. 1978. Cicero's Management of His Urban Properties. *The Classical Journal* 74: 1–6.

Frier, B., and D. Kehoe. 2007. Law and Economic Institution. In *The Cambridge Economic History of the Greco-Roman World*, ed. W. Scheidel, I. Morris, and R.P. Saller, 113–143. Cambridge: Cambridge University Press.

Garicano, L., and S.N. Kaplan. 2001. The Effects of Business-to-business E-commerce on Transaction Costs. *Journal of Industrial Economics* 49 (4): 463–485.

Geraghty, R.M. 2007. The Impact of Globalization in the Roman Empire, 200 BC–AD 100. *Journal of Economic History* 67 (4): 1036–1061.

Hollander, D. 2012. *Money in the Late Roman Republic.* Leiden: Brill.

Hopkins, K. 1978. *Conquerors and Slaves.* Cambridge: Cambridge University Press.

Isayev, E. 2007. *Inside Ancient Lucania: Dialogues in History and Archaeology.* London: University of London.

Jongman, W. 2017. The benefits of market integration. In *The Economic Integration of Roman Italy. Rural Communities in a Globalizing World*, ed. G. Tol and T. de Haas, 15–27. Leiden: Brill.

Kaser, M. (ed. R. Hackl), 1996. *Das römische Zivilprozessrecht.* Munich: C. H. Beck.

Kay, P. 2014. *Rome's Economic Revolution.* Oxford: Oxford University Press.

Kehoe, D. 1997. *Investment, Profit and Tenancy. The Jurists and the Roman Agrarian Economy.* Ann Arbor: The University of Michigan Press.

Maróti, E. 1976. The Vilicus and the Villa System in Ancient Italy. *Oikumene* 1: 109–124.

Martin, R. 1971. *Recherches sur les agronomes latins et leurs conceptions économiques et sociales.* Paris: Belles Lettres.

Marzano, A., and G.P.R. Métraux. 2018. The Roman Villa: An Overview. In *The Roman Villa in the Mediterranean Basin. Late Republic to Late Antiquity*, ed. A. Marzano and G.P.R. Métraux, 1–41. Cambridge: Cambridge University Press.

Nicholson, J. 1994. The Delivery and Confidentiality of Cicero's Letters. *The Classical Journal* 90: 33–63.

North, D.C. 1990. *Institutions, Institutional Change, and Economic Performance.* Cambridge: Cambridge University Press.

Orth, J.V. 2003. *Sale of Defective Houses. Cicero and the Moral Choice.* University of North Carolina School of Law. Available at: https://scholarship.law.unc.edu/faculty_publications/375/

Pina Polo, F. 2011. *The Consul at Rome. The Civil Functions of the Consuls in the Roman Republic.* Cambridge: Cambridge University Press.

Roselaar, S.T. 2010. *Public Land in the Roman Republic: A Social and Economic History of Ager Publicus in Italy, 396–89 BC.* Oxford: Oxford University Press.

———. 2019. *Italy's Economic Revolution. Integration and Economy in Republican Italy.* Oxford: Oxford University Press.

———. forthcoming. Status hierarchies and Economic Differentiation in Rome and Italy (IIIrd to Ist cent. BC). In *Statuts personels et main d'oeuvre en Méditerranée hellénistique*, ed. S. Maillot and J. Zurbach. Clermont-Ferrand.

Rosenstein, N. 2008. Aristocrats and agriculture in the Middle and Late Republic. *Journal of Roman Studies* 98: 1–26.

Teitler, H.C. 1993. Free-born Estate Managers in the Graeco-Roman World. In *De Agricultura: In Memoriam P. W. de Neeve*, ed. H. Sancisi-Weerdenburg et al., 206–213. Amsterdam: Gieben.

Temin, P. 2006. The Economy of the Early Roman Empire. *Journal of Economic Perspectives* 20: 133–151.

Terrenato, N. 2012. The Enigma of 'Catonian' Villas: The De Agri Cultura in the Context of Second-Century BC Italian Architecture. In *Roman Republican Villas. Architecture, Context, and Ideology*, ed. J.A. Becker and N. Terrenato, 69–93. Ann Arbor. University of Michigan Press.

Tol, G., and T. de Haas. 2017. Introduction. In *The Economic Integration of Roman Italy. Rural Communities in a Globalizing World*, ed. G. Tol and T. de Haas, 1–12. Leiden: Brill.

Toynbee, A.J. 1965. *Hannibal's Legacy: The Hannibalic War's Effects on Roman Life.* London: Oxford University Press.

Verboven, K. 2007. The Associative Order. Status and Ethos Among Roman Businessmen in Late Republic and Early Empire. *Athenaeum* 95: 861–893.

———. 2008. Faeneratores, Negotiatores and Financial Intermediation in the Roman World (Late Republic and Early Empire). In *Pistoi dia tèn technèn. Bankers, loans and archives in the ancient world. Studies in honour of Raymond Bogaert*, ed. K. Verboven, K. Vandorpe, and V. Chankowski, 211–229. Leuven: Peeters.

Walcot, P. 1975. Cicero on Private Property: Theory and Practice. *Greece & Rome* 22: 120–128.

Watson, A. 1961. *Contract of Mandate in Roman Law.* Oxford: Clarendon Press.

White, K.D. 1973. Roman Agricultural Writers I: Varro and His Predecessors. *Aufstieg und Niedergang der Römischen Welt* I. 4: 439–497.

CHAPTER 6

Domum pestilentem vendo: Real Estate Market and Information Asymmetry in the Roman World

Cristina Rosillo-López

On the outskirts of Rome, along a road, the inscribed tomb of a man proclaims how happy and easy his life would be after death. He conspicuously maintains that his body would enjoy free lodging and thus he would "no longer be indebted because of being behind in the payment of rent".[1] Meanwhile, a Roman senator was once accused of harassing a Vestal Virgin; in his defence, he declared that all what he wanted from her was to

[1] *CIL* VI.7193: *Quod superset homini requiescunt dulciter ossa/nec sum sollicitus ne subito esuriam/ et podagram careo, nec sum pensionibus arra /et gratis aeterno perfruor hospitio.*

This research has been financed by the project "El sector inmobiliario en el mundo romano: un análisis económico; s. II a.C.-s. II d.C." (HAR2016-76882-P), Ministerio de Ciencia, Innovación y Universidades, Spain. All translations are Loeb. Willems 2019 is the most recent addition to this debate, although from a juridical rather than economic point of view.

C. Rosillo-López (✉)
Universidad Pablo de Olavide, Sevilla, Spain
e-mail: mcroslop@upo.es

C. Rosillo-López, M. García Morcillo (eds.), *Managing Information in the Roman Economy*, Palgrave Studies in Ancient Economies,
https://doi.org/10.1007/978-3-030-54100-2_6

buy one of her properties at a very good price. This explanation was considered sufficient to ensure his acquittal.[2] Renting, letting, buying and selling constitute everyday actions in people's lives, whether in modern times or during the Roman Empire. Everybody needs a roof to live under, after all. As in other sectors of the economy (but perhaps even more so), questions of information asymmetry played an important role during economic exchanges.

In terms of information asymmetries, why is the residential real estate market different? Was it also this way in ancient Rome? In the first place, the houses are heterogeneous: they have a variable number of square metres, rooms, and age, as well as varying in location, access to resources, and so on. Secondly, the transactions are uncertain, namely that both the buyer and the seller (or the owner and the tenant) must identify the price that each of them is willing to receive or pay. We should not forget that the expenses related to real estate represent an essential part of each family's spending, so any alteration in prices automatically affects the living standards of the population. In addition, the real estate sector was strongly linked to the credit market in several ways: for one, it was usual to use houses and premises as a guarantee for the purchase of other goods, especially land. Secondly, the significant economic outlay involved in purchasing a house also means that current interest rates set the price trend. On more than one occasion, Cicero established a direct relationship between the devaluation of the real estate market and the difficulties of accessing credit.[3] Thirdly, a house search entails significant transaction costs, both economic and legal. It is a market in which the agents are not usually specialised intermediaries, but amateurs, namely owners and buyers or private tenants and landlords.

Likewise, it is a market in which asymmetric information is the norm, as the parties involved in the transaction have different information and one party has better (or more complete) information than the other. Asymmetries of information can lead to market failure, and thus to an inefficient economic result. In the real estate market, the asymmetry of information is usually (but not always) due to the fact that the seller generally knows more than the buyer, not only about the goods for sale, but also the characteristics of the neighbourhood and the prices within the

[2] Plut. *Crass.* 1.2.

[3] For example, Cic. *Att.* 9.9, comparing prices between 56 and 49 BCE.

area.[4] In addition, this asymmetry is not equal in all cases, since some sellers and buyers are better informed than others. These disparities in information represent a unique feature of the real estate market, compared to other markets.

For all these reasons, the real estate market is highly illiquid, slow to convey information to participants, and difficult for outsiders to value. Garmaise and Moskowitz have suggested that "information considerations may be more important in the real estate market than in Akerlof's (1970) canonical example of the used car market".[5] If information considerations are more important, it is fair to conclude that information asymmetry is also more relevant for the real estate market. Real estate is not easy to appraise; each city, each neighbourhood, each street, each building, each floor and even each apartment has a set of characteristics that make it unlike any other.

This paper thus intends to study the real estate market as an asymmetric information sphere. This objective is not a modern projection, but something that the Romans themselves specifically noted with respect to the real estate sector. Responding to a legal consultation on the inclusion or exclusion of underground pipes in the sale of a house, the jurist Proculus (mid-first century AD) based his response on the supposition that real estate transactions took place between two honest and well-informed parties, that is in a world where information is perfect and flows without restrictions (which essentially constitutes an *avant la lettre* reference to the neoclassical economists' *homo oeconomicus* of perfect information). However, when commenting on this reply, Celsus—a famous jurist from the end of the first century to the beginning of the second century AD and member of the *consilium* of emperor Hadrian—categorically discarded such an assumption. In a scathing rebuttal, he argued that in these transactions the seller and the buyer usually did not have all the information, or did not pay attention to it:

> (2) Firmus asked of Proculus whether the pipes which conduct water from a leaden reservoir underground into a brazen vessel built around the sides of a house are to be considered part of the latter? Or are they to be considered as personal property, united and stationary, which do not belong to the house? He [Proculus] answered that the intention of the parties should be

[4] Kurlat and Stroebel 2015.

[5] Garmaise and Moskowitz 2004.

> taken into account. But what if neither the purchaser nor the vendor had paid any attention to the subject, as very frequently occurs in cases of this kind? Would it not seem to be better if we should hold that what is inserted and enclosed in a building forms a portion of the same?[6]

Celsus considered the real estate sector to be governed by asymmetric information. Today, economists agree with Celsus and believe that economic interactions are characterised by asymmetries of information, a theory that received a huge boost when the Nobel Prize in economics was awarded to G. Akerlof, M. Spence and J. Stiglitz in 2001 for their work on this subject.

This paper will focus on two main questions on asymmetries of information linked to real estate: (1) how was information asymmetry handled by parties and jurists when houses were bought and sold through adverse selection; and (2) how did signalling help to distinguish and screen a good tenant from a bad one? The paper will thus analyse the asymmetry present in the system, as well as the attempts by the state and jurists to reduce the risk that it posed.

6.1 Information Asymmetry and Adverse Selection: Buyers and Sellers

The assumption that buyers and sellers are equally informed would conclude that housing prices reveal the preferences of both buyers and sellers.[7] However, as the jurist Celsus recognised, the existence of asymmetric information in real estate does not constitute an assumption; it is a fact. Prices and transactions also reflect such information asymmetry.

Anyone who has bought a house or an apartment is aware that there is an information gap between the buyer and the seller. Seller disclosure laws related to real estate have been passed in many contemporary states in order to reduce information asymmetries, going beyond the previous

[6] *Dig.* 19.1.38.2 (Celsus, *Dig.*, book 8): *Firmus a proculo quaesiit, si de plumbeo castello fistulae sub terram missae aquam ducerent in aenum lateribus circumstructum, an hae aedium essent, an ut ruta caesa vincta fixaque quae aedium non essent. ille rescripsit referre, quid acti esset. quid ergo si nihil de ea re neque emptor neque venditor cogitaverunt, ut plerumque in eiusmodi rebus evenisse solet, nonne propius est, ut inserta et inclusa aedificio partem eius esse existimemus?* Cf. Hausmaninger 1991 on the controversies between Celsus and Proculus and p. 59 regarding this case.

[7] Pope 2008.

"caveat emptor".[8] This debate was present in Roman law and Roman ethical thinking, but also in Hellenistic philosophy; in the two latter fields, it was embedded in the wider question of honesty and expediency.

Cicero discussed this at length in his *De officiis* on two occasions: first, by presenting it as a discussion between Hellenistic Stoic philosophers; second, by later framing the debate in terms that were much closer to Roman law, presenting real Roman cases, and even based on his own personal experience, in a mixture of legal, moral and practical arguments. In all instances, real estate was featured as a central component and illustration of the question.

First, Cicero posited the dilemma of whether, in times of famine, a grain merchant should disclose that other ships would soon arrive with more grain or stay silent and sell his own merchandise for a greater profit. Diogenes of Alexandria, a renowned Stoic philosopher, would argue that the seller should disclose any defects in his products, but not disclose information. In fact, he should sell to his best possible advantage as long as there is no misrepresentation: "It is one thing to conceal", Diogenes would perhaps reply; "not to reveal is quite a different thing. (...) But I am under no obligation to tell you everything that it may be to your interest to be told".[9] His pupil Antipater, on the other hand, argued (according to Cicero) that all facts should be revealed, taking into consideration the bonds of fellowship between human beings.[10] The discussion soon veered towards the disjunctive between what is expedient (*quoniam expedit*) and what is morally wrong (*turpe*).[11] In the case of the grain, uncertainty, the passage of time and the presence of risk are also important, in order to reach a decision—the other ships could sink, or could be delayed.

From a general reflection on moral matters, Cicero passed to a proper discussion on information asymmetry in real estate:

> Suppose again that an honest man is offering a house for sale on account of certain undesirable features of which he himself is aware but which nobody else knows; suppose it is unsanitary, but has the reputation of being healthful;

[8] Lefcoe 2004.

[9] Cic. *Off.* 3.52: *aliud est celare, aliud tacere. (...) Sed non, quicquid tibi audire utile est, idem mihi dicere necesse est.* Dyck 1996: 561–562 on the distinction between *celare* and *tacere.*

[10] Cic. *Off.* 3.50–54.

[11] Cic. *Off.* 3.53. Dyck 1996: 557–560 on Cicero's use of Diogenes and Antipater and a discussion of to what extent such positions were taken from Hecato's *On appropriate actions* or were mainly constructed by Cicero, with previous bibliography.

> suppose it is not generally known that vermin are to be found in all the bedrooms; suppose, finally, that it is built of unsound timber and likely to collapse, but that no one knows about it except the owner; if the vendor does not tell the purchaser these facts but sells him the house for far more than he could reasonably have expected to get for it, I ask whether his transaction is unjust or dishonourable.[12]

The dilemma is now based on legal rather than moral grounds, without any prior allusions to justice. As expected, Antipater deemed the transaction dishonourable and unjust.

Although the orator ultimately agreed with Antipater on moral grounds,[13] Cicero chose to write at length on Diogenes explanation with gusto and irony:

> "Can you say", answers Diogenes, "that he compelled you to purchase, when he did not even advise it? He advertised for sale what he did not like; you bought what you did like. If people are not considered guilty of swindling when they place upon their placards FOR SALE: A FINE VILLA, WELL BUILT, even when it is neither good nor properly built, still less guilty are they who say nothing in praise of their house. For there the purchaser may exercise his own judgment, what fraud can there be on the part of the vendor? But if, again, not all that is expressly stated has to be made good, do you think a man is bound to make good what has not been said? What, pray, would be more stupid than for a vendor to recount all the faults in the article he is offering for sale? And what would be so absurd as for an auctioneer to cry, at the owner's bidding, 'Here is an unsanitary house for sale'?"[14]

[12] Cic. *Off.* 3.54: *Vendat aedes vir bonus, propter aliqua vitia, quae ipse norit, ceteri ignorent, pestilentes sint et habeantur salubres, ignoretur in omnibus cubiculis apparere serpentes, sint, male materiatae et ruinosae, sed hoc praeter dominum nemo sciat; quaero, si haec emptoribus venditor non dixerit aedesque vendiderit pluris multo. quam se venditurum putarit, num id iniuste aut improbe fecerit?* The case of the unsanitary house had already been proposed by Carneades and was mentioned by Cicero in his *De re publica* (Cic. *Rep.* 3.29).

[13] Cic. *Off.* 3.57.

[14] Cic. *Off.* 3.55: *Diogenes contra "Num te emere coegit, qui ne hortatus quidem est? Ille, quod non placebat, proscripsit, tu quod placebat, emisti. Quod si qui proscribunt villam bonam beneque aedificatam non existimantur fefellisse, etiam si illa nec bona est nec aedificata ratione, multo minus, qui domum non laudarunt. Ubi enim iudicium emptoris est, ibi fraus venditoris quae potest esse? Sin autem dictum non omne praestandum est, quod dictum non est, id praestandum putas? Quid vero est stultius quam venditorem eius rei, quam vendat, vitia narrare? Quid autem tam absurdum quam si domini iussu ita praeco praedicet: "domum pestilentem vendo?".*

Here, Diogenes/Cicero is mixing two different legal categories. On the one hand, Roman law did not hold the seller accountable for colourful language used in the process of the sale, as long as it did not influence the price.[15] Rental announcements preserved in the cities around the Vesuvius usually employ very descriptive language, with the exception of the *balneum* located in the property of Iulia Felix in Pompeii, which is described as "elegant and distinguished" (*balneum venerium et nongentum*).[16]

On the other hand, Cicero/Diogenes mentioned a different case: the situation in which the seller failed to disclose negative facts about the house that, if known to the buyer, would change the price. In such a case, as Cicero states a few paragraphs later, Late Republican jurists considered that any seller who failed to declare defects in real estate transaction should be punished, as such a disclosure was essential to bona fide*s*.[17]

The concept of *bona fides* was introduced in public contracts at the beginning of the first century BC by the jurist Q. Mucius Scaevola *Pontifex* (cos 95 BC), author of the first systematic study on private law. During his proconsulship in Asia, where he was charged with regulating the situation of the cities and their debts towards the *publicani*, he promulgated an exception in his edict that declared illegal any contract which could not be filled *ex bona fide*. *Bona fides* opposed *fraus* and *dolus malus*, among other concepts; Scaevola extended this concept to many cases (*iudicia bonae fidei*), including guardianships, commercial societies, deposits, sales, and leases.[18]

According to such thinking, Cicero claimed, the grain trader or the owner of the unsanitary house were not right to suppress information. However, it is striking that, as a well-trained orator who was undoubtedly aware of what he was arguing, Cicero is conflating both cases, when actually they represent two different types of information asymmetry. Using Diogenes of Babylon as his mouthpiece, he had claimed that the grain trader was not hiding any defects in his merchandise, but only failing to deliver all the information he had; this is not the same as the case of the

[15] *Dig.* 18.1.43 (Florent. *Inst. 8*). The jurist Florentinus lived in the second century AD.

[16] *CIL* IV 1136 = *ILS* 5723.

[17] Cic. *Off.* 3.67. *Fides:* Cic. *Off.* 3.65: *Nam* cum *ex duodecim tabulis satis esset ea praestari, quae essent lingua nuncupata, quae qui infitiatus esset, dupli poena subiret, a iuris consultis etiam reticentiae poena est constituta; quicdquid enim esset in praedio vitii, id statuerunt, si venditor sciret, nisi nominatim dictum esset, praestari oportere.*

[18] Cic. *Att.* 6.1.15.

house, since the presence of sanitary problems would undoubtedly have an impact on the price.

This debate, pursued both by Cicero with an ethical edge as well as by jurists on legal grounds, can be contextualised with the contemporary discussion about information asymmetry and adverse selection, that is, the situation in which market participation is affected by asymmetric information. In this case, one of the parties has more information (or private information) than the other before the contract is signed (in contract theory). The risk is that the party deprived of the information fears being placed in an unfair position and may retire from the transaction, thus affecting the market. In adverse selection, parties with goods of good quality and information will leave, leaving only the "bad apples". Studies on adverse selection have also considered social preferences.[19] In the case of the real estate market, the buyer is usually the one who is adversely selected. In adverse selection, reputation and trust also play an important role: a bad transaction could involve not only economic penalties, but social ones too. This constitutes an efficient means to reduce information asymmetry.

There are two types of asymmetric information related to the real estate market: first, some sellers could possess superior information regarding current market conditions (e.g. the dynamics of the area surrounding the property, or government decisions regarding that area); second, sellers usually have more information about the possible defects or flaws of the goods.[20]

Roman sources have preserved at least three clear cases of asymmetric information in the sale of houses, related to the previous discussion on the ethical grounds of whether to disclose information or not. In all three cases, information was concealed by the seller from the buyer about the circumstances of the goods in question.

In the first case, Publius Calpurnius Lanarius bought a house in the mons Caelius; afterwards, he received a notice from the augurs stating that he had to pull down parts of the building, likely one or more floors, because they obstructed the augur's view. It is very likely that this was a building of apartments, whose value and rentability would thus be much lower than expected at the time of sale. To Lanarius' surprise, the previous owner knew about the augurs' decision, which had in fact prompted him

[19] Hoppe and Schmitz 2013.

[20] Garmaise and Moskowitz 2004: 409.

to place the house up for sale. Lanarius went to court and won the case, and the verdict stated that: "since the augurs' mandate was known to the vendor at the time of making the transfer and since he had not made it known, he was bound to make good the purchaser's loss".[21] Dated to the beginning of the first century BC, it is the first known case of a defect failing to be disclosed in Roman law.[22]

The second case is almost contemporary, since it occurred in 92 BC. Sergius Orata, a wealthy investor and famous oyster farmer, bought a property located on the Lucrine Lake and later sold it to Marcus Gratidianus (who would become praetor in 85 BC).[23] At a later date, Orata bought the property back from Gratidianus. It is a complex case, in which Orata was involved in two different lawsuits. For the sake of our study, the second of these is the most interesting to us: Orata brought Gratidianus to court, claiming that the latter had failed to disclose during the sale the existence of a *servitudo* or encumbrance. The parties were defended by the two most important orators of their time:

> Crassus pleaded the letter of the law that: "the vendor was bound to make good the defect, for he had not declared it, although he was aware of it"; Antonius laid stress upon the equity of the case, leading that, "inasmuch as the defect in question had not been unknown to Sergius (for it was the same house that he had sold to Marius), no declaration of it was needed, and in purchasing it back he had not been imposed upon, for he knew to what legal liability his purchase was subject".[24]

The defence argued that, as it was the same house, the defect (*vitium*) was known and no declaration was needed; however, this argument is not particularly solid. The accusation was based on the law, which stated that the seller had to declare all defects. The case was more complex than it appears,

[21] Cic. *Off.* 3.66: *igitur iudex ita pronuntiavit,* cum *in vendundo rem eam scisset et non pronuntiasset, emptori damnum praestari oportere.*

[22] The judge was Marcus Cato, father of Cato the Younger.

[23] *RE*, s.v. Sergius 33 (Münzer). Kay 2014: 134, n. 15 considers him an estate agent. However, from the actions described in the sources, Orata clearly acted on his own behalf. Münzer correctly described him as a "Geschäftsmann" and "ein geschickter und glücklicher Spekulant".

[24] Cic. *Off.* 3.67: *Ius Crassus urgebat, "quod vitii venditor non dixisset sciens, id oportere praestari", aequitatem Antonius, "quoniam id vitium ignotum Sergio non fuisset, qui illas aedes vendidisset, nihil fuisse necesse dici nec eum esse deceptum, qui id, quod emerat, quo iure esset, teneret".* Cf. also Cic. *De Orat.* 1.178.

however. Having information concealed from him was not the only grounds for Orata to bring the case to court, since he also wanted to regain some profits for the loss he had suffered in the first lawsuit, in which he had tried unsuccessfully to gain water access for his oyster farms.[25] In any case, for the sake of our argument, we are interested in a discussion about information asymmetries in the court of justice, and in jurisprudence that existed at the beginning of the first century BC.

Finally, Papinianus contemplated a similar case in which, during the sale, the seller had not informed the buyer about the existence of an annual payment due for an aqueduct that passed under the house. The court considered that the unexpected financial burden should be taken into account.[26]

Roman law considered not only the case of information asymmetries from the perspective of the buyer, but also from the seller. Paulus pondered on a classic case, also treated by previous jurists (Nerva, Sabinus and Cassius): what happens when someone purchases a house that is subsequently burnt down? The jurist surveyed all the possible cases of information asymmetry, including when the vendor knew about the fire but the buyer did not (the sale would be void if the entire building was destroyed before the transaction); when the buyer knew of it, but not the seller (the sale would stand at full price); when neither of the parties knew about it (the sale was void if the entire building had been burnt); and finally when both buyer and seller were aware that it had been burnt (the law considered the transaction a fraud, since both parties were guilty of deceit).[27] The case of the burnt house constitutes a special case when compared to previous cases of information asymmetry in real estate; in this instance, it is not a question of an undisclosed fault within the building, but rather an external circumstance that one of the parties may have been unaware of.

Which strategies could be used to compensate or avoid such information gaps? In a study of commercial real estate in the United States, Garmaise and Moskowitz found that people—especially those with long income histories—tried to reduce information asymmetry by purchasing

[25] On the case, cf. Dyck 1996: 579 (it is debatable who won the case, Antonius or Crassus); Bannon 2001; Marzano 2007: 76–77; Bannon 2009: 209–232; Marzano 2015.

[26] *Dig.* 19.1.41 (*Papinianus 3 resp*): *In venditione super annua pensitatione pro aquae ductu infra domum romae constitutum nihil commemoratum est. deceptus ob eam rem ex empto actionem habebit: itaque, si conveniatur ob pretium ex vendito, ratio improvisi oneris habetur.*

[27] *Dig.* 18.1.57 (Paulus 4 *Plautius*).

nearby properties, and by avoiding dealings with informed brokers.[28] In the case of real estate sales, only local buyers who knew the surrounding area of the property enough could make an accurate assessment of the market and thus solve the information asymmetry gap. The no-trade implications theory, developed by Milgrom and Stokey, posits that, faced with severe information asymmetries, uninformed agents should not trade with informed counterparts. The latter, in turn, usually prefer to trade with other informed agents.[29] We thus see the creation of market segmentation, in which informed and uniformed agents lead parallel transactions, and of a bad market in which informed agents with good assets to sell withdraw because, with uninformed agents wary of paying too much, informed agents are not paid what they consider a good price.

Who would be the informed agents in Rome? Atticus seems in general to have been an informed agent, although he was not successful in advising Cicero with his purchase of the *horti* in 45 (cf. *infra*), even though he had acted in this capacity in the past for Cicero and other senators. Cicero and Valerius Maximus mentioned the *praediatores*—the brokers and other people who bought or dealt with properties at auctions, especially properties that were pledged to the state by a debtor and forfeited. According to these authors, the jurist Q. Mucius Scaevola *Augur* considered that two of these brokers, Furius and Cascellius, knew more about legal matters of real estate than he did.[30] These informed agents, specialists in buying properties at auction, should likely be counted among Rome's informed agents on real estate sales. Did such information asymmetry lead to market segmentation and to informed agents only trading with other informed agents? The sources are not talkative on this point.

There is a second strategy to avoid this sort of information gap: inside information regarding government decisions, which can tip the scales to one side or another. After the death of his beloved daughter Tullia in 45, Cicero decided to buy a plot of land on which to erect a temple in her memory. Having surveyed several properties, he decided to purchase the *horti* owned by Scaepula at auction. However, before the auction, he received an insider tip:

[28] Garmaise and Moskowitz 2004.

[29] Milgrom and Stokey 1982.

[30] Cic. *Balb.* 45; Val. Max. 8.12.1. Cf. Castro Sáenz 2013; *RE* Suppl. XIX, s.v. *praediatura* (Wesener). On auctions, cf. Rauh 1989; García Morcillo 2005. Other mentions of *praediatores*: Cic. *Att.* 12.17.2: *Appuleius praediator liberalis* (also mentioned as *praediator* in *Att.* 12.14.2).

> Soon after came Gaius Capito with Titus Carrinas. I hardly laid a finger on their cloaks; yet they stopped, and very à propos (though by chance) Capito fell to talking about the enlargement of the city: the Tiber is to be diverted, starting from the Milvian bridge along the Vatican Hills: the Campus Martius is to be covered with buildings; while the Vatican plain is to become a kind of new Campus Martius. "What do you say?" said I, "why, I was going to the auction, to secure Scapula's pleasure-grounds if I could safely do so" "Don't do anything of the sort," said he, "for the law will be carried. Caesar wishes it." I didn't betray any annoyance at the information, but I am annoyed at the scheme.[31]

Apparently, the property that Cicero desired would be included in the new district that Caesar had in mind, part of a project that would enlarge the city by diverting the river, urbanise the Campus Martius and create a new Campus Martius on the Vatican plain.[32] If Cicero had bought the property, he would have lost money, since the *horti* would likely have been devalued or destroyed. Cicero had done his groundwork: his friend Atticus had even inspected the *horti* in situ and sent Cicero a report on them.[33] However, without senator Gaius Ateius Capito's inside tip, he would have lost a sizable amount of money. Other prospective buyers likely did not have access to such information; the uninformed buyer would purchase the *horti*. The context of the sale—an auction—is important here, since it is a moment when several buyers would confront the quality of their information, which would then be reflected in the final price. Furthermore, the question of timing is framed differently for an auction, since all participants would have the same amount of time to make their decision before the day of the sale. In other cases, in times of high demand, buyers had less time to decide whether to buy or not.

[31] Cic. *Att.* 13.33a: *Paulo post C. Capito* cum *T. Carrinate. Horum ego vix attigi paenulam. tamen remanserunt ceciditque belle. sed casu sermo a Capitone de urbe augenda, a ponte Mulvio Tiberim duci secundum montis Vaticanos, campum Martium coaedificari, illum autem campum Vaticanum fieri quasi Martium campum. 'quid ais?' inquam; 'at ego ad tabulam ut, si recte possem, Scapulanos hortos.' 'cave facias' inquit; 'nam ista lex perferetur; vult enim Caesar.' audire me facile passus sum, fieri autem moleste fero.* After the death of its owner, the *horti* had been divided by the heirs into shares. On the *horti*, Cic. *Att.* 12.40.4; 12.38a.2; 12.43.3; 12.44.2; 13.29.1; 13.31.4; 13.33a. Cf. García Morcillo 2005: 260–265 and 2019 for a detailed analysis of the affair. Capito (*RE* 7) had been a tribune of the plebs in 55.

[32] This scheme was never carried out, although both Cassius Dio (43.58) and Aulus Gellius (13.14) stated that Caesar enlarged the *pomerium*.

[33] Cic. *Att.* 13.28.1; 13.29.1.

In sum, the theories of information asymmetry and adverse selection have helped to conceptualise such situations in the Roman world. From at least the beginning of the first century BC, this was the subject of both an ethical and legal debate, grounded in real cases in which sellers and buyers attempted to get the best results for their money while being aware of the existing information gap.

6.2 Information Asymmetry and Signalling: Landlords and Tenants

In the case of the rental market, asymmetry existed on both sides, for landlords and tenants. The first was unaware of the payment intentions of the second: would the tenant disappear without paying the rent at the end of the rental period?[34] At the same time, the tenant had no knowledge of the disposition of the landlord, that is, whether they would be respectful or breach the contract. The rental market is a clear case of bilateral matching: people are interested in the object, but also in the person with whom they exchange it.

In the first case, the landlord needed to separate the wheat from the chaff, or the good tenants from the bad. Signalling constitutes an important strategy to bridge the gap of asymmetric information. Certain indices, such as race, sex or police records, constitute unalterable attributes[35]; signals, on the contrary, are observable qualities that are alterable. They imply that the informed party is able to reveal private information via individual behaviours before the agreement is signed; that signal is observed by the principal, and may influence the principal's belief about the agent's identity. For example, it may demonstrate to the principal that you have a special set of characteristics that make you fit for something.[36] Skilled agents choose to pay the price of signalling in order to transform the contract into one of symmetrical information. The classic example is a university degree: for many employers, regardless of the field of the degree, this is a signal that the candidate has acquired certain abilities during the

[34] The law allowed the landlord to seize the possessions of the tenant if the latter could not pay. Sometimes, the possessions were too meagre to make a difference. Mart. 12.32: since he could not pay, Vacerra was evicted on the 1st of July, when new leases began. However, he intended to look for another house! The only other portrait of eviction, in this case in the countryside, is Hor. *Carm.* 2.18.26, during the triumviral land confiscations of the 40s.

[35] Spence 1974.

[36] Macho Stadler and Pérez Castrillo.

degree, such as critical thinking, essay writing, and so on. A degree from a prestigious university, or from an elite private academy, also clearly signals the socioeconomic status of the individual in question.[37] Education constitutes one characteristic that can become a signal, if it influences the result of who is allocated a contract or a job.[38]

Signalling was also used in ancient Rome in order to find good tenants. Many members of the elite rented entire buildings of apartments to a contractor (*conductor*), who in turn managed the rental and subleased to individual tenants. This was advantageous for the elite, since they were paid a lump sum at the *beginning* of the rental year (the 1st of July), and did not have to involve themselves in other rental issues, while the *conductores* were, as was usual in Roman rentals, paid in annual rental instalments at the *end* of the term of contract.[39] Through such practices, the elite managed to find a convenient way to avoid the asymmetrical information problem of being paid at the end of the rental, but more importantly of transferring the risk and the transaction costs to another party, who would then be responsible for any late payments or problems that arose from the rental.

In March 45—three months before the beginning of the rental year—Cicero was studying how to finance his son's sojourn in Athens, and decided to rent his properties in the Argiletum and the Aventine. For this reason, he requested help from his friend Atticus: "therefore, please investigate who the tenants (*conductores*) are and what their rent is, and take care that the tenant is a man to pay to the day".[40] Through signalling (as well as likely by asking around), Atticus had to ascertain the moral character of the middlemen, and to estimate whether they intended to pay and had enough money to do so.[41] This was not only an investigation into the solidity of their financial position, but also whether they had a righteous moral character and would thus pay.

[37] The classic work on signalling and the job market is Spence 1974. Signalling has also been expanded to other disciplines, for example the political sciences (Banks 1991).

[38] Spence 1974.

[39] Frier 1980. On subletting for profit, cf. du Plessis 2012: 156–170; all cases preserved are about residential places, not commercial spaces. Cf. *Dig.* 19.2.7 (*Paul. ed. 22*); 19.2.30pr. (*Pompon. Sabin. 8*)

[40] Cic. *Att.* 12.32.3: *itaque velim videas primum conductores qui sint et quanti, deinde ut sint qui ad diem solvant.*

[41] Du Plessis 2012: 158–161 on how to choose middlemen.

The jurist Africanus contemplated such a case in a wider context: slaves were used as guarantees in the payment of rent (*invecta et illata*), a legal devise employed by the government to reduce information asymmetry. Offering a slave as guarantee was a clear signal to the other party that you were a reliable agent, since you were offering a valuable guarantee. In one particular instance, the jurist pondered the case of a *conductor* who had rented baths, leaving his slave Eros as a guarantee, but then pledged Eros to another creditor for a loan. We may ignore the question of whether the *conductor* had enough money to at least pay the rent (although the fact that he requested a loan could imply that he did not); the important point was that he was the kind of man who would pledge his slave as a guarantee twice.[42] Atticus should thus use signalling to avoid doing deals with this kind of people.

Finding the right tenant or middleman/*conductor* was not merely a question of getting paid on time; landlords and *conductores* had a great interest in weeding out prospective problematic tenants, as Roman law considered the tenant to be liable for the negligence of those to whom he had sublet his property. Both Pomponius and Ulpianus affirmed that the former had the *culpa* if he committed negligence in subletting his property to certain persons.[43] But what is *culpa*, in Roman law? According to Gaius, "there is no *culpa* if everything was done that a very careful and diligent man should have done".[44] Thus the Roman legal system provided them with a large incentive to decipher signalling as well as possible.

This provision not only applied to people who sublet houses, but also to innkeepers. As Ulpianus specified:

> An innkeeper is responsible for the acts of those who are in his house for the purpose of transacting his business, as well as for all permanent lodgers; he is, however, not responsible for the acts of travellers, since an innkeeper cannot select the travellers, nor can he exclude them while they are pursuing

[42] *Dig.* 20.4.9.pr. (Africanus 8 *quaestionum)* Cf. Du Plessis 2010: 55–58 (on this case and on the fluctuating value of slaves).

[43] *Dig.* 19.2.11pr (Ulpianus 32 *ad ed.)*: *mihi ita placet, ut culpam etiam eorum quos induxit praestet suo nomine, etsi nihil convenit, si tamen culpam in inducendis admittit, quod tales habuerit vel suos vel hospites: et ita pomponius libro sexagesimo tertio ad edictum probat.*

[44] *Dig.* 19.2.25.7 (Gaius 10 *ad ed. provinc.)*: *culpa autem abest, si omnia facta sunt, quae diligentissimus quisque observaturus fuisset.*

> their journey. He, however, to a certain extent, selects his permanent lodgers, if he does not reject them, and he must be liable for their acts.[45]

The distinction that the jurist established between travellers (*viatores*) and permanent lodgers (*inhabitatores*) is very interesting. The law considered that an innkeeper could not screen and reject short term lodgers, but that he has a different duty and responsibility for those who dwell in his premises for a longer time. Just as the tenant/conductor was responsible for their sublets, so the innkeeper had to be responsible for these longer-term guests (the legal term *praestare* recurs in both texts).

In sum, because of the organisation of the rental markets, landlords had a great incentive to screen prospective tenants through signalling. First, in order to be paid at the end of the rental year, and second because the legal system encouraged them to do so by making them responsible for the negligence of those to whom they had sublet a property. The intervention of the government on this scale attests to how important the question of information asymmetry was.

6.3 Conclusions

In conclusion, for all the reasons previously mentioned (heterogeneity, uncertainty, high illiquidity, transaction costs), the real estate residential market constitutes a specific case study, in which information asymmetries were especially high. Furthermore, they involved not only the buyer, as in other economic sectors, but could also be applied to the seller or the landlord.

The concept of information asymmetry is not a modern conception that has been forced upon Roman sources. In practical terms, as we have seen, Roman buyers and sellers mainly tried to bridge the gap of information asymmetry through screening, among other strategies. The government was not above such questions: Roman law punished sellers that did not declare defects in real estate transactions and made people responsible for the actions of those they sublet to. We have also seen how access to

[45] *Dig.* 47.5.1.6 (Ulpianus 38 *ad ed.*): *Caupo praestat factum eorum, qui in ea caupona eius cauponae exercendae causa ibi sunt, item eorum, qui habitandi causa ibi sunt: viatorum autem factum non praestat. namque viatorem sibi eligere caupo vel stabularius non videtur nec repellere potest iter agentes: inhabitatores vero perpetuos ipse quodammodo elegit, qui non reiecit, quorum factum oportet eum praestare.*

information could constitute a mechanism of control and selection, as in the case of those who had privileged information or were simply more familiar with the property market.

The jurist Celsus was well aware of the existence of information asymmetries in the real estate market, as he expressed in his legal opinion. Philosophers and thinkers framed it in ethical terms: how much information did you have to share when making an economic transaction? Where are the boundaries between honesty and expediency? It is remarkable that, when illustrating such ethical questions with real life cases, Cicero used prominent examples related to the purchase and sale of houses. As with other Roman senators and members of the elite, the orator bought, sold, and managed real estate during his life; in terms of the history of information asymmetry, it is remarkable that, as an author, he considered his readers would be familiar with such examples.

Bibliography

Akerlof, G.A. 1970. The Market for 'Lemons': Quality Uncertainty and the Market Mechanism. *Quarterly Journal of Economics* 84: 488–500.

Banks, J.S. 1991. *Signaling Games in Political Science*. Abingdon: Harwood Academic Publishers.

Bannon, C.J. 2001. Servitudes for Water Use in the Roman *Suburbium*. *Historia* 50: 47–50.

———. 2009. *Gardens and Neighbours*. Ann Arbor: Private Water Rights in Roman Italy.

———. 2014. C. Sergius Orata and the Rhetoric of Fishponds. *The Classical Quarterly* 64: 166–182.

Castro Sáenz, A. 2013. *¿Praediator/predator?* Una relectura de Cic. pro Balb. 20.45. *Index: quaderni camerti di studi romanistici, International Survey of Roman Law* 41: 25–40.

Du Plessis, P. 2010. The slave in the window. *Bulletin of the Institute of Classical Studies* 109 (Suppl): 49–60.

———. 2012. *Letting and Hiring in Roman Legal Thought: 27 BCE-284 CE*. Leiden: Brill.

Dyck, A.R. 1996. *A Commentary on Cicero*. Ann Arbor: De officiis.

Frier, B.W. 1980. *Landlords and Tenants in Imperial Rome*. Princeton: Princeton University Press.

García Morcillo, M. 2005. *Las ventas por subasta en el mundo romano: la esfera privada*. Barcelona.

———. 2019. Mentality, Motivation and Economic Decision-Making in Ancient Rome: Cicero and Tullia's Shrine. *The Economic History Review*, December 15, 2019, early view. https://doi.org/10.1111/ehr.12909

Garmaise, M.J., and T.J. Moskowitz. 2004. Confronting Information Asymmetries: Evidence from Real Estate Markets. *The Review of Financial Studies* 17: 405–437.

Hausmaninger, H. 1991. Celsus gegen Proculus. *Tradition und Fortenwicklung im Recht, Festschrift zum 90. Geburtstag von Ulrich von Lübtow*, 53-62.

Hoppe, E.I., and P.W. Schmitz. 2013. Contracting under Incomplete Information and Social Preferences: An Experimental Study. *The Review of Economic Studies* 80: 1516–1544.

Kay, N.M. 2014. *Martial. Book XI. A Commentary*. London: Duckworth.

Kurlat, P., and J. Stroebel. 2015. Testing for Information Asymmetries in Real Estate Markets. *The Review of Financial Studies* 28 (8): 2429–2461.

Lefcoe, G. 2004. Property Condition Disclosure Forms: How the Real Estate Industry Eased the Transition from Caveat Emptor to "Seller Tell All". *Real Property, Probate and Trust Journal* 39: 193–250.

Macho-Stadler, I., and J.D. Pérez-Castrillo. 2001. *An Introduction to the Economics of Information: Incentives and Contracts*. Oxford: Oxford University Press.

Marzano, A. 2007. *Roman Villas in Central Italy: a Social and Economic History*. Leiden: Brill.

———. 2015. Sergio Orata e il Lago Lucrino: alcune considerazioni sull'allevamento di ostriche nella Campania romana. *Oebalus. Studi sulla Campania nell'Antichità* 10: 131–150.

Milgrom, P., and N. Stokey. 1982. Information, Trade and Common Knowledge. *Journal of Economic Theory* 26: 17–27.

Pope, J. 2008. Do Seller Disclosures Affect Property Values? Buyer Information and the Hedonic Model. *Land Economics* 84: 551–572.

Rauh, N. 1989. Finance and Estate Sales in Republican Rome. *Aevum* 63: 45–76.

Spence, M. 1974. *Market Signaling*. Cambridge, MA: Harvard University Press.

Willems, C. 2019. Urbanes Mietrecht? Der römische Wohnungsmarkt zwischen Preismechanismus und Intervention. *Zeitschrift der Savigny-Stiftung für Rechtsgeschichte: Romanistische Abteilung* 136 (1): 233–270.

CHAPTER 7

Marriage and Asymmetric Information on the Real Estate Market in Roman Egypt

François Lerouxel

7.1 Introduction

Together with many others, I have long been entirely convinced of the heuristic potentials of neo-institutionalist economics for studying the ancient economy, especially for the issue of markets, whether goods or services. I belong to the generation of scholars who did their PhD in the first decade of the twenty-first century, when neo-institutionalist economics became more and more standard and mainstream in the field of economic history,[1] notably ancient history, and I wrote a book using this theory to study the credit market in the Roman world.[2] I am thus a believer.

[1] Manning 2003; Lo Cascio 2005 and 2006; Frier and Kehoe 2007; Bresson 2007; Kehoe 2007.

[2] Lerouxel 2006; Lerouxel 2012; Lerouxel 2015 and 2016a.

My warmest thanks go to Cristina Rosillo-López and Marta García Morcillo for their comments.

F. Lerouxel (✉)
Université Paris-Sorbonne, Paris, France

C. Rosillo-López, M. García Morcillo (eds.), *Managing Information in the Roman Economy*, Palgrave Studies in Ancient Economies,
https://doi.org/10.1007/978-3-030-54100-2_7

However, it is also true that neo-institutionalist economics has sometimes been applied to ancient economic history in a generalised manner, with vague assertions such as "transaction costs were high in the Roman Empire" or "markets were imperfect in the Roman world", which do not say a great deal about the historical specificity of the Roman economy, because the same could be said for almost all historical economies.[3] Books like this one[4]—which concern key notions of neo-institutionalist economics like asymmetric information that are applied to case studies within a precise geographical and historical context—are thus most welcome. They convince readers of the practical utility of neo-institutionalist economics to the ancient economic history, and further our understanding of the workings of the Roman economy.

In this paper, I study the issue of asymmetric information on the real estate market in Roman Egypt,[5] namely the selling and mortgaging of land and houses,[6] the most significant element in the estates of almost every individual at the time. In order to do so, I examine two prefectural edicts, taken by the prefect Marcus Mettius Rufus in 89, and by Servius Sulpicius Similis in 109.[7] M. Mettius Rufus made his equestrian career under Domitian, where he was prefect of the Annona, and subsequently prefect of Egypt in 89–91/92. Ser. Sulpicius Similis, meanwhile, became equestrian after a centurion career, and served as prefect of the Annona from 103–107, then as prefect of Egypt from 107–112.[8] The two edicts dealt with an institution called the *bibliothêkê enktêseôn*, a general registry of individuals' property rights, predominantly real estate.[9] I will examine the nature of the asymmetric information that the two Roman prefects were concerned with, the reason for its existence, and their reaction to these issues.

[3] Ogilvie 2007 provides an interesting criticism of the economic approaches to historical institutions.

[4] See also Kehoe, Ratzan and Yiftach 2015.

[5] On Roman Egypt in general, see Lewis 1983; Bowman 1986; Bowman and Rathbone 1992; Bagnall 1993; Riggs 2012. On the economy of the province, see Bagnall 2005; Rathbone 2007.

[6] Rowlandson 1996: 176–20; Lerouxel 2016a: 112–120.

[7] On Roman prefects of Egypt, see Jördens 2009.

[8] On Ser. Sulpicius Similis, see Christol and Demougin 1988 with bibliography.

[9] On the *bibliothêkê enktêseôn*, Wolff 1978: 222–255; Burkhalter 1990; Maresch 2002; Alonso 2010; Jördens 2010a and 2010b; Lerouxel 2016a: 152–192.

7.2 The Two Prefectural Edicts

(a) The edict of M. Mettius Rufus (89).[10]

Proclamation of Marcus Mettius Rufus, prefect of Egypt:

Claudius Arius the strategus of the Oxyrhynchite nome has informed me that neither private nor public business is receiving proper treatment owing to the fact that for many years the abstracts in the *bibliothêkê enktêseôn* have not been kept in the manner required, although the prefects before me have often ordered that they should undergo the necessary revision, which is not really practicable unless copies are made from the beginning.

Therefore I command all owners to register their property at the *bibliothêkê enktêseôn* within six months, and all lenders the mortgages which they hold, and all other persons the claims which they possess. In making the return they shall declare the source from which in each case the possession of the property devolved upon them. Wives (γυναῖκες) also, if on the strength of some local law (κατά τινα ἐπιχώριον νόμον) they have a lien on the property, shall add an annotation to the property-statements of their husbands, and likewise children to those of their parents, if the enjoyment of the property has been secured to the latter by public instruments and the possession of it after their death has been settled on their children, in order that those who make agreements with them may not be defrauded through ignorance.

I also command the drafters and keepers of contracts not [to execute] any deed without authorization of the *bibliothêkê enktêseôn*, [being warned that such a transaction has no validity] and that they themselves will suffer the due penalty for disregarding orders. If the *bibliothêkê enktêseôn* contains any property-returns of earlier date, let them be preserved with the utmost care, and likewise the abstracts of them, in order that if afterwards an inquiry should be held concerning persons who have made false returns, they may be convicted thereby. In order then that the use of the abstracts may become secure and permanent, so that another registration shall not be required, I command the keepers of the *bibliothêkê enktêseôn* to revise the abstracts every five years, transferring to the new list the last statement of property of each person arranged under villages and category. The 9th year of Domitian, the fourth day of the month of Domitianus.[11]

Μάρκος Μέττιος Ῥοῦφος ἔπαρχος Αἰγύπτου λέγει·

[10] *P. Oxy*. II 237, col. VIII, l. 27–43 = *Sel. Pap*. II 219.

[11] Trans. B. Grenfell and A. Hunt, slightly adapted.

Κλαύδιος Ἄρειος ὁ τοῦ Ὀξυρυγχείτου στρατηγὸς [ἐ]δήλωσέν μοι μήτε τὰ ἰ[δι]ωτικὰ μ[ήτε τὰ δημ]όσια πράγματα τὴν καθήκουσαν λαμβάνειν διοίκησιν διὰ τὸ ἐκ πολλῶν χρόνων μὴ καθ' ὃν ἔδει τρόπον ᾠκονομῆσθαι τὰ ἐν τῇ τῶν ἐνκτήσεων βιβλιοθήκῃ δια[σ]τρώματα, καίτοι πολλάκις κριθὲν ὑπὸ τῶν πρὸ ἐμοῦ ἐπάρχων τῆς δεούσης αὐτὰ τυχεῖν ἐπανορθώσεως· ὅπερ οὐ καλῶς ἐνδέχεται, εἰ μὴ ἄνωθεν γένοιτο ἀντίγραφα.

Κελεύω οὖν πάντας τοὺς κτήτορας ἐντος μηνῶν ἓξ ἀπογράψασθαι τὴν ἰδίαν κτῆσιν εἰς τὴν τῶν ἐνκτήσεων βιβλιοθήκην καὶ τοὺς δανειστὰς ἅς ἐὰν ἔχωσι ὑποθήκας καὶ τούς ἄλλους ὅσα ἐὰν ἔχωσι δίκαια· τὴν δὲ ἀπογραφὴν ποιείσθωσαν δηλοῦντες πόθεν ἕκαστος τῶν ὑπαρχόντων καταβέβηκεν εἰς αὐτοὺς ἡ κτῆσεις. Παρατιθέτωσαν δὲ καὶ αἱ γυναῖκες ταῖς ὑποστάσεσι τῶν ἀνδρῶν, ἐὰν κατά τινα ἐπιχώριον νόμον κρατεῖται τὰ ὑπάρχοντα, ὁμοίως δὲ καὶ τὰ τέκνα ταῖς τῶν γονέων, οἷς ἡ μὲν χρῆσεις δὶα δημοσίων τετήρηται χρηματισμῶν, ἡ δὲ κτῆσις μετὰ θάνατον τοῖς τέκνοις κεκράτηται, ἵνα οἱ συναλλάσσοντες μὴ κατ' ἄγνοιαν ἐνεδρεύονται.

Παραγγέλλω δὲ καὶ τοῖς συναλλαγματογράφοις καὶ τοῖς μνήμοσι μηδὲν δίχα ἐπιστάλματος τοῦ βιβλιοφυλακ[ίου τελειῶσαι, γνοῦσιν ὡς οὐκ ὄφελος τὸ] τοιοῦτο, ἀλλα καὶ αὐτοὶ ὡς παρὰ τὰ προστεταγμένα ποιήσοντες δίκην ὑπομενοῦσι τὴν προσήκουσαν. Ἐὰν δ'εἰσὶν ἐν τῇ βιβλιοθήκῃ τῶν ἐπάνω χρόνων ἀπογραφαί, μετὰ πάσης ἀκρειβείας φυλασσέσθωσαν, ὁμοίως δὲ καὶ τὰ διαστρώματα, ἵν' εἴ τις γένοιτο ζήτησις εἰς ὕστερον περὶ τῶν μὴ δεόντως ἀπογραψαμένων ἐξ ἐκείνων ἐλεγχθῶσι. [Ἵνα] δ' [ο]ὖν β[εβ]αία τε καὶ εἰς ἅπαν διαμένῃ τῶν διαστρωμάτων ἡ χρῆσ{ε}ις πρὸς τὸ μὴ πάλιν ἀπογραφῆς δεηθῆναι, παραγγέλλω τοῖς βιβλιοφύλαξι διὰ πενταετίας ἐπανανεοῦσθαι τὰ διαστρώματα μεταφερομένης εἰς τὰ καινοποιούμενα τῆς τελευταίας ἑκάστου ὀνόματος ὑποστάσεως κατὰ κώμην καὶ κατ'εἶδος. ...... [Ἔτους] θ' Δομειτιανο[ῦ], μηνὸς Δομιτ{τ}ιανοῦ δ'.

(b) The edict of Ser. Sulpicius Similis (8 November 109).[12]

Servius Sulpicius Similis, prefect of Egypt, says: on conducting an enquiry, I happened to find out as a result of a certain lawsuit that Egyptian women (τὰς Αἰγυπτίας γυναῖκας) in accordance with the local customs (κατὰ τὰ ἐγχώρια νόμιμα) have secured for themselves and their children, in virtue of their marriage contracts (διὰ τῶν γαμικῶν συγγραφῶν), the property of their husbands; but that very often disputes have arisen as a result of this, since people entering into contracts with married men could be in ignorance

[12] P. Mert. III 101.

(ἀγνοεῖν) as to whether their property was secured to their wives in virtue of this right, because the marriage-contracts had been filed in different registry-offices (from those containing statements about their property in general), and that (therefore) Mettius Rufus, formerly prefect over this area, had ordered copies of the marriage-contracts to be filed with the register of the husbands' property and had issued a decree to this effect, of which I have appended a copy. ().[13]

Σέρουιος Σουλπίκιος Σίμιλις ἔπαρχος Αἰγύπτου λέγει·

Διαζητοῦντί μοι μαθεῖν ἔκ τινος ὑποθέσεως ἐγένετο τὰς Αἰγυπτίας γυναῖκας κατὰ τὰ ἐγχώρια νόμιμα κατέχειν τὰ ὑπάρκοντα τῶν ἀνδρῶν διὰ τῶν γαμικῶν συγγραφῶν ἑαυταῖς τε καὶ τοῖς τέκνοις, πλειστάκις δὲ ἐκ τούτου ἀμφισβητήσεων γενομένων ἐπεὶ ἐδύναντο ἀγνοεῖν οἱ τοῖς γεγαμηκόσι συναλλάσσοντες εἰ τούτῳ τῷ δικαίῳ κατέσχηται τὰ ὑπάρκοντα αὐτῶν ταῖς γυναιξί, διὰ τὸ καὶ ἑτέροις βιβλιοφυλακίοις τὰς συγγραφὰς καταχωρίζεσθαι, κεκελευκέναι Μέττιον Ῥοῦφον, τὸν γενόμενον ἐπὶ τῶν τόπων ἔπαρχον, τὰ ἀντίγραφα τῶν συγγραφῶν ταῖς τῶν ἀνδρῶν ὑποστάσεσιν ἐντίθεσθαι, καὶ τοῦτο διατάγματι προστεταχέναι οὗ καὶ ἀντίγραφον ὑπέταξα, φανερὸν ποιῶν κατακολουθεῖν ταῖς τοῦ Μεττίου Ῥούφου...... (ἔτους) ιγ' Ἀθὺρ ιβ.

These two edicts were different: the first was enacted after a report made to M. Mettius Rufus by the head of the civil administration (*strategos*) of the Oxyrhynchite nome about the dysfunction of an important institution based in the nome capital, namely the general register of individuals' property rights (*bibliothêkê enktêseôn*). The prefect wished to set the institution back on track by ordering the inhabitants of the province to declare their property rights to the keepers of the registry. Among the population of Roman Egypt, "women" (without further precision) were specifically mentioned,[14] as owners or lenders of course, but most of all as wives who could have certain rights over the property of their husbands "on the strength of some local law". It was this second point which was the most important, as far as asymmetric information was concerned.

The edict of the prefect Ser. Sulpicius Similis was shorter, but entirely focused on the issue being studied here. For this reason, it was more precise. Contrary to M. Mettius Rufus, Ser. Sulpicius Similis has direct experience with the subject of his edict—he had to rule on a case in his tribunal involving it, as he stated at the beginning of his edict, and appeared to have a better knowledge of it. Ser. Sulpicius Similis did not merely talk of

[13] Trans. J. D. Thomas.

[14] On women in Roman Egypt, Rowlandson 1999.

"women", he also specified their social and legal status. The women in question were "Egyptian women", and their rights over the property of their husband that originated in contracts were stipulated between wives and husbands on the occasion of their marriage.

It thus appears that some "Egyptian women" had a right to the property of their husbands in accordance with their marriage contracts. The same could be true for the children of these women. For the sake of clarity, I will concentrate on the wives' rights, but the issue is essentially identical regarding those of the children. The rights of certain Egyptian wives to the property of their husbands were not automatic, nor were they not self-evident, even for those who knew the couples in question. Both prefectural edicts showed that this state of affairs could create problems in the process of exchange when, for example, somebody bought, or accepted as a mortgage, a piece of land from a man married to such an "Egyptian woman", because he could entirely ignore that the seller's rights over the piece of property he bought (or accepted as a mortgage) were not exclusive, and that the seller's wife could dispute the sale or mortgage after the transaction.

It is clear that there was:

1. A problem of information. In the first edict, the prefect M. Mettius Rufus used the expression κατ' ἄγνοιαν, "through ignorance", and in the second edict Ser. Sulpicius Similis used the verb ἀγνοεῖν, "to ignore" in exactly the same context.
2. An obvious asymmetry between the two parties involved in the transaction. In the case of a house sale for example, the buyer had no straightforward means of knowing whether the seller's wife had a right to the house, even though the seller would have known this in accordance of their marriage contract. In some cases, wives might have known what their husbands were up to and resisted, as a petition from the second c. BC shows.[15] In this document, Senesis tried to prevent her husband Didymos from alienating a house pledged to secure her marriage contract:

> To Ptolemaeus, oeconomus, from Senesis daughter of Menelaus, inhabitant of Oxyrhyncha in the division of Polemon. I lived with Didymus son of

[15] This problem of information asymmetry existed before the Roman period in Egypt.

> Peteimouthes, an inhabitant of the said village, on the terms of an Egyptian alimentary silver contract[16] for [.]1 gold pieces in accordance with the laws of the country ([κα]τὰ συγγραφὴν Αἰγυπτίαν τ[ροφ]ῖτιν ἀργυρίου χρυσῶν [ ]α κατὰ τοὺς τῆς χώρας νό[μο]υς), and for this sum and for my maintenance all his property, including a house in the aforesaid village, was pledged. Wishing to deprive me of this, the accused, approaching the inhabitants of the said village one by one, for a time desired to alienate it; but as they did not venture because I did not concur, he has subsequently contrived so as to give it to the Treasury in surety for Heraclides, tax-farmer, and thus thinks to exclude me from my rights. I therefore, being a defenceless woman, beg and request you not to suffer to be deprived of what is pledged for my dowry through the misbehaviour of the accused, but if it be your pleasure, to order a letter to be written to Ptolemaeus the *epimeletes* forbidding him to accept in surety the house of the said Didymus. If this is done, I shall receive your succour. Farewell.[17]

In other cases, however, as we may guess from the two prefectural edicts, wives were not necessarily aware of the contractual initiatives of their husbands, at least at the first stage; they discovered that their husbands had sold the house after the transaction took place. This situation thus constituted a splendid case of asymmetric information, leaving a great deal of room for the husbands' dishonesty or carelessness.

These two prefectural edicts demonstrate that the prefects of Roman Egypt were fully aware that there were information asymmetries within the real estate market that could provoke lawsuits, jeopardising some private transactions after their conclusion. Of course, they did not use the expression "asymmetric information"—they were not quoting D. North, nor did they say it was bad for economic growth as many economic historians would likely do now—but they clearly saw the problem.

7.3 Two Kinds of Asymmetric Information

In terms of sales in general, on a broader level we can distinguish between at least two kinds of asymmetric information.[18]

[16] On the different kinds of contracts in relation to Egyptian marriage, see Pestman 1961: 6–52.

[17] *Sel. Pap.* II 271 (Tebtynis, the beginning of the second c. BC) (trans. A. Hunt and C. Edgar).

[18] See Cristina Rosillo-López's contribution in this volume on asymmetric information in the real estate market, and Kehoe, Ratzan and Yiftach 2015: 7 on information costs.

The first concerns the quality of the object sold. A classic example in the Roman world was the slave-market regulated by the edict of the Curule Aediles. When a slave was sold, they could have a non-evident disease, or physical defects, or be a former fugitive; or they could be perfectly healthy with no intention of running away—the buyer had no way of knowing whether the slave he bought belonged to the first or the second category.[19] In the famous article "The market for lemons" by G. Akerlof in 1970, which constituted—among other works—the beginnings of the economics of information[20] and which put forward the notion of asymmetrical information, the author used the example of the used cars market. Within that market, there could be good cars or bad cars (known as "lemons" in the USA, at least at the time), and it is hard for a potential buyer to know if the car he planned to buy was good or bad. G. Akerlof used this simple example to illustrate his reflections on quality uncertainty, as well as the interaction of quality differences and uncertainty.[21]

In the case of the real estate market in Roman Egypt, it does not seem that this kind of asymmetrical information was the most important, at least as far as we can judge from these two prefectural edicts. The prefects did not appear to care about the quality of the pieces of real estate sold or mortgaged—whether or not a house just sold would fall apart when the seller moved in, for example. Obviously, this kind of asymmetrical information would also have existed within the real estate market in Roman Egypt, but it was not this which concerned the prefects, at least as far as we can judge from these two edicts.

Rather, it was a second kind of asymmetrical information that was the main concern for the prefects of Roman Egypt. This concerned the legal capacity of the seller to alienate the piece of property sold or mortgaged. Was he the real owner of the piece of property? Did he have the right to sell it? Did he have full rights of property over the piece of real estate sold? Could anybody else have rights over the property sold? This second type of asymmetrical information concerned sales, but also mortgages of real estate, especially when a married man sold a piece of real estate or borrowed some money by giving real estate as security, something which happened very often at the time of M. Mettius Rufus and Ser. Sulpicius

[19] See Myles Lavan's contribution in this volume.

[20] Akerlof 1970; Stiglitz 2000.

[21] See Pablo Revilla's paper in this volume.

Similis.[22] It could not be known with certainty whether his wife had rights over the piece of real estate or not.

This kind of problem was not limited to Roman Egypt. In Roman law, property transfers in connection to marriage were also an important issue.[23] In the *Institutes*,[24] Gaius wrote:

> It sometimes happens that an owner of property does not have the power to alienate it, while a non-owner can alienate it. For by the *lex Iulia* (on adultery), a husband is forbidden to alienate dowry land if his wife is unwilling, even though property is his own either through mancipation to him for the dowry or through cession in court or *usucapio*. It is disputed whether this rule applies only to Italian lands or also to provincial (land).[25]

Augustus introduced this exception in his adultery law of 18 BCE. The husband could not alienate Italian dowry land without his wife's consent. The law became even more restrictive under Justinian—a husband could not use it as security even with his wife's consent.[26]

There is no reason to believe that Roman husbands living in Italy were on average more honest than their fellow counterparts in Roman Egypt. This law protecting the wives' economic interests during marriage was thus likely also a possible source of asymmetrical information on the real estate market in Italy. Buyers and creditors had to take this into account in one way or another.[27]

Finally, as far as Roman Egypt is concerned, one must add that sales and mortgages of real estate were mostly non-professional. In many transactions, there were no professional intermediaries or brokers involved who could have gathered information on potential sellers or lenders.[28] The real

[22] Lerouxel 2016a: 112–120.

[23] On Roman law of marriage, see Kaser 1984: 284–304; Treggiari 1991: 323–396 and Frier and Mac Ginn 2004: 25–187, especially 121–153 on property of the spouses and the administration of the dowry.

[24] Gaius, *Inst.* 2.62–63: *Accidit aliquando ut, qui dominus sit alienandae rei potestatem non habeat, et qui dominus non sit, alienare possit. Nam dotale praedium maritus inuita muliere per legem Iuliam prohibetur alienare, quamuis ipsius sit, uel mancipatum ei dotis causa uel in iure cessum uel usucaptum. Quod quidem ius utrum ad Italica tantum praedia an etiam ad prouincialia pertineat, dubitatur.*

[25] Trans. Frier and Mc Ginn 2004: 153.

[26] Frier and Mc Ginn 2004: 153.

[27] It would be beyond my scope to study this issue here.

[28] In some cases, there was financial intermediation for the largest loans; see Lerouxel 2008.

estate market in the province was thus characterised by a very large number of buyers and sellers, which would only have increased the problem of asymmetric information.

7.4 "Egyptian Women": The Socio-Legal Structure of Roman Egypt

Ser. Sulpicius Similis mentioned "Egyptian women", and both prefects spoke of "local laws". M. Mettius Rufus used the expression τινα ἐπιχώριον νόμον, while Ser. Sulpicius Similis used a synonymous expression, τὰ ἐγχώρια νόμιμα. What does this mean, and why does it create asymmetrical information? To put it succinctly, this is due to the socio-legal structure of Roman Egypt.[29]

The expression "Egyptian women" refers to one of the three legal categories of the population of the province:

a) The first category comprised the small number of Roman citizens living in the province created in 30 BCE after the victory of Octavian over Antony and Cleopatra VII,[30] including the upper part of the provincial administration, the soldiers of the Roman army, and some veterans[31]; however, Roman citizens were not so numerous in Egypt around the end of the first and the beginning of the second century.
b) The second group was made up of the citizens (*astoi*) of the 3 Greek *poleis* at the time of M. Mettius Rufus and Ser. Servius Similis: Alexandria, Naukratis, and Ptolemais. We have little information on Naukratis and Ptolemais during the Roman period; it is also true that Alexandria was much more populated than Naukratis or Ptolemais. It was the second city of the Empire, after Rome, and its citizenship was very prestigious in Egypt. An Egyptian who wished to gain Roman citizenship needed to first obtain Alexandrian citizenship.[32] Many wealthy Alexandrian citizens had land interests in the province of Egypt,[33] and often bought land or lent money within the province, outside the civic territory of Alexandria.

[29] Lewis 1983: 18–35.
[30] Geraci 1983.
[31] Alston 1995.
[32] Delia 1991.
[33] Rowlandson 1996: 102–117.

c) The rest of the inhabitants of the province, comprising the vast majority, were from a Roman legal point of view "the Egyptians", irrespective of whether they were descendants from several generations of Greco-Macedonian soldiers established in Egypt under the Ptolemies since the third century BC,[34] or descendants of the Egyptian population living in Egypt before the conquest by Alexander. To put it more bluntly, from an historical, linguistic and cultural point of view it did not matter if they were Greek or Egyptian; from a legal perspective, they were all considered Egyptian. There were also Egyptians in Alexandria, since not all free inhabitants of Alexandria had Alexandrian citizenship. Of course, the urban Greek elites living in the *chôra* had some fiscal privileges, and this is how they were distinguished from villagers, but from a legal point of view they were Egyptians—the emergence of Greek urban elites in the cities of the *chôra* took time.[35]

These three categories of population were created by Augustus after the conquest in 30 BC, and were deeply and harshly separated from a legal point of view. In 1983, N. Lewis spoke of "a veritable ancient apartheid" to describe the society of the province. In 1789, the French National Assembly published a *Déclaration des droits de l'homme et du citoyen* beginning by this first article: "Men are born and remain free and equal in rights. Social distinctions may be based only on considerations of the common good", a statement that was truly revolutionary from a legal and philosophical point of view. There was no equality in rights among the society of Roman Egypt, nor in the Roman Empire in general. I believe this had consequences from a contractual point of view in that it created asymmetrical information, since the various inhabitants of the province were living under different legal systems.

All matters of status and inter-class relationship in Roman Egypt came under the jurisdiction of the *procurator* of the *Idios Logos*, an equestrian official who was in charge of the enforcement of the numerous rules and restrictions and collected the fines for infractions. A papyrus from Berlin, known as the *Gnomon of the Idios Logos* (*BGU* V 1210),[36] contains over a

[34] Clarysse and Thompson 2006; Fischer-Bovet 2014.

[35] Bowman and Rathbone 1992; Hagedorn 2007; Lerouxel 2016b.

[36] On the *Gnomon of the Idios Logos*, besides BGU V 1210 edited by W. Schubart, see Riccobono 1950 and the remarks made by J. Mélèze Modrejewski in Giuffrè 1977: 523–524.

hundred of these rules. Paragraph 42 demonstrates that the inequality of rights and socio-legal statuses that characterised the society of Roman Egypt could be a problem in private transactions as a source of possible asymmetric information. The Roman provincial authorities severely punished people who illegally claimed a legal status that was not theirs in private contracts, as this could have unpredictable and undesirable legal and economic consequences for the individuals doing business with them.

> 42. Those who claim for themselves a legal status they don't have in business and those who knowingly concur therein are fined a fourth of their estates.[37]

Other paragraphs of the *Gnomon of the Idios Logos* showed that marriage in societies where men and women were not born, and did not remain free and equal in rights, inevitably created problems of asymmetrical information between spouses. In these paragraphs can be found the same expression that the prefect M. Mettius Rufus used in his edict: κατ' ἄγνοιαν, by ignorance.[38] This was related to the marriage between people of different legal status in Roman Egypt, and were all cases of asymmetrical information, since marriage has obvious legal and economic consequences, notably in the Roman world.[39]

Riccobono 1950 contains a full translation of the *Gnomon* in Italian, Johnson 1936: 711–717, a full translation in English, Mélèze Modrejewski: 520–557 in French. On the office of the Idios Logos, see Swarney 1970.

[37] μβ οἱ ἀκαταλλήλως χρηματίζ[ον]τες τεταρτολογοῦνται καὶ οἱ εἰδότες καὶ \συν/ χρηματίσαντες αὐτοῖς [τε]ταρτολογοῦνται. (trans. A. Johnson 1936, slightly adapted). On this paragraph, see Broux, Coussement and Depaux 2010.

[38] This kind of problem also existed in Roman law and Roman legislators tried to deal with it; see Gaius, *Inst.* 1.67–97, for example paragraph 67: "Again, if a Roman citizen takes a Latin or a peregrine wife in a mistaken belief (*per ignorantiam*) that she is a Roman citizen and begets a son, that son is not in his *potestas*: for he is not even a citizen, but either a Latin or a peregrine according to his mother's status, because, except if there be *conubium* between the father and the mother, a child does not take its father's status. But by a senatusconsult the father is allowed to prove a case of mistake, and thereupon both the wife and the son attain to Roman citizenship, and thenceforth the son is subject to his father's *potestas*. The law is the same if by mistake he marries a wife who is in the class of the *dediticii*, except that the wife does not become a Roman citizen". (trans. F. De Zulueta). On these mistakes concerning personal statuses, see Moatti 2016.

[39] I leave aside the potential asymmetric information in credit transactions involving wives' property in Roman law, which would deserve a more involved treatment.

> 39. If a Roman of either sex marries any one of the status of an *astos* or of an Egyptian without being aware of their status (κατ' ἄγνοιαν), their children take the status of the inferior parent.[40]

> 47. If an *astê* marries an Egyptian husband in the mistaken belief (κατ' ἄγνοιαν) that he is an *astos*, she is not to blame; and if the declaration of birth of children is made by both, the status of citizenship is granted to the offspring.[41]

7.5 Egyptian Local Customs[42]

As a consequence of all this, from a legal point of view, Roman citizens were subjected to Roman law, while the citizens of the three Greek *poleis* lived under their respective civic law, and the Egyptians, if they wished to, lived under what was called their local laws or local customs by the Roman prefects,[43] who also protected them.

The two prefectural edicts referred to "Egyptian" women and their marriage contracts, which were part of this local law protected by the Roman provincial administration.[44] As J. D. Thomas puts it in his comment on the edict of Ser. Sulpicius Similis (P. Mert. III 101):

> It would appear that in some forms of Egyptian marriage the husband pledged all his property, present and future, as security to his wife for his performing his obligations towards her. If there was a divorce or if the man died, the wife thus had a claim on all his property and this claim took precedence over that of any other person. The husband remained owner of the property during the marriage (even if, as sometimes happened, he had gone through a form of sale of it to his wife), but could not legally alienate it unless his wife gave her consent.

[40] λθ Ῥωμαίου ἢ Ῥωμαίας κατ' ἄγνοιαν συνελθόντων ἢ ἀστοῖς < ἢ > Αἰγυπτίοις τὰ τέκνα ἥγτονι γένει ἀκολουθεῖ. (trans. A. Johnson 1936).

[41] μζ ἀστὴ συνελθοῦσα Α̣ἰ̣[γ]υ[πτίῳ̣] κατ' ἄγνοιαν ὡς ἀστῷ ἀνεύθυνός ἐστιν. Ἐὰν δὲ καὶ ὑπὸ ἀμφοτέρ̣[ων ἀπ]αρχὴ τέκνων τεθῆ̣, τηρεῖται τοῖς τέκνοις ἡ πολιτεία. (trans. A. Johnson 1936).

[42] On law in Roman Egypt, Keenan, Manning and Yiftach-Firanko 2014.

[43] Mélèze Modrzejewski 1970 remains essential. See also Mélèze Modrzejewski 1988, 1993 and 2014; Maehler 2005 and Alonso 2013.

[44] See also the subtle comments of E. Volterra, who insists on the fact that Ser. Sulpicius Similis acts according to the Roman legal mind (Volterra 1970).

These forms of marriage contracts belong to the Egyptian legal tradition of marriage, dating back to at least the New Kingdom in the second millennium BC, and were still in existence during the Roman period in the second century AD.[45] During the Ptolemaic period, which preceded the Roman period, these specific marriage contracts were often written in Demotic, that is in the Egyptian language, in opposition to the majority of private contracts (which were written in Greek), which demonstrates that these contracts belonged to the Egyptian legal tradition.[46]

This becomes even more complex from the point of view of asymmetrical information, but essentially means that during the Roman period, the use of these Egyptian marriage contracts was not systematic among "Egyptian women", understood as a Roman legal category. As a result, it was difficult for a Roman, an Alexandrian or even an Egyptian (in the legal sense of the word, namely a descendant of the Greco-Roman soldiers established in Egypt under the Ptolemies since the third century BC or descendants of the Egyptian population living in Egypt before the conquest by Alexander in 332 BC), to know if the seller of the land he bought was married to his wife under this specific type of Egyptian marriage contract.

As is clear from his edict, Ser. Sulpicius Similis had never heard of this legal tradition. As a Roman knight at the service of the Emperor, he probably lacked specialist training in the peculiarities of the legal system of the province of Egypt, unless he had previously occupied a position among the immediate subordinates of the prefect of Egypt, for example *iuridicus* (legal adviser)[47] or *procurator* of the Idios Logos,[48] almost always of equestrian rank.[49] Unfortunately, we know little of the equestrian carrier of Similis before he was prefect of the *annona* in 103–107, after which he became prefect of Egypt in 107–112; we know more about the end of his brilliant career under Hadrian.[50]

Nonetheless, Similis had advisers on his staff who were in charge of these legal aspects when he was sitting in his tribunal in full session with his *consilium*. *P. Oxy.* XLII 3015 (early second century) preserves extracts from court records about testamentary disposition. Three decisions of

[45] Pestman 1961: 115–142.
[46] On demotic documentation, Depauw 1997.
[47] Haensch 2016.
[48] Swarney 1970.
[49] Bowman 1986: 65–68; Montevecchi 1988.
[50] Christol and Demougin 1988.

justice are quoted, the second and the third of which are complete, and in both cases Similis was the judge. Whether by accident or coincidence, all three cases concern the rights of testators under local law, "the law of Egyptians", which was less strict than Roman law on this matter. The second case contains this important passage: "Sulpicius Similis, after inquiring about the case from Artemidoros the interpreter of the laws and talking with his advisers, said: 'As an Egyptian, he had the right to make his will on whatever terms he wished'".[51] This decision was taken on the 8 May 109, six months before he made his edict on the rights that Egyptian women could have on their husband's property. In the first case, he mentioned—always in the same context of testamentary disposition—"the laws of the Egyptians".[52] Artemidoros was part of the *nomikoi*, legal professionals who assisted judges in the courts of Roman Egypt.[53] Some of them were experts in Roman law, while others were trained in local law, as was the case with Artemidoros.

In Roman Egypt, the Romans protected local private law, designated by M. Mettius Rufus as τινα ἐπιχώριον νόμον or by Ser. Sulpicius Similis as τὰ ἐγχώρια νόμιμα, even when it was markedly different from Roman law. Other foreign rulers of Egypt prior to the Romans, including the Persians (from 525 to 404 and from 343 to 332) and the Ptolemies (from 332 to 30 BC) adopted the same position, and thus faced the same issue, namely the need to understand local private law in order to protect it. In 519 BC, Darius I was the first Persian ruler to order a compilation of ancient Egyptian law since the Pharaoh Amasis (570–526 BC); this order and other subsequent royal orders of the same kind produced several Demotic legal codes.[54] These collections of laws, likely kept in sacerdotal libraries, were designed for legal professionals, notaries and judges.

One of these, known as the Demotic legal code of Hermopolis West (P. Mattha),[55] was translated into Greek at the beginning of the Ptolemaic era, and this translation was copied in the second half of the second century AD (*P. Oxy.* XLVI 3285), during the Roman period. This kind of legal code was probably of great help to people like Artemidoros, who

[51] *P. Oxy.* XLII 3015, l. 8–12: Σουλ(πίκιος) Σίμιλις πυθόμενος Ἀρτεμιδώρου τοῦ ἐξηγουμένου το[ὺς] νόμους περὶ τοῦ πράγματος καὶ συνλαλήσας τοῖς συμ[β]ούλοις ἔφη· Αἰγύ[π]τιος εἶχεν ἐξουσίαν καθὼς βούλεται διαθέσθαι. (trans. P. J. Parsons).

[52] *P. Oxy.* XLII 3015, l. 3: τοὺς Αἰγυπτίων νόμους.

[53] Taubenschlag 1959; Jones 2007; Kantor 2009.

[54] Lippert 2004: 147–178.

[55] Mattha and Hughes 1975; Donker Van Heel 1990.

were supposed to advise the Roman prefects in their tribunal. The interest of the Roman administration in local Egyptian law was thus not new in Ancient Egypt. From Darius I to the Roman era, foreign rulers of Egypt allowed the Egyptians to draft their own private contracts, wills and marriages according to their own laws, and sought to understand Egyptian private law in order to settle disputes and assess its legal effects.

Some local laws remained in effect elsewhere in the Empire, especially in the Roman East[56] but also in the Roman West,[57] even after the *Constitutio Antoniniana*.[58] This was particularly true for laws concerning personal status,[59] which are known to be a highly conservative area of law, just as with landed property.[60] The interest of the Roman provincial authorities in the legislation and legal instruments of the pre-Roman period is well attested, so Ser. Sulpicius Similis was likely not an exception among Roman governors of his time.

7.6 Conclusion: Law and Economy in the Roman Empire[61]

Some supporters of the use of neo-institutionalist economics in Roman economic history sometimes describe the beginning of the Roman Empire as a period of economic unification in the Mediterranean, in the field of metrology, coinage and especially law.[62] The expansion of Roman law, especially in the sphere of contract law, is sometimes described as a means of lowering transaction costs in the Roman Empire. Even if all of this is true, it is likely too general and too optimistic—it would still be the case that the society of the Roman Empire was deeply unequal, hierarchical and segregated from a legal perspective. As far as personal legal status was concerned, Augustus was careful, in both Italy and the provinces, to restore the social and legal boundaries between men and women that composed the society of the Roman Empire; one may consider, for

[56] Mitteis 1891; Coriat 1997: 410–418; Lepelley 2001; Fournier 2010; Kantor 2015.

[57] Lepelley 2001, especially on the *Tabula Banasitana*.

[58] Mélèze Modrzejewski 1982; Kantor 2016.

[59] Fournier 2010: 358–364 on enfranchisements in the Roman East even after 212 and the *Constitutio Antoniniana*.

[60] Kantor 2013: 166.

[61] See in general, Lo Cascio and Mantovani 2018.

[62] Lo Cascio 2007: 626.

example, his legislation regarding freedmen.[63] This obsession for clear-cut social and legal boundaries in Italy and within the different provincial societies went against the legal unification of personal statuses, which was a potential obstacle to economic transactions. The Roman legal system had to develop several ways of overcoming these potential negative effects.

In Roman Egypt, the two prefectural edicts of M. Mettius Rufus and Ser. Sulpicius Similis had the same goal, that of attempting to counteract the asymmetrical information between sellers and buyers, or between debtors and creditors. They did this by ordering wives who had a right to the property of their husbands in virtue of their marriage contracts to declare these rights to the *bibliothêkê enktêseôn*. This institution was a general registry of individuals' property rights, mostly real estate, that notaries were forced to consult before drafting any private contract to avoid transactions based on shaky legal grounds. That M. Mettius Rufus failed on that precise point is obvious from the edict of Ser. Sulpicius Similis, who appears to have had more success in this respect.

Why did they do this? The main reason behind these two edicts may have been the number of lengthy, complex lawsuits that could be avoided thanks to the measure. The prefects, as governors of the province, were in charge of justice and each year they would have left Alexandria for a period of 4 or 5 months to hold assizes, travelling to two Egyptian towns—one in the Delta, the other in the Nile valley.[64] Ser. Sulpicius Similis explicitly states in his edict that he found out about these rights during a lawsuit. The measure ordered by the two prefects may have simply been because it saved them a great deal of time, in order to focus on the lawsuits that were harder to avoid.

In analysing the relationship between law and economy through the lens of neo-institutionalist economics, much attention has been paid to contract law, for example the organisation of farm tenancy or the contractual liability of property owners operating business through agents,[65] demonstrating how the law and legal institutions surrounding the economy could determine the possibility for economic development as population, technology or climate. The legal system may indeed have contributed positively to the Roman economy, but it was likely not the primary goal assigned to it by Roman authorities. In their minds, the maintenance of

[63] Mouritsen 2011 concerning freedmen in the Roman world.

[64] Haensch 1997; Kelly 2011.

[65] Aubert 1994; Kehoe 2007, 2013 and 2015; Lerouxel 2016a; Terpstra 2008.

social and legal hierarchies and the protection of patrimonial order linked to these legal structures were a condition of the stability and success of the Roman Empire, likely more so than economic development.

Bibliography

Akerlof, G. 1970. The Market for "Lemons": Quality Uncertainty and the Market Mechanism. *QJE* 84–3: 488–500.

Alonso, J.L. 2010. The Bibliotheke Enkteseon and the Alienation of Real Securities in Roman Egypt. *JJP* 40: 11–54.

———. 2013. The Status of Peregrine Law in Egypt: 'Customary Law' and Legal Pluralism in the Roman Empire. *JJP* 43: 351–404.

Alston, R. 1995. *Soldier and Society in Roman Egypt: A Social History*. London: Routledge.

Aubert, J.-J. 1994. *Business Managers in Ancient Rome, A Social and Economic Study of Institores, 200 B.C.-A.D. 250*. Leiden: Brill.

Bagnall, R.S. 1993. *Egypt in Late Antiquity*. Princeton: Princeton University Press.

———. 2005. Evidence and Models for the Economy of Roman Egypt. In *The Ancient Economy. Evidence and Models*, ed. J. Manning and I. Morris, 187–204. Stanford: Stanford University Press.

Bowman, A. 1986. *Egypt After the Pharaohs, 332 BC-AD 642*. Berkeley: University of California Press.

Bowman, A., and D. Rathbone. 1992. Cities and Administration in Roman Egypt. *JRS* 82: 107–127.

Bresson A. 2007. *L'économie de la Grèce des cités (fin VIème-Ième siècle avant J.-C.)*, 2 vol. Paris.

Broux, Y., S. Coussement, and M. Depaux. 2010. καὶ ὡς χρηματίζει and the Importance of Naming in Roman Egypt. *ZPE* 174: 159–166.

Burkhalter, F. 1990. Archives locales et archives centrales en Egypte romaine. *Chiron* 20 (1990): 191–216.

Christol, M., and S. Demougin. 1988. Notes de prosopographie équestre V: les ornements de Ser. Sulpicius Similis. *ZPE* 74: 1–14.

Clarysse, W., and D. Thompson. 2006. *Counting the People in Hellenistic Egypt*. Cambridge: Cambridge University Press.

Coriat, J.-P. 1997. *Le Prince législateur. La technique législative des Sévères et les méthodes du droit impérial à la fin du Principat*. Rome.

Delia, D. 1991. *Alexandrian Citizenship During the Roman Principate*. Atlanta: Scholars Press.

Depauw, M. 1997. *A Companion to Demotic Studies*. Bruxelles: Fondation égyptologique reine Élisabeth.

Donker Van Heel, K. 1990. *The Legal Manual of Hermopolis, Text and Translation*. Leiden: Papyrologisch Instituut.

Fischer-Bovet, C. 2014. *Army and Society in Ptolemaic Egypt*. Cambridge: Cambridge University Press.

Fournier, J. 2010. *Entre tutelle romaine et autonomie civique: l'administration judiciaire dans les provinces hellénophones de l'Empire romain, 129 av. J.-C.-235 apr. J.-C.* Athènes.

Frier, B., and D. Kehoe. 2007. Law and Economic Institutions. In *The Cambridge Economic History of the Greco-Roman World*, ed. W. Scheidel, I. Morris, and R. Saller, 113–143. Cambridge: Cambridge University Press.

Frier, B., and T. Mc Ginn. 2004. *A Casebook on Roman Family Law*. Oxford: Oxford University Press.

Geraci, G. 1983. *Genesi della provincia romana d'Egitto*. Bologne.

Giuffrè, V. 1977. *Les lois des Romains*, 7ème édition par un groupe de romanistes des 'Textes de droit romain', Tome II de P. F. Girard et F. Senn, Naples.

Haensch, R. 1997. Zur Konventsordnung in Aegyptus und den übrigen Provinzen des römischen Reiches. In *Akten des 21. Internationalen Papyrologenkongresses*, 320–391. Stuttgart/Leipzig.

———. 2010. Quelques observations générales concernant la correspondance conservée des préfets d'Égypte. In *L'étude des correspondances dans le monde romain de l'Antiquité classique à l'Antiquité tardive: permanences et mutations*, ed. J. Desmulliez, C. Hoët-Van Cauwenberghe, and J.-C. Jolivet. Lille.

———. 2016. Im Schatten Alexandrias: Der iuridicus Aegypti et Alexandreae. In *Recht haben und Recht bekommen im Imperium Romanum. Das Gerichtswesen der Römischen Kaiserzeit und seine dokumentarische Evidenz*, ed. R. Haensch, 165–182. Warsaw.

Hagedorn, D. 2007. The Emergence of Municipal Offices in the Nome-Capitals of Egypt. In Oxyrhynchus: A City and its Texts, ed. A. Bowman, R. Coles, N. Gonis, D. Obbink and P. Parsons, 194–204, London.

Johnson, A.C. 1936. *Roman Egypt to the Reign of Diocletian: An Economic Survey of Ancient Rome*. Vol. 2. Baltimore: Johns Hopkins Press.

Jones, C. 2007. Juristes romains dans l'Orient grec. *CRAI* 2007: 1331–1359.

Jördens, A. 2009. *Statthalterliche Verwaltung in der römischen Kaiserzeit: Studien zum "praefectus Aegypti"*. Stuttgart.

———. 2010a. Öffentliche archive und römische Rechtspolitik. In *Tradition and Transformation: Egypt under Roman Rule*, ed. K. Lembke, M. Minas-Nerpel, and S. Pfeiffer, 159–179. Leiden: Brill.

———. 2010b. Nochmals zur Bibliotheke Enkteseon. In *Symposion 2009*, ed. G. Thür, 277–290. Vienne.

Kantor, G. 2009. Knowledge of Law in Roman Asia Minor. In *Selbstdarstellung und Kommunikation: Die Veröffentlichung staatlicher Urkunden auf Stein und Bronze in der römischer Zeit*, ed. R. Haensch, 249–265. Munich.

———. 2013. Law in Roman Phrygia: Rules and Jurisdictions. In *Roman Phrygia: Culture and Society*, ed. P. Thonemann, 143–167. Cambridge: Franz Steiner Verlag.

———. 2015. Greek Law under the Romans. In *The Oxford Handbook of Ancient Greek Law (forthcoming)*, ed. E. Harris and M. Canevaro. https://doi.org/10.1093/oxfordhb/9780199599257.013.25

———. 2016. Local Law in Asia Minor After the Constitutio Antoniniana. In *Citizenship and Empire in Europe 200–1900: The Antonine Constitution After 1800 years*, ed. C. Ando, 45–62. Stuttgart: Franz Steiner Verlag.

Kaser, M. 1984. *Roman Private Law*. 4th ed. Pretoria: University of South Africa.

Keenan, J., J. Manning, and U. Yiftach-Firanko, eds. 2014. *Law and Legal Practice in Egypt from Alexander to the Arab Conquest*. Cambridge: Cambridge University Press.

Kehoe, D. 2007. *Law and Rural Economy in the Roman Empire*. Ann Arbor: The University of Michigan Press.

———. 2013. Roman Economic Policy and the Law of Contracts. In *Obligations in Roman Law: Past, Present, and Future*, ed. T. McGinn, 89–214. Ann Arbor: University of Michigan Press.

———. 2015. Contracts, Agency and Transaction Costs in the Roman Economy. In *Law and Transaction Costs in the Ancient Economy*, ed. D. Kehoe, D. Ratzan, and U. Yiftach, 231–252. Ann Arbor: University of Michigan Press.

Kehoe, D., D. Ratzan, and U. Yiftach. 2015. *Law and Transaction Costs in the Ancient Economy*. Ann Arbor: University of Michigan Press.

Kelly, B. 2011. *Petitions, Litigation, and Social Control in Roman Egypt*. Oxford: Oxford University Press.

Lepelley, C. 2001. Le nivellement juridique du monde romain à partir du IIIe siècle et la marginalisation des droits locaux. *MEFRM* 113–2: 839–856.

Lerouxel, F. 2006. Les femmes sur le marché du crédit en Egypte romaine (30 avant J.-C.-284 après J.-C.): une approche néo-institutionnaliste. *Cahiers du Centre de Recherches Historiques* 36: 121–136.

———. 2008. La banque privée romaine et le marché du crédit dans les tablettes de Murecine et les papyrus d'Egypte romaine. In *Pistoi dia tèn technèn. Bankers, Loans and Archives in the Ancient World: Studies in Honour of Raymond Bogaert*, ed. K. Verboven, K. Vandorpe, and V. Chankowski, 169–198. Leuven.

———. 2012. Le marché du crédit privé, la bibliothèque des acquêts et les tâches publiques en Égypte romaine. *Annales (HSS)* 67–4: 943–976.

———. 2015. The βιβλιοθήκη ἐγκτήσεων and Transaction Costs in the Credit Market of Roman Egypt (30 B.C.E. to ca. 170 C.E.). In *Law and Transaction Costs in the Ancient Economy*, ed. D. Kehoe, D. Ratzan, and U. Yiftach, 162–184. Ann Arbor: University of Michigan Press.

———. 2016a. *Le marché du crédit privé dans le monde romain (Egypte et Campanie)*. Rome.

———. 2016b. Y a-t-il des riches en Égypte romaine au Ier s.? In *Propriétaires et citoyens dans l'Orient romain*, ed. F. Lerouxel and A.-V. Pont, 213–231. Pessac.

Lewis, N. 1983. *Life in Egypt under Roman Rule*. Oxford: Oxford University Press.

Lippert, S.L. 2004. *Ein demotisches juristisches Lehrbuch: Untersuchungen zu Papyrus Berlin P 23757 rto*. Wiesbaden.

Lo Cascio, E. 2005. La 'New Institutional Economics' e l'economia imperiale romana. In *Storia romana e storia moderna. Fasi in prospettiva*, ed. M. Pani, 69–83. Bari.

———. 2006. The Role of State in the Roman Economy: Making Use of the New Institutional Economics. In *Ancient Economies, Modern Methodologies: Archaeology, Comparative History, Models and Institutions*, ed. P.F. Bang, M. Ikeguchi, and H.G. Ziche, 215–234. Bari: Edipuglia.

———. 2007. The Early Roman Empire: The State and the Economy. In *The Cambridge Economic History of the Greco-Roman World*, ed. W. Scheidel, I. Morris, and R. Saller, 619–647. Cambridge: Cambridge University Press.

Lo Cascio, E., and D. Mantovani. 2018. *Diritto romano e economia. Due modi di pensare e organizzare il mondo (nei primi tre secoli dell'Impero)*. Pavia.

Maehler, H. 2005. Greek, Roman, and Egyptian Law. *JJP* 35: 121–140.

Manning, J. 2003. *Land and Power in Ptolemaic Egypt. The Structure of Land Tenure*. Cambridge: Cambridge University Press.

Manning, J., and I. Morris. 2005. *The Ancient Economy. Evidence and Models*. Stanford: Stanford University Press.

Maresch, K. 2002. Die Bibliotheke Enkteseon im römischen Ägypten. Überlegungen zur Funktion zentraler Besitzarchive. *APF* 48: 233–246.

Mattha, G., and G.R. Hughes. 1975. *The Demotic Legal Code of Hermopolis West*. Cairo: Institut français d'archéologie orientale du Caire.

Mélèze Modrzejewski, J. 1970. La Règle de droit dans l'Égypte romaine (État des questions et perspectives de recherches). In *Proceedings of the XIIth International Congress of Papyrology*, 317–377. Toronto.

———. 1982. Ménandre de Laodicée et l'Édit de Caracalla. In Symposion 1977: Vorträge zur griechischen und hellenistischen Rechtsgeschichte , ed. J. Mélèze Modrzejewski and D. Liebs. 335–363. Köln.

———. 1988. La Loi des Égyptiens: le droit grec dans l'Égypte romaine. In *Proceedings of the XVIII International Congress of Papyrology*, vol. ii, 383–399. Athens.

———. 1993. Diritto romano e diritti locali. In *Storia di Roma*, ed. A. Schiavone, vol. iii.2, 985–1009. Torino.

———. 2014. *Loi et coutume dans l'Égypte grecque et romaine*. Warsaw.

Mitteis, L. 1891. *Reichsrecht und Volksrecht in den östlichen Provinzen des römischen Kaiserreichs*. Leipzig.

Moatti, C. 2016. Les erreurs de statut et l'idée de liberté dans l'espace judiciaire romain impérial jusqu'au IIIe siècle. In *Recht haben and Recht bekommen im*

Imperium Romanum: das Gerichtswesen der Römischen Kaiserzeit und seine dokumentarische Evidenz, ed. R. Haensch, 523–599.

Montevecchi, O. 1988. L'amministrazione dell'Egitto sotto i Giulio-Claudi. *ANRW* II 10 (1), Berlin, 412–471.

Mouritsen, H. 2011. *The Freedman in the Roman World*. Cambridge: Cambridge University Press.

Ogilvie, S. 2007. 'Whatever Is, Is Right'? Economic Institutions in Pre-industrial Europe. *Economic History Review* 60–4: 649–684.

Pestman, P.W. 1961. *Marriage and Matrimonial Property in Ancient Egypt*. Leiden: Brill.

Rathbone, D. 2007. Roman Egypt. In *The Cambridge Economic History of the Greco-Roman World*, ed. W. Scheidel, I. Morris, and R. Saller, 698–719. Cambridge: Cambridge University Press.

Riccobono, S. 1950. *Il Gnomon dell'Idios logos*. Palermo.

Riggs, C., ed. 2012. *The Oxford Handbook of Roman Egypt*. Oxford: Oxford University Press.

Rowlandson, J. 1996. *Landowners and Tenants in Roman Egypt. The Social Relations in the Oxyrhynchite Nome*. Oxford: Clarendon Press.

———., ed. 1999. *Women and Society in Greek and Roman Egypt: A Sourcebook*. Cambridge: Cambridge University Press.

Stiglitz, J. 2000. The Contributions of the Economics of Information to Twentieth Century Economics. *QJE* 115–4: 1441–1478.

Swarney, P. 1970. *The Ptolemaic and Roman Idios Logos*. Toronto: Hakkert.

Taubenschlag, R. 1959. The Legal Profession in Greco-Roman Egypt. In *Opera Minora II*, 159–165. Warsaw: Państwowe Wydawn Naukowe.

Terpstra, T. 2008. Roman Law, Transactions Costs and the Roman Economy: Evidence from the Sulpicii Archive. In *Pistoi dia tèn technèn. Bankers, Loans and Archives in the Ancient World*, ed. K. Verboven, K. Vandorpe, and V. Chankowski, 345–369. Leuven.

Treggiari, S. 1991. *Roman marriage: iusti coniuges from the time of Cicero to the time of Ulpian*. Oxford.

Volterra, E. 1970. Quelques observations sur un édit du préfet d'Égypte Servius Sulpicius Similis. In *Études offertes à Jean Macqueron*, 677–681. Aix-en-Provence.

Wolff, H.J. 1978. *Das Recht der griechischen Papyri Ägyptens in der Zeit der Ptolemaeer und des Prinzipats*. Munich: Organisation und Kontrolle des privaten Rechtsverkehrs.

PART IV

The Labour Market

CHAPTER 8

Information Asymmetry and the Roman Labour Market

Claire Holleran

Like all markets, the market for labour is imperfect and characterised by information asymmetry.[1] Those looking for work are unlikely to know about all potential employment opportunities, nor will they know all the details of the post or the expectations of the employer (e.g. Stigler 1962: 94). Likewise, employers cannot know everything about all possible candidates, their history, or their suitability for the work. Modern labour markets have, therefore, developed numerous ways of dealing with the issue of asymmetric information, particularly in relation to skilled work. A number of 'signalling devices', for example, are used to demonstrate a candidate's suitability for a particular role, such as educational and professional qualifications. Some workers, such as doctors, are licenced. References and personal recommendations, via both formal and informal channels, provide background information on potential candidates (Rees 1966). Labour

[1] My thanks to the editors, and to Paul Erdkamp, and Koen Verboven for their constructive comments on earlier drafts of this paper.

C. Holleran (✉)
University of Exeter, Exeter, UK
e-mail: C.Holleran@exeter.ac.uk

C. Rosillo-López, M. García Morcillo (eds.), *Managing Information in the Roman Economy*, Palgrave Studies in Ancient Economies,
https://doi.org/10.1007/978-3-030-54100-2_8

market intermediaries can also play an important role in linking employers with employees, through recruitment or employment agencies, the advertising of job opportunities on internet search boards, targeted e-mailing lists, newspapers, job centres, unionised hiring halls, and even street corner day labour queues (Autor 2008). None of these methods are perfect and job searches can still be lengthy and expensive, but they do go some way towards alleviating the risk, uncertainty, and high transaction costs inherent in the finding and hiring of labour.

If there were indeed a market for labour in the Roman world, it will almost certainly have been characterised by similar problems of information asymmetry. In a previous contribution, I have considered some of the ways in which workers in the city of Rome in particular may have gone about finding work (Holleran 2017); here the perspective shifts from the employees to the employers. It asks how they find workers and how they might assess their suitability for the roles on offer, as well as considering the potential mechanisms in place to assist in the search for appropriate workers, and the possible legal protections offered to employers. It explores the potential role of signalling devices, particularly for skilled work; the evidence for labour market intermediaries, such as labour contractors, employment agencies, and informal labour exchanges; the utilisation of networks and personal recommendations, including the use of letters of recommendation and both formal and informal associations and networks; and finally, the extra-economic coercion of workers and the employment of dependent labour, including the enslaved, the formerly enslaved, and clients. Central to all this is the need for workers to establish a reputation for reliability and professional competence. This was especially important for itinerant workers, as well as in larger urban centres, where workers were less likely to be known to their employers; we can suppose that in smaller places the Roman world was still very much a face-to-face society and workers were typically already known to their employers, at least by reputation.

8.1 Skilled Workers: Signalling Devices and Professionalisation

The market for skilled labour in the Roman world was notably thin, and securing workers with the appropriate skill levels for particular tasks was correspondingly difficult. Indeed, it is clear that there was a skills premium in the Roman world. In Diocletian's price edict, for example, wages reflected a worker's skill level; a figure painter, for instance, earned a maximum of 150 *denarii* a day, six times the 25 *denarii* a day stipulated for an agricultural labourer. Skilled enslaved workers were also worth more than unskilled enslaved workers (see below). Yet how did potential employers—or purchasers in the case of the enslaved—assess the skill levels of potential workers? In a modern labour market, employers can quickly gauge the skills of a job applicant by their level of educational attainment and their professional qualifications, which are used as signalling devices. In theory, such qualifications, particularly when they are supported by a recognised and respected institution, are objective and verifiable, reducing the uncertainty over the quality of an applicant (although in practice, they can mask a certain degree of variation in skill levels: Akerlof 1970: 500). Certain professions also require a licence to practice and are regulated by a professional body, providing some guarantee of competence; doctors in the UK, for example, must register with the General Medical Council in order to be provided with a licence to practice medicine, which can be removed if they are found guilty of medical malpractice or professional misconduct. Employers in the Roman world had no such guarantees, although they were not entirely without means of assessing the professional competency of workers.

While there were no clear criteria for even defining a doctor, never mind an ancient equivalent of the General Medical Council, there were, for example, various means of assessing the competency of healers for those lucky enough to be able to make a selection on criteria other than availability and price.[2] Choosing a doctor was very much an urban problem; in rural areas, patients likely had to go with whatever healing was available, and in small towns, the reputations of local doctors were presumably well known (Nutton 1990: 244). In larger cities, however, there were not only more doctors to choose from, but they were more anonymous and a potential patient had to be more cautious. According to Galen in his treatise *On Examining the Best Physicians*, a patient should be educated enough to interrogate a doctor directly on his prognosis, knowledge, anatomy, patients and performance (Nutton 1990: 244–49). Galen was, however, addressing a very restricted audience and most people had to rely on other means of assessing the quality of a doctor (Nutton 1990:

[2] On the diversity of people considered under the umbrella term 'doctor', see Nutton 2013: 254–78.

243–44, 249). The decision by town councils to grant tax immunity to doctors, a practice already common in Hellenistic cities, provided some form of external validation, particularly when the number of doctors was set by Antoninus Pius at between five and ten depending on the size of the city.[3] By late antiquity—and probably earlier in some cases, since this practice appears to be attested already among the Galatians by Strabo (4.1.5)—towns also had a number of salaried doctors.[4] These doctors were generally selected by the town council although in fourth-century Rome, they were chosen by a board of fellow doctors, suggesting a level of professional peer assessment (*CTh* 13.3.9). A certain level of skill or professionalisation could perhaps be implied by a professed adherence to a particular medical sect, or by an association with a particularly famous doctor, which in turn contributed to the reputation of certain cities as centres of medical training. Such links were part of a doctor's self-promotion and advertising (even if they were not always genuine), and acted as an assertion of authority and a sign that they were to be trusted (Leith 2016). Membership of a formal association of doctors could also be an important indicator of a doctor's standing amongst their peers and thus of their competence (Nutton 2013: 256); it should be noted, however, that there only a handful of documented formal associations of doctors in the Roman world, and some doctors were members of other professional associations (Verboven, forthcoming). Furthermore, medicine was very often practiced in public places, or in workshops that were open and visible, filled with observers and onlookers; a successful consultation with a patient could help a doctor win over new prospective clients.[5] Otherwise, personal recommendations were doubtless important wherever possible; Cicero, for example, recommended one Asclapo, a *medicus* from Patrae, to Servius (*Ad. Fam.* 13.20).

Membership of a professional association probably acted as a marker of quality in other professions also, indicating an individual with a good standing among their peers, although membership was not a legal requirement to practice a trade.[6] Membership fees were fairly substantial; in AD 160, for instance, these were 100 sesterces upon initiation to the *collegium* of Diana and Antinous at Lanuvium, followed by monthly dues of five

[3] *Dig.* 27.1.6.2 (Modestinus); Nutton 2013: 255–256.

[4] See *CTh* 13.3 for the privileges and immunities granted to doctors in late antiquity.

[5] For the public nature of medicine, see Nutton 2013: 270–71; for the street as a place of activity, see Holleran 2011.

[6] Although see Verboven 2017: 182–84 for professional associations having the potential to make life hard for non-members, as well as some of the advantages of membership.

asses, albeit for a religious rather than a trade association (*CIL* XIV 2112). Members were, therefore, most likely independent traders and craft workers, but while they were vetted before admission, crucially, this was for their character rather than for their skills.[7] Certainly when the internal rules of associations are known, these focus primarily on social interaction between members, particularly at communal dinners, and on funeral arrangements, rather than on regulating work practices. Nor is there much evidence that associations set the fees and wages of their members (although they may have shared information about these, as they surely did about many other aspects of their trade).[8] Recent scholarship, however, has tended to emphasise the role of such associations as private-order enforcement networks, imposing social norms of behaviour and regulating trust networks (e.g. Liu 2017: 203; Verboven 2017: 173). Membership of a professional association signalled that an individual was to be trusted; some may even have carried *tesserae* to confirm their membership, as we see with two personalised *tesserae* belonging to *utriclarii* (*CIL* XII *136; *283; Broekaert 2011: 229). Selecting a member of a professional association when agreeing a contract for a job may then have provided a level of assurance to an employer and helped overcome some of the shortcomings of information in the Roman world, acting as a reputation mechanism.

Indeed, there is some evidence that professional associations could act as guarantors for the work of their members. An inscription from fifth-century Sardis, for example, records an agreement between an association of builders and one Aurelianus, a civic official (*magistrianos kai ekdikos*) setting out something akin to a code of conduct for members of the association following complaints that builders had been leaving jobs unfinished and in some way obstructing their employers (*Sardis* VII I.18). Members agreed to complete all work providing the employer paid their wages promptly, but if they were unable to do so for whatever reason, another member of the association would step in and complete the work.

[7] See, for example, *CIL* VI 33885 for a clause in the *lex* of the *negotiatores eborarii et citrarii* that it was the *curatores'* responsibility to check a membership candidate's background; Broekaert 2011: 227–28.

[8] On the scarcity of evidence for wage setting and price fixing, see Broekaert 2011: 245–46. For the possibility that doctors in the collegium at Ephesos made a collective decision on fees, see *I. Ephesos* 1386 (Nutton 2013: 401, n. 19), although the inscription is badly damaged and the exact meaning is unclear. See also Broughton 1938: 849 for the suggestion that an association of building workers at Sardis advised members on suitable wage rates (*Sardis* VII 1.18, discussed later).

Furthermore, if a member somehow hindered the employer while the work was under construction, indemnities would be paid to the employer. Financial and legal penalties were set out should these rules be broken. Implicit within this is the notion that an employer could engage workers outside of the association to complete the work, but without the same protections. The agreement, therefore, offers a guarantee to employers hiring members of this particular building association that their contract will be honoured and their job completed as agreed, but how typical this was, and whether we see it in earlier periods is not clear. Furthermore, the agreement was in itself made in reaction to disputes arising from members leaving work uncompleted, indicating that membership of a professional association alone was not enough to guarantee completion of work to a satisfactory standard.

We might expect professional associations to have regulated apprenticeships within their respective crafts, but there is little evidence for this. In fact, while apprenticeships in crafts and manufacturing were likely used extensively, these did not really provide any objective way of gauging skill levels. They may have signalled some sort of competence, but were probably mainly useful only in a local sense; if you knew and trusted the skills of a particular craft worker, then you may have accepted their training of an apprentice as a guarantee of a particular skill level. Certainly the number and quality of a craftsman's apprentices appears to have enhanced his status and reputation locally (Tran 2017a: 257–60). Nevertheless, there seems to have been little, if any, formal regulation of apprenticeships. A tax list of fullers and dyers at Tebtynis mentions a *hegoumenos gerdīon* or master of weavers in connection with a *diakrisis mathētōn* or division of learners, which could perhaps indicate that the local guild of weavers, together with local government officials, had a say in the screening of apprentices, but it is not clear what the *diakrisis* in question consisted of, nor what level of involvement in the regulation of apprenticeships this implies (*P. Carlsberg 53*).[9] In any case, the motivation for the screening seems to be more about registering new craftsmen for tax purposes than about providing some objective validation of their skill level. A small number of contracts include a clause stipulating that the apprentice must demonstrate their skill at the end of the apprenticeship. For Freu (2011: 34–35), this suggests a sort of final exam, overseen by professional associations, but such stipulations are rare and probably reflect the specific situation of that particular contract

[9] On this text, see Bülow-Jacobsen 1989: 125–26. Also Freu 2011: 34–35; Liu 2017: 222.

(Bergamasco 1995: 133). There was no established progression of training of the type that we see regulated by the guilds in the medieval period, with apprentices progressing to journeymen and then to masters (Liu 2017: 222).

Informal apprenticeships within the household or workshop dominated, and many of those outside of the household were also subject to relatively informal agreements, as, for example, we see with Lucian's supposed apprenticing to his uncle as a stonecutter (Luc. *Somn.* 7; Tran 2013: 161–64). Even when apprenticeships were subject to written contracts, the terms of engagement appear to have varied enormously; the length of apprenticeships ranges from six months to six years, while there is no standard agreement regarding the responsibility for the apprentice's living costs, the provision (or not) of wages, or their rate and duration (Hawkins 2017: 46–47; Liu 2017: 222). Furthermore, the actual teaching content of apprenticeships is rarely set out in surviving contracts, other than vague allusions to a master teaching 'the whole' of a trade as that particular master knows it; the level of skill attained must have depended very much on the skill of the teacher (Freu 2016: 187). An apprenticeship contract from Oxyrhynchos, dated to AD 53, for instance, binds Pausiris' son Dioskus to Apollonios for a period of one year, 'in order to learn the whole weaver's trade, as he [Apollonios] also knows it himself' (*P Wisc.* 1.4)[10]; another from Tebtunis in AD 117 apprentices Tephersais' son Kronion to Heron for two years to learn the 'trade of weaving in its entirety, as Heron himself knows it' (*P Teb.* 2.385).[11] Essentially, apprenticeships were largely a private system with no objective form of quality control. It is highly unlikely that all apprentices reached the same level of skill at the end of their apprenticeship. In fact, it is probable that this was never the intention; apprentices were diverse, and consequently so were their apprenticeships.[12]

The legal concept of *imperitia* governing liability under contracts of *locatio conductio operis* and the *Lex Aquilia* suggests, however, that there was an externally measurable notion of an appropriate proficiency level for

[10] http://papyri.info/ddbdp/p.wisc;1;4

[11] http://papyri.info/ddbdp/p.tebt;2;385. See Freu 2016: 187, with further references. See also for so-called 'teaching contracts', which were more precise, although only three are known, two relating to shorthand and one relating to music.

[12] On the differing goals of apprenticeships and the diversity of the skilled workforce, see Freu 2011.

artisans and other skilled workers.[13] This provided some protection against damage to property caused by incompetent or poorly skilled workers. Implicit within contracts relating to the hire of a skilled worker for the fulfilment of a particular task (i.e. *locatio conductio operis*) is that the worker entering into the contract—the *conductor*—had the necessary skills to complete the work. Ulpian (*Dig.* 19.2.13.5), for example, sets out the liability if an artisan breaks a precious stone that he had been given to set or engrave; if this was caused by a defect in the stone, then he was not liable under the *actio locatio* (action on hiring), but if it occurred due to lack of skill (*imperitia*), then an action could be brought against him for the value of the precious stone.[14] For Celsus (*Dig.* 19.2.9.5), *imperitia* should be classed with negligence (*culpa*). The fact that this concept was enshrined in law by the early second century AD indicates agreements made between relative strangers that were regulated by contractual law.

The rules governing liability and *imperitia* most probably developed out of discussions surrounding liability when enslaved people were hired out for skilled work (Martin 1990: 304; 310–11). Labeo, for example, a Jurist of the Augustan age, discusses the hiring of an enslaved muleteer (*Dig.*19.2.60.7; see also *Dig.* 9.2.27.34 for a similar case).[15] A contract exists between the enslaver (*locator*) and the owner of the mules (*conductor*); the object of the contract is the enslaved muleteer, who causes the death of a mule through negligence (*neglegentia*). The issue relates to what extent the enslaver is to be held liable for the loss of the mule.[16] Labeo sets out three options for the hire of the enslaved person, all with different implications for liability: (1) The enslaved person leases himself out; (2) The enslaver leases him out 'on request'; (3) The enslaver leases out an enslaved person that he himself has selected. It is in the final scenario that the enslaver is fully liable for the value of the mule, since in selecting the enslaved person for this particular task, he is implicitly guaranteeing that he has the relevant skills.[17] The hiring of an enslaved person may offer an advantage here over the hiring of a free worker, as an enslaver

[13] On the concept of *imperitia* in Roman law, see in particular Martin 2001.

[14] See also *Dig.* 9.2.27.29 (Ulpian). See *Dig.* 9.2.7.8 (Ulpian) for a doctor being liable for the death of an enslaved person whom he treated and killed through lack of skill (also 9.2.52.pr). For *imperitia* and the *Lex Aquilia*, see also Gaius, *Dig.* 9.2.8.1.

[15] On these texts, see Martin 1990: 304–311, followed here.

[16] See also *Dig.* 19.2.45.1 (Paul.) on the issue of liability for theft.

[17] In the first scenario, the enslaver is liable but only up to the value of the enslaved person's *peculium* or to the extent that he benefitted from the transaction, whereas in the second

vouches for the skill level of the enslaved and is there to seek recompense from should any problems arise. In fact, the association of an enslaved or formerly enslaved person with a family or an individual of good reputation may in itself have acted as a signalling device, reassuring the hirer that the worker in question was skilled, and that any problems would be satisfactorily resolved; the same principal surely applies to a client with a respected patron. This would reduce the transaction costs inherent in the hiring of labour, not only in terms of enforcement costs, but also as regards search and information, and negotiating costs.

Underlying all this is the notion of good faith (*bona fides*); artisans have a good faith duty to perform with skill when they take a job under *locatio operis*, and enslavers have a duty to represent the skills of the enslaved accurately (Martin 2001: 114). A similar principle most likely applied when considering the expectation of the aptitude of a hired worker, since it was accepted that skill levels varied (e.g. Ulp. *Dig.* 46.3.31). Certainly when work was formally inspected at the end of a contract of building work by the *locator* in a process known as *probatio*, this ought to reflect the 'judgement of a good man' (*arbitrium boni viri:* Paul, *Dig.* 19.2.24.pr), a principle which can presumably be extended to cover the judgement of all skilled work, guarding against excessively harsh assessments (Martin 2001: 123–25).[18]

There were then some means of assessing proficiency levels in hired workers, and some legal protection against losses caused by incompetent employees, at least by the second century AD. What about when it came to the purchase of enslaved people with specific skills? Undoubtedly, they were more valuable than the unskilled. Cato the Elder, for example, apparently lent money to his own enslaved workers to purchase people whom they then trained and taught for a year, before selling them on for a profit (Plut. *Cato Mai.* 21.7).[19] Similarly, three centuries later, the Jurist Paulus describes a craftsman (*faber*) who purchased a man, trained him, and sold him for double the price (*Dig.* 17.1.26.8). Yet how did a buyer know that an enslaved person was really as skilled as a seller claimed? Indeed, Cicero (*Planc.* 62) writes that 'in purchasing slaves, however honest a man may

scenario, the enslaver was liable only if he could be shown to have acted in bad faith (*dolus*) or fault (*culpa*) in the lease.

[18] On *probatio*, see Martin 1989:103–113.

[19] See also Plut. *Crass.* 2.5–6 for the value of his skilled enslaved workers whose training he personally supervised; Cic. *QRosc.* 28 for an unskilled enslaved person valued at 4000 sesterces and a trained actor at more than 100,000 sesterces

be, if we have bought him as a builder or a plasterer, we are annoyed if he turns out to be ignorant of the business we had in view when we bought him…'.[20] To be sure, asymmetrical information about the enslaved was a well-known problem facing buyers, and the curule aediles already in the Republic sought to remedy this problem with an edict governing the sale of slaves. Sellers had to disclose any diseases or 'defects' of the enslaved, as well as whether they had previously run away or were prone to loitering, any capital offences, if they had been condemned to fight with beasts, or if they had made an attempt on their own life (Ulp. *Dig.* 21.1.1.1).[21] More importantly for our purposes, any assertion made by a seller about the skills of an enslaved person must be true or the buyer is subject to recompense. Again, the judgement of skill levels is understood to be somewhat arbitrary, but should match reasonable expectations: 'A seller who says that a slave is an excellent cook must supply the best in his profession; a seller who simply says that a slave is a cook does enough even if he supplies a mediocre cook. The same applies to other trades' (Gaius, *Dig.* 21.1.18.1; Joshel 2010: 104–05).[22] Ulpian (*Dig.* 21.1.19.4) follows a similar principle when he states that if a vendor promises that an enslaved person is a craftsman, he must be an adequate craftsman; he does not have to be a master, but he cannot be a beginner.[23]

The origins of enslaved people were also disclosed (Ulp. *Dig.* 21.1.31.21). This acted as a sort of signalling device for buyers, not of a precise skill level per se, but of a person's perceived suitability for a particular role. Ethnic stereotypes of physical qualities and personalities were used as a shorthand way to signal an enslaved person's supposed characteristics (Frier and Kehoe 2007: 121). Varro (*Rust.* 2.10.4), for instance, notes that workers from Baetica were not suitable for herding, but that Gauls were perfect for this role, especially for draught cattle. Similarly, if a buyer had a specific role in mind, they looked for particular physical and mental

[20] Loeb translation (adapted). *Ut nos in mancipiis parandis, quamvis frugi hominem, si pro fabro, aut pro tectore emimus, ferre moleste solemus, si eas artes, quas in emendo secuti sumus, forte nesciverit…*

[21] On this edict, see Lavan in this volume. Also Bradley 1994: 51–54.

[22] *Venditor, qui optimum cocum esse dixerit, optimum in eo artificio praestare debet: qui vero simpliciter cocum esse dixerit, satis facere videtur, etiamsi mediocrem cocum praestet. idem et in ceteris generibus artificiorum.*

[23] *Illud sciendum est: si quis artificem promiserit vel dixerit, non utique perfectum eum praestare debet, sed ad aliquem modum peritum, ut neque consummatae scientiae accipias, neque rursum indoctum esse in artificium: sufficiet igitur talem esse, quales volgo artifices dicuntur.*

characteristics when purchasing an enslaved worker. Cicero (*Planc.* 62), for example, claims that for the post of steward or shepherd, he would look for frugality, industry and vigilance, while Columella (*Rust.* 1.9) notes particular physical qualities needed in workers, such as a big voice and imposing bearing for a ploughman, or muscularity and broad shoulders for a vineyard worker (also Varro, *Rust.* 2.10.1–3; Joshel 2010:103–4).

8.2 Labour Market Intermediaries

In modern labour markets, intermediaries can play a significant role in linking employers and employees, and there are indications that some of the more rudimentary techniques were also in use in the Roman world. Labour contractors, for instance, are documented in a rural context, providing seasonal labour and even moving workers between regions as required. Suetonius (*Vesp.* 1.4), for example, claimed that some believed that Vespasian's great-grandfather was a contractor—a *manceps operarum*—for the seasonal labourers who moved annually from Umbria to the Sabine district; Vespasian's great-grandfather's involvement is to be dated to the first century BC, but Suetonius speaks as though the practice were still ongoing in his day. The well-known funerary monument from Mactaris in North Africa also records a rural labour contractor, albeit one in action as late as the fourth or even fifth century AD. He probably began as a small landowner, supplementing his income by working as an itinerant reaper during the harvest, becoming what essentially must have been a labour contractor as a leader (*ductor*) of a gang of harvesters (*turma messorum*) after 12 years, and eventually a man of some means and a member of the local town council (*CIL* VIII 11824).[24]

In urban areas, labour contractors were probably particularly important in labour-intensive and episodic industries such as construction. Construction workers were likely divided into work gangs known as *decuriae*, probably numbering around 10 although potentially larger, each led by a contractor.[25] Potentially the *collegia fabri tignuarii* played a role here, particularly in Rome and Ostia where the *collegia* were especially large;

[24] For a detailed discussion of this inscription, including an English translation, and debates about its significance and dating (which is argued here to be as late as the fourth or fifth century), see Shaw 2013: 48–73; 88–92. See also Appendix 2: 281–298 for the Latin text and commentary.

[25] For the use of work gangs (termed *decuriae* in a rural context also, see Columella, *Rust.* 1.9.7–8.

individual members perhaps headed up a group of workers, skilled and unskilled, who could then be brought together to work on large building projects, simplifying the process of finding a workforce (DeLaine 1997: 204–05; Tran 2017b). For smaller building projects, contractors like Longilius, employed by Cicero's brother Quintus to undertake some work on his house on the Palatine, may have been typical. In April 56 BC, Cicero wrote to Quintus (*Q. Fam.* 2.6.3) to tell him that he had visited the site, spoken to the contractor (*redemptor*) Longilius, and seen that work was going ahead, with 'many builders' (*multi structores*); the number is not specified, but this was perhaps a group of around five to ten workers. What isn't clear is whether these workers were Longilius' permanent workforce, or whether he employed the same or different workers on a project-by-project basis. An often-quoted passage from Venuleius (*Dig.* 45.1.137.3), however, suggests that contractors preferred flexibility, habitually maintaining only a small permanent workforce, if at all, and hiring additional workers as and when required. While labour contractors were surely essential to the construction industry, it is far from certain that they maintained permanent groups of workers, nor is there much evidence to suggest the employment of gangs of enslaved workers in building (or indeed, any other sector). Crassus' large enslaved workforce of architects and builders, numbering over 500, and the gangs of enslaved workers held by contractors engaged in the maintenance and repair of the aqueduct system appear to have been late Republican exceptions (Plut. *Crass.* 2; Front. *Aq.* 96; Anderson 1997: 22–23).

Contractors in the building industry may well have made use of more informal labour exchanges in order to obtain their workers, at least for unskilled roles (Holleran 2017: 91–95). Historically, hiring fairs, hiring halls, and the congregation of workers have all played a role in overcoming information asymmetry within the labour market, enabling potential employers and employees to connect, while also allowing both sides to see the availability of work and labour, with wages, terms, and conditions often being set accordingly. Nor are such methods of engagement confined to history, but are still prevalent in sectors like construction even in developed economies such as the USA (Valenzuela 2003: 312–14). The gathering together of workers is a cheap and effective way of enabling employers and employees to find each other. While it is fairly rudimentary in that it tells employers little about the workers, and the workers little about the employers, both sides can learn more by asking questions of each other. As a process, it is fairly well documented in the Roman world, with the most famous example surely the Parable of the Vineyard Workers in the Gospel of Matthew, a story based around the idea that potential workers could be found congregating in the agora waiting to be hired (Matt. 20.1–16). Here, the agora acted as a sort of informal labour exchange, with the vineyard owner returning repeatedly throughout the day to hire additional workers. Central urban areas such as a forum or agora probably frequently acted in this way. A story in Suetonius (*Claud.* 22) about Claudius ordering the withdrawal of slaves and *operarii* from the forum before he offered up supplication from the rostra suggests that day labourers were waiting there to be hired. In a city the size of Rome, more specialist workers may have waited in particular places, such as cooks in the *macellum* (Plin. *HN* 18.108), porters at the docks or at the gates, construction workers near to building yards, and so on. Once workers were gathered together, work opportunities could then be announced orally (e.g. Apul. *Met.* 2.21).

Collegia and other professional associations may have played a role as labour contractors in other sectors besides construction, either formally or informally, and perhaps acting too as sector-specific employment exchanges. Noy (2000: 151) also suggests an informal system of agents linking new migrants in Rome with employers, perhaps through formal associations of migrant traders, such as the Tyrians resident in Rome and Puteoli (*IG* XIV 830, lines 1–19; Holleran 2017: 96–97). This often occurs in modern migration, although there is no direct evidence for this in the Roman world.

8.3 Networks and Personal Recommendations

As we have seen, both formal and informal networks may have played a role in overcoming information asymmetry in the Roman labour market by communicating information about job opportunities and about workers. Most of this will have taken place orally, particularly in smaller face-to-face communities, and is impossible to document historically. However, there is some evidence that letters of personal recommendation were also used, and the surviving examples could point to this as a wider phenomenon, especially among migrants and in larger urban centres, where relative strangers were being employed. Indeed, as Noy argues (2000: 150), letters of recommendation were presumably the only way in which a migrant's skills could be vouched for, at least until they were able to build up a reputation of their own. Such a system relies on a certain level of literacy, at the very least on the part of an employer, if not the employee. Sidonius Apollinaris (*Epist.* 4.7) implies that workers do not always know the content of their recommendation letters, but whether in this particular case it is because the letter is sealed and unread, or because the worker is illiterate is unclear.

The letter of recommendation is in itself a fairly common phenomenon in the Roman world, found in surviving letter collections and also in documentary sources such as papyri. These have a variety of functions, including hospitality, marriage, loans, and friendship, but are also found in relation to employment. Such examples primarily concern roles within government and show us the operation of patronage at the upper levels of society, although in the empire at least, these were salaried posts, and we might think of them as part of a labour market. Certainly we are seeing the coupling of labour supply and demand, even if the holders of these posts might not necessarily want us to think of them in this way; Lucian (*Apology* 11) argues that a public post is a very different thing to wage earning in a private capacity, but this sounds rather like special pleading. A couple of literary examples should suffice to demonstrate the principle of letters of recommendation for government roles. Pliny (*Ep.* 4.4), for instance, writes a brief and formulaic letter to Sosius Senecio, probably legate of Upper or Lower Moesia at the time, recommending one Varisidius Nepos for a tribunician role; Pliny states that Nepos is hard-working, morally upright, and skilled in speaking (*vir industrius rectus disertus*), as well as being a close relative of a mutual friend. Similarly, Fronto (*Ad M. Caes*, v.37 (52)) writes to Marcus Aurelius, putting forward one Aridelus, an imperial freedman, for a position as procurator; again the potential candidate is honest, temperate, keen, and, attentive (*frugi et sobrius et acer et diligens*).[26]

Letters of recommendation also appear in the correspondence of rural landowners in late antiquity (Grey 2004). Sidonius, for example, provides a letter to Simplicius vouching for its anonymous bearer, albeit while disparaging him as a bumpkin (*rusticus*) and a poor man (*pauper*) (*Epist.* IV.7). The bearer of the letter appears to have been travelling voluntarily rather than having been sent by Sidonius to Simplicius. Indeed, he requested the letter from Sidonius himself, although the latter claims that he would have offered to write the letter anyway once he discovered that

[26] Letter 29 in Davenport and Manley 2014:108–9. For examples of letters of recommendation in the Republic, there are numerous instances in Cicero, *Ad Familiares*, e.g. 13.19–27.

the bearer was heading in Simplicius' direction. It is unclear what particular role this individual is looking for, but landowners appear to be using their links with each other to facilitate the mobility of skilled workers and ease the difficulties of employment on both sides; these workers include reapers, but also other skilled specialists, such as potters, carpenters, blacksmiths, and so on. The fluctuating demand for skilled and unskilled wage labour at certain points in the agricultural calendar was a perennial problem. Cato (*Agr.* 1.3), for example, notes in the second century BC that it is important to locate an estate near a good supply of *operarii*, while Rathbone (1991: 166–74; 392) demonstrates that specialist workers were hired as and when they were needed on the Appianus estate in third century AD Egypt. Furthermore, as we have seen, labour contractors moved rural labourers around Italy (see above), although the level of mobility of rural labour may have been higher in late antiquity, perhaps warranting the more widespread use of letters of recommendation.

Letters of recommendation for employment also survive in the papyrological material. Although outside of our period, such letters appear most frequently in the third century BC Zenon archive, where they are numerous enough for Von Reden (2010: 231) to suggest that they were 'neither exceptional nor just a polite gesture'.[27] One Ptolemaios, for example, writes to Zenon from Philadelphia (Arsinoites) to vouch for a man who has sailed down to obtain employment in the office of Philiskos, having been recommended by Phileas and other accountants (*SB* 26.16636). Others are more general in tone, such as a certain Artemidorus introducing Zenon to a man who could be useful to him in some way (*P.Col.* 4.111). Zenon himself was from Caria, and it is often Carians approaching Zenon, the secretary of Apollonios, for opportunities, implying that ethnic links with an employer could be useful in attaining positions (Cotton 1981: 2). The Carian writer of one letter thus asks Apollonius (through Zenon) for letters of recommendation to Apollodotos, Laagos, and Hikesios (*P.Cair.Zen.* 1.59037).[28]

In the Roman period, we again see official letters of recommendation for roles in public administration within the papyrological material. Ulpius Celer, for instance, an architect, wrote to Tiberius Claudius Hermeros, an imperial procurator in the later first century or early second century, recommending an imperial slave to him (*P.Ryl.* 4.608; Cotton 1981: 28–33).

[27] See also Cotton 1981: 1–2.

[28] Also *P.Cair. Zen.* 1.59045; 1.59046; 2.59284; 3.59397; 4.59590; 5.59853.

Others relate to soldiers looking for advancement. A serving soldier Claudius Terentianus, for example, wrote a letter in the early second century AD to his father Claudius Tiberianus, a veteran, which mentioned, among other things, his hope of being transferred from the Alexandrian fleet to an auxiliary cohort: '...And if god should be willing, I hope to live frugally and to be transferred to a cohort; but here nothing will be accomplished without money, and letters of recommendation have no value unless a man helps himself...' (*P.Mich.* 8.468, lines 35–41; Campbell 1994: 43).[29] Terentianus here implies that letters of recommendation and personal patronage could be useful for promotion and transfer within the army, but that a bribe could be more effective. In any case, whatever means he used, it must have worked because a later letter in the archive of correspondence between him and his father reveals that Terentianus had become a legionary soldier (*P.Mich.* 8.476).[30]

8.4 Dependent Labour

There were, then, various possible means of overcoming the information asymmetry inherent within the Roman labour market, although it is not clear how widely any of these methods were used. One response to information asymmetry and uncertainty that was undoubtedly widely used, however, was extra-economic coercion of workers and the use of dependent labour, including the enslaved and the formerly enslaved.[31] As noted above, enslaved people could be hired—or even borrowed (Ulp. *Dig.* 13.6.5.7)—for both skilled and unskilled work.[32] They could be hired out, or could hire themselves out and pay a part of their daily earnings to their enslaver (e.g. Columella, *Rust.* 1.pr. 12; Lab. *Dig.* 19.2.60.7). Depending on the form of agreement, the hiring of an enslaved worker might be beneficial, as the enslaver could potentially act as a guarantor for the skills of the enslaved. The hiring of enslaved people for skilled work in particular

[29] *.....et si deus / volueret spero ṃe frugaliter / [v]iċịturum et in cohortem / [tra]ṇsferri hic a[ut]ẹm sene aer[e] / [ni]hil fiet neque epistulae / comṃandaticiae / nihil valunt nesi / si qui sibi aiutaveret...*

[30] See Cotton 1981: 1–2 for more on letters of recommendation in the military; also 8–27 for further examples. See also Vindolanda tablets 225 and 250 for patronage within the army (http://vindolanda.csad.ox.ac.uk/); *P.Oxy.* 1666; Campbell 1994, no.48.

[31] For the scale of Roman enslavement, see, for example, Scheidel 2012: 90–96.

[32] E.g. Plaut. *Vid.* 25; Columella, *Rust.* 1.pr. 12; Sen. *Ben.* 7.5.3; *Dig.* 19.2.42–43, 45.1, 48.1, 60.7; 47.5.1.5; *P.Wisc.* 16.5; Hawkins 2016: 143.

suggests a scarcity of free skilled labour. Certainly, as we have already seen, many of the enslaved were skilled, and training was a sound economic investment on the part of the enslaver; a skilled person was potentially more useful in a domestic context, generated more profit if put to work in a business, and was worth more if sold. Crucially, since the labour was dependent, there was no danger that workers would leave and take their skills elsewhere. In this way, it offered security, more so than a contract, the terms of which could be difficult to enforce (Hawkins 2017: 38–39). Thus while the upfront costs of purchasing an enslaved person—or training one that was already part of the household—may have been higher than hiring a skilled wage worker, the long-term benefits could be greater; an enslaver knows precisely how skilled the enslaved is, particularly if trained within the household, and given their lack of agency to move elsewhere, it is largely immaterial what the worker knows about their enslaver. The downside is the lack of flexibility; in periods of fluctuating demand, the enslaved must be supported permanently. If in time an enslaved person were manumitted, they could continue to work in their particular craft, perhaps within their own business or as a hired wage worker. Legally such people were technically independent, but in many cases, it made sense for them to maintain close ties with their former enslaver as this could provide economic opportunities, access to work, to credit, to potential business partners, and so on. For their former enslavers, these freed people represented a known quantity when looking to hire workers. Similarly, 'clientelism' may have played a role in the labour market, with employees hiring workers who had other legal, economic, or social ties to their household. At the upper level at least, Lucian (*De Mercede conductis* 10) suggests that in order to get a role within one of the great houses as a salaried intellectual, it was necessary to ingratiate yourself with the household as a client first, and it is possible that this was the case with other more prosaic roles (Holleran 2017: 100–01).

In itself, the widespread use of dependent labour rather underlines the fact that the Roman labour market was characterised by information asymmetry. There are certainly other reasons for preferring the use of dependent labour, especially enslaved workers, not least social and ideological reasons such as ideals of self-sufficiency, conspicuous consumption, and competitive display, but economic concerns were central. While recent studies of the Roman economy have justifiably tended to emphasise the role of free labour, dependent labour remained important, especially in Rome and Italy, and this was surely in part a symptom of the difficulties inherent in overcoming the obstacle of information asymmetry within the market for hired labour.[33] Thus while we have seen that there were various basic means in place to help employers assess the suitability of workers, including some rudimentary signalling devices and legal mechanisms for determining professional competence, as well as the presence of labour market intermediaries such as contractors and hiring places, together with the use of networks and personnel recommendations, it is unlikely that any of these methods were effective enough to overcome entirely the issue of information asymmetry. The institution of slavery by no means precludes the presence of a labour market, but it undoubtedly distorts it, and while the use of dependent labour was one way of alleviating the problem of information asymmetry, it also lessened the need to develop anything akin to the more extensive mechanisms in place within the modern labour market.

Bibliography

Akerlof, G.A. 1970. 'The Market for 'Lemons': Quality Uncertainty and the Market Mechanism. *Quarterly Journal of Economics* 84: 488–500.

Anderson, J.C. 1997. *Roman Architecture and Society*. Baltimore: Johns Hopkins University Press.

Autor, D. 2008. *The Economics of Labour Market Intermediation*. https://voxeu.org/article/economics-labour-market-intermediation

Bergamasco, M. 1995. Le *didaskalika* nella ricerca attuale. *Aegyptus* 75: 96–167.

Bradley, K. 1994. *Slavery and Society at Rome*. Cambridge: Cambridge University Press.

Broekaert, W. 2011. Partners in Business. Roman Merchants and the Advantages of Being a *Collegiatus*. *Ancient Society* 41: 219–254.

Broughton, T.R.S. 1938. Roman Asia Minor. In *Economic Survey of Ancient Rome*, ed. T. Frank, vol. IV, 499–918. Baltimore: Johns Hopkins University Press.

Bülow-Jacobsen, A. 1989. Two Greek papyri Carlsberg from Tebtunis: P. Carlsberg 53 and 57. *Zeitschrift für Papyrologie und Epigraphik* 78: 125–131.

Campbell, B. 1994. *The Roman Army, 31 BC – AD 337*. London: Routledge.

Cotton, H. 1981. *Documentary Letters of Recommendation in Latin from the Roman Empire*. Königstein: Anton Hain.

[33] For an emphasis on free wage labour, see Verboven and Laes 2017: 6–13; also Temin 2013: 116. Cf. Scheidel 2012: 106–08 for the need to ensure that in rightly acknowledging the importance of free labour, we do not neglect the centrality of slavery to the Roman economy.

Davenport, C., and J. Manley. 2014. *Fronto: Selected Letters*. London: Bloomsbury Academic.

DeLaine, J. 1997. *The Baths of Caracalla: a Study in the Design, Construction, and Economics of Large-Scale Building*, Journal of Roman Archaeology. Portsmouth: JRA.

Freu, C. 2011. Apprendre et exercer un métier dans l'Égypte romaine (Ier-Vie siècles ap. J-C.). In *Les Savoirs Professionnels des Gens de Métier*, ed. N. Monteix and N. Tran, 27–40. Naples.

———. 2016. *Disciplina, patrocinium, nomen:* The Benefits of Apprenticeship in the Roman World. In *Urban Craftsmen and Traders in the Roman World*, ed. A. Wilson and M. Flohr, 183–199. Oxford.

Frier, B., and D. Kehoe. 2007. Law and Economic Institutions. In *The Cambridge Economic History of the Graeco-Roman World*, ed. W. Scheidel, I. Morris, and R. Saller, 113–143. Cambridge: Cambridge University Press.

Grey, C. 2004. Letters of Recommendation and the Circulation of Rural Labourers in the Late Roman West. In *Travel, Communication, and Geography in Late Antiquity: Sacred and Profane*, ed. L. Ellis and F.L. Kidner, 25–40. Aldershot: Ashgate.

Hawkins, C. 2016. *Roman Artisans and the Urban Economy* (Cambridge: Cambridge University Press)

Hawkins, C. 2017. Contracts, Coercion, and the Boundaries of the Roman Artisanal Firm. In *Work, Labour, and Professions in the Roman World*, ed. K. Verboven, C. Laes, and P. Van Nuffelen, 36–61. Leiden: Brill.

Holleran, C. 2011. Street Life in Ancient Rome. In *Rome, Ostia, Pompeii: Movement and Space*, ed. R. Laurence and D. J. Newsome, 245–261. Oxford: Oxford University Press.

———. 2017. Getting a Job: Finding Work in the City of Rome. In *Work, Labour, and Professions in the Roman World*, ed. K. Verboven, C. Laes, and P. Van Nuffelen, 87–103. Leiden: Brill.

Joshel, S.R. 2010. *Slavery in the Roman World*. Cambridge: Cambridge University Press.

Leith, D. 2016. How Popular Were the Medical Sects? In *Popular Medicine in Graeco-Roman Antiquity: Explorations*, ed. W.V. Harris, 231–250. Leiden: Brill.

Liu, J. 2017. Group Membership, Trust Networks, and Social Capital: A Critical Analysis. In *Work, Labour, and Professions in the Roman World*, ed. K. Verboven, C. Laes, and P. Van Nuffelen, 201–226. Leiden: Brill.

Martin, S.D. 1989. *The Roman Jurists and the Organization of Private Building in the Late Republic and Early Empire*. Brussels: Latomus.

———. 1990. *Servum meum mulionem conduxisti*: Mules, Muleteers, and Transportation in Classical Roman Law. *Transactions of the American Philological Association* 120: 301–314.

———. 2001. *Imperitia*: The Responsibility of Skilled Workers in Classical Law. *The American Journal of Philology* 122 (1): 107–129.

Noy, D. 2000. *Foreigners at Rome. Citizens and Strangers*. London: Duckworth with the Classical Press of Wales.

Nutton, V. 1990. The Patient's Choice: A New Treatise by Galen. *The Classical Quarterly* 40 (1): 236–257.

———. 2013. *Ancient Medicine*. 2nd ed. London/New York: Routledge.

Rathbone, D. 1991. *Economic Rationalism and Rural Society in Third-Century Egypt*. Cambridge: Cambridge University Press.

Rees, A. 1966. Information Networks in Labor Markets. *American Economic Review* 56 (2): 559–566.

Scheidel, W. 2012. Slavery. In *The Cambridge Companion to the Roman Economy*, ed. W. Scheidel, 89–113. Cambridge: Cambridge University Press.

Shaw, B.D. 2013. *Bringing in the Sheaves: Economy and Metaphor in the Roman World*. Toronto: University of Toronto Press.

Stigler, G.J. 1962. Information in the Labour Market. *Journal of Political Economy* 70 (5): 94–105.

Temin, P. 2013. *The Roman Market Economy*. Princeton: Princeton University Press.

Tran, N. 2013. Dominus Tabernae. *Le statut de travail des artisans et des commerçants de l'Occident Romain*. Rome.

———. 2017a. *Ars* and *doctrina*. The Socioeconomic Identity of Roman Skilled Workers. In *Work, Labour, and Professions in the Roman World*, ed. K. Verboven, C. Laes, and P. Van Nuffelen, 246–261. Leiden: Brill.

———. 2017b. Enterprises de construction, vie associative et organisation du travail dans la Rome impériale et à Ostia. *L'Antiquité Classique* 86: 115–127.

Valenzuela, A. 2003. Day Labour Work. *Annual Review of Sociology* 29: 307–333.

Verboven, K. 2017. Guilds and the Organisation of Urban Populations During the Principate. In *Work, Labour, and Professions in the Roman World*, ed. K. Verboven, C. Laes, and P. Van Nuffelen, 173–202. Leiden: Brill.

———. Forthcoming. Guilds and Gods. Religious Profiles of Occupational *collegia* and the Problem of the *dendrophori*. In *The Economics of Roman Religion*, ed. A. Trentacoste, N. Ray, and A. Wilson. Oxford: Oxford University Press.

Verboven, K., and C. Laes. 2017. Work, Labour, Professions. What's in a Name? In *Work, Labour, and Professions in the Roman World*, ed. K. Verboven, C. Laes, and P. Van Nuffelen, 1–19. Leiden: Brill.

Von Reden, S. 2010. *Money in Ptolemaic Egypt: From the Macedonian Conquest to the End of the Third Century BC*. Cambridge: Cambridge University Press.

CHAPTER 9

Asymmetric Information and Adverse Selection in the Roman Slave Market: The Limits of Legal Remedy

Myles Lavan

9.1 Introduction

This paper discusses the problem of adverse selection in the market for slaves in the Roman empire and the principal institutional response it elicited—legal norms that made the seller liable for latent defects.[1] My focus is on the limits of this well-known remedy in the particular context for which it was developed. I argue that the commodification of human beings always gives rise to an irreducible degree of quality uncertainty that cannot feasibly be mitigated by institutional solutions such as a system of guarantees. I will also suggest that the norm of liability for latent defects, far from being a dis-interested advance in legal sophistication, originated as a partisan innovation that served the interests of the politically dominant

[1] All translations of the *Digest* are from Watson 1998.

M. Lavan (✉)
University of St Andrews, St Andrews, UK
e-mail: mpl2@st-andrews.ac.uk

C. Rosillo-López, M. García Morcillo (eds.), *Managing Information in the Roman Economy*, Palgrave Studies in Ancient Economies,
https://doi.org/10.1007/978-3-030-54100-2_9

class. The paper draws on comparative evidence from the much better documented antebellum American South, which developed similar protections for buyers of slaves (taken directly from Roman law, in the case of Lousiana), to illustrate and explain the limits of the Roman legal remedies.

9.2 Adverse Selection

The problem of asymmetric information manifested itself in several ways in the slave market and the use of slave labour. The employment of slaves involved moral hazard—the phenomenon of agents acting against the interests of their principals because they cannot be monitored perfectly.[2] Giuseppe Dari-Mattiaci has recently used this principal-agent problem to explain variance in prevalence of manumission across different sectors of the labour market in the city of Rome.[3] He argues that the frequency of manumission in a sector is correlated with the degree of asymmetry of information between principal and agent, reflecting the use of manumission as a reward to mitigate the problem of moral hazard. This paper focuses on a different market pathology caused by asymmetric information—adverse selection.

The problem of adverse selection was highlighted by George Akerlof in his seminal discussion of asymmetric information.[4] Akerlof's paradigm was the market for used cars. Cars are an example of a good characterised by quality uncertainty. Most new cars are sound, but a few have serious manufacturing flaws. They are 'lemons' in American parlance. This does not pose a problem in the market for new cars, because neither buyer nor seller knows if a particular new car will turn out to be a lemon. The market price of a new car will be the marginal expected value of a new car, which incorporates the small risk of it being a lemon. The pathologies arise in the market for used cars, because the owner will have learned whether it is a lemon, while the prospective buyer will still be largely ignorant of its quality. The quality uncertainty is now asymmetric. At any market price, owners of lemons will be much more likely to put their cars on the market than owners of sound cars. There will thus be a higher prevalence of

[2] See Revilla's contribution to this volume.

[3] Dari-Mattiacci 2013, reframing the famous distinction (Fenoaltea 1984) between effort-intensive sectors (characterised by the use of pain incentives to motivate labour) and care-intensive sectors (characterised by the use of manumission and other rewards to motivate labour).

[4] Akerlof 1970. See also Revilla's contribution to this volume.

lemons in the used car market than among new cars. Buyers of used cars will adjust their expectations accordingly, incorporating the much higher risk of buying a lemon. This will depress the expected value of a used car relative to that of a new car, pushing down the price of used cars and making owners of sound cars even less likely to sell. Akerlof showed that equilibrium would be reached with a market that was both smaller in size and with lower average quality than would occur if the quality uncertainty was symmetric. Akerlof also discussed a number of potential remedies that could mitigate the problem, notably guarantees (which reduce quality risk by allowing buyers to recover any loss incurred by purchasing an inferior product), brands (which disincentivise sellers from exploiting the asymmetry by allowing buyers to retaliate) and licensing practices (by which the state or other institutions seek to ensure minimum quality standards).

Buyers of slaves faced quality uncertainty analogous to, but even greater than, Akerlof's paradigmatic example of used cars. Not only are human bodies much more various in their capacities and infirmities than are cars, there are also the vast imponderables involved in assessing the abilities and motivations of another human being. The uncertainty is again asymmetric: while an owner would have a good sense of a slave's quality, many important dimensions of quality would be entirely illegible to a prospective buyer. In discussing slave 'quality', it is essential not to fall into the ethical and historical trap of internalising the perspective of the slave-holding class. While it is necessary to conceptualise slaves as commodities in order to analyse the market for slaves, we should never take slave-owners' beliefs about slaves at face value. Slave-owning societies worked hard to persuade themselves not just that some human beings could be treated as property but also to reassure themselves that they had in fact reduced their slaves to objects under their control. The problem is particularly obvious with regard to the behavioural dimensions of quality uncertainty which will loom large in this paper. For a slave-owner, the quality of a slave was a function of observed characteristics such as obedience, diligence and initiative. Roman masters and jurists conceptualised these characteristics in terms of habit, moral character or even sanity. Troublesome slaves were seen as wicked or deranged. As historians, however, we should acknowledge that quality rather represents the slave-owners' interpretation of behaviour that emerged from a much more complex matrix of beliefs, preferences and calculations on the part of the slave. A 'good' slave might be one who had internalised the value system of the society of masters, accepting his or her moral duty to obey and serve; or one who had calculated that the regime of punishments and rewards made obedience the optimal strategy; or one who had strategically kept shirking, theft and resistance beneath the notice of the master and his overseers. When I write of slave 'quality', this should be taken as an analytical device, facilitating analysis in economic terms of the evaluations that loomed large in slave-owners' decisions to buy or sell slaves.

The market for slaves in the Roman empire must have shown considerable variation across the vast expanse of the empire and over the centuries of Roman rule.[5] The scale of slavery remains a major unknown, but it probably varied significantly between and within regions. One would expect the scale and complexity of local slave markets to have varied accordingly. In the best documented cases—most notably the city of Rome—intermediaries (slave dealers) played a major role, mediating between buyers and sellers of slaves (the latter including slave-owners, slavers and, in times of war, the state). But there must also have been private sales between slave-owners and these may have been more common in areas with smaller, less complex markets. Intermediaries probably had limited effect on the scale of adverse selection, since the crucial factor was slave-owners' propensity to divest themselves of more difficult or less productive slaves. A more important unknown is the structure of the slave supply. The share of warfare and entrepreneurial slaving in the slave supply should have affected the degree of adverse selection. If the vast majority of the slaves on the market had been sold on by previous masters, one would expect adverse selection to be pronounced. But if the vast majority of traded slaves were new captives, one would expect adverse selection to be more limited—though even in this case sellers of slaves would generally know more about the slaves than prospective buyers. This too must have varied over time, as intermittent warfare produced gluts of war captives, and between regions, since captives were probably funnelled towards the main centres of demand. But it is likely that slaves who had been sold on by a previous owner always remained a systemic feature of the slave market, even if there were periodic spikes in the supply of new captives.[6] Finally, the problem of adverse selection should have varied across different types of sale. For example, there should have been less scope for

[5] On the market for slaves and slave markets, see especially Chioffi 2010, Daguet-Gagey 2015: 552–9 and the articles in *JRA* 2005.

[6] On the slave supply, see Scheidel 1997, Harris 1999 and Harper 2011 ch. 2 (especially on slaving).

adverse selection in the liquidation of whole estates (e.g. after confiscation) than in the selective sale of individual slaves. On the whole, however, the market for slaves ought to have been particularly liable to adverse selection.

The legal landscape was similarly complex. This paper focuses on slave sales in Roman law. But it will become clear that the protections that Roman law offered buyers of slaves evolved considerably between their first introduction in the Middle Republic and their systematisation under Justinian. So too did their scope. At first limited to public markets in the city of Rome. they were subsequently extended to private sales and later become available across Italy and possibly also the provinces, though this remains the subject of debate.[7] In any case, in the provinces, Roman norms for the sale of slaves would have coexisted with those of other legal traditions in the regime of legal pluralism that existed before the universalisation of Roman citizenship in 212/213.[8] Indeed, some of these local usages may have persisted after Caracalla's grant.

9.3 The Aediles' Edict

Roman slave-owners and legal experts were well aware of the problem of asymmetric information in the slave market. One of the earliest developments in what became a sophisticated doctrine of the seller's liability for latent defects was the introduction by the curule aediles—probably in the late third or early second century BC—of legal remedies for persons who purchased defective slaves in the markets at Rome.[9] Sellers of slaves were required to declare any latent defects; buyers of a slave with an undeclared defect were given the right to return the slave for the price paid

[7] Jakab 1997: 119 n. 147, Daguet-Gagey 2015: 553.

[8] For example, it is noteworthy that contracts for the slave-sales in the province of Egypt seem to have often explicitly disclaimed warranty for flight, at least until the late second century (Artzt-Grabner 2010: 28–9).

[9] As with so much of the development of the rules on liability for defects, the date of the original introduction of the rules in *Dig.* 21.1.1.1 (Ulpian) is uncertain. An apparent reference to *redhibitio* in Plautus (*Merc.* 419) and a discussion of the category *morbosus* by Cato (cited at *Dig.* 21.1.10.1, Ulpian) suggest that the action for *redhibitio* of a defective slave was already possible in the early second century BC (de Senarclens 1923; Impallomeni 1955; Honoré 1959; Daguet-Gagey 2015: 623–4). But some date it as late as the early first century BC (e.g. Rogerson 1959: 116, Du Plessis 2010: 276). Jakab 1997: 128–9 is properly cautious.

(*redhibitio*) or to recover the monetary value of the defect (*actio quanti minoris*).[10] The protection of the buyer was particularly strong since the remedies were (or soon became) available against an ignorant seller: there was no requirement that the seller be aware of the defect.[11] In a series of subsequent developments, the chronology of which is profoundly uncertain, similar remedies were introduce for buyers of livestock, the protections were extended to private sales (not just those in public markets), the aedilician actions were generalised to all goods (possibly not until the time of Justinian) and some of the principles of the aedilician actions were incorporated into the civil law *actio empti* (which also had the effect of extending them to all goods).[12]

The famous Aediles' Edict is often represented as a natural response to the unscrupulousness of slave dealers.[13] But we should not take aristocratic stereotypes of the slave trade as an accurate description of economic behaviour. Stigmatising slave traders it is a typical way in which a class of paternalistic slave-owners seeks to insulate itself from the sordid commodification of human beings on which it depends.[14] 'Sharp practice' is unlikely

[10] *Dig.* 21.1, especially 21.1.1.1 (Ulpian). On the aediles' edict on the sale of slaves, see further Jakab 1997, Ernst 1999, Kupisch 2002 and Daguet-Gagey 2015 ch. 6.

[11] *Sciamus uenditorem, etiamsi ignorauit ea quae aediles praestari iubent, tamen teneri debere* (*Dig.* 21.1.1.2, Ulpian). Honoré 1959: 136 doubts that this principle of objective liability was present in the original edict and suggests that it was a later development. It was certainly established by Cicero's time (cf *scire debuit de sanitate* etc. at *Off.* 3.71).

[12] The Edict on cattle (*Dig.* 21.1.38.pr) was probably later than that on slaves, but still Republican (Kaser 1955–9: i 467; Rogerson 1959: 117). A quotation of Ulpian in the Digest states that the Augustan jurist Labeo already held that the Aediles Edict applied to the sale of all *res* (*Dig.* 21.1.1.pr with Honoré 1959: 139–40 and Parlamento 2003). In another passage, Ulpian himself asserts the same principle (*Dig.* 21.1.63). But others have rejected these texts as interpolations and held that the extension of the aedilician actions to all sales was an innovation of Justinianic law (Rogerson 1959: 117, Stein 1959: 102–11, Zimmermann 1990: 322, Jakab 1997:126 n. 16, Daguet-Gagey 2015:562). The development of the *actio empti* is discussed further below.

[13] 'Slave dealers were commonly dishonest and deceitful' (Rogerson 1959: 116). 'Slave-traders (*mangones*) were notoriously ill-reputed people, and thus one had to be particularly careful in one's dealings with them' (Zimmermann 1990: 311). 'The sharp practice of slave and cattle dealers prompted the issuing of edicts by the aediles' (Du Plessis 2010: 276). 'Le caractère volontiers dissimulateur et malhonnête des vendeurs devait ainsi conduire les magistrats et les experts en science juridique à tenter de prévenir leurs frauds et à les punir' (Daguet-Gagey 2015: 564). The idea goes back to Ulpian*: causa huius edicti proponendi est, ut occurratur fallaciis uendentium et emptoribus succurratur* (*Dig.* 21.1.1.2).

[14] See Johnson 1999: 24–30 on the American South. In the eyes of slave-owners, slave traders 'were family separators in a land of organic social relations, sharp dealers in a society

to have been the preserve of slave dealers alone. The root of the problem of adverse selection should have been slave-owners' incentive to preferentially sell on 'inferior' slaves. Hence, we should think harder about the interests served by this legal innovation. A doctrine that the seller is liable for latent defects is economically rational, insofar as it locates the risk with the party for whom acquiring information is least costly.[15] But it also has a redistributional effect, transferring risk from the buyer to the seller. It is worth asking why these protections were first developed specifically for buyers of slaves, at a time when the law of sale otherwise favoured sellers. It is surely no accident that the protections emerged at a time when the political elite were beginning to exploit their increasing wealth and the growing supply of slaves to shift towards intensive, market-oriented agriculture.[16] Slaves were both one of their largest expenses and a market in which they participated asymmetrically—predominantly as buyers rather than sellers of slaves. We might hypothesise that the aediles' intervention to redistribute risk in the slave market was driven by the imbalance of political influence between buyers and sellers in that market. This was certainly the case with similar developments in the American South. While the overall trend of English and American law of sale was towards the principle of caveat emptor, which favoured sellers of agricultural commodities, Southern legislatures and judges protected the interests of the slave-owning class that dominated politics and society by developing special protections for buyers of slaves.[17] Moreover, the degree of protection offered was correlated with the participation of local slave-owners in the slave market—strongest in South Carolina, a slave-importing state where slave-owners dealt with slave traders predominantly as buyers, and somewhat weaker in the Upper South, where slave productivity was lower and slave-owners regularly sold sales for export to higher-productivity regions.[18] As in the Roman case, protections developed to protect slave buyers were eventually extended by analogy to buyers of other goods.[19] In

of "honorable men", merchants of disease and disorder in an otherwise healthy social body. In the figure of the slave trader were condensed the anxieties of slaveholding society in the age of capitalist transformation: paternalism overthrown by commodification, honor corrupted by interest, and dominance infected with disorder' (25).

[15] Wahl 1998 ch. 2.

[16] Daguet-Gagey 2015: 561.

[17] Fede 1987; these protections are discussed further in the final section of this paper.

[18] South Carolina's 'sound price' is discussed further below.

[19] See Fede 1987: 327 on the 'sound price' rule in South Carolina.

both cases, however, the initial developments were far from neutral: they protected the interests of some economic actors at the expense of others.

The Aediles' Edict represents one of the classic institutional responses to the problem of adverse selection, as Bruce Frier and Dennis Kehoe observe in a recent survey of law and the economy: 'As is well known, the Curule Aediles, the magistrates in charge of the large-scale slave and livestock markets at Rome, attempted to counter the problem of asymmetrical information by establishing a new liability for sellers. ... The evident purpose of this new liability was to restore confidence in the market by giving buyers an opportunity to undo sales when the object of sale turned out to be defective.'[20] Besides encouraging reflection on the economic interests that the original innovation served, my focus in this paper is on the *limits* of these remedies in the context for which they were first devised—the market for slaves. I will argue that the commodification of human beings gives rise to an irreducible degree of quality uncertainty that cannot be mitigated by institutional solutions such as a system of guarantees. Human beings are far more complex than livestock or cars, and solutions that might be adequate in those markets will have more limited success in markets for human beings.

9.4 'Any Disease or Defect'

Our knowledge of the Aediles' Edict is almost entirely based on the compilation of jurisprudence in rubric 21.1 of Justinian's *Digest*.[21] The Edict required sellers of slaves to declare certain defects and gave the buyer actions against them if they failed to do so. The seller had to declare if the slave had any disease or defect (*quid morbi uitiiue*), was a runaway (*fugitiuus*) or a loiterer (*erro*) or entailed noxal liability (the owner's liability to a third party for a past action of the slave).[22] There were three further requirements that may be a slightly later addition: the seller had to declare if the slave had committed a capital crime, had attempted suicide or had been sent into the arena to fight wild animals (ibid).[23]

[20] Frier and Kehoe 2007: 120

[21] See also Cic. *Off.* 3.71, Gell. *NA* 4.2 and the so-called Romano-Syrian lawbook.

[22] *Dig.* 21.1.1.1 (Ulpian).

[23] Buckland 1908: 56. The chronology of developments from the original introduction of the edict to the late Republic is obscure. See Jakab 1997: 127–9 and Daguet-Gagey 2015: 567–81.

The interpretation of the generic protection against 'any disease or defect' (*quid morbi uitiiue*) was obviously crucial. The relatively few attempts at definition focus on the effect on the slave's usefulness.[24] What matters for this paper, however, is that there seems to have been an early consensus that they referred exclusively to physical qualities. According to Ulpian:

> Generally, the rule which we appear to observe is that the expression 'defect and disease' applies only in respect of physical defects; a vendor is liable in respect of a defect of mind (*animi uitium*) only if he undertake liability for it; otherwise, not. Hence, the express reservation of the wandering or runaway slave; for their defects are of the mind, not physical (*animi non corporis*). It is for this reason that there are those who say that animals prone to shy or kick are not to be accounted diseased; for such defects are of the mind, not the body.[25]

In the absence of express warranty (a matter I will return to), the Edict provided no remedy for buyers of slaves with 'mental defects'. This was a crucial qualification that limited the law's capacity to mitigate the problem of adverse selection in the slave market. As Ulpian's passing remark about animals illustrates, even in the livestock market quality is not just a matter of the health or disease of the animal, but extends to behavioural qualities that may not be attributable to a physical ailment. So the Edict could not even have fully addressed the problem of adverse selection in the livestock market, if as seems likely, owners preferentially chose to unburden themselves of difficult animals. This problem must have been incomparably

[24] *habitus cuiusque corporis contra naturam, qui usum eius (ad id) facit deteriorem* (Caelius Sabinus at Gell *NA* 4.2.3 and *Dig.* 21.1.1.7, Ulpian); *quod usum ministeriumque hominis impediat* (*Dig.* 21.1.1.8, Ulpian); cf. *quo ipse minus aptus sit* (Masurius Sabinus at Gell. *NA* 4.2.15). Most of the discussion in *Dig.* 21.1 is a 'wilderness of single instances' (Rogerson 1959: 121).

[25] *Dig.* 21.1.4.3 (Ulpian). See also 21.1.4.2 (Ulpian): *In summa si quidem animi tantum uitium est, redhiberi non potest, nisi si dictum est hoc abesse et non abest.* Ulpian attributes the same doctrine to his predecessor Vivianus (*magis enim de corporis sanitate, quam de animi uitiis promitti*, *Dig.* 21.1.1.9, Ulpian). Parlamento 2001: 6–7 discusses traces of arguments that sought to extend the concept of *uitium* to mental qualities that affected a slave's usefulness. She argues that medical theories of the four temperament were crucial to the eventual exclusion of *uitia animi* (as being a matter of character not pathology). I would speculate that their exclusion was also influenced by pragmatic concerns about the implications for security of sale like those that influenced the American jurists discussed in the final section of this paper.

greater in the case of slaves. For a slave-owner, the quality of a slave was a function not just of soundness of body, but also of skills (for which the edict did allow guarantees, to which I will return) and—crucially—behavioural qualities such as obedience, diligence and initiative.

The extensive jurisprudence in *Digest* 21.1 on the interpretation of 'disease or defect' can be taken as qualitative evidence for the problem of adverse selection in the slave market. The litany of examples of old, diseased and mutilated slaves suggests that masters did indeed use the slave market to offload themselves of less valuable slaves whose 'defects' were not immediately obvious to inspection. But the preferential sale of 'inferior' slaves will not have been limited to those with physical 'defects'. It can be assumed that masters would also preferentially sell slaves who they had found to be difficult, unreliable or ineffective. Indeed, some masters may have used sale as a punishment, threatening troublesome slaves with the prospect of being torn away from family and community, as in the American South, where 'I'll put you in my pocket' (i.e. trade you for cash) could be a threat.[26] To adequately address the problem of adverse selection in the slave market, the law would have had to offer a remedy for this arguably more important dimension of quality uncertainty.

9.5 Specific Behavioural Qualities Covered by the Edict

The Aedile's edict did provide remedies against certain behavioural 'defects', but these were limited to specific cases, unlike the general provision for 'any disease or defect'. As Ulpian noted, these were explicit exceptions to the rule that mental defects did not normally provide grounds for action. The Aediles required sellers to declare if a slave was a runaway (*fugitiuus*), a loiterer (*erro*), or brought noxal liability'.[27] The first two qualities concern behaviour, understood as the product of particular behavioural dispositions. The jurists interpreted a runaway (*fugitiuus*) to be any slave who had ever run away from his master. A slave who has once done so was assumed to be *fugax* and more likely to do so again. Hence the seller had to declare any history of flight. Failure to do so gave the unwitting purchaser access to the aedilican actions. The loiterer (*erro*) is a somewhat vaguer category. Ulpian glosses it as a slave 'who does not

[26] Dunaway 2001.

[27] *Dig.* 21.1.1.1 (Ulpian).

indeed run away but frequently indulges in aimless roaming and, after wasting time on trivialities, returns home at a late hour'.[28] It is striking that there is much less jurisprudence on this than on the more concrete *fugitiuus*. One suspects that it generally proved too vague to be actionable.

The Aediles' second list of qualifying defects added a third behavioural disposition: 'Again, vendors must declare at the time of sale all that follows: any capital offense (*capitalis fraus*) committed by the slave; any attempt which he has made upon his own life; and whether he has been sent into the arena to fight wild animals'.[29] The first item (having committed a capital offence) is analogous to noxal liability. It covered situations where a master sold a slave that had committed, but not yet been tried for, a criminal offence that was punishable by death, which would obviously reduce the slave's value to a new master.[30] The third item (having been made to fight with wild animals in the arena) also concerned a past event that might affect the value of the slave, though the mechanism is less clear; it was probably relevant because it was considered particularly degrading. The second (a history of attempting suicide) is different, because it was probably regarded as evidence of an undesirable behavioural disposition. A slave who had once attempted suicide might be expected to so again—with obvious implications for their value to a new master.[31] The key point is that the *fugitiuus*, the *erro* and the suicide were exceptional examples of behavioural dispositions for which the law offered the unwitting buyer a remedy. Ulpian's clear statement of the norm bears repeating: 'Generally, the rule which we appear to observe is that the expression "defect and disease" applies only in respect of physical defects. ... Hence, the express reservation of the wandering or runaway slave; for their defects are of the mind, not physical.'

Even in these cases, one might doubt the efficacy of the remedy. Besides the costs of bringing suit, the buyer always had to prove the defect. That was relatively straightforward in the case of physical defects. In the case of behavioural dispositions, however, the buyer seems to have had to prove that the slave had run away, loitered or attempted suicide under the previous owner (as opposed to having being 'corrupted' by the new master).[32]

[28] *Dig*. 21.1.17.14 (Ulpian).
[29] *Dig*. 21.1.1.1 (Ulpian).
[30] An overlapping remedy was provided by the *SC Pisonianum* (*Dig*. 29.5.8.pr, Paul.).
[31] Bellocci 1997.
[32] *Dig*. 22.3.4 (Paul.) (with Parlamento 2001: 18), *Cod. Iust*. 4.58.3pr.

Even in these three respects, masters' uncertainty about the quality of the slaves they were buying might not be wholly alleviated about the edict. But the more important point is that the Aediles' Edict offered no general solution to quality uncertainty arising from most aspects of slave behaviour.

9.6 Express Warranties

The Aediles' Edict did however protect the buyer if the seller made a false claim about a slave's behaviour. 'If a slave be sold without compliance with this regulation *or contrary to what has been said of or promised in respect of him (dictum promissumue) at the time of his sale* … we will grant to the purchaser and to all other interested parties an action for *redhibitio* in respect of the slave'.[33] Express *dicta* or *promissa* could extend to properties of the *animus*.

The very limited corpus of deeds of sale shows little or no evidence of parties offering generic warranties about character.[34] Most of the surviving examples merely stipulate against defects that were already covered by the Edict: that the slave is healthy, not a *fugitiuus* or *erro*, free from noxal liability.[35] A few add a guarantee against epilepsy, probably under the influence of Greek law, though this too would have been covered by the implicit warranty provided by the Edict.[36] Only two add an additional warranty about behaviour—in both cases a guarantee that the slave is not a thief. This admittedly small sample shows no evidence of generic warranties about character. Nevertheless, it is possible that such warranties were

[33] *Dig.* 21.1.1.1 (Ulpian).

[34] On this corpus, see further Jakab 1997:165–96 and Artzt-Grabner 2010.

[35] See, for example, *TPSulp.* 43 (… *fugit[i]uom [err]onem [non] esse [et] cetera ex edicto aed(ilis) cur(ulis)*, Puteoli AD 38), *AE* 2005 893 (*sanam traditam esse erronem fugitiuam non esse*, Londinium AD 75–125), *FIRA* iii 87 (*sanam esse a furtis noxisque solutam fugitiuam erronem non esse*, Alburnum Maior, Dacia AD 139), *FIRA* iii 132 (*sanum esse ex edicto*, Seleucia Pieria, AD 166). The description as *furtis solutum* in *FIRA* iii 87 (and *FIRA* iii 88 below, as well as the reference to *furtis* at Cic. *Off.* 3.71) probably concerns liability for theft, rather than being an additional commitment with regard to behaviour: see *Dig.* 50.16.174 (Ulpian) (*aliud est promittere 'furem non esse', aliud 'furto noxaque solutum'*) with Daguet-Gagey 2015: 578–9.

[36] See, for example, *FIRA* iii 133 (ὑγιῆ ἐκ διατάγματος [- ca. 14—ἀνέπα]φον πρὸς πάντων καὶ μήτε ῥέ[μβ]ο̣ν̣ μήτε δραπετικὸν ἱερᾶς τε νόσου ἐκτός, Side, AD 151), *P. Hamb*, 63 (ὑγιῆ ἐκ διατάγματος], [χ]ω̣ρὶς ἱερᾶς νόσου καὶ ἐ[παφῆς …], Thebais?, AD 124–5), *FIRA* iii 88 (*eum puerum sanum traditum esse furtis noxaque solutum erronem fugiti(u)um caducum non esse*, Alburnum Maior, Dacia, AD 142).

made orally. In the American South, for example, most litigation about slave character was based on claims that sellers had made an oral commitment about the slave's good character.[37] Oral claims of this sort would certainly be covered by the Edict's reference to *dicta*.

Yet the jurists' discussion of express warranties relating to behavioural qualities suggests that that they had to be very specific to be actionable—and hence could only address a small component of the buyer's uncertainty. Gaius opens his discussion with examples of what seem to be very broad warranties about character: 'that the slave is loyal or hard-working or diligent or vigilant' (*constantem aut laboriosum aut curracem uigilacem*).[38] He observes only that the seller should not be held to these commitments strictly (*amare*), without giving any sense of what would constitute a breach of such a warranty.[39] Instead, as examples of actionable warranties, he turns to much more concrete claims: that a slave is an outstanding cook or that he has amassed a *peculium*.[40] Even these are not to be interpreted too strictly: in the latter case, it would be sufficient that the slave has any *peculium* at all. Ulpian observes that there are all sorts of claims about character that are not actionable at all: 'We have, however, to realise that there are statements that a vendor might make which he does not have to validate, namely, those which simply extol the slave; for instance, that he is thrifty, upright and obedient (*frugi probum dicto audientem*).'[41] (It is not at all clear how these are qualitatively different from the examples of 'loyal or hard-working or diligent or vigilant' cited by Gaius.) To illustrate what is actionable, Ulpian falls back again on more concrete claims about past behaviour: 'The vendor would clearly be liable on an assertion that the slave is not a gambler (*aleator*) or a thief (*fur*) or that he has never sought refuge at the emperor's statue.'[42] Taken as a whole, the discussion suggests that any warranties generic enough to address a prospective buyer's uncertainty about a slave's behavioural dispositions would be too vague to be actionable.

[37] Gross 1995: 269.
[38] *Dig.* 21.1.18.pr (Gaius).
[39] Ibid.
[40] *Dig.* 21.1.18.1 (Gaius).
[41] *Dig.* 21.1.19.pr. (Ulpian).
[42] *Dig.* 21.1.19.1 (Ulpian).

9.7 The *Actio Empti*

There was one other remedy potentially available to buyers of slaves with undeclared and undesirable behavioural dispositions—the action on purchase (*actio empti*). When Ulpian states that the protection against 'any disease or defect' was normally interpreted as only applying to physical conditions, he notes that his predecessor Vivianus held the same view—but adds a significant qualification:

> Vivian says further that … [if a slave persistently engages in Bacchanalian revels] … it is still a mental, not a physical, defect and so constitutes no ground for rescission (*redhibitio*), because the aediles pronounce in respect of physical defects; *however, such facts give occasion for the action on purchase* (*actio empti*). Vivian says the same in respect of slaves who are excessively timorous, greedy or avaricious or quick-tempered (*qui praeter modum timidi cupidi avarique sunt aut iracundi*). … For all these defects, for which he says that rescission is not applicable, Vivian would give the action on purchase.[43]

The *actio empti* was a civil law action. It seems that already by the late republic it provided a remedy for buyers when a seller fraudulently failed to disclose a known defect or made express assurances that proved to be misleading (regardless of whether the seller intended to deceive). It seems to have undergone further development in the imperial period under the influence of the aedilician actions towards a doctrine of general liability for all defects even if the seller was unaware of them, though the chronology of the development is fraught.[44] Nevertheless, it seems that in the time of Vivianus and Ulpian, the *actio empti* did not yet cover defects of which the seller was ignorant. That is implicit in Ulpian's own remark on the matter:

> All in all, if the defect be only one of the mind, there will be no rescission, unless the vendor has stated that such defect does not exist when, in fact, it

[43] *Dig.* 21.1. 1.10–4.pr (Ulpian).

[44] It used to be held that this was an innovation of Justinianic law (Arangio-Ruiz 1978–80: 397–8, Stein 1959: 102–3)), but some now see its beginnings in the early empire (Honoré 1959: 137–40, Zimmermann 1990: 319–22, Hallebeek 2010: 178). The eventual outcome was considerable redundancy between the *actio empti* and the aedilician actions, though there were some important differences (e.g. there was a time limit on the aedilican actions but not on the *actio empti* and the latter would cover consequential losses in case of fraud). See Honoré 1959, Donadio 2008: 71–2, Du Plessis 2010: 278.

> does; an action on purchase, however, will lie, *if the vendor, knowing of such defect of mind, should not reveal it.*[45]

In the jurisprudence on the *actio empti* itself (*Dig.* 19.1), moreover, most of the discussion of slave sales concerns the actionability of claims the vendor made about a slave's *peculium*. There are only a handful of remarks about slave behaviour, almost all in relation to two relatively concrete categories—the runway (*fugitiuus*) and the thief (*fur*).[46] There is nothing to suggest that the gap left by the Aediles Edict was filled by the *actio empti* in the classical period. If it had been widely used to protect buyers of slaves against the risk of buying slaves with undesirable behavioural dispositions, one would have expected more jurisprudence about which undesirable characteristics were actionable. Though this is ultimately an argument from silence, it finds support in two further observations: the fact that buyers of slaves seem to have relied on very crude proxies for slave quality (suggesting considerable uncertainty about quality) and the parallel of the antebellum American South, where legislators and jurists drew the line at protecting buyers against latent defects related to slave character.

9.8 Proxies for Quality

The problem that quality uncertainty posed for buyers of slaves can be seen in the importance attributed to relatively crude proxies for quality, two of which were protected by law.[47] Ulpian says that sellers of slaves were obliged to declare the slaves' *natio* (origin): 'Those selling slaves should declare their *natio* when making the sale; for the slave's *natio* may often induce or deter a purchaser; therefore, we have an interest in knowing the *natio*; for there is a presumption that some slaves are good, coming from a *natio* with no bad repute, while others are thought bad, since they come from a notorious *natio*. If, then, the slave's *natio* be not declared, an action will be given to the purchaser and to all interested parties whereby the purchaser may return the slave.'[48] In other words, prospective buyers treated origin or ethnicity as a proxy for the character of

[45] *Dig.* 21.1.4.4 (Ulpian).

[46] *Dig.* 19.1.4.pr (*fur uel noxius*), 19.1.11.7 (*fugitiuus*), 19.1.13.1 (*fur aut fugitiuus*).

[47] Frier and Kehoe 2007: 121 discuss these as examples of 'signalling', another characteristic response to quality uncertainty.

[48] *Dig.* 21.1.31.21 (Ulpian).

the slaves they were buying.[49] This practice was so widespread and so important that it was given legal protection through a requirement that sellers of slaves disclose their ethnicity. Yet ethnicity could obviously only be a very crude proxy for quality, so the importance attributed to it indirectly testifies to the difficulty buyers faced in predicting slaves' behaviour.

The law also protected the use of another popular proxy: the distinction between the newly enslaved and those who had already served other masters. Again Ulpian explains both the law and the rationale: 'The aediles ordain that a slave of long standing is not to be sold as one newly enslaved. … It is assumed that the more recently he has been enslaved, the slave will be more malleable, more trainable to his function, more responsive to direction, and more adaptable to any service; on the other hand, it is difficult to retrain an experienced slave or one of long standing and to mould his habits.'[50] As Ulpian has it, newness is a proxy for docility; experienced slaves are assumed to be more recalcitrant.[51] This may well reflect adverse selection in the market for slaves: it is precisely what one would expect if slave-owners preferentially sold their more difficult slaves. In any case, the importance attached to this crude proxy again confirms that buyers of saves faced considerable quality uncertainty that was not mitigated by the various remedies provided by the Aediles' Edict and the *ius ciuile*.

9.9 'Pandora's Box': Explicit and Implicit Warranties for Slave 'Character' in the American South

The states of the American South developed similar remedies to protect buyers of slaves. There too, it proved very difficult to extend those protections to the aspects of quality uncertainty associated with slave 'character'. South Carolina offered the strongest protections. These were based on the 'sound price' rule developed by South Carolina judges, which held that

[49] Jakab 1997: 141.

[50] Dig. 21.1.37 (Ulpian). In the discourse of slavery 'newness' is used in several overlapping but distinct senses, including psychological (a newly enslaved slave), professional (an untrained slave) and fiscal (an imported slave). See Jakab 1997: 142 and Aubert 2011.

[51] Pliny the Elder's observation that slaves from overseas used to have their feet marked with chalk to distinguish them in the slave market (Plin. *HN* 35.199–201) can be understood in the same light. Sometimes interpreted as a mark of inferiority (e.g. Harrill 1995: 39), it may in fact have been a visual marker of a new slave (assuming that most foreign slaves were captives) and hence a signal of quality.

selling for a 'sound price' (i.e. a fair price) raised an implicit warranty of the 'soundness' of the thing sold. The judge who first articulated the rule held that 'this warranty extends to all faults, known and unknown to the seller'.[52] But courts soon decided that it was impracticable to apply it to faults of 'moral character' in the slave market. The limitation was established by Judge Abraham Nott in 1821, on grounds that bear quoting:

> The impossibility of fixing any scale by which the moral qualities can be graduated, is a conclusive reason why such a principle should not be allowed. The character of a slave depends so much upon the treatment he receives, the opportunities he has to commit crimes, and the temptation to which he is exposed, that we can form but a very imperfect opinion of it, abstracted from those considerations. A vice which would render him worthless in one situation, would scarcely impair his value in another. A habit that would render him useless to one man, would scarcely be considered a blot upon his character in the hands of another. If it should be extended to one fault, it must to all, from the highest crime which man is capable of committing, down to the smallest deviation from the strictest line of moral rectitude. Such a decision from this court, when publicly known, would be worse than opening Pandora's box upon the community. I am satisfied, therefore, that such a defence ought not to be allowed, except where it is supported by an express warranty or actual fraud.[53]

His judgement established a key limitation on the scope of the 'sound price' rule as regards slaves.

Most other Southern states rejected the sound price rule, but they did require sellers to disclose to the buyer any defects that they were aware of at the time of sale—contrary to the caveat emptor principle.[54] Moreover, across the South, most slave contracts included an explicit warranty of soundness, 'sound in body and mind and a slave for life' being the normal formula.[55] This is much more sweeping than the more specific declarations found in Roman contracts, but the warranty of mental 'soundness' was nevertheless normally interpreted narrowly as applying specifically to mental capacity (the ability to perform the ordinary duties of a slave) rather

[52] The rule was articulated in the judgement on Timrod v. Schoolbred (South Carolina, 1793), discussed at Fede 1987: 331–2.

[53] Smith v. McCall (South Carolina, 1821), quoted at Fede 1987: 333–4.

[54] Fede 1987: 340–50.

[55] Gross 1995: 268 n. 2.

than character.[56] Buyers could sue if the seller had made a more specific representation about the slave's character, but this was never straightforward. For example, a buyer in Alabama sued because a slave who was said to be 'honest and industrious' turned out to be 'a lazy liar'. The trial court rejected the evidence for the slave's character, though this was eventually reversed on appeal and the buyer secured damages.[57] Other buyers had difficulty proving that any defect of character was not the result of their own mismanagement of the slave since purchase.[58]

One state that is a particularly interesting for the Roman case is Louisiana, with its civil law tradition. Lousiana took its warranty law from the Napoleonic Code, but supplemented it with Roman law for slave sales.[59] Like South Carolina, it established an implicit warranty for latent defects, based in this case not on the 'sound price' rule but on the aedilician action for *redhibitio*. Unlike in South Carolina, the implicit warranty did extend to 'vices of character.'[60] But these vices of character were narrowly confined to specific categories (which show the influence of Roman law and practice): 'The vices of character are confined to the cases in which it is proved that the slave has committed a capital crime; or, that he is addicted to theft; or, that he is in the habit of running away.'[61] It was not necessarily straightforward to prove these even defects. In 1820, for example, a buyer brought a case for redhibition on the grounds that a slave was 'a drunk, runaway and thief'. His case was rejected by the trial court and the Supreme Court, which noted that it was not sufficient to prove regular theft, since theft was endemic among slaves: 'It is well known that most slaves will steal small articles from their owners as well as others when they find an opportunity. … If sales were set aside for that, there would be no security in slave sales.'[62]

[56] Morris 1996: 109–10.

[57] Cozzins v. Whittaker (Alabama, 1833) with Wahl 1998: 39.

[58] Gross 1995: 284–8, Wahl 1998: 39.

[59] Schafer 1987.

[60] Schafer 1987. Madness was also covered as a 'physical vice'. See Gross 1995: 291–5 on the 'medicalisation' of 'defects' in slaves.

[61] *Civil Code of the State of Louisiana* (1825) art. 2505 (cf art. 79 of the preceding *Digest of 1808*: 'The redhibitory vices and defects inherent in the disposition of slaves shall hereafter be limited to cases where it is proved that the slave has been guilty of some capital crime, or that he is addicted to robbery, or in the habit of running away').

[62] Chretien v Theard (Louisiana, 1822), quoted by Schafer 1987: 319.

In short, despite the development of norms that were very favourable to buyers of slaves, Southern legislatures and courts were consistently reluctant to extend those protections to behavioural dimensions of quality, unless the seller volunteered a warranty—and even then the buyer might have difficulty holding them to their representations. To do so would have 'opened Pandora's box', allowing potentially unlimited scope for complaint and undermining all security in slave sales.

Even with the better data of the nineteenth century American South and the Caribbean, it has not been possible to prove conclusively that there was adverse selection in the slave. Some tests suggest considerable adverse selection; others suggest little or none.[63] But the tests themselves are still relatively crude. In the absence of better evidence, we have little choice but to fall back on a priori arguments. Markets vary in the degree to which they are liable to distortion by adverse selection, depending on the extent of quality variation that is latent rather than obvious to an observer. Ackerlof's paradigm was the market for used cars, though he also discussed the insurance market, where the problems are even more severe. Even with the sophisticated economic institutions of modern western economies, residual pathologies remain. Markets for slaves must always have ranked high in their liability to adverse selection. Human beings are far more complex than livestock or cars, and solutions that might be adequate in those markets will have more limited success in markets for human beings. The level of adverse selection in particular slave markets should be related to the structure of the slave supply (the higher the proportion of

[63] Greenwald and Glasspiegel 1983 posited that adverse selection would mean that buyers in high-productivity states such as Louisiana would pay more for slaves imported from low-productivity states in the Old South than for local slaves because they anticipated more adverse selection in the local slave market. Testing the hypothesis against slave sale data from New Orleans 1830–60, they found that local slaves were indeed valued 20–40% less than imported slaves, indicating an adverse selection effect. Yet Pritchett and Chamberlain 1993 devised a different test that failed to find any adverse selection in the same data. They posited that adverse selection would cause buyers to pay a premium for slaves sold at estate sales (where these was no scope for adverse selection) compared to those voluntarily sold by their owners (when there might be adverse selection). They found no significant price difference. (Cf Pritchett and Smith 2013 for a third test, this time with the hypothesis that adverse selection would mean that slaves who were resold within a short period (8 months) would sell at a discount in the second sale, again with negative results). But, using a similar test, Dionne, St-Amour and Vencatachellum 2009 found that a significant premium of c. 45% was paid at estate sales in Mauritius 1825–7, concluding that the market expected slaves sold in voluntary sales to be of predominantly lower quality.

resale between slave-owners, the greater the effect) and to the degree of legal protection provided to buyers. But even regimes that provide relatively strong protection, such as antebellum South Carolina and Louisiana or the Roman Empire, were limited in their capacity to mitigate the effects of quality uncertainty, because it was not feasible to address the behavioural aspect of quality without undermining security of sale.

9.10 Conclusion

Like all markets for slaves, the slave markets of the Roman Empire ought to have been particularly liable to adverse selection. Scattered qualitative evidence seems to confirm the hypothesis. The numerous and varied examples of slaves with undeclared physical and mental 'defects' cited by the jurists in their discussion of the aedilician actions suggest that slave-owners did indeed attempt to sell on less valuable slaves on the assumption that buyers would not notice the difference. So too does the apparent prevalence of the stereotype that slaves who had been sold on by a previous master were likely to be recalcitrant.

Roman magistrates were clearly conscious of the problem and introduced legal remedies to protect buyers of slaves, probably in the late third century BC and probably because of the unequal political influence of buyers and sellers of slaves. These protections gradually expanded in scope from their first introduction to their systematisation under Justinian on a timeline that remains highly obscure (particularly as regards the development of parallel remedies through the *actio empti*). They also expanded in their reach, from public markets in the city of Rome to, eventually, all sales in the Roman Empire. But there were limits to what these Roman norms could achieve. The Aediles' Edict should have mitigated some of the effects of quality uncertainty related to possible physical ailments, but it could do little about the significant problem of quality uncertainty concerning slave 'character', beyond the three specific behaviours explicitly covered by the Edict (running away, loitering and attempting suicide). It seems very unlikely that express warranties or later developments in the *actio empti* filled this gap. As in nineteenth century Louisiana, classical Roman law probably left slave-buyers little scope for remedy if they were dissatisfied with the 'character' of slaves they purchased. Of course, warranties are only one possible response to the problem of adverse selection. The use of proxies for quality is another, but they are obviously of limited effectiveness when they are as crude as those mentioned by the Roman jurists. Other possibilities include institutions that might facilitate the development of trust in the context of repeated transactions. Given the very low esteem in which slave dealers were held in the Roman Empire, however, it is unlikely that trust offered a significant solution in this market.

Did it matter? The problem of adverse selection clearly did not prevent the emergence of massive markets in slaves in the Roman Empire or the American South. But it should have affected the efficiency of the market in an economic sense. First, it should have had the normal effect of holding supply and demand below their economically optimal level. In this case, oddly, we might think of this as a modest but beneficial effect. In a world with perfect information, slave-owners would have been able to optimise their income by trading slaves more frequently than they actually did. Secondly, it has implications for any attempt we might make to assess the profitability of slaves or the calculus of the choice between free and slave labour. The calculation would have to take account of the fact that the expected productivity of slaves on the market would be somewhat lower than the average productivity of slaves in the economy.[64] But there are real limits to what can be done with this insight without quantification of the degree of adverse selection in the market—which is clearly impossible in the Roman case.

The phenomenon of adverse selection also illustrates one of the limits of the practice of slavery. In both the Roman Empire and the American South, we can observe jurists and legislators grappling with the contradiction at the heart of slavery: the fact that slaves are treated as property when it is clear that they are human beings.[65] They certainly succeeded in commodifying slave bodies, such that they could be bought and sold, their quality assessed and 'defects' identified and evaluated. They would have liked to similarly commodify slaves' obedience and diligence such that they too could be valued and guaranteed, but jurists have repeatedly found that it is hardly practical to do so. The project of commodifying human beings founders when it moves from bodies to emotion and volition.

Bibliography

Akerlof, G.A. 1970. The Market for 'Lemons': Quality Uncertainty and the Market Mechanism. *The Quarterly Journal of Economics* 84: 488–500.

[64] Greenwald and Glasspiegel 1983: 496.

[65] See also Aubert 2011.

Arangio-Ruiz, V. 1978–1980. *La compravendita in diritto romano*. Naples.

Artzt-Grabner, P. 2010. 'Neither a Truant Nor a Fugitive': Some Remarks on the Sale of Slaves in Roman Egypt and Other Provinces. In *Proceedings of the Twenty-Fifth International Congress of Papyrology (Ann Arbor, July 29 – August 4, 2007)*, ed. T. Gagos and A. Hyatt, 21–32. Ann Arbor.

Aubert, J.-J. 2011. *Vitia animi*: Tares mentales, psychologiques, caractérielles et intellectuelles des esclaves en droit romain. In *I diritti degli altri in Grecia e a Roma*, ed. A. Maffi and L. Gagliardi, 236–248. Sankt Augustin.

Bellocci, N. 1997. Il tentato suicidio del servo: aspetti socio-familiari nei giuristi dell'ultima epoca dei severi. *Studia et Documenta Historiae et Iuris* 63: 259–268.

Buckland, W.W. 1908. *The Roman Law of Slavery: The Condition of the Slave in Private Law from Augustus to Justinian*. Cambridge: The Cambridge University Press.

Chioffi, L. 2010. Congressus in venalicio: spazi urbani e mercato degli schiavi a Capua e a Roma. *Mélanges de l'École française de Rome. Antiquité* 122: 503–524.

Daguet-Gagey, A. 2015. *Splendor aedilitatum: l'édilité à Rome (Ier s. avant J.-C.- IIIe s. après J.-C.)*. Rome.

Dari-Mattiacci, G. 2013. Slavery and Information. *Journal of Economic History* 73 (1): 79–116.

de Senarclens, A. 1923. La date de l'édit des édiles *de mancipiis vendundis*. *Revue d'histoire du droit* 4: 384–400.

Dionne, G., P. St-Amour, and D. Vencatachellum. 2009. Asymmetric Information and Adverse Selection in Mauritian Slave Auctions. *Review of Economic Studies* 76 (4): 1269–1295.

Donadio, N. 2008. Garanzia per i vizi della cosa e responsabilità contrattuale. In *Kaufen nach Römischem Recht: Antikes Erbe in den europäischen Kaufrechtsordnungen*, ed. E. Jakab and W. Ernst, 61–82. Berlin.

Du Plessis, P.J. 2010. *Borkowski's Textbook on Roman Law*. 4th ed. Oxford: Oxford University Press.

Dunaway, W.A. 2001. Put in Master's Pocket: Interstate Slave Trading and the Black Appalachian Diaspora. In *Appalachians and Race: The Mountain South from Slavery to Segregation*, ed. J.C. Inscoe, 116–132. Lexington: University Press of Kentucky.

Ernst, W. 1999. Neues zur Sachmängelgewährleistung aufgrund des Ädilenedikts. *Studia Zamorensia* 116: 208–221.

Fede, A. 1987. Legal Protection for Slave Buyers in the U.S. South: A Caveat Concerning *caveat emptor*. *American Journal of Legal History* 31: 322–358.

Fenoaltea, S. 1984. Slavery and Supervision in Comparative Perspective. *Journal of Economic History* 44: 635–688.

Frier, B.W., and D.P. Kehoe. 2007. Law and Economic Insitutions. In *The Cambridge Economic History of the Greco-Roman World*, ed. W. Scheidel, I. Morris, and R.P. Saller, 113–143. Cambridge: Cambridge University Press.

Greenwald, B.C., and R.R. Glasspiegel. 1983. Adverse Selection in the Market for Slaves: New Orleans, 1830–1860. *Quarterly Journal of Economics* 98 (3): 479–499.

Gross, A. 1995. Pandora's Box: Slave Character on Trial in the Antebellum Deep South. *Yale Journal of Law & the Humanities* 7 (2): 267–316.

Hallebeek, J. 2010. The Ignorant Seller's Liability for Latent Defects: One *regula* or Various Sets of Rules? In *The Creation of the Ius Commune: from Casus to Regula*, ed. J.W. Cairns and P.J. Du Plessis, 175–217. Edinburgh: Edinburgh University Press.

Harper, K. 2011. *Slavery in the Late Roman World, AD 275–425*. Cambridge: Cambridge University Press.

Harrill, J.A. 1995. *The Manumission of Slaves in Early Christianity*. Tübingen: Mohr Siebeck.

Harris, W.V. 1999. Demography, Geography and the Sources of Slaves. *Journal of Roman Studies* 89: 62–75.

Honoré, A.M. 1959. The History of the Aedilitian Actions from Roman to Roman-Dutch Law. In *Studies in the Roman Law of Sale: Dedicated to the Memory of Fraqncis De Zulueta*, ed. D. Daube, 132–159. Oxford: Clarendon Press.

Impallomeni, G. 1955. *L'editto degli edili curuli*. Padua.

Jakab, É. 1997. *Praedicere und cavere beim Marketkauf: Sachmängel im griechischen und römischen Recht*. Munich.

Johnson, W. 1999. *Soul by Soul: Life Inside the Antebellum Slave Market*. Cambridge, MA: Harvard University Press.

Kaser, M. 1955–9. *Das römische Privatrecht*. Munich.

Kupisch, B. 2002. Römische Sachmängelhaftung: Ein Beispiel für die ökonomische Analyse des Rechts'? *Legal History Review* 70: 21–54.

Morris, T.D. 1996. *Southern Slavery and the Law, 1619–1860*. Chapel Hill: University of North Carolina.

Parlamento, E. 2001. *Servus melancholicus*: I vitia animi nella giurisprudenza classica. *Rivista di diritto romano* 1: 1–20.

———. 2003. Labeone e l'estensione della redhibitio all'actio empti. *Rivista di diritto romano* 3: 10.

Pritchett, J.B., and R.M. Chamberlain. 1993. Selection in the Market for Slaves: New Orleans, 1830–1860. *Quarterly Journal of Economics* 108: 461–473.

Pritchett, J.B., and M. Smith. 2013. Sequential Sales as a Test of Adverse Selection in the Market for Slave. *Journal of Economic History* 73: 477–497.

Rogerson, A. 1959. Implied Warranty Against Latent Defects in Roman and English Law. In *Studies in the Roman Law of Sale: Dedicated to the Memory of Fraqncis De Zulueta*, ed. D. Daube, 112–131. Oxford: Oxford University Press.

Schafer, J.K. 1987. 'Guaranteed Against the Vices and Maladies Prescribed by Law': Consumer Protection, the Law of Slave Sales, and the Supreme Court in Antebellum Louisiana. *American Journal of Legal History* 31: 306–321.

Scheidel, W. 1997. Quantifying the Source of Slaves in the Early Roman Empire. *Journal of Roman Studies* 87: 156–169.

Stein, P. 1959. Medieval Discussion of the Buyer's Actions for Physical Defects. In *Studies in the Roman Law of Sale: Dedicated to the Memory of Fraqncis De Zulueta*, ed. D. Daube, 102–111. Oxford: Oxford University Press.

Wahl, J.B. 1998. *The Bondsman's Burden: An Economic Analysis of the Common Law of Southern Slavery*. Cambridge: Cambridge University Press.

Watson, A., ed. 1998. *The Digest of Justinian*. Rev. ed. Philadelphia: University of Pennsylvania Press.

Zimmermann, R. 1990. *The Law of Obligations: Roman Foundations of the Civilian Tradition*. Cape Town: Juta & Co.

PART V

Trade and Financial Markets

CHAPTER 10

Information Landscapes and Economic Practice in the Roman World

Miko Flohr

In assessing the role of asymmetric information in the Roman economy, two questions are fundamental. First, there is the question of the ways in which asymmetric information actually impacted on everyday economic processes, and which institutions or ways of doing things emerged to protect the interests of both parties in a transaction. Second, there is the question of the extent to which the shape or structure of markets in the Roman world and the way in which these developed over time, impacted on the role that asymmetric information actually could play in everyday economic practice. While most other chapters in this volume focus on issues related to the first question, the present chapter explores the second, starting from the idea that it is important to consider the ways in which increasing economic integration in the Roman world, particularly in the Western Mediterranean, changed the playing field for people buying and selling things, and how this affected the role of asymmetric information.

M. Flohr (✉)
Universiteit Leiden, Leiden, The Netherlands
e-mail: m.flohr@hum.leidenuniv.nl

C. Rosillo-López, M. García Morcillo (eds.), *Managing Information in the Roman Economy*, Palgrave Studies in Ancient Economies,
https://doi.org/10.1007/978-3-030-54100-2_10

Two starting assumptions underlie the argument of this chapter. The first of these is that there is a negative relation between the quality of the circulation of information and the potential role of information asymmetries—real or imagined—in market transactions: if more, and better information is circulating, individual sellers and buyers have to be prepared to be dealing with buyers and sellers that were relatively well-informed; if less information is circulating, or the reliability of information is low, individual sellers and buyers can expect to be dealing with buyers and sellers that are less well-informed, thus opening up the possibility to exploit information asymmetries.[1] For instance, suppose an itinerant *vestiarius* selling clothes in several places in the Roman world—a figure well attested in the epigraphic record.[2] As is clear from Diocletian's Prices' Edict, a wide variation of cloaks and tunics could be on offer on local markets, and these could differ in their material and the quality of weaving, and could be associated with widely varying in prices.[3] Evaluating the quality of what was on offer required knowledge and, to some extent, a trained eye: buyers would have to evaluate the cloak(s) on offer on the basis of (a) what the *vestiarius* in question tells them and (b) what they can see with their own eyes and feel with their hands. Yet there may be quite a bit of visual and even tactile similarity between textiles representing a quite different value. As a consequence, buyers who have a lot of knowledge—for example, because they have recently seen other *vestiarii* with similar products and thus can compare quality and prices, or who live in an environment where many people are buying such products—will be in a better position to negotiate a fair price than inexperienced buyers who have more limited access to such information. Thus, for a travelling *vestiarius*, there would be considerably less room to exploit possible asymmetries of information in circumstances where they are likely to encounter well-informed buyers, though at the same time, a thicker market also makes it a bit easier to coordinate prices with colleagues. What is true for tunics and cloaks is in fact true for a broad range of goods, including foodstuffs—when potential buyers have regular access to good information about the level of prices for wheat, oil or wine, there is less room for sellers to exploit any superior

[1] On the role of product and pricing information in the dynamics between buyers and sellers see Akerlof 1970, with Dari-Matiacci et al. 2011.

[2] On *vestiarii* see, for example, Buonopane 2003; Menella 2000.

[3] See the long lists of prices in *Ed. Diocl.* 19 (wool, 73 lines) and 26 (linen, >140 lines).

knowledge of market prices that they may have than in places where potential buyers: had more limited access to good information.

The other assumption underlying this chapter is that information circulates most easily through space via direct encounters between individuals and thus, ceteris paribus, spreads more easily in environments and regions where such direct encounters are more likely to occur, and are more likely to occur between people that do not belong to each other's personal sphere: information may spread easily within households and families, but to have a real impact on the role of information asymmetry in the economy, information, for example, about prices, or about the reliability of certain individual traders, would also need to spread, with relative ease, through the local community, and, ideally, between local communities. Obviously, there may be cultural and strategic factors inhibiting the circulation of economic information between different social groups, but as these will have varied only to a limited extent within the Roman Empire, two basic factors seem to be of key significance for the circulation of information: the sheer proximity of larger quantities of people, and the likelihood that these people encountered each other on a regular basis and had incentives to share information. This points to the importance of understanding the spatial (and temporal) dynamics of information networks, both on the macro-scale—between communities—and on the micro-scale—within communities.

The crucial role of (information) networks in everyday economic practice has, in very general terms, been broadly acknowledged by most economic historians of the Roman world: ever since Horden and Purcell's *The Corrupting Sea*, 'connectivity' has been a central concept in discourse on trade and transport over longer distances.[4] There has been ample debate about the (bad) quality of economic information in many places in the Roman Empire, and about the shortcomings of information circulation—there is ample evidence that even between neighboring cities, crucial information was not always circulating.[5] Yet, while the shortcomings of information circulation in the Greco-Roman Mediterranean may be evident, there has been very limited debate about the way in which these developed under the specific circumstances brought about by the Roman Empire. Indeed, a lot of the discourse about connectivity, traffic, and transport has remained rather theoretical in nature, and has focused on the

[4] Horden and Purcell 2000.

[5] Bang 2008: 137–138.

general problems with movement and transport over longer distances over land, river, and sea, without a lot of sensitivity to the emerging geographical realities of the Roman world.[6] Thus, there has been a lot of debate about the differences in cost, speed, and reliability between road, river, and maritime traffic, but mostly independent of real places and real traffic routes, even if occasional observations have been made.[7] This essentially even applies to Scheidel's model of the 'shape' of the Roman world which analyzes these theoretical considerations geographically, using a simplified model of the Roman world, that does not incorporate key demographic realities like the spread of urbanism.[8] It may be argued that, in debates about trade and markets in the Roman world, there also has been a certain (implicit) tendency to conflate the movement of goods with the movement of information, while in reality, goods and information may move by different means and at different speeds between similar places, with the movement of information being significantly less complicated—particularly, using lots of roads is less of an issue if you are not carrying anything. This means that price information may travel much faster than the products themselves, particularly in the case of bulk goods. Secondly, it can be argued that the focus of discourse on information circulation has remained firmly on the macro-scale—that is, on the movement of information over longer distances—without a lot of consideration for the ways in which information might have travelled on the micro-scale: recent discourse has emphasized inter-city movement, but it has had a lot less to say about the movement of information *within* cities or between cities and the surrounding countryside. Yet the circulation of information in smaller geographical contexts is not intrinsically straightforward. Particularly for economic actors operating outside their immediate social sphere, a range of practical problems began upon entering a foreign city gate, perhaps the simplest of which was finding out the way to the *forum*. Even if there were ways around this for traders, for instance by forging carefully maintained ties of trust and friendship in a range of communities, or by grouping together in trading associations, there also were occasions when traders or other economic actors arrived at a place where they had to start

[6] See esp. Bang 2008, but also Morley 2007a, 2007b, and, on the other side of the interpretative spectrum, Temin 2013.

[7] See esp. Adams 2012.

[8] Scheidel 2014.

more-or-less from scratch and had little knowledge of the local market situation in advance.[9]

It may be argued that what is lacking from the debate is, essentially, a proper network perspective on the spatial circulation of information. This chapter will explore such a network perspective, focusing on the nature of the ties between places and people, and on the nature of the dots connecting these ties. It will discuss the historical geography of information networks in the Roman world, and how the way in which the Roman world developed changed the ways in which these information networks functioned. To some extent, information simply followed the movement of goods, and it will not need elaborate argumentation that trade-routes serving the needs of major consumption centers—the Roman Metropolis, which dominated Mediterranean trade networks, and the legions on the frontiers along the Rhine and the Danube—could easily serve as information highways.[10] However, there were consumers elsewhere in the empire as well, and these equally constituted markets that could be targeted by *vestiarii* and other traders. A more challenging question is how information networks worked and developed in these contexts. One way to approach this issue is by looking at how actual social ties were used to bridge larger geographical gaps—Wim Broekaert has, in recent years, done valuable work on this aspect the Roman economy, and so have several others.[11] This chapter will, however, approach these information networks through their actual geographical shape, assessing the way in which the ties of these networks were connected at the points where they came together—in cities, through physical urban infrastructure. It will argue that over time, changes to both the geographical shape and the nodal infrastructure of information networks in the Roman world were dramatic—through road construction, the foundation or emergence of new urban settlements, and urban construction activity—and that this transformed both the information landscape and the role of asymmetric information in the Roman economy.

[9] Cf. Bang 2008: 137 on the problem of pre-industrial merchants not having accurate market information on arrival in a city.

[10] See, for example, Erdkamp 2005: 190: "good information on market conditions was much easier to obtain along the busy shipping lanes than on isolated coasts".

[11] Broekaert 2013, 2015. See also recent discourse on trading communities Bang 2008: 239–89; Rice 2016; Terpstra 2013; Verboven 2011.

10.1 Urban Networks

Starting at the macro-scale, it should be observed that, even if the city over time became a key phenomenon in virtually all parts of the Roman world, the actual evidence for urban culture is not equally divided over Rome's imperial geography.[12] In substantial parts of the Roman Empire cities remained few, and often far in between, even in the imperial period; at the same time, there were several regions where urbanism was booming, with many towns emerging at a sometimes very close distance of each other; several regions fell between these two extremes, with urban centers at regular intervals, but not necessarily within each other's direct environment. Figure 10.1 shows a distribution map of the evidence for urban culture. It has been compiled on the basis of epigraphic and archaeological evidence for key aspects of Roman urban culture, including bathing, euergetism, spectacles, spectacle architecture, and monetary culture. The inscriptions have been collected in the two leading epigraphic databases of the moment, the *Epigraphische Datenbank Clauss Slaby* and the *Packard Humanities Searchable Greek Inscriptions*, based on a range of searches.[13] The archaeological evidence, including theaters, amphitheaters, stadiums, hippodromes and public bath buildings, was compiled on the basis of the catalogues that have been published over the course of the past decades.[14] While not all inscriptions and buildings have been easily or precisely dated, both the epigraphic and the archaeological evidence have a chronological emphasis on the first two centuries AD, and essentially conform to the picture emerging from earlier scholarship.[15] The map uses a grayscale to highlight the density in the number of places where evidence is found: darker colors indicate a larger concentration of places—mostly cities,

[12] The most recent book-length survey on Roman urban geography is Hanson 2016.

[13] Search terms used, by category: monetary culture: *pecunia sua, sua pecunia, denarius, HS, nummus* (EDCS); ἐκ τῶν ἰδιων, δηναριον (SGI); statuary: *statua* (EDCS); ἀγάλμα, ἀνδριας, εἰκῶν (SGI); spectacle architecture: *amphitheatrum, circus, theatrum* (EDCS); θεάτρον, σταδίον (SGI). Spectacles: *ludus, spectaculum, venatio* (EDCS); ἀγων, ἀγωνοθετης, θεωρία (SGI); bathing: *thermae, bal(i)neum* (EDCS); βαλανεῖον, γυμνάσιον (SGI). The total amount of inscriptions underlying the map of Fig. 10.1 is 11.591. A full overview of the database used, and a live version of the map in Fig. 10.1 are available via http://www.mikoflohr.org/romanworld/

[14] For example, Golvin 1988; Humphrey 1986; Manderscheid 1988, 2004; Sear 2006; Welch 1998. The total amount of baths and spectacle buildings underlying the map of Fig. 10.1 is 1.501.

[15] See, for example, Wilson 2011: 163–167; Jouffroy 1986.

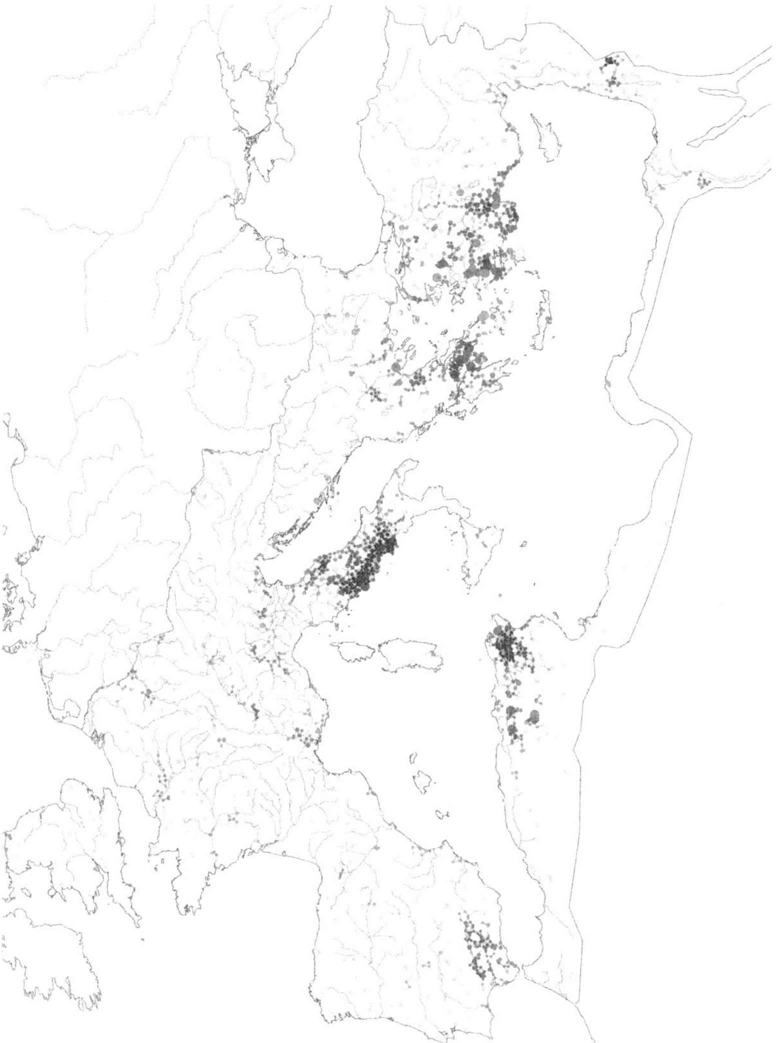

Fig. 10.1 Map of the Roman world with the spread of evidence for Roman urban culture. (Map: Miko Flohr)

sanctuaries or isolated bath spas.[16] The emerging picture is clearest in the western half of the empire, where one can easily spot three clearly articulated clusters of urbanism:

- Central Italy, basically from the Bay of Naples in the south up to Rimini in the North. This is a very dense cluster, organized around the plains of Latium and Campania, and the Tiber Valley, but including large sections of the northern Apennines, and focused strongly on the road network.
- The North part of Africa Proconsularis, with a dense scatter of settlements around the Bagradas basin and the immediate hinterland of Carthage, that to some extent continues in northern Numidia, albeit less dense—again, this cluster appears to have been organized around overland connections, and mostly lacks direct connections to the coast.
- Baetica, with a dense cluster of mostly small cities in the Guadalquivir basin, which is at two points connected to the coast of the Mediterranean (at Carteia and Malaca), but otherwise organized around a network of roads.

Besides these three key clusters of urbanism, zones of less densely clustered evidence include northern Italy, particularly Transpadana, and the lower valley and delta of the Rhone. Otherwise, however, large parts of the Iberian Peninsula, Roman Europe, and Britain appear much less densely urbanized, and the same holds true for the western part of Roman Africa, Southern Italy, and Sicily. In the eastern half of the empire, the picture is comparable, with densely urbanized zones in Greece and Asia Minor, and much less densely urbanized zones in Anatolia and in large parts of the Near East.

In terms of the spread of urbanization and urban culture, there were thus sharp differences within the Roman world, and this has implications for ways in which information could circulate at the supra-local level. Within the clusters in Italy, Africa and Baetica, circumstances for the free circulation of information were relatively good. Urban centers were often

[16] The density of settlements was measured by counting, for each settlement, the number of settlements within a radius of 30 km as the crow flies. This distance was chosen as reflecting a journey of one day on foot, or one day back and forth by cart. The map highlights cities with more than two neighbors within this distance.

literally within walking distance of each other, and the communities and economies of these cities and their territories often seem to have been well-integrated. There is quite a bit of epigraphic evidence for this: inscriptions mention patrons or patronesses active in multiple cities in a region, and there is significant evidence of people who ended up living in a neighboring city from where they were born.[17] In several regions, there were regional market circuits, and there is literary evidence for cities on the coast serving as ports for neighboring cities.[18] Moreover, these three regions also had strong and direct links with the food market of the city of Rome, with Baetica providing olive oil, Africa both oil and grain, and Italy an entire range of products, including wine.[19] Thus, within these regions, information networks were not only defined by the physical proximity of population centers and by the development of infrastructure connecting these centers, but also by direct social and economic ties between urban communities, and by their integration into the economic networks supplying the Roman metropolis. This does not mean that the circulation of information was perfect, but the concentration of urban centers and the strong and direct connections between them highlight a relative absence of impediments within these regions: information could circulate with relative ease. Outside the densely urbanized regions, obstacles to the circulation of information were more serious. Communication beyond the local horizon was less straightforward, as the distance to neighboring communities was much larger: cities were considerably more isolated. There often were fewer direct economic ties with the city of Rome, or with the wider imperial economic network. This, of course, works against the circulation of information, and it is not hard to understand the regions with the lowest densities of urbanism in primitivist terms, with economies that were to a large extent locally oriented, and with infrequent connections at the supra-local level, particularly in the winter season.[20] In terms of having frequent access to accurate information, it mattered whether

[17] For example, *CIL* 2.3278, referring to Valeria Petina, *flaminica* in Corduba, Castulo, and Tucci; *CIL* 9.2438 (169–172 AD) shows magistrates from Bovianum and Saepinum in Samnium operating together; *CIL* 9.6760 (from Aesernia, second century AD) shows these two cities had an *eques*, Flavius Celer, who was their shared *curator*.

[18] On these market circuits see De Ligt 1993. Strabo (5.3.8) recalls how Pompeii was the port city of Nuceria and Nola.

[19] On the impact of Rome see Morley 1996. On the role of Africa see Hobson 2015: 63–102; Mattingly 1995: 138–55. On Baetica see Haley 2003.

[20] See, for a vivid depiction of such a scenario, Bang 2008: 137–138.

you lived in Ucubi in Baetica, surrounded by a range of small towns like Iptuci (Torreparedones, 17 km), Ipsca (14.5 km), or Ulia Fidentia (13 km), and within a day's travelling from a large center like Corduba (30 km), or at Osca, in Northern Spain, where the nearest urban settlements—Caesaraugusta (65 km) and Ilerda (105 km)—were both more than two days of travelling away.[21]

This differentiated picture was of course the result of several social, economic, and political developments that took place over a longer period of time, but Roman imperial hegemony—and the resulting demographic explosion of the Roman metropolis—must be seen as a key factor in bringing it about.[22] While regions like Baetica and Africa were, to some extent, urbanized already before the imperial period, one clear development of the first centuries CE is the increasing differentiation between the urbanized and less densely urbanized regions of the empire, as new settlements seem to have emerged within already densely urbanized regions with higher frequency than elsewhere.[23] This process is particularly clear in Africa and Baetica, but studies of Roman Italy have equally emphasized the extent of urban growth in the early imperial period.[24] It is important to emphasize that this development was not only (or even mainly) a matter of demography: the data underlying the map reflect the existence of urban communities, but also their relative flourishing—they point to the activities of local elites involved in competitive construction and other forms of euergetism, and, thus, the presence of buying power, and of the consumer culture that characterized Roman imperial society.[25] In other words, the clusters give a rough indication not only of the spread of people, but also highlight a geography of wealth and consumption. By implication, the cities in these clusters are likely to have been attractive, low-risk destinations for *vestiarii* and other traders in consumer goods—what could not be sold in one place, could perhaps be sold in the next, and if not there, then

[21] All distances were measured as the crow flies using Google Earth. Locations of the cities mentioned were based on Ahlfeldt's *Digital Atlas of the Roman Empire*, dare.ht.lu.se, May 8, 2019. Orbis gives a travel time of 2.3 days by foot from Osca to Caesaraugusta, and 3.5 days from Osca to Ilerda; orbis.stanford.edu, May 8, 2019.

[22] On the demography of Rome see Morley 2013.

[23] On the pre-Roman urbanization of Baetica see Houten 2018: 32–36.

[24] For Baetica see Haley 2003. For Africa see Sears 2011. Italy has been intensively discussed, but see, for example, Vermeulen 2017: 108–161.

[25] See for the flourishing of euergetism in the imperial period in general Jouffroy 1986; Patterson 2006; Zuiderhoek 2009.

certainly somewhere nearby. More than the less densely urbanized and less wealthy regions, the clusters thus enabled itinerant traders to circulate, and to spread information that could feed directly into local knowledge of market situations. By implication, there was thus not only the *possibility* for information to circulate due to lower distances between urban centers, but also a clear economic drive for actors to actually move around. This was, to a much lower extent, the case outside the clustered areas—why go all the way from Osca to Caesaraugusta unless it was clear that the mission would not be in vain? In other words: there was a clear divergence between regions with increasingly low thresholds for information circulation, and regions that retained much higher thresholds for information circulation. This divergence was also known to exist: Cicero mentions how people living among the Bruttii and Sallentini in southern Italy—outside the cluster of urbanism in the center of the peninsula—were deprived of regular information flows and 'only got the news three times a year'—in Latium and Campania, he implies, things clearly were significantly better.[26]

It may be argued that, historically, the dense clusters of urbanism in Central Italy, Africa Proconsularis and Baetica were a completely new phenomenon of the Roman imperial period: the conditions for information circulation that can be reconstructed for these regions in the imperial period were unprecedented in the history of the Mediterranean region.

10.2 Urban Spaces

On the local scale, the physical organization of the built environment was of key importance for the practical, everyday functioning of information networks. Within cities, the *forum* was the obvious key node in the urban information network: this was the place where relative strangers would normally encounter each other to conduct business, exchanging relevant market information in the process; the *forum* also was the place where such information would be easily available to relative outsiders to the community.[27] Documentary evidence from the Vesuvian region confirms how business contracts were being negotiated and concluded on *fora*, or in the

[26] Cic. *Rosc. Am.* 132: '*aptam et ratione dispositam se habere existimant, qui in Sallentinis aut in Bruttiis habent unde vix ter in anno audire nuntium possunt*'. Cf. Morley 1996: 72.

[27] On the role of the *forum* see Flohr 2020a; Laurence et al. 2011: 170–202.

public buildings surrounding them.[28] The physical concentration of a lot of banking activity in urban *fora* that is suggested by some literary sources implies that a lot of market information would be available in this environment.[29] Of course, that *fora* were a critical node in urban information networks to a large extent is a product of the fact that they were the central—and in most cases the only—plaza in most Roman cities. In this sense, a Roman *forum* did not distinguish itself from a Classical Greek or Hellenistic *agora*. However, there is a little bit more to this: it can be argued that in the way in which *fora* developed architecturally, especially in the Late Republic and Early Empire, their role at the crossroads of everyday life was significantly strengthened. Three changes define this development: first, the appearance of long rows of *tabernae* around the plaza; second, the emergence of *porticus* surrounding the main forum square, and third, the introduction of the *basilica*.

Tabernae began to be constructed alongside *fora* from at least the third century BC onwards—early examples include the *fora* of Pompeii and Paestum (Fig. 10.2), and there is written evidence of early second century BC Roman *censores* surrounding urban *fora* in several places in Italy with *tabernae* in Livy.[30] Not all *fora* would have *tabernae*, and some—like at Pompeii—lost them at a later moment, but the *taberna* remained a common element around *fora* of Italy in the imperial period and it would become standard in the *fora* of Roman Europe, including, as far as it is known, Spain.[31] Only in Africa, the *taberna* remained somewhat exceptional around urban *fora*.[32] The *taberna* is so common that it is often taken for granted, but its emergence must be seen as a radical innovation, which dramatically transformed the character of urban retail and manufacturing, enhancing both the predictability and findability of retail environments, and the ease of communication between shops and workshops and the outside world.[33] Yet the open character of *tabernae* also had an impact on the information landscapes around *fora*, and not only in the sense that a lot of economic information concerning the functioning of these *tabernae* would be easily accessible, but also that there—quite simply—was a

[28] See, for example, Broekaert 2017. Cf. *CIL* 4.3340:155 (*Pompeis in foro*). *TPSulp* 1–18 (*Puteolis in foro*), 19 (*Romae in foro Augusto*). See also Flohr 2020a.

[29] For example, Vitr. *De Arch.* 5.1.2.

[30] Liv. 41.27; Lackner 2008: 271.

[31] Cf. Baratto 2003; Bouet 2012; Cavalieri 1999; Roberti 1995.

[32] Baaziz 1987.

[33] See also Ellis 2018.

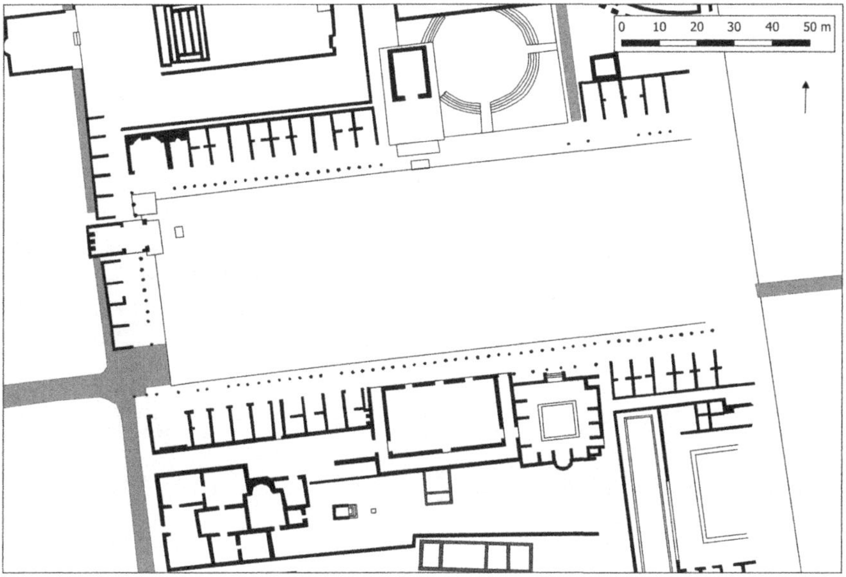

Fig. 10.2 Paestum. Plan of the forum area. (Plan: Miko Flohr)

more densely populated communication landscape in the forum area, and that information could circulate more easily.

From the second century BC onwards, most *fora* also began to be surrounded by *porticus* on all or most sides; at Pompeii, the first *porticus* appeared in the mid-second century BCE, in other Italian cities this appears to have happened around the same time or a little earlier.[34] By the first century BC, the *porticus* had become a standard hallmark of *fora* in Roman Italy (Fig. 10.3), and in the imperial period, it would become so in *fora* throughout the Roman world, particularly in Roman Europe and Africa—paradoxically, the Forum Romanum was one of very few *fora* in the Empire never to become fully surrounded by *porticus*, though the imperial fora were.[35] The practical, functional impact of *porticus* should not be underestimated: architectural historians have often emphasized

[34] On the *porticus* of Popidius at Pompeii see (Pesando & Guidobaldi 2006: 51–52. On the *porticus* in general see Frakes 2009; Lackner 2008: 271; Nünnerich-Asmus 1994.

[35] See on the *forum* and the imperial *fora* Coarelli 2008: 47–155.

Fig. 10.3 Veleia. Augustan-era forum with plaza surrounded by *porticus*. (Photo: Miko Flohr)

their role in controlling the visual appearance of the square, but, obviously, *porticus* also functioned as covered walkways, and—crucially—could do so independently of weather and season, thus guaranteeing the continuing functionality and navigability of the *forum* environment during bad weather—whether it was too hot, too cold, too windy or too rainy, the *porticus* offered a possibility for people to hang around and meet up.[36] This all-weather environment made it possible for information to circulate whatever the meteorological conditions.

What is true for the *porticus* is even more strongly the case for the *basilica*.[37] After their first appearance around the Forum Romanum in the Republican period, *basilicae* would be constructed in large numbers in Italy in the last century of the Roman republic, and by the Augustan period, the *basilica* had become a standard element in *forum* architecture,

[36] On this issue see Flohr 2020b.

[37] On the emergence and spread of the *basilica* see Gros 1996: 235–60; Lackner 2008: 266–71; Nünnerich-Asmus 1994. See also Laurence et al. 2011: 170–202.

Fig. 10.4 Grumentum. Remains of Basilica. The *forum* is directly on the left. (Photo: Miko Flohr)

to be included in the initial design of new urban *fora* all over the Roman world. Essentially, the *basilica* was little more than a large hall (Fig. 10.4), which often had an extremely open connection with the *forum* or with the *porticus* around it, and while *basilicae* are sometimes associated with certain civic and juridical processes, in general, they have a rather vaguely circumscribed functionality. Indeed, rather than being constructed for a limited number of specific functions, one should think of the *basilica* as being the covered continuation of the *forum* square, again offering an all-weather environment, but one that looks less like a corridor—as porticus did—and more like a destination space in itself. Significantly, this role of the *basilica* is made explicit by Vitruvius, who emphasized that *basilicae* should be constructed in a way that would allow business to continue in the cold season too.[38]

Thus, looking at the *tabernae*, the *porticus* and the *basilicae* of Roman *fora*—and the *fora* in places like Iuvanum and Veleia suggest that this is

[38] Vitr. *De Arch.* 5.1.4.

true for urban *fora* as well as for those built in rural contexts—it is clear that the position of the *forum* as a key node in information networks was not only recognized by communities, but it also developed in a way that was very much conducive of a continuous circulation of information.

10.3 Urban Landscapes

It is important, however, to see the development of urban *fora* as a social meeting point in a slightly broader historical context. The *forum* may have been the key interface of a city with the outside world, it was not, of course, the only urban environment where information was exchanged, formally or informally, within the community. There were other public or semi-public venues too, and particularly baths, and their *palaestrae*, were common, everyday meeting points for all kinds of people within the community; epigraphic and archaeological evidence shows how baths, in the imperial period, and particularly in the second century AD, became a common part of urban culture throughout the Roman world, with even medium-sized cities having multiple public bathing complexes.[39] Literature also suggests how baths could be used by people from different households to catch up, informally.[40] To a lesser extent, spectacle venues like theaters and amphitheaters could perform a similar role, though they were more incidentally used and not necessarily in contexts that fostered exchange of information between people that did not see each other otherwise.[41] In any case, the direction of development suggested by the construction of baths and spectacle buildings is similar: from the late Republic to the imperial period, Roman urban information networks became denser, and better integrated.

Admittedly, information relevant for everyday economic processes did not necessarily circulate through such public encounters; a lot of the more relevant, high-quality information relevant to buyers and sellers may have been disproportionally concentrated inside private houses, and thus, harder to find for people without strong social ties in the community. In this context, it is relevant to highlight the impact of the *taberna* beyond the *forum*. The *taberna* facilitated interaction between craftsmen and

[39] See esp. Nielsen 1990; Patterson 2006: 130–60; Thébert 2003.

[40] See, for example, Apul. *Met.* 9.24–26. For a demographic breakdown of the visitors to Roman baths see Fagan 2002: 189–219.

[41] On these see Laurence et al. 2011: 231–84; Patterson 2006: 130–148.

retailers and their prospective clients through their wide opening, and their spread over the urban landscape, which is particularly well-pronounced in Roman Italy, meant that it could play an important role in enhancing the circulation of information through the public sphere in the entire city (Fig. 10.5).[42] Crucially, besides interacting with the outside public, *tabernae* also interacted directly with each other, and the retailers and craftsmen operating them worked often in direct hearing distance of each other.[43] Moreover, as *tabernae* did not always have internal access to water, a lot of these people would meet regularly at public fountains.[44] Thus, the spread of the *taberna* alongside urban thoroughfares further integrated urban communication landscapes, and made it easier for information to circulate within urban neigborhoods. This already removed some of the key barriers for the circulation of information coming from private houses in these neigborhoods.

Furthermore, many of the *tabernae* lining the urban streets of Roman Italy of course also had some structural relation with an *atrium* house or a more modest form of private domestic architecture. To judge from the archaeological record it is only in Rome and Ostia that this relation is

Fig. 10.5 Pompeii. Spread of *tabernae* over the city. (Map: Miko Flohr)

[42] On the archaeology of the *taberna* see Holleran 2012: 99–158, 2017.
[43] See, for example, Flohr 2016a:168–169.
[44] As is the case with the small *fullonicae* of Pompeii. Cf. Flohr 2013: 319.

Fig. 10.6 Pompeii, House of the Faun. *Taberna* with internal connection to *atrium*. (Photo: Miko Flohr)

mostly absent. Indeed, many houses with *tabernae* also had one or two shops that had a direct connection with the main house (Fig. 10.6).[45] Arguably, such connections were made, and retained, because they could actually be used by people to go from the shop to the house, or vice versa, and as such, they imply that there were meant to be direct, and continuous information ties between the *taberna* and the household; in other words, directly connected *tabernae* integrated houses with public urban information networks. Quite possibly, therefore, many new business connections between houses and partners from outside the immediate social network of the owners first started in or through the *tabernae*—or, conversely, the existence of *tabernae* made the establishment of such ties, and the exchange of relevant information that preceded this, quite a bit easier. The ways in which *tabernae* could be used to visually advertise the quality of what was

[45] At Pompeii, 284 of ca. 900 excavated *tabernae* had a direct internal connection to a house, while the total number of *tabernae* associated with houses (including both independent and internally connected *tabernae*) is 598. See for the underlying data Flohr 2018.

on offer surely also helped in this respect; as the remains of façade paintings in Pompeii and Herculaneum make clear, this was not limited to the internal arrangement of the main room of the *taberna*, but also could include the façade.[46]

10.4 Discussion

It has been the intention of this chapter to highlight the ways in which developing urban networks and urban landscapes changed the way in which economically relevant information could circulate within and between cities in the Roman world. The argument is not supposed to imply that all obstacles for circulation were removed, or that Roman urban markets in general had access to of accurate, reliable information about what was happening elsewhere, or that all information traveled easily and freely through urban space. In absolute terms, there are clear reasons to assume that in most places in the Roman world, none of this was the case. Moreover, this chapter has neither argued that possibilities for communication were always used with a predictable frequency: it has not discussed the ways in which people actually were willing or able to share information, or whether there was a culture in which relevant information could be easily exchanged between relative strangers should they encounter each other. These are things that cannot be derived from archaeological remains or honorific inscriptions.

The point, rather, has been that in evaluating the role of asymmetric information in the Roman economy it is vital to understand how information may have been travelling through space, purposefully, or by word of mouth, and how easy it would have been for people to get essential market information when they arrived, as relative strangers, in a new place. What this chapter has argued is that throughout the Roman world, there were significant differences between cities in the quality of information that arriving traders could expect to be available locally, and that there were differences in the quality of urban information landscapes even if the general architectural tendency was toward more openness. *Porticus* and *basilica* spread throughout the Roman west, but the *taberna* was more

[46]The depiction of the activities in a textile workshop on the façade of house IX 7, 1–2 at Pompeii are a good example. Cf. Potts 2009. It has to be emphasized, however, that the actual spread of such paintings should not be overestimated.

unevenly distributed, particularly outside Italy.[47] Thus, the overall picture is one of greater divergence, not of a greater circulation of information in general. Nevertheless, it is also true that the extremely integrated information landscapes of Roman Italy, and to a lesser extent Baetica and Africa Proconsularis, had no previous parallel in antiquity, and reflect an unprecedented potential for at least regional economic integration.

So, what does this mean for the role of asymmetric information in everyday economic practice? It may be good to go back to the example of the *vestiarius* outlined at the start of this chapter and contrast the three clusters of urbanism in the Roman West with the more marginal zones of Roman Europe. Within regions like Baetica, Africa Proconsularis and Italy, the dense communication network, and the improved facilities for interaction within cities will have created a situation in which both the *vestiarii* and their prospective clients will have had reasonably reliable information about each other: clients will have been familiar with a wide range of textiles, and are likely to have had a rough idea of what these items would normally cost. Due to the nature of regional demand, *vestiarii* are likely to have been frequent guests on the urban *fora*, meaning that this information was not monopolized by individual traders—arriving traders would have to work from the idea that there might have been others before them who gave prospective customers an idea of what could be on offer against what price. This significantly limited their possibilities to exploit asymmetries of information, particularly regarding price levels, but also regarding the quality of the product. In the less densely urbanized areas, where cities were fewer and farther in between, and where regional markets were a less attractive investment in time and effort for itinerant traders, this was different. Local knowledge of products and prices would often be less up-to-date, and this generated asymmetries of information that could be exploited by traders, by pricing garments above their actual market value, or by abusing the reputation of certain clothing types or materials.[48] For instance, in a remote region where *vestiarii* were uncommon, it would be easier to sell a fine black cloak as coming from Laodicea

[47] Frakes 2009; Laurence et al. 2011: 170–202. The limited spread of the *taberna* outside Italy was not explicitly noted by Ellis 2018, but it is implicit from the virtual absence of non-Italian *tabernae* throughout his analysis.

[48] See for comparable problems Bang 2008: 138.

on the Lycus, or a white tunic as coming from Mutina without this actually being the case.[49]

Combining this differentiation in the role of information asymmetry with the historical development of the urbanized clusters in Baetica, Africa and Italy, and, indeed, in the Greek-speaking East of the empire, it becomes possible to return to the question outlined at the start of this chapter about the extent to which the changing physical shape and geographical structure of markets in the Roman world, impacted on the role that asymmetric information actually could play in everyday economic practice. Arguably, the clustered urbanization of the Roman Empire created a number of regions where asymmetries of information played an unprecedentedly small role in everyday transactions. This does not mean that they did not play a role at all, but it does mean that the growth of urbanized clusters to some extent *limited* the role of information asymmetry in the Roman economy. Arguably, this is an important development that should be an integral part of discussions about the role of information asymmetry in the Roman economy.

Bibliography

Adams, C. 2012. Transport. In *The Cambridge Companion to the Roman Economy*, ed. W. Scheidel, 218–240. Cambridge: Cambridge University Press.

Akerlof, G.A. 1970. The Market for 'Lemons': Quality Uncertainty and the Market Mechanism. *Quarterly Journal of Economics* 84 (3): 488–500.

Baaziz, S.B. 1987. Les Forums Romains en Tunisie: essai de Bilan. In *Los Foros romanos de las provincias occidentales*, 221–236. Madrid.

Bang, P. 2008. *The Roman Bazaar*. Cambridge: Cambridge University Press.

Baratto, C. 2003. Le tabernae nei fora delle città romane tra l'età repubblicana e il periodo imperiale. *Rivista di Archeologia* 27: 67–106.

Bouet, A. 2012. *Le forum en Gaule et dans les régions voisines*. Bordeaux.

Broekaert, W. 2013. Financial Experts in a Spider Web. A Social Network Analysis of the Archives of Caecilius Iucundus and the Sulpicii. *Klio* 95 (2): 471–510.

———. 2015. Recycling Networks. The Structure of the Italian Business Community on Delos. In *Structure and Performance in the Roman Economy. Models, Methods and Case Studies*, ed. P. Erdkamp and K. Verboven, 143–182. Brussels: Éditions Latomus.

[49] On wool from these regions see Flohr 2016b, 2017.

———. 2017. Conflicts, Contract Enforcement, and Business Communities in the Archive of the Sulpicii. In *The Economy of Pompeii*, ed. M. Flohr and A. Wilson, 385–412. Oxford: Oxford University Press.

Buonopane, A. 2003. Un vestiarius centonarius ad Aquileia: sulla genuinità di CIL, V, 50. *Aquileia Nostra* 74: 301–314.

Cavalieri, M. 1999. Il modello forum-basilica e la sua "evoluzione" tra la Cisalpina e la Narbonensis. *Archeologia dell Emilia Romagna* 3: 85–101.

Coarelli, F. 2008. *Roma*. Roma: Laterza.

Dari-Matiacci, G., S. Onderstal, and F. Parisi. 2011. Inverse Adverse Selection: The Market for Gems. *Social Science Research Network*.

De Ligt, L. 1993. *Fairs and Markets in the Roman Empire. Economic and Social Aspects of Periodic Trade in a Pre-industrial Society*. Amsterdam: Gieben.

Ellis, S.J.R. 2018. *The Roman Retail Revolution. The Socio-Economic World of the Taberna*. Oxford: Oxford University Press.

Erdkamp, P. 2005. *The Grain Market in the Roman Empire*. Cambridge: Cambridge University Press.

Fagan, G. 2002. *Bathing in Public in the Roman World*. Ann Arbor: University of Michigan Press.

Flohr, M. 2013. *The World of the Fullo. Work, Economy and Society in Roman Italy*. Oxford: Oxford University Press.

———. 2016a. Constructing Occupational Identities in the Roman World. In *Work, Labor and Professions in the Roman World*, ed. K. Verboven and C. Laes, 147–172. Leiden: Brill.

———. 2016b. The Wool Economy of Roman Italy. In *Textiles, Trade and Theories. From the Ancient Near East to the Mediterranean*, ed. K. Dross-Krüpe and M.-L. Nösch, 49–62. Münster: Ugarit.

———. 2017. Textiles, Trade and the Urban Economies of Roman Asia Minor. In *Wirtschaft als Machtbasis. Vormoderne Wirtschaftssysteme in Anatolien*, ed. K. Piesker, 1–41. Berlin.

———. 2018. *Database of Pompeian Houses*. Leiden: Miko Flohr.

———. 2020a. Fora and commerce in Roman Italy. In *Urban Space and Urban History in the Roman World*, ed. M. Flohr, 198–220. London: Routledge.

———. 2020b. Hilltops, Heat and Precipitation: Roman Urban Life and the Natural Environment. In *Urban Space and Urban History in the Roman World*, ed. M. Flohr, 66–85. London: Routledge.

Frakes, J. 2009. *Framing Public Life: The Portico in Roman Gaul*. Vienna: Phoibos Verlag.

Golvin, J.-C. 1988. *L'Amphithéâtre romain. Essay sur la théorisation de sa forme et de ses fonctions*. Paris.

Gros, P. 1996. *L'architecture romaine: du début du IIIe siècle av. J.-C. à la fin du Haut-Empire. 1: Les monuments publics*. Paris.

Haley, E.W. 2003. *Baetica Felix: People and Prosperity in Southern Spain from Caesar to Septimius Severus*. Austin: University of Texas Press.

Hanson, J. 2016. *An Urban Geography of the Roman World, 100 BC to AD 300*. Oxford: Archaeopress.

Hobson, M. 2015. *The North African Boom. Evaluating Economic Growth in the Roman Province of Africa Proconsularis*. Portsmouth: JRA.

Holleran, C. 2012. *Shopping in Ancient Rome: the Retail Trade in the Late Republic and the Principate*. Oxford: Oxford University Press.

———. 2017. Finding Commerce: The Taberna and the Identification of Roman Commercial Space. *Papers of the British School at Rome* 85: 143–170.

Horden, P., and N. Purcell. 2000. *The Corrupting Sea*. Oxford: Blackwell.

Houten, P. 2018. *Civitates Hispaniae: Urbanisation on the Iberian Peninsula during the High Empire*. Leiden: Leiden University.

Humphrey, J. 1986. *Roman Circuses: Arenas for Chariot Racing*. London.

Jouffroy, H. 1986. *La construction publique en Italie et dans l'Afrique romaine*. Strasbourg.

Lackner, E.-M. 2008. *Republikanische Fora. Eine städtebaulich-historische Analyse*. München.

Laurence, R., S.E. Cleary, and G. Sears. 2011. *The City in the Roman West c. 250 BC – c. AD 250*. Cambridge: Cambridge University Press.

Manderscheid, H. 1988. *Bibliographie zum römischen Badewesen*. München.

———. 2004. *Ancient Baths and Bathing: A Bibliography for the Years 1988–2001*. Portsmouth: JRA.

Mattingly, D.J. 1995. *Tripolitania*. London: Batsford.

Menella, G. 2000. Un negotiator vestiarius Cisalpinus et Transalpinus a Fara Novarese. *Epigraphica* 62: 125–135.

Morley, N. 1996. *Metropolis and Hinterland*. Cambridge: Cambridge University Press.

———. 2007a. The Early Roman Empire: Distribution. In *The Cambridge Economic History of the Greco-Roman World*, ed. W. Scheidel, I. Morris, and R. Saller, 570–591. Cambridge: Cambridge University Press.

———. 2007b. *Trade in Classical Antiquity*. Cambridge: Cambridge University Press.

———. 2013. Population Size and Social Structure. In *The Cambridge Companion to Ancient Rome*, ed. P. Erdkamp, 29–44. Cambridge: Cambridge University Press.

Nielsen, I. 1990. *Thermae et Balnea. The architecture and Cultural History of Roman Public Baths*. Aarhus: Aarhus University Press.

Nünnerich-Asmus, A. 1994. *Basilika und Portikus: die Architektur der Säulenhallen als Ausdruck gewandelter Urbanität in später Republik und früher Kaiserzeit*. Köln.

Patterson, J. 2006. *Landscapes & Cities. Rural Settlement and Civic Transformation in Early Imperial Italy.* Oxford: Oxford University Press.

Pesando, F., and M.-P. Guidobaldi. 2006. *Pompei Oplontis Ercolano Stabiae.* Roma.

Potts, C. 2009. The Art of Piety and Profit at Pompeii: A New Interpretation of the Painted Shop Façade at IX.7.1-2. *Greece and Rome* 56 (1): 55–70.

Rice, C. 2016. Mercantile Specialization and Trading Communities: Economic Strategies in Roman Maritime Trade. In *Urban Craftsmen and Traders in the Roman World*, ed. A. Wilson and M. Flohr, 97–114. Oxford: Oxford University Press.

Roberti, M.M. 1995. *Forum et Basilica in Aquileia e nella Cisalpina romana.* Udine.

Scheidel, W. 2014. The Shape of the Roman World: Modelling Imperial Connectivity. *Journal of Roman Archaeology* 27: 7–32.

Sear, F. 2006. *Roman Theaters. An Architectural Study.* Oxford.

Sears, G. 2011. *The Cities of Roman Africa.* Stroud: History Press.

Temin, P. 2013. *The Roman Market Economy.* Princeton: Princeton University Press.

Terpstra, T. 2013. *Trading Communities in the Roman World. A Micro-Economic and Institutional Perspective.* New York: Brill.

Thébert, Y. 2003. *Thermes Romains d'Afrique du Nord.* Rome.

Verboven, K. 2011. Resident Aliens and Translocal Merchant Collegia in the Roman Empire. In *Frontiers in the Roman World. Proceedings of the Ninth Workshop of the International Network Impact of Empire (Durham, 16–19 April 2009)*, ed. O. Hekster and T. Kaizer, 335–348. Leiden.

Vermeulen, F. 2017. *From the Mountains to the Sea: The Roman Colonisation and Urbanisation of Central Adriatic Italy.* Leuven: Peeters.

Welch, K. 1998. The Stadium at Aphrodisias in Caria. *American Journal of Archaeology* 102: 547–569.

Wilson, A. (2011). 'City Sizes and Urbanization in the Roman Empire', in A. Bowman and A. Wilson (eds), Settlement, Urbanization and Population. Oxford: Oxford University Press, 161–195.

Zuiderhoek, A. 2009. *The Politics of Munificence in the Roman Empire. Citizens, Elites and Benefactors in Asia Minor.* Cambridge: Cambridge University Press.

CHAPTER 11

Roman Professional *collegia* and Economic Control: A Monopoly of Information?

Nicolas Tran

In the Roman West, did professional associations hold a monopoly on economic activities? This question is almost as old as the historiography about those communities. The earlier scholarship raised the subject intensively at the end of the nineteenth century. For instance, it is an important part of the famous *Étude historique sur les corporations professionnelles chez Romains*, published by the Belgian scholar Jean-Pierre Waltzing between 1895 and 1900.[1] The same question still arouses historians' curiosity. Very recently, a paper has compared again Roman associations to medieval guilds, through the issue of monopolies, and it encourages connecting the concept of asymmetric information to monopolies potentially held by *collegia*.[2]

Most of the time, professional associations of the Roman West had no legal monopolies on a specific economic activity. At least they left no trace

[1] Waltzing 1895-1900: I, 193–195.

[2] This paper remains anonymous for the moment, but the *Revue belge de philologie et d'histoire* officially accepted it, for a publication in 2019.

N. Tran (✉)
Université de Poitiers, Poitiers, France

C. Rosillo-López, M. García Morcillo (eds.), *Managing Information in the Roman Economy*, Palgrave Studies in Ancient Economies,
https://doi.org/10.1007/978-3-030-54100-2_11

of it. Nevertheless, exceptions did exist. The re-examination of a slab engraved during Hadrian's principate indicates that boatmen sailing between Ostia and Rome (the *caudicarii nauicularii Ostienses*) had a monopoly on navigational rights.[3] The imperial power would have given them simultaneously the right to form a *corpus* and to sail on the Tiber. So the right to load merchandise on riverboats, to bring it to Rome, was probably a privilege granted to members of a few formally authorised associations. At the beginning of the third century, the collective action of five *corpora lenunculariorum Ostiensium*, together with the *corpus codicariorum Ostiensium*, in order to defend their common interests, suggests which communities held this monopoly.[4] A few family groups dominated these *corpora*, controlled admissions and thus made the monopoly profitable for themselves.[5] However, until proven otherwise, legal monopolies of this kind would have been the rare exception rather than the rule. In this case, practical difficulties caused by the traffic on the Tiber may have determined the imperial regulation.

Historians generally agree that Roman associations impacted greatly on economic activity. They exercised a form of control, which is difficult to challenge but also difficult to define precisely. It is tempting to introduce a concept of de facto monopoly, as opposed to legal monopoly, but such an expression may seem vague or even a little bit contradictory. Actually, during the last decade, historians have described Roman *collegia* as networks, whose great virtue was to lower transaction costs. C. Hawkins has insisted on this point, from his doctoral dissertation to his book of 2016, but he was not alone.[6] As usual, when a theory becomes dominant, the pendulum has started to swing back. J. Liu has published recently an important paper on the matter.[7] According to her, closed networks like *collegia* were not only assets serving economic performance. They produced also rigidity by opposing insiders and outsiders. Furthermore, it

[3] Tran 2020, revising *AE*, 1955, 184: *[Imp(eratori) Caes(ari) diui Traiani] Parthici f(ilio), diui Neru(ae) [nep(oti) / Traiano Hadriano Aug(usto), po]ntif(ici) max(imo), trib(unicia) potest(ate) X[I---, co(n)s(uli) III,] / [corp(us) codicar(iorum) nauicular(iorum) Ost(iensium) qui]bus coire et alueo Tiberis [nauigare / con]cessu(m)] est.*

[4] Tran 2015.

[5] Tran 2006: 409–500.

[6] Hawkins 2016. See also Bang 2008: 241–262 ('Communal association – the power of religious conviviality', 'A web of ties – building community'); Liu 2009: 19–21; Terpstra 2013: 112–117 ('The role and importance of coalition-membership').

[7] Liu 2017.

would be quite naïve to consider that they were built only on friendship, solidarity and benevolence amongst peers. Professional *collegia* had hierarchical structures. A narrow elite controlled them and gave access to common resources to ordinary members only according to its interests. Evidence on the associations of *fabri tignuarii* at Rome and Ostia during the early Empire makes this point clear.[8] In the building sector, entrepreneurs organised themselves in these *collegia*, under the control of the wealthiest professionals. As a result, it was probably very difficult, or even impossible, to work as a builder without complying with this control and thus without belonging to a *collegium*.

To what extent did this control exercised by associations over economic life regard information? If so-called de facto monopolies on specific activities existed, to what extent did it result from an unequal access to information, which depended on membership or non-membership in a professional association? A research on *collegia* related to long-distance trade could provide some answers. So we shall consider from this perspective two trading communities attested by Latin inscriptions, during the second and early third centuries. The first one corresponds to the *corpus splendidissimum Cisalpinorum et Transalpinorum*, an association of merchants from both sides of the Alps. The second one is very well-known and gathered long-distance merchants trading olive oil from the province of Baetica.

11.1 Associations as Space of Shared or Withheld Information

Roman *collegia* were able to foster and facilitate exchanges of information amongst traders, who were involved in the same long-distance traffics. Yet associations offered integration to their members, just as much as they organised exclusion of outsiders. The geographic distribution of documents on the *corpus* of the *negotiatores Cisalpini et Transalpini* reveals professionals who had diverse and sometimes multiple roots in northern Italy, north-western Alps and east-central Gaul. A few documents could define an even broader area, but, to be cautious, it is better not to take them into account. In Aquileia, the *merkator Transalpinus* C. Licinius Pilomusus died probably during the Augustan era, that is to say more than a century before the first evidence on the *corpus*.[9] The issue of two

[8] Tran 2017.

[9] *AE* 1994.671.

inscriptions from Aquincum, dedicated by a group of *ciues Agrippinenses Transalpini*, is less easy to solve.[10] Nonetheless it is uncertain that those individuals belonged to the *corpus Cisalpinorum et Transalpinorum*. And it is also very uncertain that the *corpus* had something to do with Cologne and Aquincum.

The altar of M. Sennius Metilus shows that these *negotiatores* were active in Lyon, in the second half of the second century.[11] The deceased was both a member and a dignitary of the *corpus*, as a *praefectus*. He came from Trier, in *Gallia Belgica*, but had strong ties with Lyon. All of his family lived here and Metilus joined the local association of builders (*fabri tignuarii*). Like other *Treuiri*, Metilus practised his trade from the *canabae* district of Lyon. His profile and another inscription suggest that the *corpus Cisalpinorum et Transalpinorum* had its seat here or, at least, one of its seats. This district, located on the peninsula shaped by the confluence of the Rhône and the Saône, was Lyon's business centre. It was beneath the civic centre founded on the hill of Fourvière. Such a concentration of economic activities and of places of professional sociability must have fostered dissemination of information, especially as merchants and transporters were from very diverse geographical origins. Through this spatial organisation, also typical of Arles and its port district of Trinquetaille, one of these 'urban information landscapes', studied by M. Flohr in this volume, emerges.

Even if he died near Novara, L. Lupercius Exessus shared common characteristics with M. Sennius Metilus.[12] This *negotiator uestiarius Cisalpinus et Transalpinus* belonged to several local societies. In the *municipium* of Novara, he bequeathed money to *collegia* and, in the *ciuitas* of the *Heluetii*, he assumed the honour of *seuir Augustalis*. Likewise, *heredes* paid final respects to an anonymous *[negotiato]r Cisalpin(us) et Transalpin(us)* in Milan, who had also ties with the city of Como, since he

[10] *Tituli Aquincenses* II 632; 743.

[11] *CIL* XIII 2029: *D(is) M(anibus) / M(arci) Senni Metili, Treue/ri, negotiatori / corporis splendi/dissimi Cisalpino/rum et Transalpino/rum, eiusdem cor/poris praef(ecto), fabro tig/nuario Lug(uduni) et Senniae / Iullae, coniugi eius dul/cissim(a)e, uiuae, paren/tibus merentissimis / fili(i) heredes f(aciendum) c(urauerunt) / et sub ascia dedic(auerunt).*

[12] Mennella 2000: 125–135 (*AE* 2000.632). *{D(is) M(anibus)} / D(is) M(anibus) / L(uci) Luperci Exessi(?), (se)uir(i) Aug(ustalis) / ciuit(ate) Heluetiorum, negoti/atoris uestiar(ii) Cisalpini et Trans/alpini, qui leg(auit) colleg(iatis) i(n) m(unicipio) N(ouariensium) HS X[-] n(ummos).* According to the editor, the deceased was not only a *seuir Augustalis*, but also belonged to the *ciuitas Heluetiorum*.

was the patron of the boatmen sailing on its lake.[13] If we turn back to the other side of the Alps, we find two possible occurrences of the *Cisalpini et Transalpini* in Augst (Augusta Raurica), in the immediate vicinity of the Rhine. It is very fragmentary evidence, but the preservation of two documents, even though modest, makes the mention of the *corpus* quite plausible. The first fragment is the most interesting, because of the high quality of the stone and of the letters. It could come from a public inscription, for instance from a tribute to a patron of the *corpus.*[14]

Such an honorific inscription provides great evidence nearby, in Avenches. A large monument, three meters high and six meters wide, honoured Q. Otacilius Pollinus a member of a very powerful family.[15] This slab is now broken into many pieces, but most of the text –except the end—is understandable.[16] Pollinus assumed all the magistracies of the *Heluetii*, under Hadrian or soon after. Outside his homeland, he was clearly linked with Lyon. Indeed, he was *inquisitor* in the federal sanctuary of the Three Gauls, near the confluence of the Rhone and the Saone. And the boatmen of both rivers chose him as patron. Besides M. Sennius Metilus' epitaph, the tribute to Q. Otacilius Pollinus also suggests that the *corpus Cisalpinorum et Transalpinorum* was based in Lyon. Moreover, this patron might have interest for the *uenalicii* of the *corpus* because of the routes that slaves walked through the Alps, between the Germanic world

[13] *CIL* V 5911: *------ / [--- negotiato]/ris Cisalpin(i) [e]t Transalpin(i), / patr(oni) coll(egii) naut(arum) Comens(ium), / hered(es) fac(iendum) cur(auerunt).* See Boscolo 2004-2005.

[14] *CIL* XIII 5303; 11547; *AE* 1988.899: *------ / coll[eg. negotiatorum] / Cisal[pin(orum) et Transalpin(orum)] / ------.* *AE* 1999.1121: *------ / Ci[s]alp[inorum et Trans]/ [al]pin[orum ---].*

[15] *AE* 1995.1141: *Q(uinto) Otacil[i]o Quir(ina) Pollino, Q(uinti) Otac[ili] / Ceriali[s] filio, omnibus honor[ibus] / apud suos functo, ter immunit[ate] / a diuo [H]adr[ian(o)] don[at]o, inquis[it]or(i)] / II[I Gall]iar(um), pa[tro]no uenal(iciorum) [corporis] / Cisal[p]ino[rum] et Transalpinorum, / item [n]autar(um) Ar[ari]cor(um) [Rho]danicor(um), / ob [e]g[re]gia eius erga re[m pub]l(icam) ergaq(ue) / sin[gu]los un[i]uerso[squ]e mer[i]ta, / Helu[etii publ(ice) p]atron[o ---]e[r]is et / [inscr]ibti[oni(bus?)] qu[---]e sunt.* See Raepsaet-Charlier 2012: few other Helvetian magistrates belonged to the same family, who may have owned a vast household (actually a palace) discovered near the *forum* of Aventicum. Furthermore, attestations of *Octacilii* in the countryside, in the surroundings of the city, implied great land properties.

[16] Raepsaet-Charlier 2012: 353, tests two restorations, '*patrono uenal(iciorum) [item corp(oris)] Cisalpinorum et Transalpinorum*' and '*patrono uenal(iciorum) [corporis] Cisalpinorum et Transalpinorum*'. She chooses finally the second one, because the abbreviation of VENAL is sure and then only a C (and not a I) seems possible.

and northern Italy.[17] C. Domitius Carassonus, *Heluetius* and *mango*, a slave merchant, fulfilled a vow to Jupiter at the Grand-Saint-Bernard Pass.[18] This place corresponded to an important stopover point on the way to Italy.

The territory of the *Heluetii* had a very favourable geographic location. Actually, Avenches was at the crossroads of main waterways. The boatmen of the Aar river (*nautae Aruranci*) had their meeting-place (*scholae*) in town.[19] They were probably based on the lake Morat, which was linked with the lakes of Neuchâtel and of Bienne. The Aar river itself connected the lake of Bienne and the Rhine, a little after Vindonissa (Windisch).[20] At the South West, Avenches was close to the lake Leman, where *nautae* operated from Lausanne. The waterway to Lyon started at Geneva and followed the Rhone valley. In sum, the traces of the *corpus Cisalpinorum et Transalpinorum* are related to multiple trade routes, from North to South and from East to West, on waterways or on roads. This system seems polycentric, since inscriptions highlight the importance of Lyon, Avenches and Milan. The name of the *corpus* and of its members reflects diversity too. It suggests that some *negotiatores* defined themselves as *Cisalpini*, and other *negotiatores* as *Transalpini*. Some of them specialised in diverse trades, as shown by the distinction between *uenalicii* and *uestiarii*.

So the *corpus* was an appropriate space to centralise and to share information about multiple and, sometimes, complex trade patterns. Its members are less noticeable by their mobility, than by their diverse and sometimes multiple geographical ties. The dissemination of information probably took place during the formal or informal meetings of the *corporati*. It is probable that a meeting-place, which served as a space of communication, was located in Lyon. But other seats may have existed elsewhere. Moreover *corporati* made less formal contacts with each other in places in direct relation with their businesses, such as inns (*cauponae*) and warehouses (*horrea*) where they rented rooms and storage facilities. Through encounters between individuals who recognised each other as colleagues, the *corpus Cisalpinorum et Transalpinorum* would have helped

[17] Wiblé 2006; Tchernia 2011: 95–96.

[18] Golosetti 2016.

[19] *CIL* XIII 5096: *In honorem domus diuinae, / [n]autae Aruranci Aramici / scholam de suo instruxerunt, / l(oco) d(ato) d(ecreto) d(ecurionum)*. The *Aramus* must be the name of a still unknown river or lake.

[20] Raepsaet-Charlier 2012: 354.

traders in their activity so much, that it created an imbalance of information between insiders and outsiders.

The exportation of olive oil from Baetica in the Roman Empire corresponds to a second example of long-distance trade, which was divided in multiple segments and branches. Because of the mass of inscriptions on stone and on amphora, research on this topic is very abundant.[21] Amongst other issues, scholars have intended to explain the diversity of occupational designations, since oil merchants are defined as *negotiatores*, *mercatores*[22] or *diffusores*. M. Christol has proposed an interpretation that I follow, after A. Tchernia before me. An inscription from Sevilla, published in 2001, suggests that a single organisation gathered all the merchants.[23] This *corpus oleariorum* would have united a large trading community, since the excavations at the Monte Testaccio provide more than 200 names painted on *tituli picti* ß between 140 and 160 approximately. This community of *negotiatores olearii ex Baetica* paid tribute to the former *praefectus annonae* M. Petronius Honoratus, in 147.[24] However some members introduced themselves as *diffusores* to emphasise a specialisation. It is difficult to define this specialisation precisely and convincingly, but it apparently implied close relations with the *praefectura annonae*.

Of course, evidence highlights intense connections between Sevilla and Rome, but other centres had their importance too. In Rome, epitaphs mention three *diffusores olearii ex Baetica*. D. Caecilius Onesimus[25] and

[21] Christol 2008 and 2016; Tchernia 2011: 73–84, 315–322. We are waiting for the book resulting from C. Rico's habilitation. See also Le Roux 1986. French scholars developed this literature in the context of a critical dialogue with J. Remesal Rodríguez (see Remesal Rodríguez 2015-2016, for a general overview of his research).

[22] On the use of the word *mercator*, see *CIL* VI 1935 (L. Marius Phoebus) and Remesal Rodríguez 2000: *D(is) M(anibus), / L(ucio) Mario / Phoebo, / uiatori / tribunicio / decuriae maio/ris, mercatori / olei Hispani ex / prouincia / Baetica.*

[23] On this important discovery, see also Rico 2003.

[24] *CIL* VI 1625b; 31834b (a. 147): *M(arco) Petroni[o M(arci) f(ilio)] / Quir(ina) Honorat[o], / praef(ecto) coh(ortis) I Raet[orum], / trib(uno) mil(itum) leg(ionis) I Miner[uiae] / P(iae) F(idelis), praef(ecto) alae Aug(ustae) P(iae) F(idelis) [Thrac(um)], / proc(uratori) monet(ae), proc(uratori) XX hered(itatium), / proc(uratori) prou(inciae) Belg(icae) et duar(um) / Germaniar(um), proc(uratori) a ratio[n(ibus)] / Aug(usti), praef(ecto) annon(ae), praef(ecto) Aegypti, pontif(ici) minor[i], / negotiatores ole[ari(i)] / ex Baetica patron[o] / curatoribu[s] / Cassio Faus[to], / Caecilio Ho[spitali].*

[25] *AE* 1980.98; 1994.194: *D(ecimo) Caecilio / Onesimo, / uiatori / apparitori / Augustoru[m], / diffusori o[lear(io)] / ex Baet[ica] / here[d(es) fec(erunt)].*

D. Caecilius Abascantus[26] belonged to a family network, which had a great influence amongst merchants from Baetica. D. Caecilius Hospitalis, one of the *curatores* in charge of M. Petronius Honoratus' tribute, was a member of it too, just as many amphora owners (and merchants) mentioned by *tituli picti*.[27] The third *diffusor olearius* known in Rome is C. Sentius Regulianus, who died with the titles of Roman knight and *curator corporis*.[28] In Sevilla, the *corpus oleariorum* erected a statue of M. Iulius Hermesianus in a meeting-place, which may have borne the name of *statio*.[29] This building hosted two other statues, of Minerva and Venus, given *in honorem corporis oleariorum*.[30]

Outside Rome and Sevilla, merchants left traces in production and transit areas. The *diffusor olearius* M. Cassius Sempronianus, from Lisbon, gave a monument in Oducia, on the bank of the Baetis.[31] Located in the valley of the Singilis, a tributary of the Baetis, the territory of Astigi produced olive oil massively. A lot of merchants came from this city, especially

[26] *CIL* VI 1885; *AE* 1994.193: *Memoriae / Caeciliae Helladis, / uxoris karissimae, / D(ecimus) Caecilius Abascantus, / lictor curiat(i)us, / diffusor olearius ex / prouincia Baetica / fecit sibi et libertis / [l]ibertabusque sui[s] / posterisque eoru[m].*

[27] D. Caecilius Hospitalis himself appears on *tituti* ß from the Monte Testaccio: *CIL* XV 3762–3764, 3769–3781.

[28] *CIL* VI 29722: *D(is) M(anibus) s(acrum), / C(aio) Sen[ti]o Reguliano, eq(uiti) R(omano), / diffus(ori) oleario ex Baetica, / curator(i) eiusdem cor/poris, negot(iatori) uinario Lugu/dun(i) in canabis consisten(ti), / curatori et patrono ei/usd(em) corporis, nautae Arari/co, patrono eiusd(em) corporis, / patrono IIIIIIuir(orum) Luguduni / consistentium, L(ucius) Silenius / Reginus, aus, et Ulattia / Metrodora et fili(i) eius/dem ponendum curauerunt, / procurante Dionysio et / Belliciano et / ------?*

[29] *AE* 2001.1186: *M(arco) Iul(io) H[e]rmesian[o], / diffusori olei ad annon[am] / Vrbis, c[urator]i corpo[ris] / olea[riorum st]ationi[s?] / Romul[ae, ---]i[---]te[---] / huic corpus [ole]ari[orum] / splend[idissi]mum / mer[entissimo s]tatu[am] / pon[enda]m iussit. / M(arcus) Iulius Hermes Fro[nti]nianus, / filius, honore accepto / impensam remisit.* See *AE* 2014.613.

[30] *AE* 2001.1187; 2002.715: *Miner[uae Aug(ustae)], / Valeria Qu[---] / Valeri Valentis [f(ilia)], / ad cultum operi[s] / a patre optumo exorna[ti], / in honorem corporis / oleariorum, d(onum) d(edit). AE* 2002.716: *Veneri Genitrici / Augustae, / Valeria Valentina, / Valeri Valentis filia, / ad cultum operis / a patre optumo exornati, / in honorem corporis / oleariorum d(onum) d(edit).* M. Valerius Valens is named between 138 and 153 on few amphora found on the Monte Testaccio (*CIL* XV 4030–4034). See Goffaux 2012: 216–218.

[31] *AE* 1984: 526: *M(arcus) Cassius M(arci) f(ilius) Gal(eria) / Sempronianus, O/lisipon(ensis), diffusor / olearius, a solo fec(it) / et dedicauit.* This marble plaque was discovered with another one, which corresponds to the epitaph of Cassia Zoe, deceased when she was twenty-seven-years-old (*AE* 1984.527). So Sempronianus may have dedicated a private and funerary monument.

the *D.D. Caecilii*. Likewise, M. Iulius Hermesianus' son and grandson, who traded oil too,[32] honoured him, on a public place given by the *ordo Astigitanus*, because here was the origin of the whole family.[33] On the other side of the Mediterranean, it is possible that few merchants or their agents were based in Ostia. No explicit evidence of the *corpus oleariorum* is preserved there. Nonetheless, the names *Decimus Caecilius* are quite rare outside. Since the publication of 'new' epitaphs from Ostia, three freedmen bearing these names are known.[34] The case of D. Caecilius Trophi[mus] is noticeable, because an epitaph from Rome is dedicated to Caecilia Helpis, *D.D. Caeciliorum Trophimi et Logi liberta*.[35] There is no mention of olive oil in this dossier. Yet the status of former *serua communis* can remind us of commercial partnerships between *D.D. Caecilii*, that *tituli picti* mention very often.[36]

It is also well-known that Baetica did not export oil only to the imperial capital. Great quantities reached the northern provinces too, through the Rhone, the Saone and the Rhine valleys. Many containers were found during underwater excavations at Fos-sur-Mer and Arles.[37] Moreover, the oil traffic between the river ports of Arles and Lyon is implicitly present on the epitaph of L. Hilarianius Cinnamus, who died in Lyon in the second half of the second century.[38] This document is lost and its nineteenth-century copy contains misreadings. Nevertheless, Cinnamus was probably a *negotiator olearius*. He and his father-in-law had very rare *nomina gentilicia*. Hence it is probably not a coincidence that another inscription from

[32] The name of M. Iulius Hermes Frontinianus appears on *tituli ß* discovered in Mainz (*AE* 1998.995a) and perhaps at the Monte Testaccio (*CIL* XV 3897).

[33] *CIL* II/5.1180: *M(arco) Iulio Hermesiano, / diffusori oleario, / patri pientissimo, / M(arcus) Iulius Hermes Fron/tinianus, fil(ius), et M(arcus) Iulius / Hermesianus, nep(os), / posuerunt, / accepto loco ab splendissimo ordine Astig(itano).*

[34] *CIL* XIV 708 and 723 (Aphrodisius); *EpOst* 1356 (Musaeus); *EpOst* 167 (Trophi[mus]).

[35] *CIL* VI 13823: *Caeciliae DD(ecimorum) Caecilior(um) / Trophimi et Logi lib(ertae) Helpidi, / D(ecimus) Caecilius Vindex auiae pientiss(imae) / fecit et libert(is) libertabusq(ue) poste/risq(ue) eius et praecepit ut ad it / sepulchrum hortus qui est cinctus / maceria et dieta aiuncta ianuae / custodiae causa sepulchro cedat, / et itum aditum ambitum sacrifi/cique faciundi causa proximis / eius recte liceat.*

[36] Broekaert 2012.

[37] Liou and Marichal 1978; Liou 1987; Liou and Gassend 1990. On a slave trading olive oil in Arles, see Tran 2014.

[38] *CIL* XIII 1996: *D(is) M(anibus) / L. Hilariani Cinna/mi, ciuis Lug(udunensis), naut(a)e / Rhodanico Rho/dano nauigantis, / curatori eiusdem / corporis, negotiato/ris <ole>ari, Q(uintus) Maspe/tius Seuerianus, s<o>/cer eius, et Cl(audius) Seueri[a]/nus, amicus, idemqu[e] / heredes p(onendum) c(urauerunt) et sub / [as]cia dedicauerun[t].*

Arles mentions both names together.[39] Cinnamus seems to have belonged to a family involved in trade along the Rhone corridor.[40] But was he a member of the *corpus oleariorum ex Baetica* or only a commercial partner in relation with some members? On his epitaph, the lack of geographical indication makes the second solution more plausible. Nevertheless, few *diffusores olearii ex Baetica* might have lived in Lyon. Fr. Bérard recently drew attention to a fragment, which had remained confidential, despite of its publication in 1973.[41] The *sanctissimus ordo* of Lyon dedicated the inscription. The upper line shows the letters *et ol(---) diff(---)*, which could not really refer to something else than a *ol(earius) diff(usor)* or the *ol(earii) diff(usores)*, even if the word order is surprising.[42]

In detail, the profile of many oil merchants reveals mobility, but not necessarily incessant journeys. Contrariwise, family epitaphs and positions of *apparitores* imply that D. Caecilius Onesimus, D. Caecilius Abascantus and L. Marius Phoebus took root in Rome. Traders' mobility looks more like residence changes. M. Iulius Hermesianus may have lived in Rome for a while. His identification on the epitaph of a freedwoman deceased in the capital seems plausible, because of the great scarcity of his *cognomen*.[43] It is not impossible either that the *corpus oleariorum* honoured him in Sevilla when he was going to settle overseas.[44] In addition to the homage to M. Petronius Honoratus, an inscription from Astigi also mentions D. Caecilius Hospitalis.[45] Through her will, Caecilia Trophime asked her heirs (D. Caecilius Hospitalis, Caecilia D. f. Materna and Caecilia Philete)

[39] *CIL* XII 851: *D(is) M(anibus) //Maspetiae / Sabinae, L(ucius) Hila/rianius Marti/dius coniugi ka/rissimae et in/comparabili.*

[40] Christol 2010: 615–621.

[41] Bérard 2016: 47–48 *------ / [---]V[--- / ---] et ol(---) diff(---) [--- / ---] ordo sa[nctissimus ? --- / ---]DE[---] / ------.*

[42] The letters DIFF appear on many lead seals discovered during the nineteenth century in the river Saône. The fragment makes stronger the hypothesis that *diffusores olearii* used such seals to identify goods sent to the Rhine area, through Lyon and the Saône valley. See also, in Arles, *CIL* XII 714a, discussed by H. Rougier in her unpublished PhD.

[43] *CIL* VI 20742: *D(is) M(anibus). / Iuliae Zotice, / uix(it) ann(is) XXVIII, / M(arcus) Iul(ius) Hermesianus / lib(ertae) bene meritae.* See Panciera 2006: 300; Remesal Rodríguez 2008; Tchernia 2011: 318–319.

[44] Christol 2008: 282.

[45] *CIL*, II/5, 1165; *AE* 1988.726: *Caecilia Trophime statuam Pietatis ex testament(o) suo ex arg(enti) / p(ondo) C, suo et Caecili Silonis mariti sui nomine poni iussit, / D(ecimus) Caecilius Hospitalis et Caecilia D(ecimi) f(ilia) Materna et Caecilia / Philete heredes sine ulla deductione XX posuer(unt).* Tchernia 2011: 76–81, 315–322.

to offer a silver statue to the *Pietas*. Hospitalis could have inherited from Trophime, because he was his patron. According to A. Tchernia, we could develop this hypothesis further. Indeed, *tituli picti* indicate that Hospitalis worked often in partnership with D. Caecilius Maternus. So Caecilia D. f. Materna could be her daughter and, thus, Caecilia Trophime could be a former *serua communis* of Hospitalis and Maternus.

These cases confirm that family groups had agents, settled at the different points of commercial routes.[46] Such an organisation fostered information flows, first within family networks. The *D.D. Caecilii* represent the most telling example of this. The *corpus oleariorum*, and the integration of multiple family networks inside it, would have complete and increase this ability to spread information. Compared to family groups, association provided a broader means to share information, through collaboration between the *corporati* and their agents. Again, we reach the hypothesis of a differential of information between *corporati* and others, between insiders and outsiders. In this context, individuals who wanted to start a business in oil trade would have wished also, automatically, to join the *corpus*. They would have been aware that the handicap was too big, if they remained outside. So, access to the *corpus* would have determined favourable conditions of access to information, which made a practice of long-distance trade sustainable.

This access was subject to a strict control. Unfortunately, no register of the *corpus oleariorum ex Baetica* is preserved. Nevertheless, the list of its members must have looked like many albums engraved in Ostia by diverse *corpora*, of port boatmen for instance.[47] These inscriptions displayed hierarchies: patrons and then magistrates were mentioned first. So the names of D. Caecilius Hospitalis, C. Sentius Regulianus, M. Iulius Hermesianus and their peers were certainly at the top part of the register. In the second part, the *plebs corporis* was listed in order of seniority. The comparison with preserved albums suggests that many *D.D. Caecilii* and perhaps many *M.M. Iulii* or *C.C. Sentii* were registered. This composition determined admissions of new members, because *corpora* proceeded to entries under the supervision of magistrates and probably through the vote of the *corporati*. For family networks, this organisation was an efficient means of

[46] Broekaert 2016. So-called *tituli* ∂ painted on amphora Dressel 20 would be linked with controls carried out by slaves, on behalf of traders, near production areas. See Tran 2013: 1010.

[47] Tran 2006.

perpetuating their dominant position, especially through the integration of sons and freedmen. And when 'actual' outsiders entered the *corpus*, they were indebted to the most powerful members of the family networks. Their relations were close to a patron-client relationship, which implied exchange of services. Sharing of information could be one of them.

In sum, the oil merchants' milieu was probably structured in concentric circles. Traders went into partnership with their closest colleagues. Many of them belonged to a broader network, which was itself a part of the *corpus oleariorum*. Information was probably shared unequally from one circle to another. At each level, merchants would have defined what they kept for themselves and what they shared outside the circle. Such a conclusion is modest, hypothetical and quite theoretical, because of the lack of evidence. Yet it is possible to be a little more concrete, by asking this question:

11.2 Which Information?

Of course, it is impossible to answer completely, especially because preserved evidence may be too poor. Nonetheless, in order to go beyond quick and abstract considerations, a particular aspect of the global issue seems important. Amongst information required by long-distance trade, the knowledge of diverse economic partners, with whom merchants had to get in contact, was crucial. It was coupled with the knowledge of areas where these partners operated. To buy and sell back: such activity required a good knowledge of producers and production areas, and/or of local merchants in business with long-distance traders. From this perspective, the *negotiatores Cisalpini et Transalpini*, just like the *negotiatores olearii ex Baetica*, offer a diversity of individual profiles. These differences suggest that *corporati* possessed complementary information and were able to share it. Amongst the *Cisalpini et Transalpini*, the specialisation of the *negotiator uestiarius*, L. Lupercius Exessus is noticeable. Gallia Cisalpina was renowned for its wool production.[48] Hence, the density of *collegia centonariorum* in the *Regio XI* and, more precisely, between Milan and the Alps, was very high. During the second century and the first decades of the third one, textile workers formed such communities in Milan, Bergamo, Como and Novara.[49] On the one hand, L. Lupercius Exessus

[48] Liu 2009: 92–94; Roncaglia 2018: 90ff.

[49] Milano: *CIL* V 5738, 5612, 5446, 5447, 5854, 5869, 5914; *AE* 1974.343. Bergamo: *CIL* V 5128. Como: *CIL* V 5283, 5658, 5701; *AE* 1951.94. Novare: *CIL* V 6515. In a few cases, textiles workers belonged to *collegia* formed by *fabri* and *centonarii*.

and other *negotiatores Cisalpini* should have known very well this professional environment. On the other hand, the *negotiatores Transalpini*, whose bases were located in northern Alps, north-eastern Gaul and/or in Lyon, were specialists in other regions, and other goods. The *uenalicii* were probably in business with the *Barbaricum*, which supplied traditionally slaves to Italy.

In the case of olive oil from Baetica, merchants coming from producer areas and those who—at first—knew above all resale regions had complementary skills. The *D.D. Caecilii* and the *M.M. Iulii* belonged to the first group; some provincials from Gallia Narbonensis to the second one.[50] *Tituli picti* found in Gaul, Germany and sometimes in Rome mention merchants with Celtic *nomina gentilicia*, such as *Connius*, *Vrittius* or *Segolatius*. Onomastics reveal that the *Connii* came from Vienna, the city just south of Lyon. The *Vritti* were also from the Rhone valley, but their city of origin is more difficult to determine. The first merchants belonging to these families started to trade oil early, since the second half of the first century. At the beginning, they certainly specialised in oil exportation to the northern provinces.[51] But they extended soon their business. The name of Q. Connius Verna appears on amphora, not only in Sainte-Colombe, very close to Vienna, but also at the Monte Testaccio.[52] And stamps on amphora suggest that, like few Hispanic merchants, the *Vrittii* got involved in oil production.[53] Their relationships with colleagues from Baetica and, what is more, inside a *corpus*, must have helped these Gauls to extend their business.

In Rome, the oil merchants were in contact with the *praefectura annonae*. Long before Septimius Severus instituted free distributions, the imperial State ensured that sufficient quantities of oil, sold at a reasonable price, reached the Roman market. Concretely, traders made a commitment to delivering merchandise in the capital and received privileges in return. The *Digest* of Justinian recalls imperial decisions made in the mid-second century.[54] As a result, it is tempting to connect the relations to

[50] Christol 2010: 577–594. See also Liou 2003.

[51] Some *dipinti* with the name of L. Vrittius Verecundus were found in Köln and Mainz. See *AE* 2002.1069a; Ehmig 2003, n°51, 52, 54; 2007, n°113, 141; 2009, n°275. On this trader, see Martin-Kilcher 2003.

[52] *CAG*, 69/1: 324; *AE* 2003.134.

[53] Broekaert 2015.

[54] Christol 2016: 42–45, especially on *Dig*. 50.4.5 (Scaevola 1 *regul*.); 50.6.6.6 (Callistratus 1 *cognit*.).

power implied by such a system and the civic titles of few merchants. C. Sentius Regulianus was a Roman knight. D. Caecilius Onesimus, D. Caecilius Abascantus and the *mercator olei Hispani* L. Marius Phoebus served as *apparitores* of Roman magistrates. Such promotions required supports in the administration. These merchants were probably the protégés of some dignitary, in office at the *praefectura annonae*. The knowledge of the administrative machinery, of the efficient personal contacts, of the useful recommendations was important information, which was helpful to share within the *corpus oleariorum*.

Moreover, to connect production and consumption regions, long-distance traders had to enter into transaction with transporters. Indeed, most of the time and even if exceptions existed, different professionals practiced commerce and transportation. As a result, the former required a good knowledge of the latter. Both occupations gave birth to many professional *collegia*, which fostered contacts between traders and transporters. A trader needed to trust a transporter to make a deal with him, and the reverse was certainly true. In this context, partners' membership in a professional association provided a guarantee, in the form of crucial information. Their community judged them dignified and respectable enough to be admitted and to remain official members, in an organisation that claimed these qualities for itself. The *corpus Cisalpinorum et Transalpinorum* called itself *splendidissimum* and, consequently, certainly did not want disreputable *negotiatores* amongst its members. To put it in more abstract words, reputation resulting from membership in an association gave information, which seemed to reduce uncertainty and risk. Hence it encourages transactions. Merchants expected transporters to bring goods from one place to another in a safe, efficient and honest manner. At least in seaborne commerce, merchants often asked their agents to ship with their cargoes, to be certain that their transporter would not cheat them.[55] But when transporters and their staff shipped alone, they should have passed messages on and, so, ensured circulation of information within trading networks. Mutual knowledge and confidence were all the more vital. Since then, there was no reason to trust an individual, whose honesty and seriousness had not been evaluated and tested by his *collegium*.[56]

[55] Tran 2013: 1011–1013.

[56] Terpstra 2013 develops this idea about Ostia and trading communities based on a same geographical origin. p. 114: 'So why would anyone have confidence in an isolated individual who, for whatever reason, was excluded from the recognized social and professional structure formed by the people from his native community?'; pp. 124–125: 'These coalitions were

Some merchants played a pivotal role between communities, because their profile implied a close relationship with transporters. They must have facilitated mutual knowledge. The anonymous *negotiator Cisalpinus et Transalpinus* deceased in Milan was a patron of the boatmen sailing on the Lake of Como. These *nautae* belonged to a dense network of associations, quite similar to the—already mentioned—network of *collegia centonariorum*. In the late second and early third centuries, *collegia nautarum* existed at least in Como, Milan, Brescia, maybe Pavia, Mantua and Arilica (on Lake Garda).[57] Boatmen played a major part at the junction of alpine routes and the Po plain. Similar professionals assumed the same crucial function on the other side of the Alps. It is all the more noteworthy that Q. Otacilius Pollinus was a *patronus nautarum Rhodanicorum*.[58] The *nautae Rhodanici* took over merchandise, when the *nautae* of the lake Leman stopped to take care of it, maybe from Geneva.[59] In any case, to have a common patron could have fostered a mutual knowledge between the *negotiatores Cisalpini et Transalpini*, on the one hand, and the *nautae Rhodanici*, on the other. Furthermore, this situation encouraged merchants and transporters to collaborate between members of client communities, and not with outsiders.

Contacts between oil merchants and transporters are also attested, even though the evidence is scarce and quite poor.[60] A few professionals have been both merchants and transporters, either successively or simultaneously. Unfortunately, we just cannot determine it with any certainty. C. Sentius Regulianus would have rather followed a two-step career. First, he would have been *curator* and then patron of the wine merchants settled

so interwoven with the Ostian mercantile fabric that traders coming to the city were obligated to use them. No native trading partner would have trusted them if they stayed outside the established foreign groups and if their business conduct was therefore not controlled by group-membership. Since geographical origin defined membership, networks had the definitive power to include and exclude'.

[57] Como (*CIL* V 5295), Milano (*AE* 2014.520, a. 233), Brescia (*AE* 1977.298; *CIL* V 4990), Pavia? (*AE* 1992.792), Mantua (D. 7265), Arilicia/Verona (*CIL* V 4016–4017).

[58] He is described as a *patronus nautarum Araricorum et Rhodanicorum*. Yet Fr. Bérard (2012: 141) is probably right, when he assumes that Pollinus protected two separate *corpora*. The *collegium nautarum Araricorum*, on the one hand, and the *collegium nautarum Rhodanicorum*, on the other hand, are well-known in Lyon.

[59] Raepsaet-Charlier 2012: 354. On the *nautae lacus Lemanni*, see *ILN*, *Vienne* 850 (Geneva); Nesselhauf and Lieb 1959, n° 26, 28, 30 (Lausanne).

[60] An association of *scaphari qui Romulae negotiantur* is attested in Sevilla, but preserved inscriptions do not indicate any link with the *olearii*. See *CIL* II 1168–1169, 1180, 1183.

in Lyon, that is to say a great dignitary of the most prestigious local *corpus*. At the same time, he would have been boatmen on the river Saone (*nauta Araricus*) and also patron of this second association. Like other businessmen settled in Lyon, he made a fortune out of trading and transporting wine from southern Gaul, to northern Gaul and the Rhine valley. He was living in opulence, when he became patron of the *seuiri Augustales* of Lyon. In a second time, he would have gone to Rome, to work as a *diffusor olearius*, and he became again *curator* of his colleagues. So, C. Sentius Regulianus could have shared information with the merchants delivering oil both in Rome and in the northern provinces, especially information about the Mediterranean-Rhine route and its transporters. The dedication of Regulianus' epitaph is a good clue that he did not cut ties with Lyon and probably its trading communities. L. Silenius Reginus, Ulattia Metrodora and Regulianus' sons paid tribute *procurante Dionysio et Belliciano et [---]*. L. Silenius Reginus also dedicated an epitaph of his sister, in Lyon.[61] Ulattia Metrodora should be related to C. Ulattius Meleager, *seuir Augustalis* and patron of all the associations in Lyon.[62] In fact, all dedicators needed procurators acting on behalf of them, because they probably lived in Lyon, and not in Rome. Yet they seem to have been still in contact with Regulianus and his freedmen.

Regarding L. Hilarianius Cinnanus, his epitaph introduces him not only as a *negotiator olearius*, but also as a *nauta Rhodanicus Rhodano nauigans, curator eiusdem corporis*. The redundant expression *Rhodanicus Rhodano nauigans* is strange and we only preserved a bad copy of this inscription, containing several mistakes. As a result, it is not impossible that Cinnamus was rather a *nauta Rhodanicus Arare nauigans*. Like other professionals, he would have belonged to the *corpus nautarum Rhodanicorum*, but his business would have included the Rhone and the Saone. Anyway, his double skill in trade and transport enables him to act as a go-between between the members of the *corpus oleariorum* and of the *corpus nautarum Rhodanicorum*.

About sea transportation, the *nauicularius* P. Olitius Apollonius represents the most interesting case. The *seuiri Augustales* of Narbonne erected

[61] *CIL* XIII 2087.

[62] *CIL* XIII 1974: *D(is) M(anibus) / et memoriae aeternae / C(ai) Vlatti Meleagri, IIIIIIuir(i) Aug(ustalis) c(olonia) C(opia) C(laudia) Aug(usta) Lug(uduni), patrono eiusdem / corpor(is), item patrono omnium / corpor(um) Lug(uduni) licite coeuntium, / Memmia Cassiana, coniunx, / sarcofago condidit et s(ub) a(scia) d(edicauit).*

a statue to honour him and mentioned his occupation of ship-owner on its marble base.[63] Moreover, his name is painted on amphorae discovered on the Monte Testaccio.[64] These documents must be connected, but many elements remain unknown. First, we ignore if Apollonius was *nauicularius* and *mercator* or *nauicularius* then *mercator*. Likewise, his implication in trade could have been occasional or regular. Last, nothing proves that Apollonius belonged to a formal community other than the community of the *seuiri Augustales.* Nonetheless, he is defined as a *nauicularius C(olonia) I(ulia) P(aterna) C(laudia) N(arbone) M(artio)*. Another inscription, which mentions another *nauicularius* during the second century, refers to the city of Narbonne.[65] Yet this indication lacks on first-century epitaphs of *nauicularii*. Actually, the reference to the colony could reflect the official recognition of a *corpus nauiculariorum Narbonensium* during the second century. So Apollonius played probably a pivotal role too, maybe as a member in two different *corpora*, whose members got to know each other and worked together.

To sum up, in long-distance trade, and probably in other economic sectors too, access to diverse information was a valuable asset that membership in a professional *collegium* provided. From this perspective, a large and irreversible gap would have separated insiders from outsiders. Such a closing, linked with a form of information withholding, was probably also typical of smaller networks, inside associations. So these organisations were not only spaces of friendship and sharing amongst equals. Information was a coveted resource that dominant individuals and dominant groups shared only according to their interest. In inter-occupational relationships too, insiders and dominants—traders and transporters belonging to different *corpora*, for instance—had interest to work only together and to withhold information on each other in closed groups. De facto monopolies would have resulted from such positions of power. It is perhaps not orthodox to describe these phenomena as 'asymmetric information'. It can be at least concluded that inequalities seemed to happen everywhere when we look at Roman professional associations, particularly when we consider how information was shared in this context.

[63] *CIL* XII 4406: *Dec(reto) IIIIIIuir(orum) / Augustal(ium), / P(ublio) Olitio / Apollonio, / IIIIIIuir(o) Aug(ustali) et / nauic(ulario) c(olonia) I(ulia) P(aterna) C(laudia) N(arbone) M(artio), / ob merita et liberali/tates eius, qui / honore decreti / usus impendium / remisit et / statuam de suo / posuit.*

[64] *CIL* XV 3975 and 3976 (a. 149).

[65] *CIL* XII 4398.

Bibliography

Bang, P.F. 2008. *The Roman Bazaar. A Comparative Study of Trade and Markets in a Tributary Empire*. Cambridge: Cambridge University Press.

Bérard, F. 2012. Les corporations du transport fluvial à Lyon à l'époque romaine. In *Collegia. Le phénomène associatif dans l'Occident romain*, ed. M. Dondin-Payre and N. Tran, 135–154. Bordeaux: Ausonius Éditions.

———. 2016. Remarques sur le commerce du vin et de l'huile à Lyon. In *"Voce concordi." Scritti per Claudio Zaccaria*, ed. F. Mainardis, 39–50. Trieste: Editreg.

Boscolo, F. 2004-2005. I battellieri del lago di Como di Como in età romana. *Atti e Memorie dell'Accademia Galileiana di Scienze, Lettere ed Arti in Padova, già dei Ricovrati e Patavina, Classe di Scienze Morali, Lettere ed Arti* 117: 221–240.

Broekaert, W. 2012. Joining forces. Commercial partnerships or *societates* in the early Roman empire. *Historia* 61: 221–253.

———. 2015. Sticky Fingers. The Investment Structure of the Spanish Oil Business. *Cahiers Mondes Anciens* 7, [online: https://journals.openedition.org/mondesanciens/1598].

———. 2016. Freedmen and Agency in Roman Business. In *Urban Craftsmen and Traders in the Roman World*, ed. A. Wilson and M. Flohr, 222–253. Oxford: Oxford University Press.

Christol, M. 2008. *Annona Urbis*: Remarques sur l'organisation du ravitaillement en huile de la ville de Rome au IIe siècle ap. J.-C. In *Epigrafia 2006. Atti della XIVe rencontre sur l'épigraphie in onore di Silvio Panciera con altri contributi di colleghi, allievi e collaboratori*, ed. M.L. Caldelli, G.L. Gregori, and S. Orlandi, 271–298. Rome: Quasar.

———. 2010. *Une histoire provinciale. La Gaule narbonnaise de la fin du IIe siècle av. J.-C. au IIIe s. ap. J.-C.* Paris: Publications de la Sorbonne.

———. 2016. Annona Urbis: la part de l'échange. In *Échanger en Méditerranée. Acteurs, pratiques et normes dans les mondes anciens*, ed. A.-F. Baroni, G. Bernard, B. Le Teuff, and C. Ruiz Darasse, 37–56. Rennes: Presses universitaires de Rennes.

Ehmig, U. 2003. *Die römischen Amphoren aus Mainz*. Möhnesee: Bibliopolis.

———. 2007. Tituli Picti auf Amphoren in Köln. *Kölner Jahrbuch* 40: 215–322.

———. 2009. Tituli Picti auf Amphoren in Köln. *Kölner Jahrbuch* 42: 393–445.

Goffaux, B. 2012. À la recherche des édifices collégiaux hispaniques. In *Collegia. Le phénomène associatif dans l'Occident romain*, ed. M. Dondin-Payre and N. Tran, 199–219. Bordeaux: Ausonius Éditions.

Golosetti, R. 2016. Les sanctuaires des grands cols alpins: entre appropriation de l'espace de marges et zone liminale. In *Franges urbaines, confins territoriaux. La Gaule dans l'empire*, ed. C. Besson and O. Blin, 553–572. Bordeaux: Ausonius Éditions.

Hawkins, C. 2016. *Roman Artisans and the Urban Economy*. Cambridge: Cambridge University Press.

Le Roux, P. 1986. L'huile de Bétique et le Prince: sur un itinéraire annonaire. *Revue des Études Anciennes* 88: 247–271.

Liou, B. 1987. Inscriptions peintes sur amphores: Fos (suite), Marseille, Toulon, Port-la-Nautique, Arles, Saint-Blaise, Saint-Martin-de-Crau, Mâcon, Calvi. *Archaeonautica* 7: 55–139.

———. 2003. QVINTVS CONNIVS VERNA: trois inscriptions peintes sur amphores Dressel 20 découvertes à Sainte-Colombe-lès-Vienne (Rhône). In *SFECAG. Actes du Congrès de Saint-Romain-en-Gal*, 589–593. Marseille: SFECAG.

Liou, B., and J.-M. Gassend. 1990. L'épave Saint-Gervais 3 à Fos-sur-Mer (milieu du IIe siècle ap. J.-C.). Inscriptions peintes sur amphores de Bétique. Vestiges de la coque. *Archaeonautica* 10: 157–264.

Liou, B., and R. Marichal. 1978. Les inscriptions peintes sur amphores de l'anse Saint- Gervais à Fos-sur-Mer. *Archaeonautica* 2: 109–181.

Liu, J. 2009. *Collegia Centonariorum. The Guilds of Textile Dealers in the Roman West*. Leiden/Boston: Brill.

———. 2017. Group Membership, Trust Networks, and Social Capital: A Critical Analysis. In *Works, Labour and Professions in the Roman World*, ed. C. Laes and K. Verboven, 203–226. Leiden/Boston: Brill.

Martin-Kilcher, S. 2003. Lucius Urittius Verecundus, négociant à la fin du Ier siècle, et sa marchandise découverte à Mayence. In *Vivre, produire et échanger: reflets méditerranéens. Mélanges offerts à Bernard Liou*, ed. L. Rivet and M. Sciallano, 343–353. Montagnac: M. Mergoil.

Mennella, G. 2000. Un *negotiator vestiarius cisalpinus et transalpinus* a Fara Novarese. *Epigraphica* 62: 125–136.

Nesselhauf, H., and H. Lieb. (1959). Dritter Nachtrag zu CIL XIII, Inschriften aus den germanischen Provinzen und dem Treverergebiet. *BRGK (Bericht der römish-germanischen Kommission des deutschen archäologischen Instituts)* 40: 120–228..

Panciera, S. 2006. *Epigrafi, epigrafia, epigrafisti: scritti vari editi e inediti (1956–2005) con note complementari e indici*. Rome: Quasar.

Raepsaet-Charlier, M.-Th. 2012. Élites politiques et économiques dans les cités gallo-romaines: l'exemple des *Otacilii* d'Avenches. Réflexion critique sur une famille de notables helvètes. In *La société romaine et ses élites. Hommages à Élizabeth Deniaux*, ed. R. Baudry and S. Destephen, 347–360. Paris: Picard.

Remesal Rodríguez, J. 2000. *L. Marius Phoebus Mercator olei hispani ex provincia Baetica*. Consideraciones en torno a los términos *mercator*, *negotiator* y *diffusor olearius ex Baetica*. In *Epigraphai. Miscellanea Epigrafica in onore di Lidio Gasperini*, ed. G. Paci, 781–797. Rome, II: Tipigraf.

———. 2008. Olearii. In *Epigrafia 2006. Atti della XIVe Rencontre sur l'épigraphie in onore di Silvio Panciera con altri contributi di colleghi, allievi e collaboratori*, ed. M.L. Caldelli, G.L. Gregori, and S. Orlandi, 349–374. Rome: Quasar.

———. 2015-2016. El monte Testaccio (30 años de investigación). *Tribuna d'Arqueologia*: 72–87.

Rico, C. 2003. *Mercatores, negotiatores* et *diffusores olearii* et le commerce de l'huile de Bétique à destination de Rome aux Ier et IIe siècles de notre ère. *REA* 105: 413–433.

Roncaglia, C.E. 2018. *Northern Italy in the Roman World*. Baltimore: Johns Hopkins University Press.

Tchernia, A. 2011. *Les Romains et le commerce*. Naples: Centre Jean Bérard.

Terpstra, T. 2013. *Trading communities in the Roman world*. Leiden: Brill.

Tran, N. 2006. *Les membres des associations romaines. Le rang social des collegiati en Italie et en Gaule sous le Haut-Empire*. Rome: École française de Rome.

———. 2013. Les statuts de travail des esclaves et des affranchis dans les grands ports du monde romain (Ier siècle av. J.-C. – IIe siècle apr. J.-C.). *Annales HSS* 68 (4): 999–1026.

———. 2014. Un esclave préposé au commerce de l'huile dans le port d'Arles. À propos de *Dig.*, 14.3.13 pr. (Ulp. 28 ad ed.). In *Les Affaires de Monsieur Andreau*, ed. C. Apicella, M.-L. Haack, and Fr. Lerouxel, 205–212. Bordeaux: Ausonius Éditions.

———. 2015. C. Veturius Testius Amandus, les cinq corps de lénunculaires d'Ostie et la batellerie tibérine au début du IIIe siècle. *MEFRA* 126 (1): 131–145.

———. 2017. Entreprises de construction, vie associative et organisation du travail dans la Rome impériale et à Ostie. *L'Antiquité Classique* 86: 115–127.

———. 2020. Boatmen and their Corpora in the Great Ports of the Roman West (IInd – IIIrd c. AD). In *Roman Port Societies through the Evidence of Inscriptions*, ed. P. Arnaud and S. Keay, 85–106. Cambridge: Cambridge University Press.

Waltzing, J.-P. 1895-1900. *Étude historique sur les corporations professionnelles chez les Romains*. Louvain: Ch. Peeters.

Wiblé, F. 2006. Le trafic commercial par le Grand Saint-Bernard à l'époque romaine. L'apport de l'épigraphie et de quelques données archéologiques. In *Alpis Graia. Archéologie sans frontières au col du petit Saint-Bernard*, ed. L. Apollonia, Fr. Ballet, M.-P. Feuillet, and D. Herrero, 285–289. Aoste.

CHAPTER 12

A Case of Arbitrage in a Worldwide Trade: Roman Coins in India

Dario Nappo

12.1 Introduction

> The Roman economy was too complex to be reduced simply to the label market economy. The challenge is to explore the interplay of several modes of economic organization, market trade being only one important element among several in institutional fabric of the empire.[1]

Scholars engaged in the study of the ancient economy have often shown a preference for looking at the economic phenomena, assuming that these

[1] Bang 2012: 303. On the same subject, see also Hingley 2005: 106; Lo Cascio 2007: 622; 2009: 208; Tchernia 2016: 72–96.

This research was carried out in the framework of the STAR programme, funded by UniNa and Compagnia San Paolo. I would like to express my gratitude here to Prof William V. Harris and Prof Domenico Fausto for their willingness to read an earlier version of this work and give me their extensive feedbacks.

D. Nappo (✉)
Università degli Studi di Napoli Federico II, Naples, Italy

C. Rosillo-López, M. García Morcillo (eds.), *Managing Information in the Roman Economy*, Palgrave Studies in Ancient Economies,
https://doi.org/10.1007/978-3-030-54100-2_12

phenomena might somehow be self-explanatory, in a sort of natural, ideology-free manner.[2] Unfortunately, this is almost never the case. In order to gain a satisfactory interpretation of the ancient evidence, we need to make a conscious use of the models and tools that history and, in this case, economics have devised to interpret data.[3] The aim of this work is to contribute to the ever-heated debate on some of the peculiar structures of the ancient economy, focussing on some aspects of the Roman imperial economy. In particular, this paper will investigate a case of arbitrage in the context of the international maritime trade, between the Roman Empire and India, taking as an example a specific case study, which will be used to make it clear what this particular case can tell us to improve our understanding of the ancient Roman imperial economy. In doing so, some methodological frameworks which have been devised by students of economics and history will be put in use. Different models can help us to understand different features of economic phenomena, as long as we are careful when combining ideas and approaches with diverse theoretical backgrounds.[4] We must also keep always in mind, on the one hand, the undeniable difference of the Ancient from the Modern World, while conceding that economic theories and models conceived in the Modern World can, if properly calibrated, explain some of the features of the Ancient World.[5] Methodological awareness is the only way to avoid becoming trapped in the shortcomings of an 'anachronistic' approach.[6]

[2] In economic history, this tendency is even more pronounced, because of the inclination of economists to describe economic activities in mathematical terms. An interesting and updated debate on such a leaning can be found in Boer and Petterson 2017: 1–48; Blanton IV and Hollander 2019: 9–11.

[3] See the classic Hicks 1969: 1–8 for an economist's purview on the matter.

[4] On the topic, see for example the discussion in Meikle 2002; Bang 2012: 301–302.

[5] For an interesting treating of the issues related to the application of economic theories and models on the ancient economy, see recently for example Verboven 2015a and Erdkamp 2015; see also the very recent and extremely compelling collective book edited by Hollander, Blanton IV and Fitzgerald 2019, which is full of stimulating new insights aimed at breaking the limits of a 'market-oriented' scholarship on the ancient economy.

[6] The problem of describing non-modern economic activities in modern terms is already fully discussed by Karl Marx in his *Grundrisse*: Marx 1973: 105–106; see also Marx 2002. See recently Boer and Petterson 2017: xi–xxi for an engaging discussion on the usefulness of applying modern approaches to the study of Antiquity.

12.2 The State of the Debate

Understanding the functioning, the structure, and (as was more fashionable until some 30 years ago) the nature of the ancient economy is a challenge that has been intriguing historians over the last two centuries. Our current comprehension of the true dynamics that regulated the economy in Antiquity is still far from adequate, let alone complete.[7] This is of course only a part of a much wider problem, the unbridgeable distance between Antiquity and Modernity, an issue which is far beyond the limits of this paper.[8]

At least at a very general level, it is worth pointing out how ancient Mediterranean societies were governed by different sets of values and rules, when compared to equivalent modern societies. These deep differences encompassed every human activity, including economics. Also for this reason, while some of the contemporary dispute is somehow still affected by the old quarrel between *primitivist* vs *modernist* view of Antiquity, other scholars have preferred to stay above the fray and look for different interpretations.[9]

The Roman economy, albeit comparatively developed when confronted with other pre-modern economic systems,[10] was still a conventional pre-modern economy, largely based on agriculture and household production.[11] There are of course a number of economic activities and behaviours

[7] Morris 1994.

[8] I will refer to Morley 2009 and Manning 2018 for a very elegant discussion of the issues related to this huge topic.

[9] See for instance Frederiksen 1975: 10: "the old debate between primitivists and modernists (is) a small and rather unimportant duel (...) Neither thesis (is) really acceptable without a good deal of emendation". The attempts to shift the debate intensified since the '90s of the last century: see Harris 1993. An interesting overall rethinking of the economy of Antiquity is in Andreau and Maucourant 1999; Bresson 2000. In the new millennium, see the monumental *Cambridge Economic History of the Greco-Roman World* (Scheidel et al. 2007), followed by a considerable step forward thanks to the works of for example Erdkamp and Verboven 2015; Kehoe et al. 2015; Boer and Petterson 2017; Manning 2018; Hollander et al. 2019.

[10] Among the most interesting cases of comparative history of the last few years, Scheidel's and Bang's works are definitely noteworthy. See Scheidel 2009 and 2015 for a contrast between the Roman Empire and ancient China. See also Morris and Scheidel 2009 for a wider range of comparisons among pre-industrial societies. See instead Bang 2008 for a comparison between the Roman Empire and the Moghul Empire. See also Bang and Kołodziejczyk 2012 for a comparison between Eurasian empires.

[11] Bowman and Wilson 2009; Scheidel 2012b: 1; Jongman 2014: 75–77; Lo Cascio 2018: 117–118; Zuiderhoek 2019: 51.

which can be scrutinised to investigate the functioning and development of the Roman economy. Scholarship on phenomena such as modes of production, labour, banking, slavery, agriculture, farming, and so on has grown significantly over the last two centuries. Yet even if there is some (very little) general consensus on some of these activities and their role in shaping the context of the Roman economy, one of the main objects of disagreement is the role of trade, defined as an exchange of goods in which a desire for profit is the motive of one party or both,[12] and especially long-distance trade, to define the features of the ancient economy.[13] This leads us to ask ourselves what was the real role played by trading activities in Antiquity.

All works concerning such topic have to some extent to deal with what is known as 'the Great Debate' on relevance of trade in the ancient economy. There is no agreement on whether (long-distance) trade was a matter of luxuries and/or special merchandise, therefore having a minor impact on an otherwise agrarian-based economy, or instead there was a steady and strong commercial ongoing flow that made a major impact on the overall performance of the Roman economy.[14]

Literary sources do not normally give us much help to obtain a clear picture. In fact, they seldom refer to movements of merchandise between hubs in the Mediterranean basin and even when they do, they generally talk only of big cities, such as Rome or Alexandria, often overlooking small-scale regional trade. Even more problematic in our surviving sources is the irremediable lack of any sort of statistical presentation of any given economic phenomenon, though we can be reasonably sure that this class of document was available at the time:[15] all we find are occasional records of single events, taken out of their economic context. Nevertheless, some

[12] Harris 2011: 156.

[13] It should be noted incidentally that even the importance of trade as a proxy to understand the structures of the ancient economy is a concept that has always been taken for granted. See now on this subject Hollander et al. 2019.

[14] For a survey of the different points of view and interpretations on the subject, see for example the chapter "A Forum on Trade" in Scheidel 2012a: 287–317. The idea that eastern merchandise were only luxury items dates back as far as Gibbon (1776), and, despite being proved wrong by many scholars (see e.g. Sidebotham 1986; Morley 2007, 573–574) still has some supporters among modern scholars: see for example McLaughlin 2010.

[15] Appian (*Introduction* 15) explicitly refers to such documents. Other hints in Suet. *Vita Aug.* 101; Stat. *Silv.* 3.3.85–108. See also Nicolet 1982; Wilson 2009.

scholars of Antiquity have become accustomed to using these impressionistic data, a habit which has received severe criticism by others.[16] Still, the reference to exceptional forms of commerce in our sources can shed some light on the establishment of particular trade routes, otherwise undocumented. This particular interpretation was first popularised by the works of M.I. Rostovtzeff, who held true the belief that trade is a kind of activity strictly connected to human nature.[17]

This view has been fiercely opposed by scholars such as Polanyi, Weber, Finley, and more recently Bang, according to all whom trade in Antiquity was not just limited to a smaller scale than in Modernity, but it was in fact a completely different kind of phenomenon.

The main problem with the 'Great Debate' is that the available evidence is inconclusive, and its interpretation is arbitrary, to some extent.[18] It is therefore yet too soon to hope to settle the debate in a conclusive manner, but it is also true that carefully selected models and theories can help us make some progress towards understanding several aspects of the functioning of the ancient economy.[19]

For this reason, in this paper I have chosen to clarify some facets of the trade between the Roman Empire and the Indian Ocean, using the tools provided by selected economic theories, first of all asymmetric information theory. The starting point will be evidence I have already examined in a previous paper,[20] to which I will refer, to avoid redundant duplications. I will only summarise here the most important parts of it, which are necessary to follow the present argument. What I am focussed on here is applying asymmetric information theory to a concrete case, to verify how this theoretical tool can help us to clarify certain aspects of already known economic phenomena, to put them into a proper context, and therefore give a contribution to achieve a wider interpretation of the ancient economy and its peculiar features.

[16] See for example the classic criticisms of Braudel 1979; Finley 1985: 61.

[17] Rostovtzeff 1926 and 1957. See also Hopkins 1983; Cartledge 1998; Morley 2004; Temin 2001, 2013.

[18] Morley 2007: 5. Similarly, see also Vivenza 2012.

[19] Again, I have specifically in mind the recent works of Erdkamp and Verboven 2015; Kehoe et al. 2015; Hollander et al. 2019.

[20] Nappo 2018.

12.3 The Theoretical Framework

Asymmetric information theory was developed in the 1970s and 1980s in order to explain some common phenomena of economic transactions, which cannot be understood in the framework of the general equilibrium theory. In 2001 the Nobel Memorial Prize in Economic Sciences was awarded to the three economists who had built and developed the theory over the years: George Akerlof, Michael Spence, and Joseph Stiglitz.[21] Asymmetric information is a situation where some participants in an economic transaction have access to more, or better, relevant information than the other parties. This situation can be a reason for market failure. Economic agents with superior information might attempt to gain advantage from this, and inefficiency may result.[22]

This concept itself is intuitive and can be easily understood even by people with limited or no background in economics. Asymmetric information in economic transactions is in fact a very common phenomenon, which anyone would experience very often in their life. A typical example of asymmetric information is a transaction between a skilled worker and his customer. The skilled worker normally has a greater knowledge in his own field than the customer, due to the former's theoretical studies and/or practical experience.

As argued by Akerlof, if information is unevenly distributed in a certain market, it follows that the latter cannot be considered an 'integrated market'.[23] Later on, Stiglitz has observed that information asymmetry can be a common feature to all markets, and he also added that an uneven distribution of information is not only dependent on a lack of technological resources, but it can very well be a product of hierarchies of power and societal organisation.[24] Growing asymmetrical information can even be considered a desirable outcome of a mature market economy, since a highly specialised worker can offer a better service to his customers. On the other hand, asymmetric information can generate situations in which one of the parties takes an economically irrational decision, due to his own lack of knowledge on a certain matter. A typical example is known as adverse selection, which occurs when a buyer is unable to observe charac-

[21] A very short synthesis of the most important works of the three Nobel laureates can be found in Löfgren et al. 2002.

[22] Eatwell et al. 2000: 133–135.

[23] The theory was first developed in Akerlof 1970. See Eatwell et al. 2000: 133–135.

[24] Stiglitz 1989.

teristics of the seller or his product: this leads to a situation in which either the products or the sellers with higher quality are selected (or even self-selected) out of the market.[25]

A point that it is worth stressing at the beginning is that many asymmetric information situations have a temporal dimension, an element that will prove essential to our analysis. Since information is revealed over time, the likelihood of repeated interactions among parties is important, as a source of information for buyers, and as a source of profit for sellers.[26] Behaviours of individuals in one-shot economic interactions may dramatically differ from behaviours of the same individuals over a repeated transaction. In fact, each party in a repeated transaction will have a more prudent approach to the business, taking into account the fact that a non-honest behaviour may hamper the ability to keep doing business with the other party, over time. Since its codification, asymmetric information theory has been applied to a number of different contexts, either in the field of economics, or even in politics and sociology.

12.4 Exposition of the Case Study

In the second century AD, having to address the emperor with an official speech, the rhetor Aelius Aristides pronounced a long oration, which was to be remembered as the archetypical celebration of the Roman Empire and its cultural, political, and economic achievements:

> ὅσα γὰρ παρ' ἑκάστοις φύεται καὶ κατασκευάζεται, οὐκ ἔστιν ὡς οὐκ ἐνταῦθα ἀεὶ καὶ περιττεύει. τοσαῦται δ' ἀφικνοῦνται δεῦρο κομίζουσαι παρὰ πάντων ὁλκάδες ἀνὰ πᾶσαν μὲν ὥραν, πᾶσαν δὲ φθινοπώρου περιτροπὴν, ὥστ' ἐοικέναι τὴν πόλιν κοινῷ τινι τῆς γῆς ἐργαστηρίῳ. φόρτους μὲν ἀπ' Ἰνδῶν, εἰ βούλει δὲ, καὶ τῶν εὐδαιμόνων Ἀράβων, τοσούτους ὁρᾶν ἔξεστιν ὥστε εἰκάζειν γυμνὰ τὸ λοιπὸν τοῖς ἐκεῖ λελεῖφθαι τὰ δένδρα καὶ δεῦρο δεῖν ἐκείνους ἐλθεῖν, ἐάν του δέωνται, τῶν σφετέρων μεταιτήσοντας[...]. γεωργίαι δὲ ὑμῶν Αἴγυπτος, Σικελία, Λιβύης.
>
> Whatever is grown and made among each people cannot fail to be here at all times and in abundance. And here the merchant vessels come carrying these many products from all regions in every season and even at every equinox, so that the city appears a kind of common emporium of the World. Cargoes from India and even Arabia the Blessed, one can see in such num-

[25] Akerlof 1970.

[26] Jones 2014: 236.

> bers as to surmise that in those lands the trees will have been stripped bare and that the inhabitants of those lands, if they need anything, must come here and beg for a share of their own [...]. Your farmlands are Egypt, Sicily and all of cultivated Africa.[27]

In order to make an impression on his audience, Aelius Aristides did not fail to underline the large amount of cargo that reached the Empire from regions as far as Arabia and India, whose merchandise were poured into Rome to satisfy the appetites of the imperial customers. Aristides' enthusiastic remarks were not a *hapax* in the Roman official propaganda: Augustus himself, in his *Res Gestae*, had started the long list of writers who were to exalt the ability of the Roman Empire to stretch its political influence as far as India.[28]

In fact, trading relations between the Roman Empire and India are a historical phenomenon which is still attracting the attention of scholars, an attention that has been growing constantly over the last roughly one hundred years.[29] Apparently, Indo-Roman trade would fit very well in the category of luxury trade. This is, at least, the way our available ancient sources consistently describe it to us. According to all of them, in fact, this kind of trade was fuelled by the decadent tastes of an élite unworthy of their own ancestors' *mos maiorum*.[30] This interpretation of Indo-Roman trade as a business in luxury was originally taken at face value by many modern scholars, at least until the publication of S. Sidebotham's first monograph on the Roman trade with India. Sidebotham started to challenge the traditional interpretation of this trade as luxury trade: he rightly pointed out that some of those substances of trade could not simply be classified as pure luxury merchandise: frankincense, pepper and many other spices were widely used in the Roman Empire, for everyday

[27] Ael. Arist. *Oration* 6.12–13.

[28] Aug. *Res Gest.* 31: *Ad me ex India regum legationes saepe missae sunt non visae ante id tempus apud quemquam Romanorum ducem.*

[29] The first to deal with the subject was Gibbon, in his *The History of the Decline and Fall of the Roman Empire* (1776–1789); see also Warmington (1928, revised edition 1974). But the turning point for such studies was the excavations made by Wheeler at Arikamedu, in India, that for the first time provided some actual archaeological evidence of the trade between the two areas of the world (Wheeler 1976). Since then, the number of papers and works published on the topic has constantly increased.

[30] See Young 2001 for a full discussion.

purposes, and by heterogeneous social clusters.[31] Since Sidebotham's remarks, scholarship started to reconsider the economic relevance and the meaning of Indo-Roman trade in the wider context of the Roman economic system. Its importance and impact have been the subject of several major works.[32] The further step has been analysing this trade as a proxy to investigate some of the "big themes" in the ancient economy, such as World Trade Economy and Globalisation. Although an interpretation of Indo-Roman trade in such terms might be legitimate and stimulating, studies on World Trade and (even more) on Globalisation in Antiquity are probably still at a very embryonic stage of development,[33] therefore much more theoretical thinking is needed, before we can safely apply these categories to the Ancient World.[34]

The real economic impact that such a trade would have had for the Roman Empire is something very difficult for us to estimate, since we almost completely lack reliable figures associated with this business. Notoriously, one of the few exceptions are two places of Pliny the Elder's *Naturalis Historia*, which indeed are burdened with heavy and trite moralistic comments.

In book six, Pliny assesses a flow of 50,000,000 sesterces per year paid by the Empire in order to buy Indian merchandise, and he also adds that it was sold in the Empire at 100 times its purchase price.[35] He then returns

[31] Sidebotham 1986: 20–21. Most of the following scholarship has now accepted this important point. See for example Ball 2000: 130; Young 2001: 14–17. Yet the old approach to the Indian trade as merely a trade in luxury items is still present in some recent works unwilling to engage with the progress of modern scholarship (e.g. McLaughlin 2010: 7–10; and again 2016: 1).

[32] Every attempt to list all the relevant monographs appeared after Sidebotham's first book is doomed to be incomplete. Among the most relevant studies on the subject, it is certainly necessary to mark out the works of De Romanis 2006, 1998, 2020; Young 2001; Sidebotham 2011; Power 2012; Seland 2008, 2010, 2014; Gurukkal 2016; Boussac et al. 2016; Mathew 2016; Manzo et al. 2018; Cobb 2015a, 2018a, c.

[33] For an engaging discussion on the applicability of concepts such as globalisation and world economy to Antiquity, see Hingley 2005; LaBianca and Scham 2006; Jennings 2011; Pitts and Versluys 2015; more recently Terpstra 2019: 1–32. On the definition of Global History, see for example Conrad 2016.

[34] See for example the works of McLaughlin 2010 and 2016; Manzo et al. 2018, which all in their titles rather ambitiously refer to the concepts of World Economy and Globalisation, while not specifically addressing such sensible topics. More interesting is the purview of Seland (2008, 2010: 18–20; 2014: 386–387), who prefers to speak of 'oikoumenisation'. See also Cobb 2018b: 5–7.

[35] Plin. *NH* 6.101.

to the same topic in the twelfth book of his work, again complaining about the excessive amount of money wasted in such a trade:[36]

> *Verum Arabiae etiamnum felicius mare est; ex illo namque margaritas mittit. Minimaque computatione miliens centena milia sestertium annis omnibus India et Seres et paeninsula illa imperio nostro adimunt: tanti nobis deliciae et feminae costant.*
>
> But it is the sea of Arabia that has even a still greater right to be called "happy", for it is this that furnishes us with pearls. At the very lowest computation, India, the Seres, and the Arabian Peninsula, withdraw from our empire one hundred millions of sesterces every year—so dearly do we pay for our luxury and our women.[37]

Despite the moralistic attitude of Pliny toward the Eastern trade,[38] many modern scholars have been attracted by his statements, which have generated rich debate, and the trustworthiness of his figures has long been discussed: it is obvious that they cannot, in any case, be taken at face value.[39]

The fact that they are round figures suggests that they are not very reliable. Still, in both passages, Pliny provides us with a minimum rather than precise amounts, something that would give a reason for the round figures.

[36] Plin. *NH* 12.84 (trans. Bostock and Riley (1855)).

[37] See Tac., *Ann.*, 3.53 (reporting Tiberius' words): *Promiscas viris et feminis vestis atque illa feminarum propria, quis lapidum causa pecuniae nostrae ad externas aut hostilis gentis transferuntur.* ('The apparel worn indiscriminately by both sexes, or that peculiar luxury of women which, for the sake of jewels, diverts our wealth to strange or hostile nations'). As pointed out by Tchernia (2016: 239), the words of Pliny and Tiberius are very similar, suggesting that "either Pliny was directly influenced by an idea actually expressed in Tiberius' discourse, or it was a *topos* widely used in the middle decades of the first century, or more precisely, an adaptation of an old *topos* on luxury and autarky to a particular set of circumstances."

[38] More examples of such a point of view are to be found in the ancient literary sources, such as Dio Chrysostom, *Orations* 79.5–6: Ἆρα ἐνθυμεῖσθε ὅτι πάντες οὗτοι, λέγω δὲ τοὺς Κελτοὺς καὶ Ἰνδοὺς καὶ Ἴβηρας καὶ Ἄραβας καὶ Βαβυλωνίους, φόρους παρ' ἡμῶν λαμβάνουσιν, οὐ τῆς χώρας οὐδὲ τῶν βοσκημάτων, ἀλλὰ τῆς ἀνοίας τῆς ἡμετέρας; [...] πλὴν ὅτι λίθους μικροὺς καὶ ἀσθενεῖς καί, νὴ Δία, θηρίων ὀστᾶ διδόντες λαμβάνουσιν ἀργύριον καὶ χρυσίον, ἀντὶ χρηστῶν ἄχρηστα ἀντικαταλλαττόμενοι. ('Are you aware that all these peoples—the Celts, Indians, Iberians, Arabs, and Babylonians—exact tribute from us, not from our land or from our flocks and herds, but from our own folly? [...] They do offer tiny, fragile pebbles and, forsooth, bones of wild beasts when they take our silver and gold, exchanging useless things for useful').

[39] Raschke 1978: 604–608; Veyne 1979; De Romanis 1982-87: 199; Tchernia 2016: 238–239.

They are meant as a rough indication of the scale, rather than a precise evaluation.

Instead, the real problem with Pliny's figures lies not in their scant reliability, but in the fact that we have no clue what they actually meant to him, since he provides us with no terms of comparison to really appreciate the order of magnitude of the outflow he is talking about. Much debate has also risen about whether we should consider Pliny's data as his estimate of the value of the Roman coins exported to buy exotic items in the Indian Ocean, or rather a rough indication of the value of all the Roman items leaving the Empire bound East.[40]

Despite such uncertainty, scholars have always assumed that coins were the most important Roman export, the only means through which Roman traders could pay for the eastern commodities they sought.[41] Such a scenario should probably be partially corrected, since it is plainly attested by the *Periplus Maris Erythraei* that Romans were also trading their own merchandise in India.[42] Anyway, the fact that coins were an important part of the Roman exports is also reported by the same *Periplus*,[43] which often refers to exports of money and metals from the Roman Empire to India, but which also makes some differences. When talking about Roman

[40] See the interesting discussion of De Romanis 2006 on the topic. Also, see MacDowall 2003b: 39. See also recently Cobb 2015b: 199.

[41] Note the different opinion expressed by Harris (2011: 227) who argues that payments could also be done in bullion.

[42] Yet, our sources make reference also to the possibility of trading with Indians through the means of barter. See for instance Pausanias, *Descriptio Graeciae*, 3.12, 3–4: Λακεδαιμονίοις δὲ κατὰ τὴν ὁδὸν ταύτην ἐστίν, ὡς ἤδη λέλεκταί μοι, τὰ ὀνομαζόμενα Βοώνητα, Πολυδώρου ποτὲ οἰκία τοῦ βασιλέως: ἀποθανόντος δὲ παρὰ τοῦ Πολυδώρου τῆς γυναικὸς ἐπρίαντο ἀντιδόντες βοῦς. ἀργύρου γὰρ οὐκ ἦν πω τότε οὐδὲ χρυσοῦ νόμισμα, κατὰ τρόπον δὲ ἔτι τὸν ἀρχαῖον ἀντεδίδοσαν βοῦς καὶ ἀνδράποδα καὶ ἀργὸν τὸν ἄργυρον καὶ χρυσόν: οἱ δὲ ἐς τὴν Ἰνδικὴν ἐσπλέοντες φορτίων φασὶν Ἑλληνικῶν τοὺς Ἰνδοὺς ἀγώγιμα ἄλλα ἀνταλλάσσεσθαι, νόμισμα δὲ οὐκ ἐπίστασθαι, καὶ ταῦτα χρυσοῦ τε ἀφθόνου καὶ χαλκοῦ παρόντος σφίσι.

'On this road the Lacedaemonians have, as I have already said, what is called the Booneta, which once was the house of their king Polydorus. When he died, they bought it from his widow, paying the price in oxen. For at that time there was as yet neither silver nor gold coinage, but they still bartered in the old way with oxen, slaves, and uncoined silver and gold. Those who sail to India say that the natives give other merchandise in exchange for Greek cargoes, knowing nothing about coinage, and that though they have plenty of gold and of bronze.'

[43] For the references to the text of the *PME*, I used here the version of Casson 1989. For a complete overview on the nature and problems of this text, see now Boussac et al. 2012.

exports to Barbarikon (North India), the author lists χρῆμα[44] (which can be translated as money),[45] and silver plate. At Barygaza (still North India), the metals in demand are copper, tin, lead, antimony, gold and silver money (δηνάριον χρυσοῦν καὶ ἀργυροῦν).[46] At Limyrike (South India), we are told that there is a market for a 'great amount of money' (χρήματα πλεῖστα), antimony, copper, tin, and lead.[47]

To corroborate even further the assessment of the *Periplus*, it is worth remembering that there is abundant evidence of Roman coins found in India, confirming that coins were actually exported there, evidently for trading purposes.[48] Although the most obvious way for Roman traders to make use of their coins would certainly be to trade them in exchange for local merchandise, there is evidence to postulate that some more refined way of investing these coins was also possible. This possibility is openly suggested in a crucial sentence of the *Periplus Maris Erythraei*.[49]

In brief, when the anonymous author of the *Periplus* writes about Barygaza and the items which it is possible to trade there, he says that Roman traders bring there δηνάριον χρυσοῦν καὶ ἀργυροῦν, ἔχον ἀλλαγὴν καὶ ἐπικέρδειάν τινα πρὸς τὸ ἐντόπιον νόμισμα ('gold and silver Roman coins, which commands an exchange at some profit against the local currency').[50]

This sentence has been studied by several scholars, and it has been put in context with an Indian inscription from Nasik, dated to year AD 42.[51] Most scholars interpreted such inscription as inferring an exchange ratio between gold and silver in Western India 1:10.[52] In the same period, in

[44] *PME* 39.

[45] Casson 1989: 75.

[46] *PME* 49.

[47] *PME* 56.

[48] An updated and amended catalogue of all the Roman coins found in India is still missing. So far, the best available accounts are Turner 1989 and Suresh 2003.

[49] Nappo 2018 for the full description of the case study.

[50] *PME*, 49. Transl. Casson (1989: 81). Note that the Greek text has the word 'denarion' which Casson (with reason) takes as meaning generally 'Roman coin.'

[51] First published in Senart 1905/1906: n. 12, 82–85. For amendments and intepretations, see Lüders 1912: n. 1132; Mirashi 1981: n. 38, 95–100; MacDowall 1991: 151–152.

[52] Rapson 1908: clxxxiv; Altekar 1940: 4–5; MacDowall 1996: 92; MacDowall 2003: 43–44. *Contra* Bhandrkar (1921: 191–192), who assumed a gold:silver ratio of 1:14. A different opinion is now in De Romanis (2020: 327–332), although it is not really clear to me what the ratio should be, according to him.

Rome, the gold:silver ratio was 1:12.[53] This means that Roman traders could make a good profit using silver (rather than gold) as a metal for trade in India. And it also gives the reason why, until the reform of Nero, Roman traders used mostly *denarii* rather than *aurei* for their business in India.[54] It was simply much more profitable.

The reforms of Nero and later Vespasian changed the gold:silver ratio first to 1:11 and then to 1:10, exactly the same as India. That made the old pre-reform *denarii* a currency much more valuable (for their intrinsic value) than the new *denarii* (which still had the same face value). It is easy to understand that at this point the use of the old pre-AD 64 *denarii* was no longer attractive for transactions within the empire: the best way to make use of them would be either to melt them down or to export them somewhere where they could still be appreciated for their intrinsic value, such as India.

If this hypothesis is sound, the implication is that for the first century of the trade between the Roman Empire and India, coins (mostly silver) played a key role, not just as a means of exchange, but as a proper financial tool to make some profit.[55]

What is now left to determine is the definition of such financial activity. I think the most suitable one is arbitrage. According to the *New Palgrave Dictionary of Economics*: "An arbitrage opportunity is an investment strategy that guarantees a positive payoff in some contingency with no possibility of a negative payoff and with no net investment. (…) In other words, an arbitrage opportunity represents a money pump. A simple example of arbitrage is the opportunity to borrow and lend costlessly at two different fixed rates of interest. Such a disparity between the two rates cannot persist: arbitrageurs will drive the rate together."[56]

Before we engage in commenting on this definition, it is worth pointing out the reference to an important notion, that will be the object of further analysis *infra*: transaction costs. As for the applicability of the concept of arbitrage to our case-study, the question is here twofold. First of all, can we truly define the silver coins transaction in India as a risk-free

[53] Butcher and Ponting 2015: 451.

[54] It is indeed true, as pointed out by De Romanis (2020: 328) that the *Periplus* explicitly talks of gold and silver coins to be traded in Barygaza, but the corpus of Roman coins found in India, so far, does not endorse such claim. For the inaccuracies of the Periplus, see Arnaud 2012, more precisely page 40 for the problems with the area of Barygaza.

[55] That is how I interpret the words ἐπικέρδειάν τινα used by the Periplus.

[56] Eatwell et al. 2000: 100.

business? Secondly, can we actually consider the two phases of it (acquiring the coins within the Empire and selling them in India) as happening simultaneously?

A straightforward answer to both questions is a plain no. This type of transaction was definitely not simultaneous, for it would take a few months at least for the whole process of purchasing-and-selling to be completed.[57] Nor was it risk-free: first of all, there was the obvious risk of shipwrecks along the journey;[58] secondly, there was the huge risk of finding that the ratio between gold and silver had meanwhile changed in India, thus eroding the margin of profit for the merchants.

In fact, the best conceptual framework to describe this situation is the one provided by P. Bang in his monograph on the Roman Bazaar. According to him, an ideal-type of bazaar would have these features: "As a form of trade, the bazaar has taken shape from the many irregularities characteristic of pre-industrial peasant societies. Compared to modern markets, the bazaar is distinguished by high uncertainty of information and relative unpredictability of supply and demand. This makes the prices of commodities in the bazaar fairly volatile. As a consequence, the integration of markets is often low and fragile; it is simply difficult for traders to obtain sufficiently reliable and stable information on which effectively to respond to developments in other markets. [...] Most merchants operating in a bazaar environment are small and household-based. However, they were and are not passive victims of uncertainty. Instead they tend to pursue strategies which do not aim to eradicate the general condition of uncertainty, but rather reproduce them as part of the solution. One such strategy, as observed by Clifford Geertz, is *clientelisation*. Merchants in the bazaar seek to cultivate personal and lasting relations of exchange with particular business partners. This serves to shelter them against the all-pervasive risks and uncertainties of the bazaar, but on the basis of specially trusted and favoured relations."[59]

The theoretical framework provided by Bang describes very well the problems of the transaction we are dealing with, rightly pointing out that the only way out of those problems is to rely on a network of trust.

[57] See De Romanis (2020: 59–80) for a detailed description of the timing of the Indian commercial enterprises.

[58] On the economic implication of the risk of wrecking, see Harris 2019a. See also Duncan-Jones (1990: 47), referring to Fronto assessing the high risk of shipwreck embedded in sea-transport.

[59] Bang 2008: 4–5.

Therefore, the key to understanding the phenomenon must lay in its temporal dimension.

The only way Roman traders would perceive the risk as acceptable would be if they could have some means to verify the different and favourable silver:gold ratio to be consistent over a long period of time. If this was the case, consistency in pricing difference would allow Roman traders some degree of confidence to keep finding the exchange ratio unchanged year after year, when they reached Barygaza. From this perspective, the time variable of the asymmetric information theory can be of help in comprehending the situation: repetition of the same economic transaction, in consistent conditions, over a long period of time, would overcome the objective lack of constantly updated information, therefore driving Roman traders to trust their business to still be worthwhile. Also, the perpetuation over the years of the same gold:silver ratio would have worked to counterbalance the other missing factor, i.e. the simultaneity. Transactions were not simultaneous, but the reasonable certainty of finding in India an unchanged economic scenario would crystallise in a permanent present the temporal element.

In fact, we can add that the *Periplus* presents this as a standard type of trade happening in Barygaza, not an exceptional one,[60] allowing us to infer that this kind of business had been going on for quite some time.

If this interpretation of the whole phenomenon is acceptable, two preliminary observations are in order. The first, obvious one, is that Roman traders had a knowledge, at least at a rudimentary, practical level, of the concept of arbitrage and of the risks involved in it.[61] The second, possibly more interesting, is that if they made use of arbitrage when dealing with India, the most likely thing is that they did not devise this tool just for Indian trade, but instead they must have had a grasp of the concept for a long time, possibly applying it to other transactions within and without the Empire.

The temporal dimension and its repetitiveness is also illustrated, in my opinion, by another feature of the *corpus* of Roman coins found in India. Most of the Roman *denarii* found in India are dated to the Julio-Claudian dynasty, specifically to the reigns of the first two *principes*, Augustus and Tiberius, only one is dated after Nero's reform, and just a few are from the

[60] *Pace* De Romanis 2020: 332.

[61] Bresson 2015: 382–384 reports a case for arbitrage happening between the city of Athens and grain traders, in the second half of the fourth century BC.

Republican period. But the really unusual aspect is that a large share of them belong to only two types, one for each emperor: the *Gaius et Lucius Caesares* type for Augustan *denarii*,[62] and the *Pontifex Maximus* type for Tiberian *denarii*.[63]

The production of the *Gaius et Lucius Caesares* type started in the year 2 BC and went on at least until AD 12[64] and, according to Turner, they account for about a quarter of all the Augustan *denarii* found in India.[65] Many theories have been put forward to explain these features of the *corpus* of Roman coins in India. The oldest available overview of the corpus was done by S. Bolin, who suggested that Roman coins exported to India had never previously circulated in the Roman market. Traders would have acquired them either "direct from the mint or from money-changers with large stocks of newly minted *aurei* and *denarii*, and taken on board and shipped to India".[66] Later on M. Crawford pushed Bolin's idea further, arguing that only members of the imperial family would have regular access to freshly minted coins and therefore the eastern trade must have been controlled by them.[67]

Both these interpretations have been severely criticised for at least two main reasons. First of all, both *Gaius et Lucius Caesares* and *Pontifex Maximus* types were minted for a very long span of time, therefore they had to be very common on the market.[68] Secondly, and most importantly, the absence of die linkages among the ones found in India makes it very difficult to believe that they were packed together before leaving the mint, to be eventually exported.[69]

MacDowall has analysed the topic in several publications.[70] Overall, he has pointed out that the composition of hoards of *denarii* in India is different from that of hoards from inside the empire; the *denarii* in the 'Indian' hoards were carefully selected, which can be inferred from the fact

[62] *RIC* 2.207.

[63] *RIC* 2.25.

[64] Sutherland and Carson 1984: 97.

[65] Turner 1989: 21.

[66] Bolin 1958: 73. See also Burnett 1998: 181–182.

[67] Crawford 1979: 207–218. It should be noted that his idea of a significant involvement of the imperial entourage in the trade is overall confirmed by the documentary sources. See Sidebotham 1986.

[68] Cobb 2018c: 259.

[69] MacDowall 1991: 146–147; MacDowall 1996: 83.

[70] MacDowall 1996, 2003, 2003b.

that most of them have the same reverse; there are few Republican *denarii*, and those that are found mainly come from hoards in India dated to the second century AD, when Republican *denarii* disappear from hoards inside the empire.

Starting from these points, MacDowall claims that Julio-Claudian *denarii* only arrived in India in the Flavian period and that the worn Republican *denarii* arrived after Trajan's debasement in AD 107. Albeit interesting, MacDowall's theory seems too rigid, because in fact we have evidence of Republican *denarii* which arrived well before the second century AD: unworn Republican coins from Ajaigadh, Krishnagiri, and Tiruppur.[71]

Finally, F. De Romanis suggested a new interpretation of the monetary evidence from India. He starts from the texts of Tacitus and Pliny to assess that the outflow of Roman coins had already started and reached a huge level during Tiberius' and Claudius' reigns, respectively.[72] On the ground of these accounts, De Romanis rules out the possibility that the outflow was triggered by Nero's reform of AD 64. According to him, the best way to understand the Indian evidence would be to contrast it with the parallel contemporary evidence from the Vesuvian area, where in fact all pre-64 imperial *denarii* are very scarce: Duncan-Jones calculated that they represent around 2–3% of the available coins, while in the provinces the median is 15.9%.[73] Finally, De Romanis inserts in the equation also a passage from Strabo, where the writer would refer to an "imbalanced trade between Alexandria and Puteoli", that would allow us to infer that a lot of Alexandrian merchandise were bought by Campanian buyers, resulting in huge numbers of coins moving from Campania to Egypt.[74] In conclusion, De Romanis claims that the scarcity of the Augustan-to-early-Neronian-*denarii* in the Vesuvian area is certainly to be ascribed to the presence there of many traders involved in Red Sea trade, who would have generated an unbalanced flow of currency between Puteoli and Alexandria, as

[71] Suresh 2003: 29. See also the discussion in Lo Cascio (1980: 445–470) on the effects of Gresham's Law after Nero's devaluation of the *denarius*. Lo Cascio points out that *denarii* from Augustus, Tiberius, Caligula, and Claudius are rare in the hoards during the Flavian era: according to him, the best coins must have either been melted down or sent abroad for trade.

[72] Tac., *Ann.*, 3.53; Pliny, *NH*, 6.85.

[73] Duncan-Jones 1994: 121.

[74] Strab. 17.1.7.

confirmed indirectly by Strabo. For this reason, most of the giulio-claudian pre-64 *denarii* were transferred to Egypt and from there to India.[75]

De Romanis' theory is undoubtedly intriguing. I agree with his general point of view, that we should make an effort to read the Roman trade with India within the wider context of the ancient economy or, at least, trade dynamics. Nevertheless, I see some problems with his overall reconstruction. First of all, the sources. Tacitus' account is stuffed with moralistic judgments, so his opinion on the matter are at least biased.[76] As for Pliny, the passage is the famous narration of Annius Plocamus' adventures, and it does not really say much about any outflow of coins from Rome to India. Furthermore, the interpretation offered of the account of Strabo seems far-fetched. In fact, Strabo does not acknowledge the existence of a special unbalanced trade line between Puteoli and Alexandria, but he rather claims that all trade-lines involving Alexandria are unbalanced, since every ship that leaves from there, then comes back lighter than when it departed. In this context, Strabo quotes the case of Puteoli and Alexandria as a meaningful example.[77] Another problem I see is the utilisation of the Vesuvian data. De Romanis uses them as an evidence to understand the economic situation in Puteoli, something which, although not exactly accurate, is still understandable, but then he goes further to using it as a proxy to describe the situation of 'central Italy', which is rather unconventional, due to the geographical position and the cultural background of both Puteoli and the Vesuvian towns.

The final and more decisive point, in my opinion, is the analysis of the numismatic data themselves. De Romanis, building on Duncan-Jones,[78] notes that the median presence of giulio-claudian pre-64 *denarii* in the Vesuvian area is 2–3% of the total, in contrast to a provincial median of 15.9%. The problem here is that (a) these figures refer to all the pre-reform *denarii*, regardless of their specific type; (b) the *corpus* of the Roman coins found in India dramatically overrepresents only the Augustan and the Tiberian *denarii*, not all the pre-64 ones, reaching the out-of-scale level of 80% of the total; (c) within the *corpus* of the 'Indian' *denarii*,

[75] De Romanis 2020: 127–132.

[76] For the text, see *above*, n. 38.

[77] Strab. 17.1.7: ταύτῃ δὲ καὶ τὰ ἐκκομιζόμενα ἐξ Ἀλεξανδρείας πλείω τῶν εἰσκομιζομένων ἐστί: γνοίη δ᾽ ἄν τις ἔν τε τῇ Ἀλεξανδρείᾳ καὶ τῇ Δικαιαρχείᾳ γενόμενος, ὁρῶν τὰς ὁλκάδας ἔν τε τῷ κατάπλῳ καὶ ἐν ταῖς ἀναγωγαῖς ὅσον βαρύτεραί τε καὶ κουφότεραι δεῦρο κἀκεῖσε πλέοιεν.

[78] Duncan-Jones 1994: 118–123.

the *Caius and Lucius* type and *Pontifex Maximus* type are 25% of the total. All this means that the Indian sample is in no way aligned with the Roman provincial one, therefore the idea that the Indian situation derives directly from the Mediterranean one is to be rejected.[79]

Even more, even if we were to accept De Romanis' overall interpretation, we would only have a solution that might in fact solve the rebus of the *scarcity* of *Caius and Lucius* and *Pontifex Maximus* types in Campania, not the one of the overwhelming *presence* of such types in India. In other words, why Roman traders would mostly pick those two types, partially overlooking the others available.

I think that one key to reading this phenomenon can be the temporary dimension of the asymmetric theory. Roman and Indian traders would find themselves, as said before, in a position in which both parties might in principle be interested in trading with the other, but with limited knowledge of the quality of the reciprocal goods. In particular, Indian traders would be in the position of having to check for the quality of Roman coins at any single transaction, a very tedious, and also a very time-consuming task. More than that, this technical difficulty can be seen as a transaction cost.

Transaction costs is a concept deeply intertwined with the New Institutional Economics (therefore NIE) theoretical framework. Using the theoretical tools of the NIE is not a neutral action, for the methodological and even ideological implications that this theory carries along. This is not the place to go through the complexities of the use of NIE as a theoretical framework,[80] so I will try to explain how and why I see it appropriate to make use of the transaction costs element.

The concept of transaction costs is quite ill-defined, and we can roughly say there are different meanings of transaction costs. The basic definition is Coase's: the cost of using the price mechanism.[81] Some of the earlier studies have focussed on concrete opportunity costs, while a more modern tradition has seen transaction costs as arising from the cost of information.[82] Coase later returned on the importance of transaction costs in trad-

[79] De Romanis 2012 and 2020. For a more traditional interpretation of the Pompeian evidence, see Lo Cascio 1980.

[80] See Ménard and Shirley 2018 for an up-to-date discussion of this issue. In particular, see the chapter of Terpstra 2018 in the book, on NIE and the ancient economy. See also Blanton IV and Hollander 2019: 14–18.

[81] Coase 1937: 390.

[82] Coase 1960: 15; Kehoe et al. 2015: 5–7.

ing activities, stating: "if the costs of making an exchange are greater than the gains which that exchange would bring, that exchange would not take place and the greater production that would flow from specialization would not be realised. In this way transaction costs affect not only contractual arrangements but also what goods and services are produced."[83] D. North has notoriously built on the concept, constructing the theoretical framework of the NIE, assessing that transaction costs are a key to understand why some Countries are rich and some others are poor:

> The costliness of information is the key to the costs of transacting, which consist of the costs of measuring the valuable attributes of what is being exchanged and the costs of protecting rights and policing and enforcing agreements. These measurement and enforcement costs are the sources of social, political, and economic institutions.[84]

North's definition widens the spectrum of the transaction costs, giving them a new meaning "the costs of running an economic system". This view implies that all transactions have necessarily to be regulated by some institutional agreements or rules, and therefore that every set of rules or institutions is fit to cope with a particular set of transaction costs.

All this should to some extent give reason for the poorly determined definition of transaction costs. Notwithstanding, for the sake of the argument, we can summarise by agreeing that a transactional cost is any kind of cost we need to face in order to acquire the necessary information to carry on a business. This information can concern the quantity of the item one wants to trade, or its propriety, or its fair price, or its actual quality, and so on.[85]

There is no complete agreement on whether the concept of transaction costs should be applied to the study of the ancient world without any further theoretical scrutiny,[86] and I would not personally share the view embedded in the NIE theoretical framework, that trade is a pervasive

[83] Coase 1992: 716.

[84] North 1990: 27.

[85] Tchernia 2016: 91–96; Lo Cascio 2018.

[86] There are many works which carefully explain the most evident issues with the NIE model. For an example of a severe and ideologically motivated criticism, see Boldizzoni 2011; for an alternative view, see Verboven 2015b.

activity in any economic system, including the ancient one.[87] Anyway, it seems legitimate to recognise that some of the fundamental features of transaction costs can be sensibly applied to the study of the ancient economy.[88] As pointed out by Kehoe, Ratzan, and Yiftach, these are: (1) Information is not free; (2) The goods exchanged are alterable and variable in quality; (3) A plurality of partners must seek (and be known to seek) to extract value from opposite parties in exchanges while simultaneously seeking (and being known to seek) to protect or retain value they themselves control.[89]

What we are now left to check is whether these three points apply to Indo-Roman trade, specifically. As for point 1, it is rather intuitive that acquiring information is a transaction cost, and that such a cost applied to Indo-Roman trade must have been unavoidably huge. Nevertheless, needless to say, it was also crucial to have access to the proper information by both parties, Indian and Roman, in order to have fruitfully taken part in this sort of trade.

As for point 2, again it is perfectly applicable to our case study: Indian traders could not have been sure about the purity of Roman coins over time, because they could not have been up-to-date with every debasement of the coinage happening within the Empire. On the other hand, Roman traders could not always have been sure of finding the profitable silver:gold exchange ratio in India year after year.

As for point 3, it involves the concept of trust between the parties and again it is applicable to our case.

So, we are apparently in a very complex situation, where it would have been difficult for individual traders to make a rational economic choice, in terms of wealth maximisation, if the information they had was imperfect and did not give them the necessary tools to understand the reality around them.[90] Nevertheless, the exchange was indeed happening, which means that a system must have been devised, to overcome the difficulties. For this

[87] The topic of the natural inclination of men to trade, as well as the possibility of using the concept of 'market economy' to usefully describe any economic system are very sensitive ones. There is a rich and very heated debate going on these subjects. See for instance Temin 2013, who advocates for the presence of a strong integrated market economy in the Roman World; Bang 2008 for a completely opposite view on the topic.

[88] A classic exposition of how the burden of transaction costs would have weighted premodern economies is in North and Thomas 1973.

[89] Kehoe et al. 2015: 9, adapted from Allen 1991.

[90] For more theoretical thinking on this, see Lo Cascio 2006: 219; 2018: 118–120.

reason, the importance of institutions was paramount, to reduce the nebulousness of the exchange and consequently decreasing the transaction costs.

In the general theoretical framework of the NIE, a solution is offered to overcome transaction costs, the concept of *institutions*. According to D. North: "Institutions are the humanly devised constraints that structure political, economic and social interaction. They consist of both informal constraints (sanctions, taboos, customs, traditions, and codes of conduct), and formal rules (constitutions, laws, property rights). Throughout history, institutions have been devised by human beings to create order and reduce uncertainty in exchange. Together with the standard constraints of economics they define the choice set and therefore determine transaction and production costs and hence the profitability and feasibility of engaging in economic activity. They evolve incrementally, connecting the past with the present and the future; history in consequence is largely a story of institutional evolution in which the historical performance of economies can only be understood as a part of a consequential story. Institutions provide the incentive structure of an economy; as that structure evolves, it shapes the direction of economic change towards growth, stagnation, or decline."[91]

Again, I would like to point out that institution is only one of the possible means to give an interpretation of the actual economic phenomenon. In my view, this is not at all the only possible way to decipher it.[92] Anyhow, if we are to utilise the institution concept, we can usefully do it, allowing that the practise to preferably use a limited type of silver coins would indeed represent an institution, generated by a deal between private parties, and not guaranteed by any public or state regimentation. Moreover, it is precisely for the absence of any possibility of carrying on this trade under the umbrella of some sort of "international commercial law" protecting the rights of the parties involved,[93] that the same parties had to resort to a private institution in order to complete the transaction.[94] The scheme would be roughly as follows:

[91] Quotation from North 1991: 97. On the same subject, see also North 1981.

[92] It should be noted as well that the definition of institution went through evolution and revision in the thinking of D. North. On the subject, see Wallis 2014.

[93] Even the existence of a proper "Commercial Law" within the Empire is a hotly debated problem. See Cerami, Di Porto, and Petrucci 2004; Aubert 2015; Sirks 2018.

[94] See Hollander 2015 (especially pages 148–155) for an overview of the main private institutions devised to overcome transaction costs by Roman traders.

Phase 1: Roman traders take notice of the difference in the gold:silver ratio between the Roman Empire and Barygaza.
Phase 2: Therefore, they try to sell Roman coins in the local market, hoping to make a profit out of the deal.
Phase 3: Local traders might be keen to take the deal, but they have to face the transaction cost to verify the purity of the Roman coins offered to them as items of trade.
Phase 4: Given the abundance of such types (i.e. *Gaius et Lucius Caesares* and *Pontifex Maximus* coins) in the Roman currency, it is likely that they were the majority of the first coins that reached India. Once local traders realise that some types are good quality, they seal the deal.
Phase 5: Here the temporal element is essential. Since the transaction is repeated over time, local traders would ask the Roman counterparts to keep using the same types of coin, which have already been tested, therefore creating a private institution that allows the overcoming of a transaction cost connected to the checking of the purity of the coins.

The preference for some specific types of coin would be determined by the creation of an institution, in the sense expressed by D. North.[95] The applicability of such a model to the general context of the Indo-Roman trade is also confirmed by the structure of one of the most famous documents related to this business, the Muziris Papyrus.[96] This papyrus contains two incomplete texts, one on the *recto* and one on the *verso*, written by different hands, and it is overall dateable to the mid-second century CE.[97] The part which is relevant for the present discussion is the *recto*: it shows a text in one column, reporting the final part of a contract of a maritime loan for a trading voyage from Alexandria (Egypt) to Muziris (India, supposedly modern Pattanam).[98] The *recto* of the papyrus is a very good example of a private agreement between a financier and a trader, aimed at

[95] I think that Cobb (2018a, b, c: 259) has come to a very similar conclusion, pointing out that these types of coin were selected for the confidence they would inspire on those receiving them. Cobb does not however link this practice to the concept of institution.

[96] Harrauer and Sijpesteijn 1985: 124–155; Thür 1987: 229–245; 1988: 227–233; Casson 1986: 73–79; 1990: 195–206; Foraboschi and Gara 1989: 280–282; De Romanis 2006: 183–196; 1998: 11–60; 2010/11: 75–101; 2014: 73–90; 2017; Rathbone 2000: 39–50; 2002: 179–198; Morelli 2011: 199–236; De Romanis 2020.

[97] The papyrus was bought in 1980 for the Austrian National Library, but its provenance is unfortunately unknown. See Rathbone 2000: 39.

[98] On Pattanam-Muziris, see Cherian 2007, 2008, 2009; Cherian et al. 2009.

the reduction of transaction costs to the smallest possible level. In fact, the financier offers the traders the possibility of using many facilities along the journey from Alexandria to Coptos and then the Red Sea. For using these facilities, traders would not pay in cash upfront when reaching them: the cost of the usage for these facilities would be included in the contract they had signed in Alexandria with the financier. This type of agreement would save the traders much trouble, while looking for a trustworthy transport-lender, bargaining over the price of renting animals to deliver goods from one place to another, or looking for safe shelters along the journey. On the other hand, it is also true that the financier greatly benefitted from this arrangement too, keeping the trail of the traders under the constant control of his business associates, therefore protecting his own investment from both internal and external dangers. The key element, in the private institutions to overcome unbearable transaction costs, is the trust bond between a businessman (in this case, the financer) and his partners (in this case, the network supporting the traders along their journey from Alexandria to the Egyptian ports on the Red Sea). If these private institutions built on trust and *clientelisation* worked within the Empire, it is plausible, in my opinion, that the same pattern was duplicated, to some extent, in Indian territory, this time creating a trusting bond between Roman and local traders.[99]

12.5 Conclusions

It is now time to draw together all the threads of this work. If all my arguments are acceptable, I think that a few remarks are in order.

1. First of all, we must acknowledge the ability of Roman traders to deal with sophisticated economic tools such as arbitrage, a form of financial business which is normally associated with the more modern stages of economic history. The presence of phenomena such as arbitrage in the ancient economy should be carefully considered when trying to assess the performances of the ancient economy.
2. A second point I would like to stress is the crucial importance played by coins in this case of arbitrage. This point would probably need to be further developed, but here I must at least point out that the role

[99] On the importance of familiar and friendly ties in ancient trade, see Verboven 2002. Also, Harris 2019b.

of monetisation in the fostering of the Roman economy has already been acknowledged by scholarship in the last two decades. In particular, the rise of monetisation has been put in context with the development of a more sophisticated finance.[100]

3. A third point, more connected to the actual case-study taken into account, is that despite the huge, objective difficulties of conducting this trade over such a long distance, Roman traders were able not only to successfully buy and import Indian merchandise, but were even able to take advantage of the difference in the silver:gold ratio in Rome and in Barygaza, and to realise a gain through arbitrage. This is a very sophisticated financial action that requires great skills in overcoming the lack of the necessary information to complete the transaction.
4. This leads us to another issue addressed in this paper, the role of private institutions to set up commercial rules that allowed an international business to continue for a long time. The private institution devised rises from the preference for the use of specific types of coins, which were presumably recognised as trustworthy by all the parties involved in the trade. Such an institution would have overcome the problem of the asymmetric information about the purity of the Roman coins. On this last point, I would like to add a few more final considerations.

The analysis carried out so far seems to shed some light on how Indo-Roman trade fits into the model of international trade. As said before, trade between Romans and Indians is often assumed to be an example of World Trade, a big unified market that encompassed places and actors scattered over three continents. From what we have seen, more than on a global unified market, it seems to have rested on a number of juxtaposed, although somehow interconnected, separated markets. For this reason, again, I think that the Bazaar Model devised by P. Bang, carefully calibrated to match the available evidence, can be of great help to understand the actual functioning of this trade: "In contrast to market in the abstract, generalised, modern sense, it is customary to speak of concrete, individual marketplaces existing in isolation."[101] In this context, asymmetric theory is a perfect tool to give reason for some apparently irrational behaviours of

[100] See Hollander 2007: 104–111; Kay 2014: 143–144, and 314–318; Terpstra 2019: 4–8.
[101] Bang 2008: 140.

the involved economic actors. The shortage of reliable information forced the traders to devise alternative means to carry on the international trade. These means, although not perfectly 'economically rational' allowed them to carry on sophisticated transactions on a worldwide scale. Even more, all this was achieved in the framework of an agrarian pre-modern economy, an economy which would be very unwise to define according to parameters such as modernity or primitivity, and whose characteristics we must describe for what they were.

In doing so, the use of modern economic theories and models can be of great help, as long as we manage to remember that those theories and models were not originated by the same economic world we are trying to describe. Therefore, to make use of an example familiar to all students of ancient history, analysing the ancient Mediterranean economy is somehow similar to reading ancient fragmentary texts written in Greek or Latin: when interpreting them, sometimes the fact that the texts are written in a different language adds to the complexities deriving from their poor state of preservation.

Bibliography

Akerlof, G. 1970. The Market for 'Lemons'. *Quarterly Journal of Economics* 84: 488–500.

Allen, D.W. 1991. What Are Transaction Costs. *Research in Law and Economics* 14: 1–18.

Altekar, A.S. 1940. The Relative Prices of Metals and Coins in Ancient India. *The Journal of the Numismatic Society of India* 2: 1–13.

Andreau, J., and J. Maucourant. 1999. À propos de la rationalité économique dans l'Antiquité gréco-romaine. Une interprétation des thèses de D. Rathbone (1991). *Topoi* 9 (1): 47–102.

Arnaud, P. 2012. Le Periplus Maris Erythraei: une oeuvre de compilation aux préoccupations géographiques. *Topoi* Suppl. 11: 27–61.

Aubert, J.-J. 2015. Trade. In *The Cambridge Companion to Roman Law*, ed. D. Johnston, 213–245. Cambridge: Cambridge University Press.

Ball, W. 2000. *Rome in the East. The Transformation of an Empire*. London/New York: Routledge.

Bang, P.F. 2008. *The Roman Bazaar*. Cambridge: Cambridge University Press.

———. 2012. A Forum on Trade. Bazaars, Empires, and Roman Trade, in Scheidel 2012, 296–303.

Bang, P.F., and D. Kołodziejczyk. 2012. *Universal Empire. A Comparative Approach to Imperial Culture and Representation in Eurasian History*. Cambridge: Cambridge University Press.

Bhandarkar, D.R. 1921. *Lectures on Ancient Indian Numismatics*. Kolkata: The University of Calcutta.

Blanton IV, T.R., and D.B. Hollander. 2019. The Extramercantile Economy, in Hollander, Blanton IV and Fitzgerald, 8–28.

Boer, R., and C. Petterson. 2017. *Time of Troubles. A New Economic Framework for Early Christianity*. Minneapolis: Fortress Press.

Boldizzoni, F. 2011. *The Poverty of Clio. Resurrecting Economic History*. Princeton: Princeton University Press.

Bolin, S. 1958. *State and Currency in the Roman Empire to 300 AD*. Stockholm: Almqvist and Wiksell.

Boussac, M.-Fr., J.-Fr. Salles, and J.-B. Yon. 2012. *Autour du Périple de la mer Érythrée*. Paris.

———. 2016. *Ports of the Ancient Indian Ocean*. New Delhi: Primus Books.

Bowman, A., and A. Wilson. 2009. *Quantifying the Roman Economy. Methods and Problems*. Oxford: Oxford University Press.

Braudel, F. 1979. *Civilisation Matérielle, Économie et Capitalisme, XVe–XVIIIe siècle*. Paris: Armand Colin.

Bresson, A. 2000. *La cité marchande*. Pessac: Ausonius Éditions.

———. 2015. *The Making of the Ancient Greek Economy: Institutions, Markets, and Growth in the City-States*. Princeton: Princeton University Press.

Burnett, A. 1998. Roman Coins from India and Sri Lanka. In *Origin, Evolution and Circulation of Foreign Coins in the Indian Ocean*, ed. O. Bopearachi and D.P.M. Weerakkody, 179–189. Manohar.

Butcher, K., and M. Ponting. 2015. *The Metallurgy of Roman Silver Coinage: From the Reform of Nero to the Reform of Trajan*. Cambridge: Cambridge University Press.

Cartledge, P. 1998. The Economy (Economies) of Ancient Greece. *Dialogos* 5: 4–24.

Casson, L. 1986. P.Vindob. G. 40822 and the Shipping of the Goods from India. *BASP* 23: 73–79.

———. 1989. *The Periplus Maris Erythraei: Text with Introduction, Translation, and Commentary*. Princeton: Princeton University Press.

———. 1990. New Light on Maritime Loans: P. Vindob. G. 40.822. *ZPE* 84: 195–206.

Cerami, P., A. Di Porto, and A. Petrucci. 2004. *Diritto Commerciale Romano. Profilo Storico*. 2nd ed. Turin: Giappichelli.

Cherian, P.J. 2007. The Muziris Heritage Project: Excavation at Pattanam – 2007. *Journal of Indian Ocean Archaeology* 4: 1–11.

———. 2008. The Muziris Heritage Project and the Archaeological Research at Pattanam: An Overview. In *The Living Dead and the Lost Knowledge*, 5–20. Thiruvananthapuram.

———. 2009. *The Exchanges between Early Historic Ports on the Malabar Coast and the Red Sea Port of Berenike*. Mumbai.

Cherian, P.J., G.V. Ravi Prasad, K. Dutta, D.K. Ray, V. Selvakumar, and K.P. Shajan. 2009. Chronology of Pattanam: A Multi-Cultural Port Site on the Malabar Coast. *Current Science* 97 (2): 236–240.

Coase, R.H. 1937. The Nature of the Firm. *Economica* 4: 386–405.

———. 1960. The Problem of Social Cost. *Journal of Law and Economics* 3: 1–44.

———. 1992. The Institutional Structure of Production. *The American Economic Review* 82 (4): 713–719.

Cobb, M. 2015a. The Chronology of Roman Trade in the Indian Ocean from Augustus to Early Third Century. *JESHO* 58 (3): 362–418.

Cobb, M.A. 2015b. Balancing the Trade: Roman Cargo Shipments to India. *OJA* 34 (2): 185–203.

———. 2018a. *The Indian Ocean Trade in Antiquity*. London/New York: Routledge.

———. 2018b. The Indian Ocean in Antiquity and Global History, in Cobb 2018a, 1–14.

———. 2018c. *Rome and the Indian Ocean Trade from Augustus to the Early Third Century CE*. Leiden/Boston: Brill.

Conrad, S. 2016. *What is Global History?* Princeton: Princeton University Press.

Crawford, M. 1980. Economia Imperiale e Commercio Estero. In *Tecnologia, Economia e società nel Mondo Romano: Atti del Convegno di Como,* 27–29 Settembre 1979, Como, 207–218.

De Romanis, F. 1982-87. Roma e i Nótia dell'India, ricerche sui rapporti tra Roma e l'India dravidica dal 30 a.C. all'età Flavia. *Helikon* 22–27: 143–210.

———. 2006. *Cassia Cinnamomo Ossidiana*. Rome: L'Erma di Bretschneider.

———. 1998. Commercio, metrologia, fiscalità. Su P. Vindob. G 40822 Verso. *MEFRA* 110: 11–60.

———. 2006. Aurei after the Trade: Western Taxes and Eastern Gifts. In *Dal Denarius al Dinar. L'Oriente e la Moneta Romana*, ed. F. De Romanis and S. Sorda, 55–82. Rome.

———. 2010/11. Playing Sudoku on the verso of the Muziris papyrus: pepper, malabathron and tortoise shell in the cargo of the Hermapollon. *Journal of Ancient Indian History* 27: 75–101.

———. 2012. Julio-Claudian Denarii and Aurei in Campania and India. *AIIN* 58: 161–192.

———. 2014. Time to repay a maritime loan: A Note on SB III 7169 and SB XVIII 1367 Recto. *Sileno* 40: 73–90.

———. 2017. A Muziris Export: Schidai or Ivory Trimmings. In *Imperial Rome, Indian Ocean Regions and Muziris: Recent Researches and New Perspectives on Maritime Trade. Proceedings of the International Seminar Held at Irinjalakuda, Kerala, India 8-12 September 2013*, ed. K.S. Mathew, 369–380. London/New York.

———. 2020. *The Indo-Roman Pepper Trade and the Muziris Papyrus*. Oxford: Oxford University Press.

Duncan-Jones, R. 1990. *Structure and Scale in the Roman Economy*. Cambridge: Cambridge University Press.

———. 1994. *Money and Government in the Roman Empire*. Cambridge: Cambridge University Press.

Eatwell, J., M. Milgate, and P. Newman. 2000. *The New Palgrave Dictionary of Economics*. Vol. 1–4. London: Palgrave Macmillan.

Erdkamp, P. 2015. Structural Determinants of Economic Performance in the Roman World and Early Modern Europe. A Comparative Approach, in Erdkamp and Verboven 2015, 17–32.

Erdkamp, P., and K. Verboven. 2015. *Structure and Performance in the Roman Economy. Models, Methods and Case Studies*. Bruxelles: Editions Latomus.

Finley, M.I. 1985. *Ancient History: Evidence and Models*. London: Pimlico.

Foraboschi, D., and A. Gara. 1989. Le direttrici del commercio alessandrino. *Quaderni Ticinesi di Numismatica e Antichità Classiche* 18: 280–282.

Frederiksen, M.W. 1975. Theory, Evidence, and the Ancient Economy. *Journal of Roman Studies* 65: 164–171.

Garnsey, P., K. Hopkins, and C.R. Whittaker, eds. 1983. *Trade in the Ancient Economy*. London.

Gibbon, E. 1776–1789. *The History of the Decline and Fall of the Roman Empire*. London.

Gurukkal, R. 2016. *Rethinking Classical Indo-Roman Trade. Political Economy and Eastern Mediterranean Exchange Relations*. Oxford: Oxford University Press.

Harrauer, H., and P. Sijpesteijn. 1985. Ein neues Dokument zu Roms Indienhandel, P. Vindob. G 40822. *Anzeiger der Österreichischen Akademie der Wissenschaften, Phil.-Hist. Klasse* 122: 124–155.

Harris, W.V. 1993. Between Archaic and Modern: Problems in Roman Economic History. In *The Inscribed Economy: Production and Distribution in the Roman Empire in the Light of Instrumentum Domesticum: The Proceedings of a Conference Held at the American Academy in Rome on 10-11 January, 1992*, ed. Id, 11–29. Ann Arbor.

———. 2011. *Rome's Imperial Economy. Twelve Essays*. Oxford: Oxford University Press.

———. 2019a. A Strange Fact about Shipboard Coin Hoards Throws Light on the Roman Empire's Financial System. *Athenaeum* 107.

———. 2019b. Credit-Money in the Roman Economy. *Klio* 101 (1): 158–189.

Hicks, J. 1969. *A Theory of Economic History*. Oxford: Oxford University Press.

Hingley, R. 2005. *Globalizing Roman Culture: Unity, Diversity and Empire*. London/New York: Routledge.

Hollander, D.B. 2007. *Money in the Late Roman Republic*. Leiden: Brill.

———. 2015. Risky Business: Traders in the Roman World. In *Traders in the Ancient Mediterranean*, ed. T. Howe, 141–172. Chicago: Ares Publishers Inc.

Hollander, D.B., T.R. Blanton IV, and J.T. Fitzgerald. 2019. *The Extramercantile Economies of Greek and Roman Cities. New Perspectives on the Economic History of Classical Antiquity*. London/New York: Routledge.

Hopkins, K. 1983. Introduction, in Garnsey, Hopkins and Whittaker 1983, ix–xxv.

Jennings, J. 2011. *Globalizations and the Ancient World*. Cambridge: Cambridge University Press.

Jones, D.W. 2014. *Economic Theory and the Ancient Mediterranean*. Chichester: Wiley Blackwell.

Jongman, W.M. 2014. Re-constructing the Roman Economy. In *The Cambridge History of Capitalism. Volume I. The Rise of Capitalism: From Ancient Origins to 1848*, ed. L. Neal and J.G. Williamson, 75–100. Cambridge: Cambridge University Press.

Kay, P. 2014. *Rome's Economic Revolution*. Oxford: Oxford University Press.

Kehoe, D.P., D.M. Ratzan, and U. Yiftach. 2015. *Law and Transaction Costs in the Ancient Economy*. Ann Arbor: University of Michigan Press.

LaBianca, Ø.S., and S.A. Scham. 2006. *Connectivity in Antiquity. Globalization as a Long-Term Historical Process*. London: Equinox.

Lo Cascio, E. 1980. La riforma monetaria di Nerone: l'evidenza dei ripostigli. *MEFRA* 92: 445–470.

———. 2006. The Role of the State in the Roman Economy: Making Use of the New Institutional Economics. In *Ancient Economies Modern Methodologies*, ed. P.F. Bang, M. Ikeguchi, and H.G. Ziche, 215–234. Bari: Edipuglia.

———. 2007. The Early Roman Empire: The State and the Economy, in Scheidel, Morris, and Saller 2007, 619–647.

———. 2009. *Crescita e Declino: Studi di storia dell'economia romana*. Roma: L'Erma di Bretschneider.

———. 2018. Market Regulation and Transaction Costs in the Roman Empire, in Wilson and Bowman 2018, 117–131.

Löfgren, K.-G., T. Persson, and J.W. Weibull. 2002. Markets with Asymmetric Information: The Contributions of George Akerlof, Michael Spence and Joseph Stiglitz. *The Scandinavian Journal of Economics* 104 (2): 195–211.

Lüders, H. 1912. A List of Brahmi Inscriptions from the Earliest Times to about AD 400 with the Exception of those of Asoka. *Epigraphica Indica* 10: 1–203.

MacDowall, D.W. 1991. Indian Imports of Roman Silver Coins. In *Coinage Trade and Economy*, ed. A.K. Jha, 145–163. Maharashtra: Indian Institute of Research in Numismatic Studies.

———. 1996. The Evidence of the Gazetteer of Roman Artefacts in India. In *Tradition and Archaeology: Early Maritime Contacts in the Indian Ocean*, ed. H.P. Ray and J.-F. Salles, 79–95. Lyon/New Delhi.

———. 2003a. Foreign Coins found in India. In *Foreign Coins Found in the Indian Subcontinent*, ed. D.W. MacDowall and A. Jha, 9–14. Maharashtra: Indian Institute of Research in Numismatic Studies.

———. 2003b. The Indo-Roman Metal Trade. In *Foreign Coins Found in the Indian Subcontinent*, ed. D.W. MacDowall and A. Jha, 39–44. Maharashtra: Indian Institute of Research in Numismatic Studies.

Manning, J.G. 2018. *The Open Sea. The Economic Life of the Ancient Mediterranean World from the Iron Age to the Rise of Rome*. Princeton: Princeton University Press.

Manzo, A., C. Zazzaro, and D.J. De Falco. 2018. *Stories of Globalisation. The Red Sea and the Persian Gulf from Late Prehistory to Early Modernity*. Brill, Leiden and Boston.

Marx, K. 1973. *Grundrisse: Foundations of the Critique of Political Economy*. Trans. M. Nicolaus. Harmondsworth.

———. 2002. *Pre-Capitalist Economic Formations*, ed. E. Hobsbawn. Geneve.

Mathew, K.S. 2016. *Imperial Rome, Indian Ocean Regions and Muziris: New Perspectives on Maritime Trade*. London/New York: Routledge.

McLaughlin, R. 2010. *The Roman Empire and the Indian Ocean*. Barnsley.

———. 2016. *The Roman Empire and the Silk Routes. The Ancient World Economy and the Empires of Parthia, Central Asia and Han China*. Pen and Sword, Barnsley.

Meikle, S. 2002. Modernism, Economics and the Ancient Economy. In *The Ancient Economy*, ed. W. Scheidel and S. von Reden, 233–250. Edinburgh: Edinburgh University Press.

Ménard, C., and M.M. Shirley. 2018. *A Research Agenda for New Institutional Economics*. Cheltenham/Northampton: Edward Elgar.

Mirashi, V.V. 1981. *The History and Inscriptions of the Sātavāhanas and the Western Kshatrapas*. Maharashtra State Board for Literature and Culture, Mumbai.

Morelli, F. 2011. Dal Mar Rosso ad Alessandria. Il verso (ma anche il recto) del 'papiro di Muziris' (SB XVIII 13167). *Tyche* 26: 199–236.

Morley, N. 2004. *Theories, Models and Concepts in Ancient History*. London/New York: Routledge.

———. 2007. *Trade in Classical Antiquity*. Cambridge: Cambridge University Press.

———. 2009. *Antiquity and Modernity*. London.

Morris, I. 1994. The Athenian Economy Twenty Years after the Ancient Economy. *Classical Philology* 89: 351–366.

Morris, I., and W. Scheidel, eds. 2009. *The Dynamics of Ancient Empires. State Power from Assyria to Byzantion*. Oxford: Oxford University Press.

Nappo, D. 2018. Money and Flows of Coinage in the Red Sea Trade, in Wilson and Bowman 2018, 557–578.

Nicolet, C. 1982. Il Pensiero Economico dei Romani. In *Storia delle Idee Politiche, Economiche, Sociali*, ed. L. Firpo, 877–960. Turin.

North, D.C. 1981. *Structures and Changes in Economic History*. New York: Routledge.

———. 1990. *Institutions, Institutional Change, and Economic Performance*. Cambridge: Cambridge University Press.

———. 1991. Institutions. *Journal of Economic Perspectives* 5: 97–112.

North, D.C., and R.P. Thomas. 1973. *The Rise of the Western World*. Cambridge: Cambridge University Press.

Pitts, M., and M.J. Versluys. 2015. *Globalisation and the Roman World. World History, Connectivity and Material Culture*. Cambridge: Cambridge University Press.

Power, T. 2012. *The Red Sea from Byzantium to the Caliphate. AD 500-1000*. Cairo: American University in Cairo Press.

Rapson, E.J. 1908. *Catalogue of the Coins of the Andhra Dynasty, the Western Kṣatrapas, the Traikūṭaka Dynasty, and the 'Bodhi' Dynasty*. London: British Museum.

Raschke, M.G. 1978. New Studies in Roman Commerce with the East. In *Aufstieg und Niedergang der Römischen Welt* 2.9, 604–1076. Berlin.

Rathbone, D. 2000. The 'Muziris' Papyrus (SB XVIII 13167): Financing Roman Trade with India. *BSAA* 46: 39–50.

Rathbone, D.W. 2002. Koptos the emporion. Economy and society, I–III AD. In *Autour de Coptos. Actes du colloque organisé au Musée des Beaux-Arts de Lyon*, ed. M.-F. Boussac, 179–198. Lyon: Topoi.

Rostovtzeff, M.I. 1926. *A History of the Ancient World*. Vol. I. Oxford: Oxford University Press.

———. 1957. *The Social and Economic History of the Roman Empire*. 2nd ed. Oxford: Oxford University Press.

Scheidel, W. 2009. *Rome and China. Comparative Perspectives on Ancient World Empires*. Oxford: Oxford University Press.

———. 2012a. *The Cambridge Companion to the Roman Economy*. Cambridge: Cambridge University Press.

———. 2012b. Approaching the Roman Economy, in Id. 2012, 1–21.

———. 2015. *State Power in Ancient China and Rome*. Oxford: Oxford University Press.

Scheidel, W., I. Morris, and R. Saller. 2007. *The Cambridge Economic History of the Greco-Roman World*. Cambridge: Cambridge University Press.

Seland, E. 2008. The Indian Ocean and the Globalisation of the Ancient World. *Ancient West and East* 7: 67–79.

———. 2010. *Ports and Political Power in the Periplus: Complex Societies and Maritime Trade on the Indian Ocean in the First Century AD*. Oxford: Oxford University Press.

———. 2014. Archaeology of Trade in the Western Indian Ocean, 300 BC-AD 700. *Journal of Archaeological Research* 22: 367–402.

Senart, E. 1905/1906. The Inscriptions in the Caves at Nâsik. *Epigraphica Indica* 8: 59–96.

Sidebotham, S.E. 1986. *Roman Economic Policy in the Erythra Thalassa. 30 B.C.–A.D. 217.* Leiden: Brill.

———. 2011. *Berenike and the Ancient Maritime Spice Route.* Los Angeles: University of California Press.

Sirks, B. 2018. Law, Commerce, and Finance in the Roman Empire, in Wilson and Bowman 2018, 53–115.

Stiglitz, J.E. 1989. Markets, Market Failures, and Development. *American Economic Review* 79: 197–210.

Suresh, S. 2003. *Symbols of Trade.* New Delhi.

Sutherland, C.H.V. and Carson, R.A.G. 1984. Roman Imperial Coinage Vol. I: From 31 BC to AD 69 - Augustus to Vitellius. London: Spink.

Tchernia, A. 2016. *The Romans and Trade.* Oxford: Oxford University Press.

Temin, P. 2001. A Market Economy in the Early Roman Empire. *Journal of Roman Studies* 91: 169–181.

———. 2013. The Roman Market Economy, Princeton University Press, Princeton.

Terpstra, T. 2018. Neo-Institutionalism in Ancient Economic History: The Road Ahead, in Ménard and Shirley 2018, 233–240.

———. 2019. *Trade in the Ancient Mediterranean. Private Order and Public Institutions.* Princeton: Princeton University Press.

Thür, G. 1987. Hypotheken-Urkunde eines Seedarlehens für eine Reise nach Muziris und Apographe für die Tetarte in Alexandria. *Tyche* 2: 229–245.

———. 1988. Zum Seedarlehen κατὰ Μουζεῖριν. *Tyche* 3: 227–233.

Turner, P.J. 1989. *Roman Coins from India.* London: Royal Numismatic Soc.

Verboven, K. 2002. *The Economy of Friends: Economic Aspects of Amicitia and Patronage in the Late Republic.* Bruxelles: Latomus.

———. 2015a. Models or Muddles? What are Theories Good for in Ancient Economic History? *in Erdkamp and Verboven* 2015: 9–14.

———. 2015b. The Knights who Say NIE. Can Neo-Institutional Economics Live up to Its Expectation in Ancient History Research?, in Erdkamp and Verboven 2015, 33–58.

Veyne, P. 1979. Rome devant la prétendue fuite de l'or: Mercantilisme ou politique disciplinaire? *Annales ESC* 34 (2): 211–244.

Vivenza, G. 2012. Roman Economic Thought, in Scheidel 2012, 25–44.

Wallis, J.J. 2014. Persistence and Change in Institutions. The Evolution of Douglass C. North. In *Institutions, Property Rights, and Economic Growth. The Legacy of Douglass North*, ed. S. Galiani and I. Sened, 30–49. Cambridge: Cambridge University Press.

Warmington, E.H. 1928. *The Commerce between the Roman Empire and India*. 1st ed. Cambridge: Cambridge University Press.

Warmington, E. H. 1974. *The Commerce between the Roman Empire and India*. 2nd rev. ed. Curzon Press, London.

Wheeler, R.E.M. 1976. *My Archaeological Mission to India and Pakistan*. London: Thames & Hudson.

Wilson, A. 2009. Approaches to Quantifying Roman Trade, in Bowman and Wilson 2009, 213–249.

Wilson, A., and A. Bowman. 2018. *Trade, Commerce and the State in the Roman World*. Oxford: Oxford University Press.

Young, G.K. 2001. *Rome's Eastern Trade*. London/New York: Routledge.

Zuiderhoek, A. 2019. Benefactors, Markets, and Trust in the Roman East, in Hollander, Blanton IV, and Fitzgerald 2019, 51–62.

CHAPTER 13

Information Governance in Roman Finance

Koenraad Verboven

Does information matter? The question seems superfluous. The importance of information for economic transactions is hardly disputed. It is the central study-object in Information Economics, a cornerstone of New Institutional Economics, and built-in in the very world-view, of Complexity Economics according to César Hidalgo: *The universe is made of energy, matter, and information, but information is what makes the universe interesting. Without information, the universe would be an amorphous soup. It would lack the shapes, structures, aperiodic orders, and fractal arrangements that give the universe both its beauty and its complexity.*[1] Yet, curiously, ancient economic historians have not yet conceptualised it as an important determinant of economic performance.

Datasets documenting levels of trade and production show that the Roman Empire was a success at least in terms of its economic output: shipwrecks, lead pollution levels in Greenland ice, fish salting factories, water-mills and water-lifting devices, olive- and wine presses, settlement

[1] Hidalgo 2016: 1; for NIE see for instance North 1990, 2005: 120 (and *passim*).

K. Verboven (✉)
Universiteit Gent, Ghent, Belgium
e-mail: Koen.Verboven@UGent.be

C. Rosillo-López, M. García Morcillo (eds.), *Managing Information in the Roman Economy*, Palgrave Studies in Ancient Economies,
https://doi.org/10.1007/978-3-030-54100-2_13

densities, building inscriptions, honorific inscriptions, and many more.[2] None are straightforward but they all show the same picture of growth towards the early Empire, regionally differentiated declines in the third century, recoveries in the fourth, and renewed growth in the eastern Mediterranean until the middle of the sixth century. As we should expect in an empire as large and diverse as the Roman, some sets peak earlier, others later, some grow faster, some slower, and there are clear regional differences. The resolution is low and the datasets only allow a general impression but that impression is solid. It suggests that economic performance peaked in the first half of the second century at roughly the level of sixteenth or (maybe) early seventeenth-century Europe, considerably below that of developed nations even in the eighteenth century but impressively high for a pre-industrial empire.

While there is a broad agreement on this fuzzy outline, however, there is none on the determinants behind it. Some interpret the growth as the dividend of political unification and argue that most or all of it was extensive growth. In this view, flourishing markets were merely by-products of a larger and more stable political structure and of demographic growth.[3] Others argue there was real growth supported by market-oriented technical and logistic improvements. In this view, markets positively contributed to growing integration and increased resource production.[4]

In this paper, I want to look at the role of information as a structural determinant of growth. I am not interested here in possible strategies to acquire and use information but in the opportunities and constraints that determined how information could be generated, coded, stored, and transmitted and in how this affected attainable levels of performance.[5] As far as I am aware the problem has never been conceptualised in this way, but much of the ground work has been done. To denote this web of constraints and possibilities I use the concept of 'information governance system' (IGS) and ask how Roman IGS structurally affected the availability and reliability of information.

[2] For a general discussion of the possibilities, limitations and pitfalls see Cf. Wilson 2009a, b; Verboven 2018.

[3] Scheidel 2009, 2012; Bang 2007, 2008.

[4] Erdkamp 2001, 2016; Jongman 2016, 2017; see Temin 2013 for an economist's view.

[5] Douglass North calls this the 'incentive structure' of society; the concept is central throughout his work, see particularly North 1990, 2005; for a brief introduction see North 2008.

I will focus on the financial aspects of trade as a suitable case-study. Long-distance trade depended on credit to finance operations, to cover temporary losses, or to arrange transfer of funds. Information is crucial in credit transactions. Creditors want prior information regarding the reliability and solvency of debtors and sureties, and where they can be found if necessary. Information on transactions needs to be recorded and stored to avoid disputes, to inform parties that might later become involved (such as heirs), and to inform third party enforcers.

In addition to being vulnerable to future events, credit transactions are beset by incomplete, imperfect, and asymmetric information. Information control is almost by definition asymmetric because debtors are better informed of their ability and willingness to repay a loan than creditors. Agents provided representation services for long-distance credit transactions in pre-industrial societies, but exceedingly slow communication meant that principals had little means to monitor their agents' integrity or verify information. Structural uncertainty drives up transaction costs, increases moral hazard, and gives rise to adverse selection. With few means to distinguish solvent and reliable debtors from insolvent and unreliable ones, creditors are unwilling to extend loans except at excessively high interest rates and under unfavourable conditions.[6] Thus, the efficiency of a credit market, and whether or not it outperforms non-market credit transactions, depends on the organisations and institutions that facilitate access to and storage and retrieval of reliable information, and thereby determine the level of transaction costs that agents face.

Historically, market relations have rarely dominated credit systems. In most historical societies (and many even today) credit and sureties were easiest to obtain from close kin or from co-members of close-knit social groups. Credit transactions were embedded in pre-existing relational contracts, enforced by social sanctions and (ideally or ideologically) emotional commitments. Information exchange in such contexts is fast and its reliability is easily checked. Pure market transactions cannot compete because the formal institutions required to back them up are more costly and less efficient than the informal ones governing relational contracts. Hence the general tendency throughout history to graft business relations on personal ones or to cultivate personal relations with interesting business partners.

[6] Akerlof 1970; North 1990: 28–30, 41; Temin 2013: 97–100. See also North 1990: 108–109; 2005 (esp. 13–18) on the effect of uncertainty on economic development.

However, relational contracts are inevitably limited in scope. Social networks can comprise many weak ties ('just-someone-I-know') but the kind of strong ties needed to consolidate interpersonal trust by embedding it in multi-stranded interactions including material interests, affections, and moral obligations, are never very numerous. Social sanctions and emotional commitments work well only in small homogenous communities with strong shared beliefs regarding respect for commitments.

These limitations of personalised credit create theoretical opportunities for specialised intermediaries willing and able to invest resources to obtain and safe-keep information in exchange for fees and commissions. Commercial intermediaries extend the efficiency and the range of reputation-based sanctions because they inform potential partners of each other's previous conduct. In addition, by recording agreements in legally prescribed terms and safe-keeping these records intermediaries facilitate recourse to third party enforcers. They consequently reduce enforcement costs and help to settle disputes. The intermediaries are vulnerable to reputation damage and often incur legal liabilities themselves, which acts as a deterrent against fraud and an incentive to verify information carefully and to record it for future usage. Such opportunities for intermediaries, however, and the credit markets they create are merely a theoretical *potential*. Whether and how this potential materialises depends on the institutional context and presence or absence of organisations (including but not limited to the state) with opposed or converging interests to those of the intermediaries. This brings us back to the role of 'information governance systems'.

13.1 Information Governance Systems

Information Governance (IG) is a concept coined in corporate governance studies, where the aim is to establish 'instituted processes' that increase the effectiveness of information management. It broadly indicates all socially or formally instituted processes that regulate the production, circulation, valuation, storage, retrieval, and processing of information.[7]

[7] Cf. Kooper, Maes, and Lindgreen 2011: 195–196: 'Information governance involves establishing an environment and opportunities, rules and decision-making rights for the valuation, creation, collection, analysis, distribution, storage, use and control of information; it answers the question "what information do we need, how do we make use of it and who is responsible for it?"'.

The concept of IG *system* denotes how these processes are structured and which rule sets define them.

The efficiency of an IGS is defined by the quantity of data it is able to produce, store, and circulate, the speed with which it is able to process information, and the quality of the data it is able to ensure, that is the reliability of the valuations it makes. This efficiency, however, depends not only on the structure of the system and its rule sets but also on the resources that are available to make it work. These include material ones, such as money and goods (for instance writing material, means of transport) but also immaterial ones such as the skills possessed by agents (for instance literacy and numeracy) and moral entitlements they have (for instance to honesty and pro-activeness on the part of family or friends). Without a public postal system, for instance, Roman long-distance traders had to invest in couriers (usually slaves) or rely on friends or partners to take letters with them if they happened to travel in the right direction. Basic numeracy was low in Roman society, so successful traders had to invest time to upgrade their own skills and train or buy a specialist slave accountant.[8]

Conceptually we can distinguish private order IGS and public order IGS. The former are created by social networks; the rules governing the creation, distribution, processing, storage, and retrieval of information are social norms and conventions. The Roman ethics of friendship strongly emphasised the importance of sharing news and giving honest and reliable advice.[9] Within private associations (*collegia*) members were similarly expected to inform and advise each other on all matters of interest.[10] Public order IGS are open to agents regardless of the networks in which they participate. They often (but not necessarily) rely on regulation by public authorities. Codification systems such as writing or accounting are public domain, but largely unregulated. The *Acta Diurna* in Rome announced decisions by public institutions.[11] Laws and decrees were published via inscriptions. The contents were carefully controlled by public authorities. In reality most systems are a mix of both and (may) use the

[8] On Roman numeracy and accounting techniques see Minaud 2004; 2005a, b.

[9] Verboven 2002; cf. De Salvo 2002 for long-distance trade.

[10] Terpstra 2013; Broekaert 2017 on the importance of merchant *collegia* and foreign resident communities to share or withhold information.

[11] Baldwin 1979; but see Behrisch 1996 for a more nuanced view.

same instituted processes such as accounting systems, written registrations, archives and so on.

Informal trust networks are by far the most pervasive and powerful information governance systems in human history. Information communicated within relations of trust—especially when these are multiplex relations—is easily accepted as trustworthy. The rule sets that govern trust networks *qua* IGS are primarily moral imperatives pertaining to information sharing and acting upon information received. These rules determine the network's information potential, that is the effectiveness with which information inside the network is spread, assessed, stored, and retrieved. The effectiveness of trust networks as IGS depends on the density of ties within the network, the strength of the ties between the agents, and the degree of closure of the network. The first (density) ensures rapid dissemination of information, the second (strong ties) the effectiveness of moral imperatives to share and act upon information received, the third (closure) the relative absence of alternatives for agents who wish to defect. Thus Terpstra argued that ethnically defined trade diaspora's—mercantile foreign resident communities—dominated trade in the in the Roman Mediterranean because they pooled information without which itinerant traders with the same ethnic background could not operate.[12] Information management based on trust networks can be enhanced by using available technology. Letters, note-books, or accounts increase information storage capacity, geographic range, chronological durability, reliability of the information retrieved, and its persuasiveness when disclosed to members or third party enforcers.

Consciously or not social groups and organisations create their own private IGS. They adopt, reject, or interact with parts of public systems, such as codification standards (in accounting for instance) or open information repositories (libraries for instance). Sometimes different group-specific IGS use similar rule sets, as in the case of kinship-based social groups, each forming their own IGS. Sometimes they are qualitatively different. Some peacefully co-exist, others compete for power, money, or glory. Increase in overall efficiency is not the inevitable outcome of trajectories through time; nor is it always perceived as being desirable. Governing bodies may wish to curtail improvements in specific IG-Systems. In modern societies the press constitutes an IGS that authoritarian regimes prefer to curtail. Privacy laws affect the efficiency of the IGS a state's security

[12] Terpstra 2013, 2019. But see the critical remarks in Verboven 2020b.

services is able to develop. Social and wealth elites may be adverse to or merely uninterested in the creation of effective public order institutions that would support IG-Systems independent from the elites' own social networks.

But social/trust networks as IGS have their limitations. Their potential is first of all limited by the resources controlled by network members. Social networks that consist largely of illiterate agents cannot use written documents; adequate levels of numeracy are required to use accounting tools. Secondly, the larger a social network becomes, the more weak ties it comprises and the more room it gives to cliques. This decreases the efficiency of the network as a coherent IGS. The cliques have their own group-specific IGS but they are smaller and less closed to other members of the parent network. Thirdly, IGS based on trust networks can be effective only within the network itself. The rules—for instance determining which information is confidential, which can be divulged and to whom—apply only to insiders. Outsiders are not bound by them.

In the following pages I will first discuss the potential of Roman private order IGS based on personal networks, communities and *collegia*. Next we will survey aspects of public IG that merchants could use to enhance their operations. In the last part I will show how commercial intermediaries responded to facilitate this and thereby boosted the development of credit markets.

13.2 Roman Private Order Information Systems

13.2.1 Personal Networks

Roman social culture stimulated the formation of strong and large personal networks through the formal and informal institutions supporting slavery, freedmanship, patronage, and *amicitia*. This allowed businessmen to build large extended-family based networks. Slaves could be given autonomy as agents, allowing them to share in the profits they made for their master. They continued to belong to the *familia*, however, and could freely be punished or rewarded. Legally, everything an independently working slave acquired, whether property, money, or legal claims belonged to his master. The ultimate reward for loyal and successful slaves was manumission. Freedmen's reputation hinged upon deference (*obsequium*) towards their patron (and his/her *domus*). Defection to other freedman-based networks was impossible. Conversely being in the core of their former master's personal network gave freedmen a vested interest in their patron's success because it provided them with opportunities to further their personal interests.[13]

Hovering around these high density multiplex cores were relations to friends, clients, and (in some cases) independent freedmen who had been successful in developing their own business and capital base. They were tied to the core ideologically because public transcript stressed reciprocity ethics (*gratia*) and reputation (*existimatio*). Presumably many had interiorised this ideology early in their lives. However, they had also a vested interest in maintaining the network because any breach risked cutting them off from the core.[14] Roman type personal networks, therefore, were a mix of hierarchically structured involuntary relations based on personal power (*familia*), and 'voluntary' relations ranging from semi-dependent patron client relations to *amicitia* relations between social equals, with freedmen situated somewhere in the middle. As IGS such networks were highly effective because they combined size with density and strong ties. The key characteristic of the core networks (hierarchy, lack of formal rights, personal power) supported information control. The middle-range of clients, protégés, and close 'friends' added size and flexibility. The emphasis on *amicitia* and its link to *existimatio* made defection to alternative clusters costly in terms of reputation damage. The size of the core-cluster facilitated control over middle-range ties because it allowed for multiple supervision. It also raised the stakes for middle-rangers and outliers because a break with a core-member, risked provoking a reaction from the entire core-cluster and other middle-ranges that would deny the defector future access to the cluster. In addition, Roman personal networks benefitted from a legal backup. Business associates were routinely connected through family relationship or instrumental friendship (*amicitia*) but the agency services they exchanged were interpreted legally as *mandata* or exchanges in the frame of *societas*.[15]

[13] Broekaert 2016; Verboven 2012.

[14] Verboven 2002.

[15] See Verboven 2002: 227–286 for the view that key features of Roman agency contract can only be understood as functioning against the backdrop of the dominance of *amicitia* and patronage in organisations; see also Michel 1962; Kirschenbaum 1987; Nörr 1990; on *societas* see Verboven 2002: 275–287; Broekaert 2012; *socii* shared profits and losses but were also tied to each other by bonds of personal trust and solidarity (*fides*) rooted in close family relationships or friendships

However, there were also limitations and disadvantages to Roman personal networks. As is the case for all person-based or family based trust networks the core remained closed to outsiders. *Amici* could gradually shift their alliance. Maintaining personal bonds required time and resources. The larger the network, the greater the costs involved in maintaining it. Last but not least, personal networks are always vulnerable to demographic events such as the death of core-members or important middle-rangers, or the coming-of-age of particularly skilled or inept core-members.

13.2.2 Communities and Guilds

Close-knit communities characterised by a strong sense of shared identity and insider morality generate a different type of IGS. Sanctions for defection (ideally) comprise emotional costs, such as shame or feelings of guilt or sin, that are underpinned by social sanctions ranging from gossip and public shaming (tarnishing the reputation of defectors) through shunning and exclusion from the community and the benefits attached to membership, including access to information.

Geographically defined mercantile communities were relatively common in the Hellenistic and Roman world.[16] Some of these congregated in formal voluntary associations. The 'Shippers, Merchants, and Warehousemen from Beirut Residing on Delos', for instance, possessed a large building with storage and lodging facilities, meeting rooms, and religious shrines.[17] The Tyrians in Puteoli were organised through a *statio* established by their home city in the first century BC or AD, which still represented the community in the late second century.[18] Merchant and shipper *collegia* created closure through clearly defined membership criteria, by-laws and formal positions of leadership and authority. This strengthened trust relations internally and thereby increased the efficiency and reliability of information transmission, verification, and storage. From Trajan onwards the imperial administration encouraged the formation of

[16] Terpstra 2013, 2019.

[17] Bruneau 1978, 1991; Trümper 2002; Hasenohr 2007; Trümper 2011; Harland 2013: 56 for more references. Other examples include the Aradians, the Tyrians, and the Alexandrians, see Rauh 1993 and for a critical view Verboven 2020b.

[18] Sosin 1999; Aliquot 2011: 88–91, no. 6; Terpstra 2013: 70–87; Soricelli 2007: 137; Verboven 2020b.

merchant and shipper *collegia* to ensure the capital's food supply.[19] They were recognised as corporate bodies and mediated imperial privileges and immunities to individual merchants and shippers.

In contrast to their medieval successors, however, Roman *collegia* never attained formal positions of power and received no delegated authority from local or imperial public administrations to punish defectors.[20] Guild(-like) groups of merchants and shippers are not widely documented. Most foreign resident communities were only loosely structured through common cults. Contrary to religious minority groups in medieval and early Modern Europe (such as the English Calvinists in Amsterdam), and in the Arab world (such as the 'Maghribi' Jews in old Cairo) religious oppositions were rarely strong enough to impose themselves on societal structure before late Antiquity.[21] Cultural or religious solidarity played an important role in the daily lives of mercantile communities, underpinning personal trust relations but religious or ethnic identity was rarely strong enough to impose closure on these communities.[22] So we should beware of exaggerating the potential of the IGS generated by these groups.

13.3 Roman Public Order Information Systems

Public order IGS set universalistic standards to specify and record *ex ante* expectations and facilitate a posteriori enforcement—for instance by stipulating formal requirements for registration of contracts or attaching tacit but legally enforceable implications to transactions. The rules that define them apply to agents regardless of the social networks or communities they belong to, even though significant differences can exist related to personal status (most of all citizenship and freedom) and gender. Public order IGS reduce transaction costs between agents who are not embedded in strong social networks, thereby stimulating the development of market-based information services.

[19] De Salvo 1992; Sirks 1991; Broekaert 2008; they might go back in some form to the Augustan period, cf. *AE* 1955, 178; *CIL* 14.3603; *AE* 1987, 180 (De Fino 1994); possibly also *CIL* 6.29725.

[20] Verboven 2020b.

[21] On the Calvinists in Amsterdam see Grafe and Gelderblom 2010: 490; on the maghribi see Greif 1991, 2006: 58–91, but see also the critique by Edwards and Ogilvie 2012, the reply by Greif 2012 and Goldberg 2012 for a new interpretation.

[22] Verboven 2020b; contra Terpstra 2013.

Characteristic of public order IG in the Roman world was the gradual spread of Roman law and customs; first as a legal system superimposed on local systems (for instance Hellenistic or Jewish law), then in the early Principate as the dominant system to which also non-roman citizens could have recourse. Eventually, when Roman citizenship was extended to all inhabitants of the empire in AD 212, Roman law became the only valid legal system.

Roman public order IG always remained less important than private order in terms of quantity of information and speed of transmission but for storage, retrieval and verification processes the procedures it laid down had become dominant by the second century BC when it became common practice for all property holders to keep written accounts. Cicero feigns surprise that Verres would have kept his accounts only intermittingly. Some people supposedly never kept accounts (says Cicero) but this was highly exceptional.[23] Even within trust networks, relevant information was commonly codified following the (simple) principles of Roman accounting, expressed in legal terms, triggering (in principle) legal effects, written down in sealed documents, deposited for safe-keeping with bankers, scribes or public registration offices. The validity of the information thus stored in accordance with the principles of public order governance was easily accepted in later dispute settlements, dividing up inheritances, transferring entitlements and obligations, and so on, regardless of whether or not public authorities were involved. In that sense they became part of Roman business culture.[24] In defending Q. Roscius the actor Cicero challenged his opponent, Fannius Chaerea, to show his account books to prove that he had paid out 100,000 sesterces to Roscius. Chaerea admitted that he had not entered the sum in his ledger (*codex accepti et expensi*), but argued that he had registered it in his daybook. Cicero laughed Fannius away; daybooks were nothing but careless notes, the ledger on the contrary provided a meticulous account of income and expenses.[25]

How efficient was public order IG in the Roman world compared to that of other pre-modern societies? I will focus here on accounting

[23] Cic. 2 *Verr.* 1.60. On Roman accounting see Thilo 1980; Minaud 2005b.

[24] On the importance of culture in codification practices following public prescriptive norms see Meyer 2004; Terpstra 2013.

[25] Cic. *Rosc. Com.* 7.

practices, registration offices, and financial instruments because these mattered most for commercial services offered by specialised intermediaries.

13.3.1 Roman Accounting

Speeches in court, legal and literary sources, documentary texts, and iconographic sources show the centrality of account books in Roman patrimonial management and business practice. Account books were a cornerstone of information management by Roman public administration, elite households, and businessmen. They were mostly private documents but followed common standards intended to ensure use in case of disputes (see above). A senatorial decree from AD 61 prescribed how tablets needed to be sealed in order to be valid in court.[26] The technical language used in connection with the account books and the skills involved in drawing them up and interpreting them imply a considerable investment in training. In large households and public administrations 'accountant' (*ratiocinator*) was a specific office, usually filled by slaves or freedmen, distinct from that of the *dispensator*, the 'pay-master' or 'treasurer', who was in charge of payments and receipts. Liabilities and claims were technically conceptualised as *nomina* and registered in the account books to keep track of affairs and to support business operations.[27]

There has been considerable debate on the efficiency of Roman (and Greek) accounting practices. Double bookkeeping was not used, nor was the concept of amortisation familiar.[28] Trying to establish the efficiency of ancient accounting in comparison to modern accounting practices, however, is meaningless given the latter's development to accommodate the needs of modern industrialised economies. Nevertheless, accounting was central to Roman trade and finance. Long-distance trade was hardly imaginable without it. Businessmen (*negotiatores*) were respected by patrimonial elites for their ability to read and interpret accounts.[29] Atticus—a former businessman but still active investor—supervised the affairs and

[26] Camodeca 1993.

[27] The literature on Greco-Roman accounting is vast; on legal and technical aspects see Thilo 1980; for accounting as a management tool see Rathbone 1991; on how accounting practices reflected and influenced mental and ideological perceptions of reality see Minaud 2005b; a; regrettably most scholars have focused on agricultural estates, not on trade or finance; for deposit bankers see Andreau 1987: 615–626.

[28] de Sainte-Croix 1956; Carandini 1983; Macve 1985.

[29] Verboven 2004.

accounts of several of his aristocratic friends, among whom Cicero.[30] The businessman M. Mindius assisted his brother (or cousin?) L. Mescinius Rufus in supervising the provincial accounts of Cilicia as *proquaestor*.[31]

Accounts codified transactions and stored information for later use in making decisions, controlling agents and partners, and handling disputes. Accounts also created instruments and procedures that could be used to manage financial and commercial transactions. Thus, they provided the legal basis for a common procedure to transfer debts. When a debtor 'A' wished to pay his creditor 'B', he could transfer a claim he owned on 'C' to 'B'. The registration was called a *nomen transcripticium* and created a new enforceable debt that annulled the two previous ones.[32] It was a flexible way to arrange payments and balance accounts.[33]

13.3.2 Public Registration Offices

The concurrence of the account books of payer and payee constituted proof in court but could easily be forged. It was common therefore to use trustworthy third persons to register transactions. We will return to them later in this paper. Interestingly, however, in Egypt public registration offices (*grapheia*) offered third party registration. The institution existed in Ptolemaic times but was greatly expanded under Roman rule when offices were created in every town and village. These were leased out to private scribes, who recorded contracts in exchange for a fee and sent summaries to their district's (*nome*) capital. Only one registration list is partly preserved for the year AD 44/45 from the village/town of Tebtynis, (c. 4500 people). The preserved parts list 836 contracts, 21% of which are loans.[34]

The institution worked well. The number of recorded loans in the early Roman period increased compared to the Ptolemaic period and whereas the majority of loans under the Ptolemies had been loans in kind (60%), the vast majority now was in money (85%). The sums lent, however, were

[30] Nepos, 15.1; see Rauh 1986: 7–12; Verboven 2002: 227–274 (here also for other examples).

[31] Cic. *Fam.* 5.20.2; 13.26.

[32] Gaius 3.30; there were also *nomina transcripticia a re in personam* used to register sales on credit.

[33] Cf. Verboven 2009.

[34] *P.Mich.* 2.121; 123; 5.238.

still relatively small and the transactions recorded are all local.[35] That changed after the creation c. AD 70 of the 'registers of holdings' (*bibliothèkai enkteseoon*) in the district capitals. It now became obligatory to register real property, slaves, mortgages, and claims guaranteed by real security in the 'register of holdings'. The scribes of local *grapheia* had to consult the register for each contract they drew up in which real property or slaves were involved. The registers were probably intended to facilitate levying taxes but greatly boosted also private credit markets. The number of credit contracts increased, the median sums borrowed tripled, women became active creditors, and local credit markets opened up with elites becoming prominent creditors at regional levels.[36]

We have no proof that similar innovations occurred also elsewhere but it is tempting to believe they did. The 'register of holdings' was a Roman innovation. There is no reason to think that this reform was limited to Egypt. Although the registration offices (*grapheia*) had non-Roman precursors their generalisation was a Roman administrative measure that would have suited also other provinces. The fragments of reliefs and inscriptions showing cadastres indicate that registration of real property was ubiquitous long before the tax reforms of Diocletian.

13.3.3 Financial Instruments

In addition to the proper registration of transactions in account books and registration offices, it was customary to draw up *cautiones* sealed by witnesses recording the relevant (legal) details of a transaction. They followed models devised by jurists and used a highly formulaic language.[37] Forgery was a criminal offence punished by the *lex Cornelia de falsis* (81 BC).[38] A *senatus consultum de falsarios* (c. AD 61) stipulated how tablets had to be sealed to be allowed in court.[39] The tablets found in Pompeii show that the decree was adhered to in practice.[40]

[35] Lerouxel 2012, 2015.

[36] Lerouxel ibid.; Jördens 2010a; b for the view that the *bibliothèkai enkteseoon* were part of a policy to stimulate private interests.

[37] See Meyer 2004 for the cultural significance of this formulaic language.

[38] See *Dig.* 48.10 (Paulus, *Sent.* 5.25); Septimius Severus eventually included unsealed accounts (ibid.); obviously a victim of forgery could also use the (private) *actio doli* to obtain compensation.

[39] Suet. *Ner.* 17; Paulus, *Sent.* 5.25.6; Meyer 2004: 163–168.

[40] Camodeca 1993, 1999.

Legally *cautiones* merely documented the existence or dissolution of obligations but in practice the issue was largely academic. By far the most important type of *cautio* was the *chirographum*, a term borrowed from Greek law where it referred to a common type of written contract. The fact that the word found its way into Roman legal parlance illustrates the thin divide. By the third century (but perhaps much earlier) debts recorded in properly sealed *chirographa* could only be denied the first year after they had been drafted.[41]

A similar blurring between written and non-written contracts is visible in the case of what the jurist Gaius (second century AD) called *nomina arcaria*. These are not mentioned in later law. Presumably because they became obsolete as legal innovations improved the use of chirographs. Some examples, however, are preserved among the remains of the archives of the Sulpicii—bankers active in the port of Puteoli—in the form of sealed tablets recording sums paid out to a borrower, and referring explicitly to the account books (*codices accepti et expensi*) of creditor and debtor.[42] Gaius notes that people often confused *nomina arcaria* with written contracts but legally the obligations were created by the recorded paying-out and receiving of money.[43] As in the case of the chirographs, the difference was academic from the view-point of the users.

The blurring between sealed documents as 'proof of contract' and 'contract in itself' facilitated the sale of debts or the transfer of debts in lieu of payment. The legal procedure behind this was the *delegatio debitoris* but tellingly even jurists commonly referred to it as *venditio chirographi*.[44] The procedure had become common by the late Republic. The basic principle was that a creditor handed over the *chirographum* and instructed (*denuntiatio*) his debtor to repay his debt to the new holder of the chirograph. Contrary to the transfer of *nomina* described above, *delegationes debitoris* did not require the consent of the debtor who received the instruction. Originally the original creditor had to appoint the assignee of

[41] Zimmermann 1990: 93–94; Sirks 2016; Verboven 2020.

[42] Camodeca 1999: 151–160 (*TPSulp*. 60–65); on the question of whether these *nomina arcaria* indicate that the Sulpicii were deposit bankers see Verboven 2003b: 436–439.

[43] Gaius 3.132; Camodeca 1992: 199–235.

[44] Although they stressed that legally speaking it was a *venditio nominis*; *Dig*. 30.44.5 (Ulpianus, 22 *Ad Sabinum*): *Eum, qui chirographum legat, debitum legare, non solum tabulas argumento est venditio: nam cum chirographa veneunt, nomen venisse videtur*; the oldest attestation is Cato, *Agr*., 149.2; Verboven 2002: 134–135; 2020; Harris 2008: 192–193; 2006; on legal technicalities see Thilo 1980: 276–318; Zimmermann 1990: 60–63; 158–160.

the debt as 'legal representative in his own interest' (*procurator in rem suam*), giving him the right to sue the debtor contained in the chirograph in the original creditor's name (but in his own interest). This was a very imperfect solution because the appointment ended with the death of either the original creditor or the assignee (*cui delegatus est*). The debtor, moreover, was still free to discharge his obligation by paying the initial creditor (or his agents), which made it vulnerable to fraud and errors. In addition, the original creditor formally retained his rights. In practice, this meant that *delegatio debitoris* required drawing up several additional formal contracts (*stipulatio*) with penalty clauses to cover unintended or undesirable eventualities.

From the second century AD onwards jurists simplified the procedure, extended its applications, and strengthened its legal implications. Around the middle of the second century purchasers of inheritances acquired the right to sue on the claims in the inheritance, without requiring separate *delegationes debitoris* from the heir who sold the estate.[45] This principle was later extended to other cases. Towards the middle of the third century the requirement of a separate appointment as *procurator in rem suam* was accepted as inherent in the act of selling or transferring a *chirographum/nomen*. By that time also the *denuntiatio* notifying a debtor that his creditor had changed, had become legally binding for the debtor. It seems unlikely (although it has recently been argued) that *chirographa* now became fully negotiable instruments, that is that they could freely circulate as 'paper' money but they were clearly very common instruments and within business communities were used routinely to handle payments at a distance and to balance business accounts.[46]

13.3.4 Enforcement

The discussion above shows how accounting practices, registration offices, and legal instruments provided common standards to support an IGS with advanced storage, processing, and valuation processes. The system relied both on public domain standards and codifications (such as writing, calculus, sealed tablets, and so on) and on formal regulations designed by public authorities regarding the use of these.

[45] *Dig.* 2.14.16. pr. (Ulpianus 4 *ad edictum*).

[46] Pro free circulation Harris 2006: 15; Sirks 2016; contra Verboven 2020.

But how robust was this system against future contingencies? Written *cautiones* informed the parties concerned on future claims and obligations but what was this information worth if they were not enforceable? What was the point of a legally waterproof contract if the creditor could not rely on its enforcement to prevent the debtor from reneging on the contract? To put this in information terms: without enforcement possibilities the documents informed on predictable claims, not on predictable outcomes.

Traditional views of Roman law are sceptical about the enforceability of legal obligations. Summons to appear before the judicial magistrate had to be made by the prosecuting party directly to the defendant. If the defendant ignored the summons, it was up to the prosecuting party to find means to force him. When a verdict was passed, it was again up to the winner to enforce it. In this view, the Roman legal system only worked because it ultimately relied on an informal reputation mechanism enforced by social sanctions inflicted by the community to which the wrongdoer belonged.

There is little doubt that private order enforcement via social sanctions was an important part of Roman legal dispute management. Roman legal culture in general was strongly embedded in social culture. As argued by Elisabeth Meyer, sealed tablets were more than just legal instruments. They were a part of social rituals that fortified interpersonal commitments and triggered strong social disapproval when breached. The provinces lacked this specific cultural background but it was an integral part of Roman military culture and of social life in citizen colonies. To provincials aspiring to participate in Roman power, the culture of sealed *tabulae* signified 'Roman-ness'.[47]

Private order sanctions, however, work well only in relatively closed communities that combine strong norms of fairness towards group members with norms imposing altruistic punishment of norm-breakers—that is group members are expected to punish cheaters even when they have not experienced a personal disadvantage and even when doing so comes at an emotional or material cost to themselves. Failure to perform altruistic punishment constitutes a breach of the group's norms and risks triggering sanctions.[48] Apart from being strongly dependent on cultural specificities,

[47] Meyer 2004; Terpstra 2013.

[48] On private order sanctions working well only within closed communities see Ogilvie 2011: 250–268; on altruistic punishment Verboven 2015: 43–47; Fehr and Gächter 2002; Boyd et al. 2005.

however, this type of social behaviour governance works well only if the group is small and homogenous enough to detect free-riders and defectors effectively. In addition, the relative benefits of group membership need to outweigh the relative costs, which implies that there must be exclusive 'club goods' that defectors risk losing. For private order sanctions to be an effective alternative to public order sanctions, therefore, long-distance traders need to be able to rely on closed communities and limit their business dealing as much as possible to insiders. Thus, for instance, scholars have pointed to the absence or weakness of public institutions to explain the importance of medieval merchant guilds and foreign resident communities.[49] Can we find similar solutions in the Roman world? Roman merchant and shipper *collegia* fostered norms of group solidarity that were very similar to those of their medieval counterparts but with very few exceptions they never received similar privileges or delegated authority from public authorities to punish cheaters.

Taco Terpstra advocates a model of 'trade diaspora communities' that would have provided efficient social sanctions to deter cheaters and free-riders. According to this model, long-distance traders set up ethnically and geographically defined trading stations (*stationes*) run by and representing foreign mercantile communities. These assisted traders by offering them information in addition to material support. Traders who broke agreements or breached faith were denied access to the communities' institutions, making it impossible in practice to continue doing business.[50]

But this model is not without problems. While reputation was highly important in Roman business networks and foreign mercantile communities were common, few of these constituted identitarian groups characterised by religious or cultural closure. The model is heavily based on what we know of the Tyrian resident communities in Puteoli and Rome, which had a formal representation via *stationes* (cf. above n. 18). Phoenician communities in late Hellenistic Delos as well established formal associations with statutes, officers, and valuable communal assets that set these groups apart from other communities (see above n. 17). These were obviously important trading groups, but similar social institutions are rarely

[49] Greif 2006; Ogilvie 2011; Grafe and Gelderblom 2010; note, however, the very different approaches: a response to ineffective public institutions (Greif), collusion between merchants and rulers to prevent the development of efficient public institutions (Ogilvie); Gelderblom and Grafe argue that both are not incompatible and that guilds can be a driving force to improve public institutions.

[50] Terpstra 2013, 2019.

found among non-Phoenician residents. Most *stationes* we know from Ostia were geographically defined, grouping shippers and merchants from various cities in northern Africa and Gaul. They were not ethnically or religiously specific. So closure based on religious or ethnic identity cannot have been strong for these groups. Even for the Tyrians in Puteoli and Rome the interpretation of strong social norms providing private order sanctions is problematic. The reason why we know these two groups so well is because they came into conflict around AD 170 and appealed to the *public* authorities in the mother-city of Tyre to resolve their dispute. Among the tablets of the Sulpicii, Roman bankers at Puteoli, we find a freedman agent of a Tyrian merchant borrowing money. This seems to indicate that at least some Tyrian traders had access to business networks outside their own community.[51] Athenodorus is said to have observed that Romans and other foreign residents in Petra, capital of the Nabataeans, 'frequently engaged in litigation, both with one another and with the natives', while the natives themselves 'lived together in perfect harmony'.[52] We are not told what procedures were used but they were clearly public and intended to resolve disputes between members of different communities.

Does this imply that Roman long-distance trade was effectively curtailed or depended on protection from powerful aristocrats to supplement the otherwise inadequate legal protection? I am not convinced this was the case. We should beware to take too pessimistic a view of Roman legal practices. While *stricto iure* the formulary procedure used for litigation in early imperial Italy did not comprise public arrests or state enforcement of verdicts, Roman magistrates did have the discretionary power to provide these services. The provision of justice was a central duty of the Roman magistrates and the corner stone of imperial ideology. Even second and third century rabbis stressed that the Roman Empire provided justice.[53]

The 'coercive power' of government, moreover, should not be defined narrowly as only the exercise of physical violence. A creditor facing a

[51] *TPSulp.* 4.

[52] Strab. 16.1.22: εὑρεῖν γὰρ ἐπιδημοῦντας ἔφη πολλοὺς μὲν Ῥωμαίων πολλοὺς δὲ καὶ τῶν ἄλλων ξένων. τοὺς μὲν οὖν ξένους ὁρᾶν κρινομένους πολλάκις καὶ πρὸς ἀλλήλους καὶ πρὸς τοὺς ἐπιχωρίους, τῶν δ᾽ ἐπιχωρίων οὐδένας ἀλλήλοις ἐγκαλοῦντας, ἀλλὰ τὴν πᾶσαν εἰρήνην ἄγοντας πρὸς ἑαυτούς.

[53] Cf. Ando 2000: 55–56.

debtor who refused to come to court could request a so-called *missio in possesionem rei servandae causa* from the judicial magistrate, giving the plaintiff legal possession of the defendant's property. A similar *missio in possessionem* was available if the defendant was convicted but refused to execute the verdict.[54] Technically *missiones in possessionem* provided only a 'right to seize', not a confiscation on the part of public authorities but they gave the plaintiff a claim to whatever the defendant or convicted party wished to sell or pledge. A businessman might have felt duly 'coerced' by such a measure.

There is no need to doubt that disputes were rarely brought to court. Businessmen generally prefer not to litigate if possible. It is time consuming and expensive. Yet, the Sulpician archives abound with documents relating to litigation. The obvious conclusion is that informal negotiations in these cases had failed and the Sulpicii (or their adversaries) had come to the conclusion that they needed help from public authorities. It illustrates that the law served its purpose as ultimate enforcement mechanism, when private attempts to settle a dispute had failed.

In terms of information management this implied that the available IGS on which creditors relied not only informed on current and future claims but on future outcomes and that it did so not merely because it documented entitlements to social sanctions but because it provided the information required to access public order enforcement procedures.

13.4 Commercial Credit Intermediaries

In the previous pages, I argued that Roman IGS provided scope to transcend the level of network embedded transactions by providing common procedures and institutions that guaranteed information storage, retrieval, and verification that was robust against future contingencies. Many of the instruments and procedures, however, were highly technical and required special skills and expertise. This section will discuss the role of specialised intermediaries who capitalised on these opportunities and consider to what extent they stimulated credit markets for trade ventures. We will first discuss deposit bankers and then turn to other intermediaries.

[54] Kaser 1996: 427–32.

13.4.1 Deposit Bankers

Deposit banking emerged in fifth century BC Greece and spread to Rome during the third century BC.[55] The basic service provided by ancient deposit bankers was to test and accept coins in deposit and assist customers in making and receiving payments. By doing so they alleviated the inconveniences of using heavy metal currency and the risks of counterfeiting. In addition, however, they extended bank loans (mostly short term and low risk) from the deposits they held, lent out their own private funds, and assisted private lenders and borrowers as go-betweens, brokers, and/or registrars and safe-keepers of contracts. By the middle of the second century BC the utility of deposit banking was officially recognised. Their services as coin assayers, safe-keepers of funds, payment intermediaries, and scribes gave bankers a reputation of trustworthiness. Specific legal rules were devised to regulate and uphold their activities. Among these the *edictum de edendi* (second century BC) was crucial: it stipulated that deposit bankers had to present the accounts of their clients in court.[56] These bank accounts enjoyed a special status as proof in court. For businessmen it implied that involving a banker in their affairs guaranteed that reliable information on transactions would be securely stored and could be used in later litigation.[57]

Roman deposit bankers are mentioned in the works of Plautus and Terentius in the late third and early second century BC.[58] Their importance for long-distance trade, however, is first documented on late Hellenistic Delos, where we find several wealthy bankers (*trapezitai*) providing services to merchants and shippers. Shortly after the island had been returned to Athens with an imposed status as a free-port (in 166 BC), 'the bankers on Delos' set up a statue to Apollo on the 'Agora of the Italians'.[59] The location suggests many were Romans or came from Italian

[55] For a history of Roman banking see Andreau 1999; for Greek banking Bogaert 1968.

[56] Cf. *Dig.* 2.13.10.1 (Gaius) "only bankers … are required to present their accounts because their office and service have a public cause and their foremost task is that they diligently draw up accounts of their affairs" (*argentarios tantum neque alios ullos absimiles eis edere rationes cogit, quia officium eorum atque ministerium publicam habet causam et haec principalis eorum opera est, ut actus sui rationes diligenter conficiant*); see also *Dig.* 16.3.8 (Papinianus 9 *quaestionum) necessarium usum argentariorum ex utilitate publica receptum est*); *Dig.* 42.5.24.2 (Ulpianus 63 *ad edictum*) *qui pecunias apud mensam fidem publicam secuti deposuerunt*); on the role of bankers' archives see Andreau 1995; 1996.

[57] For the legal framework see Petrucci 2002.

[58] Andreau 1968.

[59] *IDélos* 1715; Bogaert 1968: 190.

communities allied to Rome. A good example is Maraeus Gerellanus, who was honoured by the merchants and shippers of Athenian, Roman and other business communities on the island for 'his virtue and uprighteousness' (*aretè kai kalokagatheia*) towards them. His father had been *magister Neptunalis* a generation before.[60] Another, M. Minatius Sex. *filius*, helped the guild of the 'Worshippers of Poseidon from Beirut on Delos, Merchants, Shippers, and Warehousemen' to finance their grandiose guild-house. He was a wealthy man; in addition to remitting the interest on funds he had collected from other lenders, he donated 7000 *drachmai* towards the completion of the project.[61] The ex-banker, L. Aufidius, was honoured by all merchants, shippers and fellow-bankers on Delos. In the 90s BC he settled on nearby Tenos where he, and a generation later also his son, helped the debt-burdened city financially.[62]

Deposit bankers (*argentarii*) at this time belonged to the business elite. That changed after the crises of the 80s BC when many financial fortunes were destroyed. Deposit bankers no longer belonged to the financial elite later[63] but they continued to be important in assisting businessmen. In Italy and the western provinces, deposit bankers specialised in organising auctions.[64] We don't know how common it was for them to auction off incoming cargoes but by extending credit to local craftsmen and retailers to buy supplies *argentarii* boosted the circulation of money and goods.

Important for us here, however, is that their services were never limited to auctioneering. The jurists prescribed how bankruptcy had to be dealt with: creditors of non-interest bearing deposits were to be repaid first, before those who had practised money-lending with the banker's help—either by simply entrusting money in the hands of their banker as interest bearing deposits (*apud nummularios*), or by becoming his co-creditor (cum *nummulariis*), or by using him as a go-between (*per ipsos*).[65] There are no examples attested of bankers extending bank loans (from deposits)

[60] *IDélos* 1725; 1726; 1727; he is mentioned among the contributors to reconstruction works on the agora of the Italians (*IDélos* 2612); not everyone liked him: he is the target of a curse tablet (*IDélos* 2534); Bogaert 1968: 189.

[61] *IDélos* 1520; Bogaert 1968: 187–188.

[62] *IDélos* 1729, mentioned also in *IDélos* 1728; Bogaert 1968: 190; Tenos: *IG* 12.860; Bogaert 1968: 193–196; Migeotte 1986: 221–226.

[63] Andreau 1987: 333–356 (late Hellenistic period); 1987: 359–438 (late Republic and early Empire); 1999: 30–49; Kay 2014: 235–265.

[64] Andreau 1974; Petrucci 2008; García Morcillo 2005, 2008.

[65] *Dig.* 16.3.7 (Ulpianus 30 *ad edictum*).

to long-distance traders but financial mediation through bankers did provide merchants with working capital. Bankers in Roman Egypt, for instance, are often attested as go-betweens between private creditors and borrowers, including in the case of long-distance trade.[66] A famous example is a papyrus from AD 149. It records a maritime loan contract between two prominent notables from the town of Theadelphia, deep inland in the Fayum, and four merchants from the Phoenician city of Askalon. It seems unlikely that without their banker the notables would have considered investing their money in a maritime loan.[67]

Because they provided services to different population classes, from wealthy land-owners to craftsmen and small entrepreneurs, bankers were able to establish contacts between potential creditors and prospective debtors who were otherwise unconnected.[68] Bank accounts and other supporting documents drawn up and safe-kept by a banker provided valued information support for business transactions. Involving a banker in the conclusion of business deals, therefore, greatly improved all aspects of information management connected with the deals. The system was backed up both by the fact that bankers depended on their reputation of trustworthiness and by specific legal regulations.

13.4.2 Other Intermediaries

Deposit bankers, however, were never the only intermediaries. Brokers and bankers sensu *largo*—that is businessmen who specialise in the provision of financial services, including but not limited to loans—are well attested as financial intermediaries for merchants. Arranging *delegationes debitorum*, for instance, was considered to be inherent to commercial moneylending.[69] When Seneca tells his friend Lucilius that he will teach him a fast way to become rich, the necessity to borrow via a middleman (*per intercessorem*) or broker (*proxeneta*) in order to do business is seen as

[66] Only three examples of bank loans are attested: Bogaert 2000: 265–266; on deposit bankers brokering private loans see Lerouxel 2008, 2016: 85–86, 133–143.

[67] *SB* 14.11850; see also *PSI* 7.735; *P. Oslo* 3.89 for one of the creditors; cf. Casson 1986a: 13.

[68] Cf. Cic. *Off.* 3.58 on the immoral banker Pythius who was *ut argentarius apud omnes ordines gratiosus*.

[69] *Dig.* 14.3.19.3 (Papinianus 3 *responsorum*) shows it is implied in the *praepositio faenerandis causa*, the institution of a slave agent as moneylender; see Verboven 2008, 2020.

self-evident.[70] The jurist Ulpianus discusses the liabilities and fees due to brokers (*proxenetae*) who had offices (*officinae*) in large cities and made themselves useful in accomplishing purchases, sales, and commercial deals.[71] The famous 'Muziris papyrus' (documenting a maritime loan for a voyage from Egypt to India and back) mentions only one nominal creditor with his agents or managers (ἐπ[ι]τρ̣όπων ἢ φροντιστῶν). In view of the enormous amount at stake (the cargo was valued at seven million sesterces), however, multiple investors are likely to have been involved.[72]

The best known example of skilled credit intermediaries is provided by a batch of writing tablets discovered in Pompeii. The tablets attest the activities of three businessmen from Puteoli, C. Sulpicius Faustus, his freedman Cinnamus, and his brother and probably heir Onirus.[73] Faustus had a background in trade and a few transactions still record his involvement in trade deals (although possibly only as a sleeping partner). The other tablets attest Faustus or Cinnamus lending money, assisting creditors, and acting as go-between. Sometimes no Sulpicius at all is mentioned, which probably indicates they provided brokerage services and safe-kept contracts and related documents. Sixty-one payments or debt acknowledgments are preserved representing a total value of more than one million sesterces.[74]

Some scholars have argued that the C. Sulpicii were deposit bankers (*argentarii*) but nothing in the tablets substantiates this interpretation. It stems from a mistaken belief that all bankers are deposit bankers and all loans provided by bankers are bank loans drawn from deposits. Neither of this is historically correct.[75] Nevertheless, the Sulpicii were clearly highly specialised businessmen who sold financial services to long-distance traders and to Roman aristocrats or their representatives, including imperial freedmen. The latter looking for lucrative investments, the former for working capital to run their business. The tablets of the Sulpicii present various types of legal documents, ranging from loan contracts and contracts to rent storage space, to documents relating to legal trials and sales

[70] Sen. *Ep.* 119.

[71] *Dig.* 50.14 (Ulpianus).

[72] Casson 1986b, 1990; Rathbone 2001, 2003; Verboven 2020.

[73] Camodeca 1999; Andreau 1999: 71–79.

[74] We hear of debts of 94,000 sesterces (*TPSulp.* 69), 125,000 (*TPSulp.* 49) and even 130,000 sesterces (*TPSulp.* 74). The average value is 10,791 sesterces. Some debts are repaid in installments, some are consolidated.

[75] For a discussion see Verboven 2003a, b, 2008, 2020 (and there for further references).

of real sureties. The documents are highly technical and must have required basic legal training or legal advice.

Both the case of the Sulpicii of Puteoli and Seneca's letter to Lucilius show how specifically trained and specialised intermediaries allowed money from landed (and political) wealth to flow to long-distance trade. While many clearly had a background in trade financing trade was nevertheless a separate business specialisation.

13.5 Conclusion

The institutional framework of the Roman Empire supported IGS that offered ample opportunities for the development of a market for financial services, including to long-distance traders. These systems relied on universalistic standards of codification and formal regulations that enabled credit operations between anonymous or (rather more commonly) weakly linked agents. While personal trust networks continued to dominate long-distance trading organisations, as they did in all pre-industrial societies, the public order dimensions of the IGS available to Roman creditors and credit intermediaries allowed these organisations a greater scope in arranging and handling financial needs. By framing transactions in accordance with prescribed norms regarding the creation, registration, and extinguishing of obligations, mutual expectations were clarified and future contingencies protected against—even when these obligations were not embedded in multiplex social relations. The overall effect was that creditors and debtors had access to more and better information, including safeguards against future contingencies. The development of Roman IGS allowed swift identification of cheaters and thereby facilitated social sanctions. In addition, the instruments and the procedures used followed legal requirements and thus made litigation possible.

The public order dimensions in IGS available to Roman finance, however, required considerable knowledge and skills. As in late medieval Europe this led to the emergence of financial specialists, offering a range of services catering to the specific needs of long-distance traders. Both deposit bankers and other intermediaries further reduced problems of information asymmetries. They alleviated debtors and creditors (at least in part) from having to acquire specialist technical knowledge and obtain information on each other's solvency and reliability. Instead, the intermediaries invested in acquiring these skills and in creating their own information network regarding the clients they worked with.

The development of Roman IGS thus constituted a qualitative improvement in terms of information control and distribution. While IGS were obviously linked to political structures, they cannot be reduced to a mere side-effect of improved safety conditions, or of advantages of scale, or population increase. They independently supported the expansion of credit markets for long-distance trade. As such they were a positive determinant for the economic growth we see documented in the material record.

However, a last word of caution is in order. We should beware not to overestimate these developments. The overall development of public-domain rules and standards and the implication of public authorities in their enforcement is comparable to what happened in medieval Europe from the twelfth century onwards. In the Roman Empire this evolution culminated in the dominance of Roman law and provincial and imperial institutions. Contrary to ideological discourses, these were generally favourably disposed to long-distance traders and financiers without whom the cities could not be provisioned and life-styles not be maintained. But political elites remained firmly tied to patrimonial elites. To some extent they shared interests because credit intermediaries could be useful to raise money or to invest it, but they never identified with business elites. In early modern Europe on the other hand merchants and businessmen gradually won a greater grip on institutions, giving them leverage on the further development of public IGS: newspapers, gazetteers, maps, price-lists—all made possible by the invention of printing[76]—postal systems,[77] double-entry accounting, improved financial instruments,[78] and so on. These were all developed by and for a new bourgeois elite. Eventually by the seventeenth century early modern Europe had definitely surpassed the Roman Empire in terms of the capacity of its IGS.

Bibliography

Akerlof, G.A. 1970. The Market for 'Lemons': Quality Uncertainty and the Market Mechanism. *The Quarterly Journal of Economics* 84: 488–500.

[76] See the special issue of *Media History* 22.3–4 (2016) on 'Managing the News in Early Modern Europe, 1550–1800'.

[77] Cf. Veluwenkamp 2006 (134: "The postal revolution of the seventeenth century removed the need for business trips, expatriate agents and, eventually, commission agents as it disseminated information, expertise and trust. It paved the way to direct trade between local businessmen in different countries").

[78] Cf. Geva 2011.

Aliquot, J. 2011. Les Tyriens dans le monde romain. In *Sources de l'histoire de Tyr: textes de l'Antiquité et du Moyen Âge*, ed. P.-L. Gatier, J. Aliquot, and L. Nordiguian, 73–115. Beyrouth: PUSJ, Presses de l'Université Saint-Joseph.

Ando, C. 2000. *Imperial Ideology and Provincial Loyalty in the Roman Empire*. Berkeley: University of California Press.

Andreau, J. 1968. Banque grecque et banque romaine dans le théâtre de Plaute et de Térence. *MEFRA* 80: 461–526.

———. 1974. *Les affaires de Monsieur Jucundus*. Rome: Ecole Française de Rome.

———. 1987. *La vie financière dans le monde romain: les métiers de manieurs d'argent (IVe siècle av. J.-C.-IIIe siècle ap. J.-C.)* (Bibliothèque des Ecoles Françaises d'Athènes et de Rome 265). Rome: École française de Rome.

———. 1995. Pouvoirs publics et archives des banquiers professionels. In *La mémoire perdue: à la recherche des archives oubliées, publiques et privées, de la Rome antique*, ed. C. Nicolet and S. Demougin, 1–18 (Histoire ancienne et médiévale 30). Paris: Publications de la Sorbonne.

———. 1996. Les archives des banquiers romains et leur conservation. In *Archives et sceaux du monde hellénistique = Archivi e sigilli nel mondo ellenistico; Torino, Villa Gualino, 13–16 Gennaio 1993*, ed. M.-F. Boussac and A. Invenizzi, 423–437. Athènes: Ecole française d'Athènes.

———. 1999. *Banking and Business in the Roman World*. Cambridge/New York: Cambridge University Press.

Baldwin, B. 1979. The acta diurna. *Chiron* 9: 189–203.

Bang, P.F. 2007. Trade and Empire: In Search of Organizing Concepts for the Roman Economy. *Past and Present* 195: 3–54.

———. 2008. *The Roman Bazaar: A Comparative Study of Trade and Markets in a Tributary Empire*. Cambridge/New York: Cambridge University Press.

Behrisch, L. 1996. Die Acta Diurna: eine römische Staatszeitung. *Das Altertum* 41: 55–68.

Bogaert, R. 1968. *Banques et banquiers dans les cités grecques*. Leiden: A.W. Sijthoff.

———. 2000. Les opérations des banques de l'Égypte romaine. *Ancient Society* 30: 135–269.

Boyd, R., H. Gintis, S. Bowles, and P.J. Richerson. 2005. The Evolution of Altruistic Punishment. In *Moral Sentiments and Material Interests: The Foundations of Cooperation in Economic Life*, ed. H. Gintis, R. Boyd, S. Bowles, and E. Fehr, 215–229. Cambridge, MA: MIT Press.

Broekaert, W. 2008. 'Creatio ex Nihilo'?: The Origin of the 'Corpora Nauicularioram' Reconsidered. *Latomus* 67: 692–706.

———. 2012. Joining Forces. Commercial Partnerships or *Societates* in the Early Roman Empire. *Historia* 61: 221–253.

———. 2016. Freedmen and Agency in Roman Business. In *Urban Craftsmen and Traders in the Roman World*, ed. A. Wilson and M. Flohr, 222–253. Oxford: Oxford University Press.

———. 2017. Conflicts, Contract Enforcement, and Business Communities in the Archive of the Sulpicii. In *The Economy of Pompeii*, ed. M. Flohr and A. Wilson, 385–412 (Oxford Studies on the Roman Economy). Oxford: Oxford University Press.

Bruneau, P. 1978. Les cultes de l'établissement des Poseidoniastes de Bérytos à Délos, I. In *Hommages à M. J. Vermaseren, I–III*, ed. M.B. de Boer and T.A. Edridge, 160–190. Leiden: E.J. Brill.

———. 1991. Encore le sanctuaire et les cultes des Poseidoniastes de Bérytos. Deliaca, IX, 67. *BCH* 115: 377–388.

Camodeca, G. 1992. *L'archivio puteolano dei Sulpicii*. Napoli: Casa ed. Dott. E. Jovene.

———. 1993. Nuovi dati dagli archivi campani sulla datazione e applicazione del 'S.C. Neronianum'. *Index* 21: 353–364.

———. 1999. *Tabulae Pompeianae Sulpiciorum: TPSulp. : edizione critica dell'archivio puteolano dei Sulpicii*. Roma: Ed. Quasar.

Carandini, A. 1983. Columella's Vineyard and the Rationality of the Roman Economy. *Opus* 2: 177–204.

Casson, L. 1986a. New Light on Maritime Loans. P. Vindob. G. 19792 (=SB VI 9571). In *Studies in Roman Law in Memory of A. Arthur Schiller*, ed. R.S. Bagnall and W. Harris, 11–17. Leiden: Brill.

———. 1986b. P. Vindob. G 40822 and the Shipping of Goods from India. *Bulletin of the American Society of Papyrologists* 33: 73–79.

———. 1990. New Light on Maritime Loans: P. Vindob. G 40822. *ZPE* 84: 195–206.

De Fino, M. 1994. Dedica dei « nauclarii » ad un duoviro di Ostia. In *Epigrafia e territorio, politica e società: temi di antichità romane. III*, ed. M. Pani, 37–50. Bari: Edipuglia.

de Sainte-Croix, G.E.M. 1956. Greek and Roman Accounting. In *Studies in the History of Accounting*, ed. A.C. Littleton and B.S. Yamey, 14–74. London: Sweet & Maxwell Limited.

De Salvo, L. 1992. *Economia privata e pubblici servizi nell'impero romano: i corpora naviculariorum*. Messina: Samperi: Ecole française de Rome.

———. 2002. Mare, commercio e informazione privata nella tarda antichità. In *L'information et la mer dans le monde antique*, ed. J. Andreau and C. Virlouvet, 299–319 (Collection de l'Ecole française de Rome 297). Rome.

Edwards, J., and S. Ogilvie. 2012. Contract Enforcement, Institutions, and Social Capital: The Maghribi Traders Reappraised. *Economic History Review* 65: 421–444.

Erdkamp, P. 2001. Beyond the Limits of the « Consumer City » : A Model of the Urban and Rural Economy in the Roman World. *Historia* 50: 332–356.

———. 2016. Economic Growth in the Roman Mediterranean World: An Early Good-Bye to Malthus? *Explorations in Economic History* 60: 1–20.

Fehr, E., and S. Gächter. 2002. Altruistic Punishment in Humans. *Nature* 415 (6868): 137.
García Morcillo, M. 2005. *Las ventas por subasta en el mundo romano: la esfera privada*. Barcelona: University of Barcelona.
———. 2008. Auctions, Bankers and Public Finances in the Roman World. In *Pistoi dia tèn Technèn: Bankers, Loans, and Archives in the Ancient World: Studies in Honour of Raymond Bogaert*, ed. K. Verboven, K. Vandorpe, and V. Chankowski, 257–275. Leuven: Peeters.
Geva, B. 2011. *The Payment Order of Antiquity and the Middle Ages a Legal History*. Oxford/Portland: Hart Publishing.
Goldberg, J. 2012. *Trade and Institutions in the Medieval Mediterranean: The Geniza Merchants and Their Business World*. Cambridge/New York: Cambridge University Press.
Grafe, R., and O. Gelderblom. 2010. The Rise and Fall of the Merchant Guilds: Re-thinking the Comparative Study of Commercial Institutions in Premodern Europe. *Journal of Interdisciplinary History* 40: 477–511.
Greif, A. 1991. The Organization of Long-Distance Trade: Reputation and Coalitions in the Geniza Documents and Genoa During the Eleventh and Twelfth Centuries. *The Journal of Economic History* 51: 459–462.
———. 2006. *Institutions and the Path to the Modern Economy: Lessons from Medieval Trade*. Cambridge/New York: Cambridge University Press.
———. 2012. The Maghribi Traders: A Reappraisal? *Economic History Review* 65: 445–469.
Harland, P.A. 2013. *Associations, Synagogues, and Congregations: Claiming a Place in Ancient Mediterranean Society (Second revised edition with links to inscriptions)*. 2nd ed. Kitchener (Ontario).
Harris, W.V. 2006. A Revisionist View of Roman Money. *JRS* 96: 1–24.
Harris, W. 2008. The Nature of Roman Money. In *The Monetary Systems of the Greeks and Romans*, ed. W.V. Harris, 174–207. Oxford: Oxford University Press.
Hasenohr, C. 2007. Italiens et Phéniciens à Délos : organisation et relations de deux groupes d'étrangers résidents (IIe-Ier siècles av. J.-C.). In *Etrangers dans la cité romaine*, ed. R. Compatangelo-Soussignan and C.-G. Schwentzel, 77–90. Rennes.
Hidalgo, C. 2016. *Why Information Grows: The Evolution of Order, from Atoms to Economies*. New York: Basic Books.
Jongman, W. 2016. Italian Urbanization and Roman Economic Growth. In *L'Italia dei Flavi (atti del convegno, Roma, 4–5 ottobre 2012)*, ed. L. Capogrossi Colognesi, E. Lo Cascio, and E. Tassi Scandone, 105–117. Roma: L'Erma di Bretschneider.
———. 2017. The Benefits of Market Integration: Five Centuries of Prosperity in Roman Italy. In *The Economic Integration of Roman Italy: Rural Communities in a Globalizing World*, ed. T.C.A. de Haas and G.W. Tol, 15–27 (Mnemosyne,

Supplements, History and Archaeology of Classical Antiquity 404). Leiden/Boston: Brill.

Jördens, A. 2010a. Öffentliche Archive und römische Rechtspolitik. In *Tradition and Transformation: Egypt under Roman Rule: Proceedings of the International Conference, Hildesheim, Roemer- and Pelizaeus-Museum, 3–6 July 2008*, ed. K. Lembke, M. Minas-Nerpel, and S. Pfeiffer, 195–179. Leiden/Boston: Brill.

———. 2010b. Nochmals zur Bibliotheke Enkteseon. In *Symposion 2009: Vorträge zur griechischen und hellenistischen Rechtsgeschichte*, ed. G. Thür, 277–290 (Seggau, 25.-30. August 2009). Wien: Verlag der Österreichischen Akademie der Wissenschaften.

Kaser, M. 1996. *Das römische Zivilprozessrecht*. München: Verlag C.H. Beck.

Kay, P. 2014. *Rome's Economic Revolution* (Oxford Studies on the Roman Economy). Oxford: Oxford University Press.

Kirschenbaum, A. 1987. *Sons, Slaves and Freedmen in Roman Commerce*. Jerusalem: Magnes Press.

Kooper, M.N., R. Maes, and E.E.O.R. Lindgreen. 2011. On the Governance of Information: Introducing a New Concept of Governance to Support the Management of Information. *International Journal of Information Management* 31: 195–200.

Lerouxel, F. 2008. La banque privée romaine et le marché du crédit dans les tablettes de Murécine et les papyrus d'Egypte romaine. In *Pistoi dia tèn Technèn. Bankers, Loans, and Archives in the Ancient World: Studies in Honour of Raymond Bogaert*, ed. K. Verboven, V. Chankowski, and K. Vandorpe, 169–198. Leuven: Peeters.

———. 2012. Le marché du crédit privé, la bibliothèque des acquêts et les tâches publiques en Égypte romaine. *Annales (HSS)* 67: 943–976.

———. 2015. The βιβλιοθήκη ἐγκτήσεων and transaction costs in the credit market of Roman Egypt (30 B.C.E. to ca. 170 C.E.). In *Law and Transaction Costs in the Ancient Economy*, ed. D.P. Kehoe, D.M. Ratzan, and U. Yiftach, 162–184. Ann Arbor: University of Michigan Press.

———. 2016. *Le marché du crédit dans le monde romain (Égypte et Campanie)* (Bibliothèque des Écoles françaises d'Athènes et de Rome). Rome.

Macve, R.H. 1985. Some Glosses on Ste. Croix's Greek and Roman Accounting. *History of political thought* 6: 233–264.

Meyer, E.A. 2004. *Legitimacy and Law in the Roman World. Tabulae in Roman Belief and Practice*. Cambridge/New York: Cambridge University Press.

Michel, J.H. 1962. *Gratuité en droit romain*. Bruxelles: Université Libre de Bruxelles: Latomus.

Migeotte, L. 1986. *L'emprunt public dans les cités grecques: recueil des documents et analyse critique*. Québec/Paris: Ed. du Sphinx/Les Belles Lettres.

Minaud, G. 2004. Regard sur la comptabilité antique romaine. La mosaïque de l'aula des mensores à Ostie, des doigts et des comptes. *Mélanges de l'école française de Rome* 116: 437–468.

———. 2005a. Rationalité modulable des comptabilités. *Topoi* 12: 271–281.

———. 2005b. *La comptabilité à Rome: essai d'histoire économique sur la pensée comptable commerciale et privée dans le monde antique romain.* Lausanne: Presses Polytechniques et Universitaires Romandes.

Nörr, D. 1990. Reflections on Faith, Friendship and Mandate. *Irish Jurist* 25/27: 302–310.

North, D.C. 1990. *Institutions, Institutional Change, and Economic Performance.* Cambridge/New York: Cambridge University Press.

———. 2005. *Understanding the Process of Economic Change.* Princeton: Princeton University Press.

———. 2008. Institutions and the Performance of Economies over Time. In *Handbook of New Institutional Economics*, ed. C. Ménard and M.M. Shirley, 21–30. Heidelberg: Springer-Verlag Berlin Heidelberg.

Ogilvie, S. 2011. *Institutions and European Trade: Merchant Guilds, 1000–1800.* Cambridge/New York: Cambridge University Press.

Petrucci, A. 2002. *Profili giuridici delle attività e dell'organizzazione delle banche romane.* Torino: G. Giappichelli.

———. 2008. Riesame del ruole dei banchieri nelle auctiones private nel diritto romano. In *Pistoi dia tèn Technèn. Bankers, Loans, and Archives in the Ancient World: Studies in honour of Raymond Bogaert*, ed. K. Verboven, K. Vandorpe, and V. Chankowski, 277–300. Leuven: Peeters.

Rathbone, D. 1991. *Economic Rationalism and Rural Society in Third-Century A.D. Egypt: The Heroninos Archive and the Appianus Estate.* Cambridge/New York: Cambridge University Press.

———. 2001. The Muziris Papyrus (SB XVIII): Financing Roman Trade with India. *BSAA* 46: 39–50.

———. 2003. The Financing of Maritime Commerce in the Roman Empire, I-II AD. In *Credito e moneta nel mondo romano: atti degli Incontri capresi di storia dell'economia antica: Capri, 12–14 ottobre 2000*, ed. E. Lo Cascio, 197–229. Bari: Edipuglia.

Rauh, N.K. 1986. Cicero's Business Friendships. Economics and Politics in the Late Roman Republic. *Aevum* 60: 3–30.

———. 1993. *The Sacred Bonds of Commerce: Religion, Economy, and Trade Society at Hellenistic Roman Delos, 166–87 B. C.* Amsterdam: J.C. Gieben.

Scheidel, W. 2009. In Search of Roman Economic Growth. *Journal of Roman Archaeology* 22: 46–70.

———. 2012. Approaching the Roman Economy. In *The Cambridge Companion to the Roman Economy*, ed. W. Scheidel, 1–22. Cambridge: Cambridge University Press.

Sirks, A.J.B. 1991. *Food for Rome: The Legal Structure of the Transportation and Processing of Supplies for the Imperial Distributions in Rome and Constantinople*. Amsterdam: J.C. Gieben.

Sirks, B. 2016. Chirographs: Negotiable Instruments? *ZRG* 133: 265–285.

Soricelli, G. 2007. Comunità orientali a Puteoli. In *Étrangers dans la cité romaine : actes du colloque de Valenciennes (14–15 octobre 2005) : 'Habiter une autre patrie' : des 'incolae' de la République aux peuples fédérés du Bas-Empire*, ed. R. Compatangelo-Soussignan and C.-G. Schwentzel, 129–144. Rennes.

Sosin, J.D. 1999. Tyrian 'Stationarii' at Puteoli. *Tyche* 14: 275–284.

Temin, P. 2013. *The Roman Market Economy* (The Princeton Economic History of the Western World). Princeton: Princeton University Press.

Terpstra, T.T. 2013. *Trading Communities in the Roman world: A Micro-Economic and Institutional Perspective* (Columbia Studies in the Classical Tradition 37). Leiden: Brill.

———. 2019. *Trade in the Ancient Mediterranean: Private Order and Public Institutions*. Princeton: Princeton University Press.

Thilo, R.M. 1980. *Der Codex accepti et expensi im römischen Recht: ein Beitrag zur Lehre von der Litteralobligation*. Göttingen: Muster-Schmidt.

Trümper, M. 2002. Das Sanktuarium des 'Établissement des Poseidoniastes de Bérytos' in Delos : zur Baugeschichte eines griechischen Vereinsheiligtums. *BCH* 126: 265–330.

———. 2011. Where the Non-Delians met in Delos. The Meeting-Places of Foreign Associations and Ethnic Communities in Late Hellenistic Delos. In *Political Culture in the Greek City After the Classical Age*, ed. O. van Nijf, R. Alsten, and C.G. Williamson, 49–100. Leuven: Peeters.

Veluwenkamp, J.W. 2006. International Business Communication Patterns in the Dutch Commercial System, 1500–1800. In *Your Humble Servant: Agents in Early Modern Europe*, ed. H. Cools, M. Keblusek, and B. Noldus, 129–134. Hilversum: Verloren.

Verboven, K. 2002. *The Economy of Friends: Economic Aspects of « Amicitia » and Patronage in the Late Republic* (Collection Latomus 269). Bruxelles: Latomus.

———. 2003a. The Sulpicii from Puteoli and Usury in the Early Roman Empire. *Legal History Review* 71: 7–28.

———. 2003b. The Sulpicii from Puteoli, 'Argentarii' or 'Faeneratores'?. In *Hommages à Carl Deroux III – Histoire et Epigraphie, Droit*, ed. P. Defosse, 429–445 (Collection Latomus 270). Brussels: Latomus.

———. 2004. Mentalité et commerce : le cas des 'negotiatores' et de ceux 'qui negotia habent'. In *Mentalités et choix économiques des Romains*, ed. J. Andreau, J. France, and S. Pittia, 179–197. (Scripta antiqua ; 7). Bordeaux: Ausonius.

———. 2008. Faeneratores, Negotiatores and Financial Intermediation in the Roman World. In *Pistoi dia tèn Technèn. Bankers, Loans, and Archives in the Ancient World: Studies in Honour of Raymond Bogaert*, ed. K. Verboven,

K. Vandorpe, and V. Chankowski, 211–229 (Studia Hellenistica). Leuven: Peeters.

———. 2009. Currency, Bullion and Accounts. Monetary Modes in the Roman World. *Revue belge de numismatique* 155: 91–124.

———. 2012. The Freedman Economy of Roman Italy. In *Free at Last! The Impact of Freed Slaves on the Roman Empire*, ed. S. Bell and T.R. Ramsby, 88–109. London: Bristol Classical Press.

———. 2015. The Knights Who Say NIE. Can Neo-Institutional Economics Live Up to Its Expectation in Ancient History Research? In *Structure and Performance in the Roman Economy. Models, Methods and Case Studies*, ed. K. Verboven and P. Erdkamp, 33–57. Brussels: Latomus.

———. 2018. Ancient Cliometrics and Archaeological Proxy-Data. Between the Devil and the Deep Blue Sea. In *Cuantificar las economías antiguas. Problemas y métodos. Quantifying ancient economies. Problems and methodologies*, ed. J. Remesal Rodríguez, V. Revilla Calvo, and M. Bermúdez Lorenzo, 345–371 (Col.lecció Instrumenta 60). Barcelona: Universitat de Barcelona Edicions.

———. 2020a. Capital Markets and Financial Entrepreneurs in the Roman World. In *Capital, Investment, and Innovation in the Roman World*, ed. P. Erdkamp, K. Verboven, and A. Zuiderhoek, 381–416 (Oxford Studies in the Roman Economy). Oxford: Oxford University Press.

———. 2020b. The Structure of Mercantile Communities in the Roman World. How Open Were Roman Trade Networks?. In *Roman Port Societies. The Evidence from the Inscriptions*, ed. P. Arnaud and S. Keay, 326–366 (British School at Rome Studies). Cambridge: Cambridge University Press.

Wilson, A. 2009a. Approaches to Quantifying Roman Trade. In *Quantifying the Roman Economy: Methods and Problems*, ed. A. Bowman and A. Wilson, 213–249 (Oxford Roman Economy Series). Oxford: Oxford University Press.

———. 2009b. Indicators for Roman Economic Growth: A Response to Walter Scheidel. *Journal of Roman Archaeology* 22: 71–82.

Zimmermann, R. 1990. *The Law of Obligations: Roman Foundations of the Civilian Tradition*. Cape Town: Juta.

PART VI

Conclusions

CHAPTER 14

Concluding Remarks

Jean Andreau

People who participate in economic life, whatever the circumstances, need information, as Pablo Revilla rightly remarks in the opening of his chapter. They find part of this information themselves. For example, each participant in the economy is, in theory, capable of deciding upon their own objectives and consumer choices. But other kinds of information must inevitably be provided by third parties. In a perfectly efficient economic model, there would be the best possible allocation of information. There would be no inequalities in the distribution of information, or, if there were, the purpose of these would be to enable the perfect distribution of this asset among different participants.

However, in real life, in the Ancient World just as today, it is not like that. Instead of the perfect distribution of information within the framework of an efficient economy, we find information asymmetry. Those who benefit from this asymmetry have reason to be pleased with this advantage. As Marta García Morcillo and Cristina Rosillo-López note in their Introduction, they may be inclined to exclaim: "I know something that

J. Andreau (✉)
École des Hautes Études en Sciences Sociales, Paris, France
e-mail: jean.andreau@ehess.fr

C. Rosillo-López, M. García Morcillo (eds.), *Managing Information in the Roman Economy*, Palgrave Studies in Ancient Economies,
https://doi.org/10.1007/978-3-030-54100-2_14

you don't know." In contrast, if the other parties are aware of this asymmetry, they may feel wronged by this kind of distribution. This is true in the current period, but information asymmetry has also existed in all societies throughout history. This book reveals similar situations of asymmetrical distribution of information under the Roman Empire—that is, during the first three or four centuries of our era and the centuries immediately preceding it.

Information asymmetry was certainly not equally strong in all periods, and it varied as well by location and sector. Some Romans themselves were aware of its strength within the real estate sector. Cristina Rosillo-López stresses, in her chapter, this distinctive characteristic of the real estate sector. The seller of a house is, indeed, better informed than the buyer concerning the property in question; he is also better informed about the neighbourhood and the prices in the neighbourhood. Even so, this asymmetry is a phenomenon that spreads far and wide, to most places, most of the time.

The chapters in the book have been ordered according to the major sectors of economic life. To begin with, following the Introduction, there are three chapters concerned with whole of economic life in the city and the Empire. The first, by Pablo Revilla, presents the main concepts used by economists to explain the role of information in economic contexts; the second chapter, by Alejandro Díaz Fernández and Francisco Pina Polo, deals with the Treasury (*aerarium*); and the third chapter, by Marta García Morcillo, is about auctions, which were very important in the Roman world, for public authorities as well as private citizens.

Next, we move on to real estate and land ownership, the topic of the following three chapters, by Saskia T. Roselaar, Cristina Rosillo-López and François Lerouxel. Then come two chapters about the relationships in work (Claire Holleran) and about slavery (Myles Lavan). Finally, three other chapters deal respectively with social space and the relationship between space and information (Miko Flohr), with professional companies and associations (Nicolas Tran) and with long-distance trade with India (Dario Nappo).

And to finish off, just before these concluding remarks comes the chapter by Koenraad Verboven which, in a way, presents a synthesis. In fact, Verboven takes as a starting point the belief (now shared by many specialists in the Roman economy) that the economic performance of the Empire was a real success. He aims to demonstrate the formal or informal procedures through which people were able to produce information, circulate such information, store it and transmit it. At the end of this conclusion I will return briefly to Verboven's chapter.

I fully appreciate the way in which the different chapters in the book have been set out. However, in my brief concluding remarks, I will not regroup them in the same way. I will distinguish between two categories of chapter. The authors in the first category have chosen to analyse information in a single kind of transaction, which brings two protagonists together and into opposition with one another. If the transaction is a sale or an auction (sale of a property, a piece of land to be farmed or a slave), the two protagonists are the seller and the buyer. If the transaction is a tenancy (*locatio rei*), they are the owner and the tenant. In the case of a work contract (*locatio operis faciundi, locatio operarum*), they are the employer and the worker. When the sale of merchandise takes place in a market, does the buyer of the merchandise have as much information as the seller? Usually not. But this is not an absolute rule. Sometimes the information asymmetry leans in favour of the buyer, at the expense of the seller. In both cases, we find ourselves facing a transaction which simultaneously brings together and puts into opposition two protagonists: the buyer and the seller. They come face to face with one another, in a way. Neither does one have access to the same information, nor the same amount of information, as the other. When the transaction is not a sale, the two protagonists are the owner and the tenant, or the lender and the borrower, or once again the employer and the employee.

It is interesting to analyse the role of information within each of these kinds of transaction, and this is just what six of the authors in this book have done. Three of these six cases are concerned with the seller and buyer of a building or a piece of land (Saskia T. Roselaar, Cristina Rosillo-López and François Lerouxel). In the other cases, it is the seller and the buyer at an auction (Marta García Morcillo), the seller and buyer of a slave (Myles Lavan) and finally, when a work contract is involved, the employer and employee (Claire Holleran). It is also very instructive to compare the role of information and asymmetry in these different categories of transaction. There is asymmetry in all of these cases, but perhaps above all in the case of real estate, as I have already noted above.

The chapter by Claire Holleran occupies a somewhat special place. In fact, although she has dedicated herself to the way in which employers find their workforce, rather than to labourers and unskilled workers looking for work (a theme on which she has previously written), the chapter contains a number of social and practical details. These detailed analyses focus, for example, on apprenticeships (in houses or workshops), the purchase of slaves in order to train them in a particular skill, the role of intermediaries and of associations and networks. Several professional sectors are considered in succession, such as medicine, weaving and construction. And yet there is little question of either flagrant abuses or major strategising. With regard to the workforce, information asymmetry certainly creates difficulties, but these can be resolved in the ways mentioned above.

Marta García Morcillo's chapter on auctions is very different. We know that both private and public auctions were important in the Roman world. Ancient authors stressed the need to ensure that they were publicised and transparent, and that information about them was controlled. A whole series of measures were put in place to respect these requirements: the presence of a public auctioneer (*praeco*), a sales register, compulsory guarantees, regulations emanating from magistrates. But all this did not prevent some from taking part in shrewd or even fraudulent transactions. García Morcillo focuses on two of these: first, the collusion among different bidders and second, the participation of a 'shill bidder', that is, a bidder whose specific aim is to raise the bid in favour of the seller.

The contribution by Myles Lavan is dedicated to the sale of slaves. The seller is either an individual or a professional, whereas the buyer is usually a private citizen. Whether the seller is an individual or a professional, such sales can provide typical examples of information asymmetry between the two protagonists, the seller and the buyer. This is because normally, the slave vender, regardless of who he is, knows the slave better than the buyer. Moreover, if the slave has any defects or physical or mental deficiencies, it is obviously in the vender's interest not to disclose them, since the price of the slave depends largely on the absence or presence of these defects or deficiencies.

Lavan, who is interested in the comparison between ancient slavery and American slavery, adds that this information asymmetry between the seller and buyer of one or more slaves can be observed in the United States as well as in ancient Rome. He is likely thinking in particular of the comparison between ancient Rome and Louisiana, since that state adopted legal regulations inspired by Roman law. Unfortunately, he does not fully explain this comparison between slavery in Rome and Louisiana, limiting himself to a brief outline in a sentence or two. In any event, he believes that in both cases this asymmetry could have led to the phenomenon of 'adverse selection', especially, perhaps, when the seller was a private citizen. Indeed, slave owners tended to dispose of slaves with whom they were not satisfied by reselling them. Slaves who belonged to private citizens and were resold by their owners were likely seldom of the best quality.

Slave sales have three particular features. We just spoke of the first: they very much lend themselves to 'adverse selection'. The second specific feature has to do with the fact that, notwithstanding the presence of private individuals—prominent citizens—among slave venders, slave owners were more often buyers than sellers of slaves. This was true to such an extent that it was not very difficult to place the blame on intermediary sellers and slave merchants, and to condemn their greed. The first remedy against these ills was introduced by curule aediles. In their edict, they placed the blame for hidden defects on sellers, by giving buyers the opportunity to appeal in cases of slaves who were not of good quality (this was probably dated from the end of the third or beginning of the second century BC). The edict of the curule aediles was especially favourable to the buyer in the case of slave sales.

The third special feature of slave sales rests in the fact that, notwithstanding the existence of the institution of slavery, human beings cannot be reduced to pieces of merchandise like any other, whether in ancient Rome or in the United States before abolition—and even if many contemporaries refused to acknowledge this truth. Lavan makes this fact felt in the very details of what he writes, and this adds greatly to the value of his contribution.

For certain categories of goods sold, whether at auction or by mutual agreement, we have notably more information than for others. This is the case of the property and real estate sectors. There are several reasons for this situation. On one hand, these two sectors, which are linked to one another, result in very high expenses for the household. Moreover, they are linked to the practice of credit, in two ways: because it is often necessary to borrow money at interest in order to purchase a piece of land or a building, and also because estates and buildings are quite often provided as guarantees for financial loans. On the other hand, the social and political elite have a special interest in these sectors, because the assets of the most powerful families are always based on property and real estate.

Saskia T. Roselaar, whose chapter looks at the last two centuries of the Republican period, stresses that the desire for profit and wealth accumulation, whether through land or urban investment, was widespread. She reviews the writing of Cato the Elder and Varro regarding their estates and agricultural property. But she also emphasises how much information major Roman property owners received word-of-mouth and from visits to villas and farms, in addition to these agronomic treaties.

As for public lands (*ager publicus*), she stresses that a real problem arose from their uncertain legal status. In this case, according to her, it is not so much a question of information asymmetry as an information deficit, or even an information vacuum. What Roselaar writes in this regard is interesting. Nevertheless, I think some senators, and even some knights, who were highly engaged in the political and financial affairs of the city, were much better informed than others about the *ager publicus*. This in turn helps to explain the sequence of serious political crises in republican Rome, especially the crisis during the period of the Gracchi.

Cristina Rosillo-López's chapter, about which I have already written briefly at the beginning of my comments, emphasises the importance of information asymmetry in relation to property sales as well rentals. Should those who have access to information always disclose this to the other parties in the transaction (e.g., when selling or buying from them an apartment or building)? Rosillo-López relies on a number of examples taken from Cicero and on fragments featured in the *Digest*.

These texts are rich and well chosen, because they show the extent to which information was important for these Roman writers. I would like to make a comment on the first among them, an excerpt from the *Digest* in which Celsus had critiqued a conclusion made by Proculus. This concerned the pipes which conducted water from a leaden reservoir underground to a vase, where it had to be heated before it was used. Should these pipes be judged to belong to the house in which they are found, or not? Proculus replied that the will of the participants had to be taken into account. But, writes Celsus, what if the seller and the buyer have paid no attention to this question, as often happens in cases such as this? Would it not be better to judge that pipes that are part of a building belong to that building?

It seems to me that this passage, in spite of its brevity, touches upon at least two different themes, and even three, which are intimately connected. One of these is precisely information, a theme which Rosillo-López emphasises. But this first theme is linked to a second, which reduces, in a way, the importance of the first: neither the seller nor the buyer has considered the question. In this particular case, no one has taken an interest in this information, and Celsus adds that such a lack of interest is not exceptional. And finally, the third theme, which may be at the centre of Celsus's concerns in the text. This is the question of knowing whether these pipes belong to the house in which they are registered or whether, juridically, they exist independently.

Next, Rosillo-López examines the purchase of the Scapula gardens, which Cicero wanted to acquire in 45 BC as a place to build a funerary monument to his daughter Tullia, who had recently died. In the end, the purchase did not go through, after Cicero learned that Caesar had restructuring projects for the city of Rome, particularly in the area of the Vatican plain (which, ultimately, were never realised).

François Lerouxel's chapter also deals with the real estate sector. But in contrast to the other chapters discussed just above, this one is about the inhabitants of Roman Egypt, who had Egyptian legal status. The inhabitants directly concerned were married women with Egyptian status. If a man owned a house and wanted to sell it, according to the terms of their marriage contract and under local law, he needed his wife's permission—even if he, not she, was the owner. The chapter focuses on two prefectural edicts: the edict of the prefect M. Mettius Rufus (AD 89) and that of the prefect Ser. Sulpicius Similis (AD 109), which are concerned with this aspect of the status of married women in Egyptian law, in relation to the administrative system called the 'property library' (*bibliothêkê enktêseôn*). This is where all transactions relating to the ownership of buildings, and all guarantees and mortgages which had been signed in relation to them, were registered.

The authors of the chapters belonging to the first category, which I have discussed so far, have thus chosen to analyse the question of information in a single type of transaction, which brings two protagonists together and into opposition with one another.

The authors of the chapters upon which I have not yet commented, or about which I have limited myself to a mention, have adopted a larger subject. They study, from the perspective of information, an entire aspect of economic life or an entire part of Roman life. These chapters—by Alejandro Díaz Fernández and Francisco Pina Polo, Miko Flohr, Nicolas Tran, Dario Nappo and Koen Verboven—are five in number and are relatively different from one another. In my opinion, the chapters in the first category, which analyse only one type of operation, treat the topic of information asymmetry—and above all asymmetry between the two protagonists—more directly. The five chapters which have taken on a larger subject, and about which I will now say a few words, tend to speak about the diffusion of information in its totality.

The chapter by Alejandro Díaz Fernández and Francisco Pina Polo poses two questions about the Roman Treasury, the *aerarium Saturni*, during the period of the Republic. What documents were kept in the *aerarium*? In the first few pages of their chapter, the authors outline a very brief history of the Treasury and a list of the different documents found there. Understandably, they do not claim this list to be exhaustive. But they ask a second question: who had the right to consult these documents, some of which concerned economic affairs? This is a very difficult question. Could these documents be consulted and reproduced? The answer is yes, according to the two authors, because of the example of Cato after his quaestorship. But Cato had just been a quaestor and, in any case, was already a senator. Some passages in Cicero (e.g., *De Oratore*, 2, 116), imply that advocates such as Cicero could have access to all these public documents in order to prepare their defence work before the *quaestiones*. The authors of the chapter admit that not all citizens had access to these documents in the *aerarium*, and they are surely correct. At the same time, they do not think that this access was limited to ancient magistrates.

Next, they ask what effect this partial opening of the official documents of the *aerarium* had on economic and financial transactions. They speak of these effects in relation to the societies of publicans, and I think the authors are right to conclude that, if there was competition among various groups of publicans over an adjudication, the public authorities would make an effort not to give official favour to one group of publicans over another. These documents were not conceived as economic documents; they were conceived as administrative and political documents. In principle it was necessary to assure that the adversaries were treated equally, for reasons to do with the legality of public proceedings.

Miko Flohr believes that two questions can be addressed in relation to information asymmetry. The first of these is "the ways in which asymmetric information actually impacted on everyday economic processes, and which institutions or ways of doing things emerged to protect the interests of both parties in a transaction". The majority of the chapters in this book, he says, look at this first question. He, in contrast, wants to dedicate himself to the second question. What does this involve? It is "the question of the extent to which the shape or structure of markets in the Roman world and the way in which these developed over time, impacted on the role that asymmetric information actually could play in everyday economic practice".

His chapter is very interesting but, to tell the truth, it is not really dedicated to the structure of markets in the Roman world, the way in which they developed and the impact they had on the role of information asymmetry. It is first and foremost about social space and the relationship between space and information. Does information spread equally throughout the expanse of the Empire? Flohr is convinced that it does not, and he is right. He deals only with the western part of the Empire, and finds there three regions that were particularly active, three regions where information circulated particularly well: Central Italy, from the region of Rimini to the Golf of Naples; the province of Baetica; and the northern part of the province of Africa and one part of the north of Numidia. These were also the most urbanised regions, "the three clusters of urbanization". In the eastern part of the Empire, there were also very active regions in Greece and Asia Minor, but Flohr deliberately limits himself to the West. He also dedicates several pages to the places where information circulates in the interior of each region and each city: the *fora*, shops and porticos, and basilicas. Flohr has a number of inspiring ideas about how information circulates. For example, information does not travel by the same routes, nor at the same speed, as goods; it circulates much faster. What's more, the more information circulates, the more information asymmetry is reduced. The three most economically active regions have the lowest levels of information asymmetry.

Nicolas Tran's chapter focuses on the *collegia*, that is, the Roman professional associations. What is particular about these associations is that we know much about their names, their geographical location and their dignitaries, and very little about their functions. Did they play an active economic role, or did they have an exclusively social mission? Based on two important examples—the *negotiatores Cisalpini et Transalpini* and the olive oil merchants of Baetica—Tran underscores their role in regard to information and, at the same time, insists they were exclusive in nature. More hierarchical than has sometimes been claimed in modern historiography, these associations constituted networks in which the 'insiders' were noticeably different from those who were not members, the 'outsiders'. The existence of these networks therefore marked out a social geography in the world of traders, in which "insiders" enjoyed significant advantages, notably in regard to information.

The last two chapters in the volume, by Dario Nappo and Koen Verboven, treat very different topics; but what they share in common is that they evoke, unlike the other chapters, the major late nineteenth- and twentieth-century debates about the ancient economy. Moreover, in relation to these debates, they adopt positions which seem to me quite close to one another. Both authors manifestly refuse to enter into these old debates, and they admit wholeheartedly to using tools from contemporary social sciences and, most notably, neo-institutionalist economics. As Nappo writes, it is a question of making "a conscious use of the models and tools that history and, in this case, economics have devised to interpret data". At the same time, however, it is a question of avoiding anachronisms and measuring the distance between the ancient and modern worlds. Nappo is very conscious of defining the concepts he uses, and his chapter contains numerous reflections which I find invaluable on the notion of the costs of transaction. With regard to the specific character of commerce between Roman traders and Indians, Nappo explains it by the difference in corresponding value between gold and silver at the beginning of the Empire. In that period, the ratio was 1 to 10 in India and 1 to 12 in Rome, which could result in great advantages for traders setting out for India with a substantial quantity of silver currency. Moreover, Nappo's explanation as to why the *Gaius et Lucius Caesares* and *Pontifex Maximus* types are so common among Roman coins found in India is very astute and convincing.

As I said above, Koen Verboven's chapter is a kind of synthesis. His chapter fulfils, in effect, two functions. On one hand, Verboven takes as a starting point the belief (now shared by many specialists in the Roman economy) that the economic performance of the Empire was a real success. He aims to demonstrate the formal or informal procedures through which people were able to produce information, circulate such information, store it and transmit it, and what role information played in the economic results achieved. He believes that the different aspects of this function constituted a whole, which he designates the 'Information Governance System', an expression borrowed from studies in business management. On the other hand, within this framework, he devotes the rest of his chapter to different categories of financial intermediaries, as informed by Latin texts, inscriptions and tablets from the cities in the region of Vesuvius.

Verboven concludes that information played a primary role in the economic and social success of the Roman world. Indeed, the whole of the book we have just finished, edited by Cristina Rosillo-López and Marta García Morcillo, is testimony to this importance. We have in fact observed that, according to the sources upon which the authors have relied, some Romans themselves were aware of this. The authors of this book have researched and analysed first and foremost information asymmetry. Did this information asymmetry make information less effective? Did it always lead transactions to fail? The interpretation of the different chapters in this book, it seems to me, lead to a much more balanced conclusion. Information asymmetry—an inevitable product of a complex and unequal society, composed of distinct social milieu, a number of aspects of which we have analysed here—contributed, in contrast, to the very success which Verboven stresses at the opening of his chapter.

Index[1]

[1] Note: Page numbers followed by 'n' refer to notes.

C. Rosillo-López, M. García Morcillo (eds.), *Managing Information in the Roman Economy*, Palgrave Studies in Ancient Economies,
https://doi.org/10.1007/978-3-030-54100-2

I

K

L

The manufacturer's authorised representative in the EU is Springer Nature Customer Service Centre GmbH, Europaplatz 3, 69115 Heidelberg, Germany. If you have any concerns regarding our products, please contact ProductSafety@springernature.com

Printed and bound by CPI Group (UK) Ltd, Croydon, CR0 4YY
30/09/2026
02225459-0016